CONFESSIONS

AUGUSTINE

A NEW TRANSLATION BY
SARAH RUDEN

THE MODERN LIBRARY

NEW YORK

Published in the United States by Modern Library, an imprint of Random House, a division of Penguin Random House LLC, New York.

MODERN LIBRARY and the TORCHBEARER colophon are registered trademarks of Penguin Random House LLC.

Originally published in hardcover in the United States by Modern Library, an imprint of Random House, a division of Penguin Random House LLC, in 2017.

Grateful acknowledgment is made to the *National Review* for permission to reprint "Translators" by Sarah Ruden (*National Review,* December 31, 2009), copyright © 2009 by National Review, Inc. Reprinted by permission.

LIBRARY OF CONGRESS CATALOGING-IN-PUBLICATION DATA
Names: Augustine, Saint, Bishop of Hippo, author. | Ruden, Sarah, translator.
Title: Confessions / Augustine; a new translation by Sarah Ruden. Other titles: Confessiones. English
Description: First edition. | New York: The Modern Library, [2017] | Translation of Confessiones. | Includes bibliographical references.
Identifiers: LCCN 2016033647 | ISBN 978-0-8129-8648-8 | ISBN 978-0-8129-9657-9 (ebook)
Subjects: LCSH: Augustine, Saint, Bishop of Hippo. | Christian saints—Algeria—Hippo (Extinct city)—Biography. | Catholic Church—Algeria—Hippo (Extinct city)—Bishops—Biography. | Hippo (Extinct city)—Biography.
Classification: LCC BR65.A6 E5 2017 | DDC 270.2092 [b]—dc23
LC record available at https://lccn.loc.gov/2016033647

Printed in the United States of America on acid-free paper

randomhousebooks.com
modernlibrary.com

8 9

This book is dedicated to my husband, TOM CONROY, and I'm sorry, Tom, that the previous book dedicated to you was *The Golden Ass*; but you understand that, and all the other hazards of translating, such as I wrote about in my poem "Translators":

In the beforetime, under a different administration,
There were marsupial words, chameleon words in trees,
Words shedding their wings and tunneling in the sea—
Clever and strong, out-thronging all our small associations.

Among them went the poor hunters of words, into a stark
And dreary contest. Most dissolved when spat on.
Or imagine being hopeful, small and sat on
By a behemoth epic myth lured from the dark.

Yet efforts did persist, since words were useful things,
As proven by certain midden-heaps of note
That show the bones of comedy cooked with votes;
Also oration hides made into slings.

Once in a while a tender soul took home
A gold-hoofed lyric antelope to feed—
Winsome, admired, but it would not breed.
Now all these creatures' habitat is gone.

But wonder on wonder: maybe cynically,
They left what could be hounded in the dust
By the henchmen of their perished captors—us.
From the ruins of that strange menagerie,

We sift the endless pailsful for a hoary
Vertebra or a molar, the single part
Left in the flattened cage of the world's heart—
Evidence of a story of a story.

CONTENTS

INTRODUCTION

During the transition of the West from a pagan to a Christian society, two personal accounts of conversion rose monumentally, and would have vast influence on popular thinking and institutional authority. These accounts were the mid-first-century A.D. epistles, or letters, of Paul of Tarsus (which would in time be established in the biblical New Testament beside a third-person narrative of Paul's mission that makes up most of the book of Acts); and the *Confessions* of Augustine, bishop of Hippo Regius (a Roman provincial city within the territory of present-day Algeria), written at the very end of the fourth century.

The shattering conversion of Paul, who was from the Jewish Diaspora but attached to the Jerusalem Temple, changed him from a persecutor of the earliest Christians on behalf of fellow

Jews to the main early propagator of what was to be the Christian church in Europe. Augustine was born in North Africa, into a mixed pagan-Christian household, and in early adulthood he moved to Italy to further his career as a rhetor, an entrepreneur or state functionary who used traditional pagan Roman and Greek literature to teach public speaking, at times performing in this genre himself. Rhetoric was the mainstay of Greco-Roman education, the readiest means of social mobility, and the most important nexus of politics and popular entertainment. Augustine got as far in the profession as settling in as official rhetor of Milan, the Western Imperial capital, before decisively answering a Christian calling.

His movement toward devout commitment as a follower of Christ was decades long, rather plodding and dithering, and occasionally silly, not sudden and dramatic like Paul's. But the results were perhaps no less momentous for the history of ideas and institutions. Here was a second eloquent popularizer, radical critic of the power structure, and no-nonsense proponent of order and conformity at the same time; both men emerged as public personalities at just the right time to help set Christianity on a basis that would survive tremendous shocks of history. Both—intrinsically to the kind of religion Christianity became, I would argue—made their cases most powerfully through the stories of their own lives as examples of sin and salvation.

Augustine lived (354–430) during an era in which Christianity enjoyed official toleration under the Roman Imperial administration—toleration authorized by the emperor Constantine's Edict of Milan in the year 313—after centuries of on-and-off persecutions, some within living memory. State support of the church was quickly established in the form of privileging laws, subsidies, and even magnificent basilica churches and deluxe editions of the complete Bible. Priests and bishops,* such as Augustine was to become, evolved into de facto Imperial functionaries, particularly when the ties of the state per se weakened under violent pressures from inside and outside the Empire. However, these clerics often resisted the power of the state, calling secular officials to account, and some clerics continued to suffer for their intransigence. The recent consensus of scholars holds that there was no hard division between the pre-Constantinian "pagan" and the post-Constantinian "Christian" Roman Empire. Dissonance, conflict, and confusion prevailed for a considerable time—as Augustine's life shows.

But the general movement was in only one direction: toward greater authority for the church. In Augustine's own accounts, functions such as dispute resolution, economic and social patronage, and the dole—as well, of course, as public ceremony—can be seen devolving more and more onto the church. Of apparently overarching influence was the Roman *clientela* system, a daily enacted hierarchy that shadowed and intersected the state throughout Romanized regions (which included North Africa).† The church's respectful community gatherings, fixed reciprocal duties, and charities naturally resonated with *clientela* as well as testifying to specifically Christian principles. Augustine depicts himself, during his rapprochement with mainstream Christianity, making formal calls on the bishop Ambrose—but having no opportunity to discuss troubling is-

---

* These are titles we derive from the Greek words for "elder" and "overseer" respectively, which stood for offices providing administrative and moral leadership since Pauline times, and later evolving exclusive ritual roles.

† A *patronus* received ceremonial visits from his *clientes,* used them as a retinue, and distributed a private dole to them. Their support for him was a major basis for his political, business, and social dealings.

sues because of the crowds of people having business with the prelate (*Confessions,* book 6, chapters 3 and 4).

The church wasn't yet ideologically coercive, however; hence Augustine's emphasis on voluntary conversion, his own and that of others. Nor did he consider the church anything like what we would call "the establishment." In fact, Augustine makes very clear in his climactic treatise, *The City of God,* his opposition to any such regime. In the earlier *Confessions,* he stresses that the crucial choice of his own life was *not* to acquire wealth and power through the old means of forensic and display oratory, marriage alliance, and public administrative appointments. It may seem odd to many modern readers that he considered marriage incompatible with the highest kind of Christian life, but this makes more sense in light of contemporary facts. The church did not preside over marriages to the extent it now does: the essential legal, financial, and social arrangements were all holdovers from pagan culture. This left a spiritual and psychic gap in which a rather extravagant cult of virginity and celibacy could flourish, so that aspirants like Augustine and his friends believed that they would be outranked as Christians if they lived in sexual and household partnerships. (Ironically, this was an attitude more in keeping with certain pagan philosophers, and with certain outré Christian sectarians like the Manichaeans, than with the Palestinian Jew Jesus—at least on the evidence preponderating in the Gospels.)

Hence, to Augustine, full Christian commitment seemed a zone of daunting sacrificial withdrawal from the world. However, as ties between the church and state strengthened, and as the Christian population grew, with conversions spreading up the social scale and so becoming more respectable, the authority of the church, and hence its attractions to ambitious young intellectuals, did grow significantly. Even before Augustine's time this was marked by something that would prove to be of great interest to him: guidance toward uniformity of belief.

If we were to be transported back to late antiquity, we would struggle to recognize some groupings as Christian at all, despite their claims to represent the only valid Christianity. But in the fourth century, Imperial auspices strengthened the cause of conformity. The First Council of Nicaea in 325, convened by Constantine, produced a "creed," or formal assertion of normative belief, and the Nicene Creed of 381 is actually still shared among most modern-day churches. Nicene Christianity settled (though hardly right away) certain conceptual problems that were difficult enough to have made their sectarian answers far-flung and serially vulnerable over the centuries. Most important, how could God—regarded as a definite part of history, and indeed the most vital part, rather than as a mere invocation of myth and ritual—have lived and died as a human being? The creed states that there is a single God, and that his only Son, Jesus Christ, is "begotten, not made" and of "one substance with the Father." A third part of divinity is specified: the Holy Spirit. Thus the universe is ruled by a Trinity, or Three in One.

It would take an encyclopedia just to summarize all the fragmentation in early Christianity, or even all that Augustine was concerned with over the course of his religious career. ("Heresy," most literally "choice," was a term in use since Paul; "schism" designated the "splitting" that could be merely on moral or ritual grounds.) Setting itself against this, the mainstream church called itself *catholicus* in Latin, from the Greek word for "universal"; hence the name of the religion now understood in relation to the various Protestant and Eastern Orthodox churches, which of course didn't exist in Augustine's time. This is why I don't use the word "catholic," let alone "Catholic," in my translation, except with expansion: "catholic or universal." The "universal" church was supposed to be for everyone, of all classes and ethnic groups, and required no special knowledge but what was imparted to the catechumens ("those under instruction"), who were preparing for baptism; and baptism was the only rite essential for membership. Augustine strongly advocated for infant baptism and against a very long catechumenate such as he had experienced, which was common at the time. Christianity needed, to his mind, to be even simpler than it had been for him as a questioning, hesitating convert to the public, common, relatively egalitarian religion.

He converted some time after rejecting the Manichaean sect in which he had spent most of his young adulthood, and the Manichaeans make for a broadly instructive example among alternatives to the universal church. They are the only alternative he is substantially concerned with in the *Confessions,* so we get quite an intimate account of their attractions for him, as well as his grounds for disgust. It is possible to extrapolate a little, speculatively, toward the whole of dissenting Christianity (I would not say "vanishing forms of Christianity," as there are, for example, Gnostic sects that endure to this day)—as long as I make it clear that this *is* speculation, drawing mainly on a single author's experience. In any event, I'm committed to an effort to see circumstances through Augustine's eyes; and I hope this effort will allow me to avoid the anachronistic language of political dissidence and religious freedom that appears in some accounts.

To the still dominant pagan culture, Christianity was exotic and baffling, having little in common with the ways pagans worshipped and understood the meaning of life. Their traditional religion was basically nature worship, observed with sacrifices and explained by elaborate mythology. But mystery cults required initiation and secrecy and promised special, individual relationships with the divine, and a privileged afterlife. And philosophical religions pursued broader and more logical explanations of existence, from physics to metaphysics to ethics.

Manichaeism suggests congeniality with all three of these experiences—traditional public cults, mystery cults, and philosophizing—in that all three entailed a certain exclusivity, whether of geography and nationality, demanding ritual, fee-paying initiation, study, or some combination thereof. Manichaeism has been associated with Gnosticism ("knowingness"), whose name connotes belief and practice for special people; certainly the Manichaean theology of stark dualism, good and evil, stressed the importance of being on the right side of the universe. The copious pseudoscientific Manichaean literature and the fantastic Manichaean mythology would at first have appealed to the precocious, ambitious, and fun-loving Augustine as a way to split the difference between a morally repugnant paganism, alien to his Christian mother's teachings, and a "universal" Christianity distinctly short on glamour, prestige, and entertainment. But over time he could not stomach the self-serving absurdities of Manichaean doctrine; and as for the sect's cultural pretensions, he actually found himself introducing a much-touted Manichaean leader to solid literary studies.

Yet on the other side, where he was headed, the internal strains of a very inclusive church membership policy manifested with a vengeance—but in ways that offered him a special role and purpose. Scientific and philosophical knowledge might be deemed unnecessary for the uneducated people this church embraced, but some of the most celebrated leaders had it, continued to be interested in it, and displayed it in their sermons and popular publications—including Augustine's *Confessions,* the last four books of which depart from his life story and are filled with metaphoric and abstract discourse. Congregations must have been in the thrall of this expertise; Augustine's ordination was mobbed, and he proved a superstar preacher and polemicist. Nor could ordinary people's mere reception into the church show them how to live. Leaders from Peter, James, and Paul onward hammered out the rules and their rationales, an influential collection of which Augustine left in his writings. (While visiting the U.S. Naval Academy recently, I found that his writings on the ethics of warfare were part of the curriculum.) Pastoral authority was unavoidable, and probably sterner than in Christian sects whose members were on a closer social footing.

But to class Augustine as a "preacher" on these grounds, and to put him aside as sensible characters in Jane Austen put aside tomes such as Fordyce's sermons in favor of novels, is dead wrong. He is—as I hope to show—more vivid than any gothic tale. Not that his historical importance alone doesn't merit a careful consideration: During his lifetime, under his hyperintelligent gaze, the Roman Empire ceased existing in any recognizable form; Rome itself was sacked by the Visigoths in 410. Augustine died while Hippo was under siege by another barbarian tribe, the Vandals, twenty years later—but as Christians (though of the heretical Arian variety), they preserved his archive when they prevailed. Augustine was able, through his words, to imagine and to some degree ensure what happened afterward: The Christian church became the center of civilization.

But as his translator, I am more interested in Augustine as a literary figure than as a reporter and a shaper of his times, no matter how fascinating these were, and no matter how insightfully and energetically he dealt with them. But there is no either-or. As a man of letters, he probably shows more deeply and sweepingly what a successful Christian leader was at the time, and thus what Christianity itself was, than he would have as the ancient embodiment of CNN.

The *Confessions* demonstrates why. The work sets forth an individual life from its very start (and this itself would have been striking to his readers: babyhood was no common preoccupation of the ancients) and assigns it universal and eternal meaning. This is a logical conclusion toward which Christian literature had long been moving, but for which it had until now lacked the requisite genius.

In every passage, the author aims at the quintessential Christian equipoise between being everything and being nothing: everything, because God has been born and has died for him; and nothing, because it took something this momentous to justify the author's existence, sordid and meaningless as it is in itself. The brilliance, flashiness, and subtlety of pagan literature, especially oratory, which Augustine had formally renounced in leaving his professional post, was brought to bear on the task of dramatizing this contrast and its resolution through faith in God's love and power.

In this way, Augustine pursues the narrative of the two main conflicts in his life. One is his struggle with his erotic impulses, a struggle that did not end but did largely subside after he retired to a contemplative community. I will spare the reader

Freudian or other speculative interpretations of Augustine's state of mind and note only that he found it difficult to reconcile the influence of his very pious mother, Monica, and her church with his strong sex drive and his deep attachment to the woman (to us, nameless) who was the mother of his adored son Adeodatus ("Given by God") and his exclusive mistress for more than a decade, until the year before his conversion. (His sexual adventures, in his few months of living independently in metropolitan Carthage before this liaison began, seem hardly to have merited, on objective grounds, the language of horrified remorse he uses much later. Outwardly, whatever he did was likely quite ordinary for a Roman Imperial student.) She undoubtedly lacked the status that would have allowed a legal marriage to him, but his difficulties went beyond this fact. He also gave up his engagement to a wealthy, well-connected, and appealing girl (chosen by his mother) in order to take up his calling as a contemplative and ascetic Christian. The Bible passage he read in the garden during the famous showdown between his incompatible drives, the passage that pushed him into an inspired conversion after years of indecision, was a Pauline exhortation to leave behind the life of sensuous and competitive self-indulgence (Romans 13:13–14).

He himself (at a stage of his life the *Confessions* does not cover) ended up bringing a new arrangement to the priesthood. If the church wanted him as an official, he insisted, it must not separate him from his celibate lay religious community; all monastic communities so far, including his own, had been founded and run independently of the institutional church. The church complied with his wishes and helped him accommodate his spiritual brothers. He subsequently produced the model "rule," or collection of guidelines for monastic living, which would be named Augustinian after him. With the help of this document and the practical examples he and his friends set, monastic life was to come more fully under the auspices of bishops.

Besides the physically based struggle for celibacy, his other great struggle was intellectual. Hence, the departure from autobiographical narrative to metaphysical analysis and speculation in the final four books of the *Confessions* is not at all a strange or trivial digression. In these books, he gleefully displays the treasures that his conversion and his resolute adherence to it have given him in the decade and a half since it occurred—and he also displays biblical commentary of the kind that lay at the heart of his role as a bishop. These final four books (on average, far longer than the previous nine) treat memory, time, and allegorical interpretations of the Bible's creation story at the beginning of Genesis.

The treatment is challenging for any English speaker (not excepting me) who does not have specialized theological or philosophical training; but to anyone interested in Augustine, I would strongly suggest not only reading these discourses— though it is tempting to disregard them after the much more personal, literally sexier, life narrative—but also reading them as integral to Augustine's view of his life's development and purpose.

To consider this view, in outline, from the beginning: In book I, Augustine carefully and plausibly discusses himself as a baby, recounting how he must have misbehaved and started to learn language, though he admits he can remember nothing. His earliest memories center on school and its traumas; his earliest memories of self-regard and self-direction refer to evidence of his superior oratorical talent, which was, aside from his mother's piety, the main thing setting him apart for a special purpose in life.

His analytical drive in the *Confessions* is wildly ambitious even at this early stage of the work—not in the ordinary or expected way but rather in an ironic and paradoxical one. His purpose is always to show human worthlessness extravagantly blessed with gifts from God (as a fretful, demanding baby is blessed with instinctive care and nurturance, and as a selfish, distractible child is given the full benefit of a traditional education), and appalling human sinfulness showered with God's grace, which if accepted leads to blissful eternal life. It's necessary, in this schema, for the author to denigrate his own expressive genius even as he parades it, and he makes this reversal many times with considerable wit and charm.

Behind the schema is a painful but fertile cultural contrast: the ancient prestige and cosmopolitan flashiness of the Greco-Roman heritage versus the earnest, crude, but more humane innovations of Christianity, a religion imported from a nation widely despised in the first place and actually subject to Roman extirpation in A.D. 70. For dramatizing and at the same time pooh-poohing the contrast, Augustine marshals a quintessence of rhetorical skill unrivaled in early Western Christian literature. He is familiar with the higher reaches of traditional pagan intellectualism, in which Plato (for instance, on the Greek side, about which Augustine knew mainly through Latin authors) might make up elaborate myths to suit the argument of the moment, or Lucretius (on the Roman side) might coast in verse back to the beginning of the universe and declare what must have happened to start the endless actions and reactions of nature. But to Augustine, unless the adoption and adaptation of any such analysis is effectively a form of prayer—a humble and grateful celebration of the human mind, the physical universe, and the transcendent realms; a celebration that cedes all real understanding to God—the effort is frivolous and wrongheaded. Seemingly by preference, at least in the *Confessions,* he plays instead of hammering away: he paints one picture and then another, hypothesizes poetically, withdraws, laughs at himself, takes a few potshots at those whose ideas are theoretically impossible within the compelling equations of divine grace—but always he returns to submissive praise of and thanks to God.

Everything most enticing to his intellect is stacked on the altar, less as a combustible sacrifice than as a bundle of fireworks: the way the mind works, the very memory he relies on to write this very autobiography; time, that powerful and mysterious thing, seemingly both inside and outside himself; and reading and interpreting, those psychologically fascinating, ultraprestigious, defining acts of a Roman gentleman.

The last four books are almost a narrative resolution of Augustine's personal ideological history as set out in the *Confessions.* To back up to book 2 and start again from there: From his late teens, when he was sorely exercised about what to do with his body—his fundamental, long-term confusion, in fact, was over how the physical could be related to the transcendent—he found several cerebral recourses that, in their partial satisfactoriness, he was to experience as great frustrations and wastes of time.

He apprenticed himself to the Manichaeans, with their elaborate materialistic dualism. He soon divined that they had made everything up; their cosmology had none of the logical, predictive justification that many pagan scientific philosophers could offer, through their understanding of eclipses, for example. Moreover, by systematizing at whim, the Manichaeans could derive an entirely self-serving morality.

On reading the Roman Republican orator Cicero's philosophical dialogue *Hortensius* (which is no longer extant), Augustine conceived a passion for philosophy, as virtuous and exalted, but the absence of Jesus in the work was for him a significant fault. He was looking for a way back to his mother's piety, but it needed to be his own way, a literary and intellectual one.

He snubbed the Latin scriptures on his first encounters with them: their language was lowly and their assertions inconsistent. Later, in Milan, Ambrose's sermons introduced him to flexible, allegorical methods of learning and teaching from scripture that we can see throughout the *Confessions,* and especially in the final two books.

But though he came to revere the Bible, the critical *intellectual* resources for him were from pagan philosophy. He not only began his quest with Cicero as a popularizer of this field; he also came close to the end of that quest when Latin translations of the Greek Neoplatonic works of Plotinus and his student Porphyry were made available to him.

He could then become more at home with the idea of transcendent being (reflected in the power of the mind to transcend the material world, and in the unchangeable truths of mathematics) that dated back to Plato (and further back to certain pre-Socratic philosophers). If God is the being superior to time and space and everything in it, then all that God created with his perfect will must be good, and evil is only a willful—though for humankind sadly universal, ever since Adam's rebellion— self-twisting in the direction of disintegration and nothingness.

For Augustine, however, Neoplatonism did not instill ultimate and lasting truth. His entry into religious experience itself was a largely emotional surrender to the teaching of the Word incarnate and God made humble for humankind's sins—the teaching he recalls (at the very beginning of the *Confessions*) as delivered to him from God "through the ministry of your preacher," Ambrose, a prominent bishop of the "universal" church.

My main justification for this new translation, after several learned and serviceable ones have become established, is the previously hidden degree to which Augustine makes his life and ideas vivid in the style of his Latin. (The fusion of form and content in ancient literature has become something of a specialty for me in the course of translating a variety of Latin, Greek, and now Hebrew works.) In Augustine, the manner of presentation is especially compelling, because of his stress on beauty and joy on the one hand, and intellectual helplessness on the other.

Both his mind and "inward ear" are freely exercised for his own delight and put on display for the world's benefit; here, he is squarely in pagan literary territory. But unlike pagan writers, he demurs in alarm from any pretense to comprehensive understanding or a rounded or even privileged view: he repeats that he is no better off spiritually than the *parvuli*, the simple-minded "little children" of the church—and he can be (in fact, has been) much worse off because of arrogance and self-satisfaction separating him from God.

His style (especially in this work about his own life's past and its purpose) is quite jagged and convoluted—but thematically so, and not in a way a translator should try to mitigate. She should instead hear the author saying, as he always does more or less explicitly, "*I* am not the guide for your minds; *I* am not the proper object of praise or admiration. I write in this impressive way (as I was trained to do since early boyhood), but everything from my personal memories to my cosmic reflections is really just a joke—so I fill it with little jokes and keep explicitly backing off it to return to prayer and praise of God, where I started." The *Confessions* is a book that cannot easily be reconciled with the theological systematizing in other Augustinian works or in later great religious thinkers such as Thomas Aquinas. An objective, scientific tone is seldom warranted here.

In this work, Augustine usually *performs* his relationship with God. His account of it is crammed with puns and other wordplay, alliteration, clever allusion, abrupt self-correction, whimsical digression, and self-deprecating rhetorical questions. He even bases figurative language on the feminine gender of certain nouns in Latin and their pronouns, depicting himself as erotically repelled by or attracted to an abstract quality or a general situation, as if it were a woman.

A favorite example of mine (in book 6, chapter 6) may amount to a burlesque of the image of falling into the pit of destruction (as in the biblical book of Psalms, a favorite inspiration of Augustine's prose poetry): "I was, you see, holding my heart back from any admission of the truth, as I feared the sheer drop into it; but hanging (myself) in the air above it was more like killing myself." I banged my head on my desk after seeing that several previous translators had treated the Latin word *suspendium* so as to deprive the English rendering of any punch whatsoever. True, the word comes from the Latin root for any kind of hanging, and Augustine himself uses words with this root for emotional suspense and intellectual or moral suspension between different alternatives—a notion clearly at play here. But the

Oxford Latin Dictionary has a single definition heading for *suspendium:* "The act of hanging oneself."

Augustine's philosophical discourse is challenging, not least because its original terms are Greek, a language in which he never felt fully confident. It is necessary to balance between fixed philosophical terms, without which references will be opaque, and Augustinian metaphors, which can be quite quirky. If this means playing with English vocabulary by using two or more different translations of one word, in sequence (as in book 4, chapter 30, in which Aristotle's *Categories* meets the prodigal son [Luke 15:11–32]), then so be it. The words in question are italicized in this example:

> But I didn't employ [academic disciplines, including the study of "substances" for philosophical categorizing] to make offerings to you, and that's why they had more capacity to doom me than to be of any use, because I meddled in trying to keep such a good part of my own substance, my property, in my own possession, and I didn't keep my strength in stock for you, but I left you and traveled to a distant country, to waste that strength on the whores that were my desires.

Such flexibility in word choice is an absolute necessity for literary faithfulness in translating this author. As for purported conflicts this creates for showing his religious single-mindedness, I have to protest that patristics scholars have in general allowed anachronistic misunderstanding of both ancient writing and ancient Christianity to influence their dictates on what is proper.

Ancient literary languages, especially Latin, had tiny vocabularies. The basic work of developing ideas in writing involved using the same word in widely different contexts and meanings—

even to demonstrate the most simple and deeply held beliefs; in scripture itself, this method was rife, on the evidence of the original texts.* There is no way in English to represent this but through word choice flexibility, which also serves an aesthetic principle that the ancients embraced but that is much more important for acceptable English style: *variatio,* or the deliberate varying of word choice for stylistic purposes.

When modern *Confessions* translators insist on the "consistency" and "discipline" of either translating a Latin single word with a single, traditionally established English one throughout this long work or footnoting any exceptions, they are really talking about top-down, academically elaborated and enforced ideological and doctrinal consistency and discipline, which are much later than Augustine, and the imposition of which greatly frustrates his speaking with both perceptible religious fervor and authentic rhetorical ingenuity to a very broad readership in his time and beyond it. I appeal to professors who may be inclined to anathematize my translation because it is different from the familiar ones: Would not Augustine have wanted flexibility? What would he have thought of "habit of the body," for example, given that "habit" has in this case turned out to be a largely sonic resonance of the Latin *habitus* and would suggest to the nonspecialist reader the daily workout or bath, and not a physical shape or other condition, which is plainly the meaning?

These are only the more familiar and ordinary headaches Augustine infuses into a translator. His use of scripture constitutes at the same time the main and the extraordinary challenge

---

* See my own accounts of this in *The Face of Water: A Translator on Beauty and Meaning in the Bible* (New York: Knopf, 2017).

of translating the *Confessions*. Here again I mediate quite differently than other translators have—I feel I must.

Augustine's protean exposition of the Bible is in conformity with a vast, immemorial, literary tradition—pagan, Jewish, and Christian; European and Middle Eastern—with which the modern method of careful, word-for-word quoting and objectively accurate citation could hardly be more at odds. Recourse to previous literature, especially to scripture among Christians, was frequent, but word-for-word quotation was, first of all, difficult. There were no standard, uniform texts with numbered small divisions. Nor was access to books a given in the first place. There is no reason to suppose that during his education and his teaching career, Augustine even had enough books around him to make "looking things up" a habit that would have been practical to develop, should it have occurred to him to develop it. Later, in the midst of his substantial library, he probably still operated as most other literate people did, quoting and making other references from memory and not worrying about any sharp tangents he might make from the words' context or the author's purpose. Even leaving aside Augustine's thirdhand remove from the original text of much of what he was quoting, for him, "quoting" is likely not an accurate term; it seems more like distant echoing, both in evident practice and in the results.

But that is only a modern, academic, rationalist take on him. A translator has to get beyond that to his inspired synthesis. In his eyes, the Latin Bible was a providential miracle, a safe intellectual enclosure (with simple wording that even the lowliest inquirers could understand literally), and yet a permitted means of wide-ranging speculative interpretation. The upshot was that he was never, in our sense, "freethinking" on the basis of the Bible; he was sure that if he was not "faithful," by the church's sole judgment, he would be wrong, however he read. But on the other hand, he was sure that such faithfulness would cover any factual mistake he might make. He had nothing in common with modern fundamentalists who conflate the truth of the Bible with scientific accuracy. Instead, Augustine was extremely *poetic*, in the ancient sense (the word "poetic" taking its origins from a Greek word for "making"): confidently, within a fixed tradition, he *created*.

I've therefore been concerned that my numerous citations, which are necessary to show the Bible's rich resources for Augustine, not get in the way of the highly literary, personal character of his exposition. In my footnotes, I do not cite individual scriptural "tags," or short phrases that are no striking part of the author's train of thought; these seem to be merely incorporated into his language, so that I cannot see the point of citing all possible sources of them. I also do not put quotation marks around biblical language that is blended and integrated (as it almost always is) into Augustine's rhetoric, but only cite the Bible in the New Revised Standard Version if the connection seems important.

Also, I do not impose the language of that or any other standard English Bible on Augustine's words. This would suggest categories of discourse and styles that didn't exist in his time. When Augustine writes that he has found the Bible lowly in expression, and that it is easy for ordinary people to read (book 6, chapter 8), he means it. For example, the biblical Latin word *spiritus*, which we almost always translate as "spirit," also meant simply "breath" or "wind": it thus had certain wide expressive possibilities (corresponding to those of the likewise triply significant *ruach* in Hebrew and *pneuma* in Greek), but it was more pedestrian than a number of other Latin terms for respiration and air currents. Augustine did intuit and develop a sense of the Bible's grandeur and mystery, but that's a special literary operation that our normally stilted, archaic-sounding language of biblical translation is unsuited to represent. The Latin in his passages that is closest to the Bible is like his Latin everywhere: new, bold, synthetic, very much his own.

The biggest challenge in accommodating Augustine—as opposed to trying to correct him or just translating past him—comes whenever he bases an entire disquisition on a Bible verse quite different in meaning, in its contemporary Latin state, from the modern result, in English, of centuries of philological research and textual restoration. I could merely refer the reader to a Bible verse in a gesture toward what is going on, but the reader would naturally take that as a reference to a standard English Bible that of course did not exist for Augustine.

An instance of the magnitude this problem can attain is that Augustine in book 12 of the *Confessions* bases an important part of his speculation around the Genesis creation story on a Bible verse most of us would notate as Psalms 115, verse 16, and which the NRSV translates (correctly) from the Hebrew as "The heavens are the Lord's heavens, but the earth he has given to human beings." But Augustine drew on a text of the Psalms from the "Old Latin" tradition, which was all but oblivious of Hebrew; the centuries-old (and not supremely accurate) Greek Septuagint translation of the Hebrew Bible was the only antiquarian source ever called on. (Letters Augustine wrote to Jerome show that though the former knew of the work that would become the improved, Hebrew-mediated Latin Vulgate Old Testament, he did not cede to the commonsensically overriding authority of the original language.) In this way, Augustine fixated on what is, technically, the collapse of a Hebrew subject and predicate into two Latin nouns attached to each other, *cae-lum caeli,* or "heaven of heaven" or "sky of sky." (Latin, like He-brew and Greek, doesn't distinguish by mere vocabulary between the physical sky and the celestial regions.) He then proceeded to build a poetic description and a theological ratio-nale for *two* areas: one—the sky—merely cosmological, and the other—the sky of sky—divine. In the conceptual background are probably expressions like "king of kings"—that is, the over-arching being, supreme over what it possesses or controls.

Obviously, Augustine is the author here, and gets his way; I'm not his schoolmarm. In fact, I find it rather wonderful that a vision caused by human limitations—notably, cultural narrow-ness and scholarly nonchalance in himself and his predecessors—can speak to an author and his readers so profoundly as this vision has. (How consonant with his own theme of outrageously beneficent providence!) He gets his lofty "heaven of heaven." But I don't think I can avoid explaining respectfully in a foot-note the gap modern readers will find if they look for his inspi-ration in a standard modern Bible.

Splitting differences this way produces splitting headaches, and in the end even the best efforts may look rather comical. But I would rather fail openly, fall while going out on a limb for him, than leave him up there with no chance. I'm perhaps most awkward where he thematically applies extended wordplay and conceits to single words. For example, there's *firmamentum,* which the Latin scripture says divided the two heavens from each other at the start of creation (Genesis 1:6–8). "Firmament" is a traditional biblical translation, but it takes only a baby step from the Latin, and ignores the fact that the English "firma-ment" was never a word in common use and offers no image. In contrast, a *firmamentum* in Latin is a support or prop, mainly one used in building, so that a cunning author could riff on and on about physical and spiritual support. "Firmament or support" or "firmament or prop" thus seems the proper translation at least in introductory passages. Just "firmament" suggests that Augustine is reciting Bible verses in Sunday school.

Here is a sort of glossary, including justification of either a consistent nonstandard choice throughout for a word, or varied choices for words translated consistently in the past. I discuss the first item at considerable length, as Augustine uses the word constantly in the same important way, yet I'm convinced that the traditional translation is wrong. I hope this discussion will exemplify the kind of reasoning behind my other decisions laid out here, all of which I don't have room to explain in such detail.

This list itself, by the way, is a severely truncated one. Augustine's vocabulary roams the registers and is extremely shrewd and expressive; here I mention only what I think are my most interesting departures from the usual renderings. But every passage of the text requires similar lexical twists and turns.

Dominus, in my translation, always "Master," not "Lord": The latter suggests a ruler, a nobleman, or another political authority, or the enthroned God of imagery starting in the Hebrew Bible. The Latin Bible's *dominus,* however, was far different in its contemporary associations.

Stemming from the word for "house" or "home," *domus, dominus* primarily and ordinarily refers to that home's head and the owner of its slaves, who would address him with this title. The unavoidable English translation seems to be "Master."

Sometimes in Roman history a *dominus* was a political leader, but in circumstances that make it hard to imagine that this was the analogy Christian Latin authors had in mind when they used this word. The emperor Domitian (A.D. 81–96), a tyrant, had innovatively styled himself *dominus et deus*, "Master and God." To the Romans, who had been enrolling emperors among the immortals for generations but were very attached to outward semblances of their old participatory government of free men, it was the "Master" part that was more offensive. Domitian was deposed bloodily and suffered *damnatio memoriae*, or expunging from official history and public imagery. Diocletian, who was one of the last three pagan Roman emperors and initiated the climactic persecution of Christians (303–311), also styled himself *dominus et deus*. When Augustine refers to an unambiguously political leader as an analogy to God, he refers to a "king" (*rex*), not a *dominus*.

It thus seems impossible that Augustine consciously and fervently prayed to a *dominus* in the symbolic form of a political ruler, instead of a householder like so many highly respected adult males he knew—and like himself, whose inheritance of a small estate (that would, as usual, have included slaves) had allowed him to set up a contemplative community. Moreover, "Master" is one meaning of the Greek mirror of *dominus* in scripture, *kyrios;* verses such as Mark 13:35 and Luke 14:21 speak of the *kyrios* of a slave or even "the *kyrios* of the house."

But most important, Augustine's own conception, at least in the *Confessions,* of the human relationship to God fits householding. When the author sets out how sacred law applies differently in different circumstances, he does not picture a whole city or a nation, but an ordinary household in which members—most of whom would have been slaves—are commanded and forbidden to do different things in different places and at different times (book 3, chapter 13). The household's commander was the *domi-*

nus. Augustine's humorously self-deprecating, submissive, but boldly hopeful portrait of himself in relation to God echoes the rogue slaves of the Roman stage. In book 3, chapter 5, he shows himself being justly whipped by God for defrauding the deity of his services and conferring them on demons, and preferring the false liberty of a runaway.

This imagery, with its reminders of American plantation slavery, may be harsh and off-putting, but a translator must govern her distaste and try to make her author's thought and experience as vivid and sympathetic as it plainly was to his contemporaries. Otherwise, there can be no limits to the demands of a condescending, manipulative, and anachronistic political correctness.

Servus, servire, nearly always "slave," and "to be a slave" or "to serve as a slave": These meanings follow on the correct translation of *dominus* and are lexically unexceptionable. Whatever the looser versions of servitude in Palestine and in the Greek world, and the accordingly more nuanced and less harsh constructions possible for the relevant vocabulary in Hebrew and Greek, for the Romans, a slave was a slave, a piece of property, and any recent marginal legal rights slaves had obtained (partly under the influence of Christianity) had apparently not disturbed Augustine's view of a slave's fate as naturally abject (book 7, chapter 8). Augustine considers himself God's slave; he exists at God's pleasure, he exists only to do God's will, and only his death will deliver him from such an existence.

Confessio, confiteor, usually "testimony," "testify": The title of Augustine's autobiography is the plural of the noun, the standard translation being *The Confessions,* and I have had to retain this title just to keep my translation from being misidentified. But lexically, contextually, *The Testimonies* would be more accurate. Early Christians had procedures for penitence (though nothing like the Catholic rite in its later form), but that is not what Augustine is doing in his book. Moreover, the Latin word at this stage of the language still has a strong judicial tinge and links back to the "testimony" prescribed in the New Testament for missionaries and the persecuted: fearless public declaration of faith. This *is* what Augustine is doing in this book. In any case, Augustine heads with the word *confessio* not just revelations of his own sins but celebrations of his salvation, praise of God, metaphysical speculation, and much else. The testimony is that his life, his mind, and everything else in the universe belong to God.

Convertere, conversio, always "to turn around" and "turning around," not "to convert" and "conversion": The great event of Augustine's life was, granted, a conversion, but to translate the terms this way is to misrepresent both the state of Latin and Augustine's use of the language. This pair of Latin terms was not until much later isolated in the religious realm and stripped down to a single reference. Thus, Augustine can play dramatically with the still clear physical meanings: he was halted in running away from God; he and others must turn and face God to acknowledge reality and escape destruction (see particularly book 5, chapter 2). Sticking with the most basic rendering also allows an authentic reproduction of some telling effects: in book 1, chapter 7, for instance, Augustine speculates about the possibility of *God* "turning around" and pitying him; the imagery is moving and memorable, but only if the reader is allowed to dwell on it *as imagery,* as an imagined scene of God turning back and stooping to help: the notion of God "converting" is merely bizarre.

Doctrina and a number of other nouns and verbs for teaching, always the simplest English translation, never "doctrine": An extract from my translation (book 12, chapter 31) may explain this best. Augustine is quoting a potential interlocutor on the meaning of the creation story at the start of Genesis:

> "Thus, even if Genesis is silent about God's having made something, neither sound faith nor solid comprehension allows any doubt that God made it; and it follows that no sober teaching [*sobria doctrina*] will dare to assert that those waters are equal sharers in eternity with God just because we hear them mentioned in the book of Genesis without, however, finding there any indication that they were made."

Augustine regards the search for and promulgation of truth as active, interactive, and ongoing, though it must stay within the limits of emotional and experiential commitment (here, "sound faith") and logical necessity (here, "solid comprehension"). The church wishes to preside over the search, but has few resources for intellectual coercion. It is also important to note that the search is often occupied with matters that seem abstract or abstruse to a modern sensibility—there was apparently a lot of literary and philosophical gamesmanship in such discussions. This is all very different from voluminous, detailed "doctrine" on the conduct of life formulated and handed down legalistically from a church hierarchy.

Vanitas, vanus, "emptiness," "empty-headedness," "pretentious," etc., never "vanity" or "vain": Pounded in by Ecclesiastes, the scriptural concept is, basically, lack of substance or lastingness. The Latin words, though translating this concept adequately, incline (to judge from their own previous literary history, including pagan authors) toward what we would term "no center" or "nothing between the ears." Notions of physical primping and strutting don't figure here, but intellectual pretension does: People who pride themselves on their learning may be merely full of themselves. This is Augustine's obsessive characterization of his youthful self and of the non-Christian mentality generally.

Species, speciosus, pulchritudo, pulcher, forma, formosus, the core of a highly poetic and thematic collection of expressions for beauty: Augustine's first venture into authorship was a work called "On the Beautiful and the Fitting," and he remained preoccupied with how things fit together as wholes, and with the connection between outward impression and inward purpose. God as the creator and ruler of the good and beautiful universe was a natural resting place for the mind of a man who was fundamentally a literary artist, putting words together to attract and lead, as well as to help him figure out what he himself thought.

So intricately and ingeniously does Augustine deploy this set of words that a translator has to develop them in something like the way he does, to try to maintain at least a little of the sense. *Species* is an appearance (real or not) or representation, an attractive or splendid appearance, a thing looked at, the act of looking, a category, and a Platonic archetype. *Speciosus* is mainly "worth looking at" or beautiful. This allows for a great deal of play on, for example, the stages of creation in book 13 (i.e., when the universe could be seen at all, different divisions of it that could be seen, and when it was worth looking at).

The rhetorical structure of *forma* and *formosus* (with the help of the verb *formare*) is similar in book 13: basically, God shapes the universe to make it really shapely, or both physically attractive and metaphysically worthy of his creative activity.

Pulcher and *pulchritudo* concentrate on physical and sensual beauty, but by no means refer to this exclusively. In fact, Augustine's famous cry to God, "I took too long to fall in love with you, beauty so ancient and so new" (book 10, chapter 38), uses the word *pulchritudo* with the rather erotic verb *amare* (see immediately below). How's that for a metaphor?

Caritas, amor, amare, diligere, diligentia, terms with connotations ranging from transcendent love to rampant lust to dutiful devotion: *Caritas* is (though not exclusively) the divine love that humans must imitate, of 1 Corinthians 13; *amor* and *amare*, though evolving, had hardly yet shed their connotations of eroticism; *diligere* and *diligentia* were both personal and impersonal, warm and cool, abstract and concrete. Most shocking in the poetic complex of emotion—and I maintain that the Augustine of the *Confessions* was a feeling man more than a thinking one—are images of God as the ultimate seducer and ravisher. Therefore, I've found myself unable to translate everything as "love." Terms like "passion" and "losing my heart" appear even in strictly religious connections wherever I think they're called for by Augustine's own word choice and the context.

Continentia, contineo, continens, words hovering steadily over the topic of sexual abstinence, but in my translation almost always "self-control" or "self-restraint" or a similar general term: Our "chastity" and "celibacy" are narrower than these words: chastity tends to be about the avoidance of premarital and extramarital sex, and celibacy about the exclusion of sex from an institutional religious vocation. Moreover, our terms concentrate on states of life, whereas the Latin *continentia* semantic group concentrates on the psychological, on willpower and self-control—literally "holding back" or "holding in"—not its results. "Abstinence" is technically the closest word in English, but it is unfortunately freighted with the distracting reminder of a long-running American public education controversy.

I can offer only brief, general justifications for the ways I treat Augustine's most challenging compositional quirks. Mostly, the translation must speak for itself.

He was educated to the highest level of literary eloquence, but other influences on him also seem profound. Among these are the rather commonplace and flat style of the Latin scriptures and early Christian Latin liturgy, the dryness and succinctness of certain philosophical writing (especially that of Aristotle), and the clerical day's sheer rush and strain. This author must have dictated routinely to an amanuensis (or a team of them) and lacked time to revise. Once, at Thomas Aquinas College, I confronted a rare complete collection of Augustine's surviving works—sermons, letters, treatises, biblical commentaries—in their large cabinet. No one human being can write that much by hand or put it through multiple versions.

In a couple of connections, remediation through translation is needed. Augustine is not generous with nouns, especially not with proper nouns; he relies on hearers and readers to follow lengthy, varying discourse about someone or something mentioned only at the start, or not mentioned at all. The Manichaeans, for example, are sometimes just "those [people]"—that's the classic forensic manner of contempt as well as of brevity. I fill in a lot of blanks, believing it to be very tiresome behavior to send readers to footnote after footnote just so that I can try to simulate a degree of cursoriness that can't exist in formal English writing except under the headings "careless" and "bad." Any representation of Augustine that gives that impression is not authentic.

I do *not* fill in blanks with elaborations in unmitigated modern liturgical or theological terms. A passage on metaphysics (such as that in book 13, chapter 27) crammed with different "things" may be exasperating, but it serves Augustine's emphatic intention in the *Confessions* not to pronounce definitively on matters he can't definitely know. It could not conceivably be correct to "translate" from such a passage that the Trinity has "persons"—from *personae,* standing mainly for "mask" or "role," or "personality," and used in some combination of those ancient senses in Augustine's *On the Trinity,* books 5–7, but very certainly not with the common modern meaning of "human being," which is what the great majority of English speakers would innocently understand.

As a partly folksy, sometimes smirking writer—or just as a man of his time—Augustine sometimes commits himself where his translators have wished he wouldn't, and this has led them to gloss over what he does plainly express. He speaks, for instance, contemptuously of women as women, merely because they're not expected to let their men disappear into an ascetic community, or to come along themselves: they're "little women," the diminutive, not just "women" (book 6, chapter 24). The lexical history of this word could easily have justified my writing "the girls" or "the little ladies." And Augustine really does talk about the embarrassment of nocturnal emissions for a man called to celibacy (book 10, chapter 41). He can't have meant his readers in any language to chew a fingernail and ask, "Could he be saying—*that?*" Yes, he's saying it. But I would have had trouble picking this up from even the best current translations on their own.

Finally, I think a translation's pacing and layout need to challenge any impression of Augustine—in this work, anyway—as a plodder or systematizer rather than a poetic, organically branching, rather whimsical author. Within the very different conventions of English writing, choices in sentence division, punctuation within sentences, and paragraphing can all freely reflect a translator's sense of an ancient author's train of thought. I actually felt that for Augustine a whole new physical structure was warranted.

Or maybe I should state that less boldly. I personally experienced that I could make more progress in difficult passages when I thought about the Greek *Meditations* of the Roman philosopher-emperor Marcus Aurelius (who reigned from A.D. 161 to 180). It's doubtful that the *Meditations,* a sort of private intellectual journal, circulated much in antiquity, and even more doubtful that Augustine knew the work. But the digressive, piecemeal manner of a great thinker reflecting on matters personal and emotional as well as abstract and general, and the familiar post–Golden Age tendency away from cohesive and single-minded exposition, seemed similar in these two authors. And I found it much easier to get through tough passages of Augustine when I began to lay them out in a more Aurelian manner, in short paragraphs like the *Meditations'* independent entries.

This layout allows Augustine more explicit latitude, whereas the long paragraphs of previous English translations hardly separate prayer, narrative, homily, and speculation, jamming all these together both physically and, as implied, logically. It also allows the general reader more freedom from the notion that an author should just get on with streamlined thought.

Often I felt I could see more clearly Augustine's dance steps when I tried to mark his rhythms with the white space so useful in modern poetry and novels, but greatly circumscribed in ancient literature, because the cadences of oral delivery expressed so much so effectively, and writers assumed that even individuals reading alone would rely on these cadences. Perhaps some of these divisions are themselves clumsy, but if they only provoke debate and thereby bring more attention to the task of translating this astonishing author, I'll count that as progress.

CONFESSIONS

BOOK 1

1. You are mighty, Master, and to be praised with a powerful voice: great is your goodness, and of your wisdom there can be no reckoning.* Yet to praise you is the desire of a human being, who is some part of what you created; a human hauling his deathliness in a circle,† hauling in a circle the evidence of his sin, and the evidence that you stand against the arrogant.‡

But still a mortal, a given portion of your creation, longs to extol you. In yourself you rouse us, giving us delight in glorifying you, because you made us with yourself as our goal, and our heart is restless until it rests in you.

---

* As throughout the *Confessions*, Augustine draws phrases from the Psalms; here he echoes Psalms 48:1, 96:4, 145:3, and 147:5.
† 2 Corinthians 4:10.
‡ 1 Peter 5:5, quoting Proverbs 3:34.

Grant me, Master, to know and understand whether a person ought first to call on you or to praise you; and which of the following is first, to know you or to call on you? But who invokes you without knowing you? In his ignorance, he might call on the wrong thing. Or instead, are you invoked in order to be known? But how will people invoke a being in whom they don't believe already? And how will they believe without a preacher?*

But those who search for God will praise him, since by seeking him they will find him,† and by finding him they will praise him. Let me search for you, Master, even while calling on you, and while believing in you, let me call on you. The faith you gave me—which you breathed into me through your son's human life and through the service your preacher performed—calls on you, Master.‡

2. So how will I call on my God, my God and my Master, since inevitably calling *on* him is calling him *in*to myself? But what place is there in me to come into for my God—for *God* to come into *me*—the God who made heaven and earth? Is it as if, God my Master, there is anything in me that could hold you? Could in fact the sky and the earth, which you created, and in which you created me, hold you? Or, because without you whatever is would not be, does it come about that whatever is holds you? Since, therefore, I also exist, why do I beg that you come into me, when I wouldn't exist in the first place unless you were in

---

* Romans 10:14.
† Matthew 7:7–8, Luke 11:10.
‡ The preacher was probably Ambrose, bishop of Milan, who was instrumental in Augustine's conversion. See pages xxxi–xxxiii of my introduction concerning the use of "Master" instead of the traditional "Lord."

me? I am not now in hell, and yet you are there, too, because if I go down into hell, there you are.*

To sum up, I would not exist, my God, I would not exist at all, unless you existed in me. Or is it rather that I would not exist unless I existed in you, from whom, through whom, in whom, everything exists?† That's it, Master, that's it. To what place can I call you, if I am *in* you? And from what place can you come into me? Where would it be, outside heaven and earth, that I could withdraw, so that God could come into me there—the God who said, "Heaven and earth are filled with me"?‡

3. So then do the sky and the earth hold you, since you fill them? Or do you fill them, with some left over, since they don't hold you? And where do you pour back what remains of you after you've filled earth and sky? Or do you not need to be held within anything—you who contain everything, since the things you fill, you fill by containing them? The vessels that are full of you don't make you stationary, because you don't spill out even though they break. And when you spill out over us,§ you don't lie inert on the ground but instead lift us up. You don't scatter in all directions but instead gather us together. But the everything that you fill, you fill with all your being. Or, because everything that exists can't hold the whole of you, does everything contain a part of you, with everything containing the same part at the same time? Do single things hold single parts of you, and larger things larger parts, and smaller things smaller parts? Then is

* Psalms 139:8.
† Romans 11:36.
‡ Jeremiah 23:24.
§ Joel 2:28, Acts 2:17–18.

some part of you larger, and some part smaller? Or are you everywhere whole, and can no thing hold the whole of you?

4. Then what are you, my God? What are you, I ask, except God
the Master? Who is a master except—the Master? Or who is a
god except our God?* The highest, the most excellent, the most
powerful, all-powerful beyond all-powerful, most merciful and
most just, most remote and most present, most beautiful and
most powerful, unmoving but ungraspable, unchangeable but
changing everything, never new, never old, but making all
things new† while leading the arrogant into decrepitude, though
they are unaware of it. You are always active and always at rest,
gathering in but not in need, carrying and filling and protecting,
creating and nurturing and bringing to fulfillment, searching
though you lack nothing. You love, but you do not burn with
love, you are jealous yet carefree, you repent but you do not
grieve, you are angry yet serene,‡ you change your works but
you do not change your plan, you take back what you find but
have never lost. You are never poor, but you rejoice in what you
gain, never greedy, but you exact interest;§ more is paid to you
than owed, but the result is that you owe us. Yet who has anything that doesn't belong to you? You pay your debts though
you owe no one, you remit your debts but lose nothing. And
what have we said now, my God, my life, my holy sweetness, or
what does anyone ever say in speaking of you? But woe to those
who are silent about you; however garrulous they are in general,
they are mute about what counts.

---

* Psalms 17:32.
† Wisdom of Solomon 7:27.
‡ See, by contrast, the "jealous" God of the Ten Commandments and Genesis 6:6, where
the deity repents, grieves, and is destructively angry.
§ Matthew 25:27.

5. Who will grant me repose in you? Who will grant your arrival in my heart and the drunkenness that comes from you, making me forget the evils that are mine˙ and embrace the single good that belongs to me, which is you?

Have pity on me and let me speak. What am I to you, in myself, that you command love for yourself from me?—but unless I give it to you, you inveigh against me and menace immense miseries. Is my misery a petty thing if I don't love you? Pitiful me, in that case!

Tell me, in the name of your mercies, you, Master, who are my God, what you are to me. Say to my soul, "I myself am your rescue."† Say it in such a way that I hear it. Here before you are the ears with which my heart hears, Master. Open them and say to my soul, "I myself am your rescue." I will run after the sound of your voice and lay hold of you. Do not hide your face from me.‡ Let me die, to keep me from dying, and let me see your face.§

6. My soul's house is too meager for you to visit; enlarge it. It is falling down; rebuild it. Inside it are things that would disgust you to see: I confess this, and I know it. But who's going to clean it? Or rather, to whom else am I going to shout, "Clean away from me, Master, the hidden things that are my own, and spare your slave from the hidden things coming from others!"?¶

˙ Jeremiah 44:9.
† Psalms 35:3.
‡ Psalms 27:9.
§ In Exodus 33:20–23, God protects Moses from the deadly sight of the divine face.
¶ Psalms 19:12–13; the modern English version is somewhat different.

I believe, and because I believe, Master, I speak;* you know it, Master. Didn't I openly divulge to you my offenses, my God, confronting myself, and didn't you acquit my heart's guilt?† I won't contest the matter in court with you,‡ who are the truth, and I don't want to mislead my own mind and let my wrongdoing commit perjury against itself.§ So I won't contest the matter with you in court, because if you, Master, are witness to my wrongdoings—who can make that stand up?¶

7. But nevertheless allow me to speak in the face of your mercy. I am dust and ashes,** but nevertheless let me speak; because here is your mercy—and not a human being who will only make fun of me—to which I am speaking. Maybe you too make fun of me, but you will turn around and pity me.

What is it, after all, that I want to say, Master, except that I don't know where I came from to this place, into this—do I call it a deathly life or a living death? I don't know. But taking me in their arms to rear up as their own were the solaces of your mercies—as I heard from the parents of my body, the man from whom and the woman in whom you shaped me in the realm of time; I myself don't remember, naturally.

Yes, the comforts of human milk took me under their care, but it wasn't my mother or my nurses who filled their own breasts; you yourself gave me, through them, the nourishment of in-

---

* Psalms 116:10. The New Revised Standard Version reads, "I have kept my faith, even when I said, 'I am greatly afflicted.'" The verse is quoted in 2 Corinthians 4:13.
† Psalms 32:5.
‡ Job 9:2–4.
§ Psalms 27:12.
¶ Psalms 130:3.
** Genesis 18:27, Job 42:6.

fancy, according to your dispensation; you gave me your riches, which you've allocated clear down to the lowest place in the universe. You gave me the gift of not wanting more than you gave me, and to those who nursed me, you gave the desire to give to me what you gave to them. They wanted, through the feelings you ordained, to give to me what overflowed in them, coming from you. Their good was my good coming from them, because it wasn't actually from them, but only through them.

All good things, in fact, are from you, God, and from my God is my full deliverance. I became aware of this later, when you shouted at me through these very things you bestow inside me and outside me. But at first, back then, I knew enough to suckle, and to find satisfaction with pleasures, and to cry at physical annoyances—and I knew nothing else.

8. Later I started to smile as well, first while I was sleeping, and then wakefully. People have told me this about myself, and I believe it, since this is what we see babies in general doing; I myself certainly don't remember doing it.

And there I was, gradually perceiving where I was, and desiring to make my desires known to people who could grant them—but I couldn't show my desires, because they were inside me, whereas other people were outside, and no perception that they possessed had the power of entering into my consciousness; so I threw around my arms and legs, and I threw off sounds, making signs resembling my wishes—the few signs I could make, that is, and as good as I could make them; there wasn't really any resemblance. And when compliance was not forthcoming, either because people didn't understand me or wouldn't do something to my disadvantage, I was wrathful that my elders wouldn't submit themselves to me, and that free people wouldn't be my slaves, and I wreaked vengeance on them—by crying.

I've been instructed, by those babies in a position to instruct me, that this is how they are; and they, though hardly knowing the facts, have informed me that I was like them, and informed me better than those knowledgeable people who nurtured me.

9. So here we are: my babyhood died long ago, but I myself am still alive. But you, Master, who live forever, and in whom nothing dies; since before the origins of all ages, and before anything that could even be called "before," you exist, and you exist as the God and the Master of all things, which you created, and in your presence every impetus of unstable things stands fast, and the immutable sources of all mutable things remain unmovable, and the reasons for all unreasoning and time-bound things have their eternal life: God, tell me, your suppliant, in your pity tell me, a pitiful human being belonging to you, whether my babyhood followed on some other, expired stage of my life?

Was that the stage I spent inside my mother's womb? About that age a certain amount has been told me, and I personally have seen pregnant ladies. My delight, my God, tell me what took place even before that? Was I anywhere or anyone? I have no one who can tell me this. My father and mother couldn't, nor could other people's experience or my own memory. But are you laughing at me as I ask these questions, and commanding praise and testimony from me for yourself that draws on what I do know?

10. I testify to you, Master of the sky and the earth, reciting praise to you out of the earliest days of my babyhood, which I don't remember. You have granted to a human being the power to conjecture about himself based on the evidence of others, and to trust as authoritative many utterances even of trivial womenfolk about him.

At any rate, I existed and I lived even then, and already near the end of babyhood, in its borderland, I was seeking the signals by which I could make my perceptions known to others. Where would such an organism come from, if not from you, Master? Will anyone emerge as the craftsman who makes himself? Or is any channel drawn from anywhere else, by which existence and life can run into us? Is this channel anything except your making of us, Master, for whom being and living are not two different things, because to be, in the highest sense, and to live, in the highest sense, are one and the same?

You are the highest, and you do not change,* and the day that is today does not pass by in you—and yet it does pass by in you, because in you are also all these lower things: they would not have their paths on which to pass by, unless you contained these paths. And since your years do not fall short,† your years are the day that is today. How many days, our own and our ancestors', have passed through your today, and from it have taken their limits, and in whatever way have existed! And other days will pass through and take their limits and in whatever way will exist.

---

* Malachi 3:6.
† Psalms 102:27, quoted in Hebrews 1:12.

You, however, are yourself, the same one, and all things that are tomorrow and beyond, and all that are yesterday and before, you will make to be today, you have made to be today. What is it to me, if someone doesn't understand? Let even the one who says "What is this?" have joy. Let him have joy even in saying it, and let him love finding you through not finding you out, rather than not find you by trying to find you out.

11. Listen to me, God! Tragic, the sins of humankind! A human being says this, and you have pity on him, since you made him yet didn't make the sin in him. Who will bring to my mind the sin of my infancy, since no one is clean of sin in your eyes, not even a baby whose life on earth is only a day long? Can any tiny little one at all recall this for me, a child in whom I see what I don't remember about myself?

So how was I sinning at that time? Was it because I strained, greedily drooling and wailing, toward my nurses' breasts? If I did that now, fixating in this way not on breast milk but on some food suitable to my age, I would be laughed at and very rightly taken to task. Back then, therefore, I was doing things that merited a scolding, but since I couldn't have understood anyone scolding me, custom and common sense didn't allow me to be scolded. As we grow up, we pull up behavior of that sort by the roots and toss it out. I haven't seen anyone, when cleaning something out, consciously throw away good things.

But could even that temporary behavior have been good: weeping for something that would have been harmful if handed over; getting bitterly angry at free people and grown-ups, the baby's own progenitors, who refuse to subject themselves to him; striking at and struggling to hurt, to the limits of his powers, many people besides who know better than him and don't submit to the slightest gesture that indicates his sovereign will—because they won't obey commands that it would be disastrous to obey?

Being weak, babies' bodies are harmless, but babies' minds aren't harmless. I myself have observed (carefully enough that I know what I'm writing about) a tiny child who was jealous: he couldn't speak yet, but his face was pale and had a hateful expression as he glared at the child who shared his nurse. Who doesn't know that this happens? Mothers and nurses say that they avert this curse with one kind of cure or another. The alternative would be to believe that *this* is really "harmlessness" or "innocence": where a wellspring of milk is flowing and overflowing from the very bosom of abundance, he doesn't tolerate an adjunct who absolutely needs this resource and is still drawing his life from this single food. But these things are gently put up with, not because they're nothing, or because they're small matters, but because at a more advanced age they'll disappear. You can confirm this by the fact that you can't calmly endure the very same faults when you detect them in someone older.

12. You, therefore, Master, who gave life to that baby, and gave him a body, which, as we perceive, you fitted out with the physical senses, you composed from its various parts, you beautified with its shape, and for its wholeness and wholesome security you placed in its bosom all the impulses of a living being: you command me to praise you even for these small things, and to make my testimony to you and chant psalms to your name, to you the most high, because you are God, all-powerful and good—and this would be the case even if you'd made nothing

but these small things, as no one but you, the One, can make them. From you comes every form, from you who are most sublimely becoming—the most beautiful, that is—you who form all things and arrange all beings in order through your law.

This was an age, then, Master, through which I don't remember living, and for an account of which I trust others, and through which only on the evidence of other babies I can conclude that I passed (though the conclusion seems highly reliable): so I shrink from placing this age in the same category as this conscious life of mine that I live in the world. To the degree that babyhood belongs to the darkness of my forgetting, it is like the time during which I lived in my mother's womb. But if I was conceived in wrongdoing and in her sins my mother nourished me in her womb,* then where—I beg you to tell me, my God and my Master—where and when was I your slave innocent? Well then, let me leave aside that time: What, after all, does it have to do with me now, since I can't recollect any trace of it?

13. Didn't I move onward from there, from babyhood, and come to boyhood? Or rather did boyhood come into me and take over from babyhood? Babyhood didn't leave me—what "away" did it have to go to? Yet now it wasn't there. I wasn't an "in-fant," or "non-speaker," any longer but a boy, talking.

And I do remember this, and afterward I realized how it came about that I learned to talk. Older people didn't teach me, purveying the words in a fixed order in lessons, as they taught me to read and write later on. Instead, I used the mind you gave me,

* Psalms 51:5.

my God. With various murmurs and other sounds, and with parts of my body moving in different ways, I tried to deliver the impressions of my heart, in order to enforce obedience to my will. When I couldn't prevail in everything, or with everyone, I would grab with my memory. That is, when people around me named some object and, in accordance with that word, moved their bodies toward something, I saw, and I grasped that they were naming the object in this way, by the sound that they made when they wanted to indicate it. The evidence of this was their physical movements, a sort of natural worldwide language arising from facial expressions and movements of the eyes, and actions of other parts of the body, and the voice's pitch that shows the mind's disposition in seeking out, retaining, discarding, and avoiding things.

In due course, when I had heard words often in their proper places in a variety of sentences, I gradually deduced what they were symbols for; and once I had tamed my mouth and made it use these symbols, I could announce my wishes through them. Thus I began to share with those around me the symbols for making wishes known, and I ventured farther from shore on the stormy sea of our common human life—depending on my parents' authority and the power of people older than myself.

14. God, my God, what wretchedness I experienced there, what a mockery was made of me; but this was in fact set before me, as a boy, as the proper way to live. I was to submit to those guiding my views, that I might flourish in this world and excel in the science of garrulity, which would pander slavishly to the penchant for prestige you find among humankind and to wealth that was in reality no such thing.

Hence, I was handed over to a school to learn reading and writing—though I was woefully unfamiliar with what use there could be in these things. Nevertheless, if I was sluggish in learning, I found myself being pounded. This recourse was in fact praised by our ancestors, who, as they before us passed through this poor life in their multitudes, built ahead of themselves pathways of anguish that we were forced to walk to the end, with multiples of hardship for the sons of Adam.*

However, Master, we did encounter people who prayed to you, and we learned from them. We understood—as far as we could understand—that you were a mighty someone who, though not evident to our physical senses, could give ear to us and come to our aid.

As a boy, then, I began to pray to you, my help and my refuge, and in invoking you I broke the knots around my tongue. As a little one, I prayed to you with no little fervor to keep me from a pounding in school. When you didn't listen, because you didn't want to indulge me into idiocy, my welts were a source of laughter for older people, including my parents, who didn't want any fisticuffs of misfortune to come my way—but to me the beating was a tremendous, grievous evil.

15. Is anyone's courage so great, because it clings to you with mammoth devotion; is there anyone, I ask—and come to think of it, a certain kind of cement-headedness could achieve this, so in fact there is someone—who in clinging to you reverently is so enormously devoted that he can pooh-pooh, in this grown-

* Genesis 3:16–19, Sirach 40:1.

up manner, racks and hooks and similar devices for torture, panicked pleas to escape which rise to you from all over the earth? Could he love those harboring a razor-sharp fear of such things and yet, as our parents did, laugh at the torments our teachers inflicted on us? We boys didn't fear these torments any less than we would have feared full-blown torture, and we didn't entreat you less passionately to let us evade them.

Nevertheless, we did sin by writing or reading or thinking about our studies less than the school was trying to exact from us. Our memory was adequate, and we were bright enough: it was your will that we be well enough provided, for our age. But we enjoyed playing, and were punished for this by those who, for their own part, were busy with similar activities. The inanity of adults is called "business," but when boys behave like that, adults punish them, and no one has compassion for the boys—or for the adults, when it comes to that.

But no—some respectable man weighing up matters may well approve of my being beaten because as a boy I played ball, and by playing ball I was blocked from a swifter training in letters, with which as an adult I could play in a much uglier way. Did the activities of the actual man who beat me show a different attitude? He was the sort who, if his partner in teaching defeated him in some silly debate, was tortured by greater gall and envy than I felt when my partner in play conquered me in the contest of a ball game.

16. But nevertheless I sinned, Master, my God, creator and regulator of all natural things, but only the regulator of sins; Mas-

ter, my God, I sinned in acting against the instructions of my parents and those teachers. I could in fact make good use of literacy later on—no matter the spirit in which those around me wished me to imbibe it. And it wasn't from superior judgment that I was disobedient, but from a passion for playing, as I was hot for swaggering victories in our contests, and I lusted to have my ears tickled, until they burned and itched incrementally, with tales that weren't true.*

It was the same kind of burning interest that flashed in my eyes when they were directed toward shows, at which adults play. The producers, however, are endowed with such preeminent prestige that almost all parents hope their little ones will take up the same profession. The parents—however—are quite happy to let their children be assaulted if such shows get in the way of their studies—through which the parents are keen to have the children reach the goal of producing shows.†

Look on this sort of thing with pity in your heart, Master, and set free those who already call on you, and have pity also on those who still don't, so that they call on you and you can set them free.

17. Before I was out of my boyhood, I had heard of the eternal life promised to us by the lowly embodiment of the Master, our God, who came down to meet our lofty pride. The sign of his cross was repeatedly made on me, and I was again and again

---

* 2 Timothy 4:3–4.
† One of the principal duties of high public office was to fund and manage public entertainment.

"preserved" with his salt,* right from the time I came out of my mother's womb, as my mother had a strong hope in you.

You saw, Master, that when I was still a boy I had some sort of stomach affliction and a fever that brought me close to death; you saw, my God, because you were already my guardian, how excitedly and with how much trust I demanded baptism in the Anointed One, who is your son and my God and Master; I demanded it in the name of my mother's duty to God, and the duty of your church, which is the mother of us all.

The mother of my body's life was deeply shaken. With her pure heart and her faith in you, she was already in labor with more love than before, at the start of my life, and now it was to save me for an endless life as well. Now she would have seen to it, in a great flurry, that I was inducted and washed in the saving sacraments while I testified to your power, Jesus my Master, for the pardoning of sins.

But just then, I recovered. Therefore my cleansing was delayed—as if it were required that I continue getting dirty if I was going to live; the reason for the delay being, clearly, that after that cleansing the liability for dirty crimes of mine would be graver and place me in greater jeopardy.

That's what I already believed then, and so did my mother and the whole household—except for a sole person, my father; he, however, didn't prevail against the right over me asserted by my mother's piety; he couldn't keep me from believing in Christ, in line with his own unbelief at the time. In fact, she made a con-

---

* These are rites administered to a catechumen, or person receiving instruction before baptism.

siderable bustle to ensure that you, my God, were my father, rather than him. And in this you helped her conquer her husband, to whom she was enslaved even though she was a better person. Even in replacing him, she was his dutiful slave, because at any event she was obedient to your command.*

18. I beg of you, my God: I want to know, if you also want me to know, what the rationale was in putting me off from being baptized then. Was it for my own good that the reins holding me back from sinning would be let loose, so to speak? Were they not in fact let loose? On the same rationale, even now, all around me the cry echoes in my ears concerning one person or another, "Let him alone, let him do it: he's not baptized yet."

Yet where physical health is concerned, we don't say, "Let him go on being injured: he isn't healed yet." How much better if I had been healed quickly, and my treatment had been conscientiously carried out by those around me, and by myself, so that my soul's rescue, once in my possession, would have been safe under the guardianship of you who had rescued me.

Better, for certain. Yet how many huge waves of temptation seemed to be looming for me after childhood; indeed, my mother was aware of them already, and she preferred to launch on them the earth out of which I was still going to be formed in the time to come, rather than the baptized image of my maker.†

---

* These rather disturbing assertions are quite telescoped and ambiguous in their wording. I have gone for the maximum paradoxical pointedness, which I believe is strongly supported by both the literal meaning here (as far as it is accessible) and by Augustine's typical vivid wit.

† Baptism, the one-time cleansing and regenerating ritual, was during this period often delayed until the deathbed, as in the case of the emperor Constantine. Augustine attributes to his mother the most idealistic reason for the delay: those likely to lack self-control would dishonor their baptism by their behavior.

19. But in my boyhood itself, which gave rise to less dread than my youth did about what I might do, I had no passion for reading and writing and hated to be pushed into them, yet I *was* pushed into them, and this turned out to be for my good. I didn't *do* good, as I didn't learn unless I was forced to; no one does good against his will, even if what he does is good. Nor did those who were pushing me do good, but rather good gradually arose for me from you, my God. People didn't examine the purpose to which I was putting what I learned, unless that purpose was to sate insatiable greed for what was in reality poverty aplenty and degrading glory.

But you, who know the number of hairs on our heads, put to use the wrongheaded pressure everyone was putting on me to learn, and turned it to true utility for me. My wrongheadedness, on the other hand, in not wanting to learn, you used to punish me, because I did deserve to be worked over with the penalties, tiny boy yet immense sinner that I was. In this way you did right by me through those doing wrong, and you requited me justly for my sins. This is your command, and it is carried out in full, that every mind not conforming to your law is its own punishment.

20. But what was the reason I hated studying Greek, in which I was initiated as a very small boy? Even now, I haven't fully solved this mystery. I was infatuated with Latin—not the part taught by primary school teachers, but by those called grammarians. The rudiments, or the instruction in reading, writing, and arithmetic, I treated as just as burdensome, and just as much of a punishment, as the whole of the Greek curriculum.

* Matthew 10:30 and Luke 12:7.

Where would the blame be, if not in my sinfulness and my nugatory nature, by virtue of which I'm nothing but flesh and breath walking on its way and never returning to where it's been?*

At any event, those rudiments are better, because they're more solid. Through them developed in me, and came to fruition, and remains in my possession, the ability to read any piece of writing I come across and to write something if I want to; that's better than the training in which I was forced to memorize the wanderings of some Aeneas or other, while I had no sense of my own wanderings; and to bewail the death of Dido, because she "died for love,"† when all the time I endured dry-eyed the utter misery of myself dying away from you, God, my life.

21. What was more pitiful than me, a pitiful person not pitying himself but weeping for the death of Dido, which came about through her "love" of Aeneas; while I didn't weep for my own death, which was coming about through not loving you, God, the light of my heart and the bread I eat within my soul, and the manliness that actually marries my mind and is a legitimate husband to the bosom of my meditations?

I didn't love you, and I cheated on you like a true slut,‡ and as I cheated there rang around me the words "Excellent, excellent!" A "loving" attachment to this world *is* cheating on you, and that expression "Excellent, excellent!" makes a person ashamed if it doesn't describe him. But I didn't cry for these reasons; I cried

* Psalms 78:39.
† Vergil's *Aeneid,* an epic poem about the legendary founding of Rome; in book 4, the Carthaginian queen Dido commits suicide when abandoned by her lover, Aeneas.
‡ The imagery also accords with Psalms 73:27, which in the Latin Bible has the wording of erotic unfaithfulness.

about Dido and her life quenched when she sought to end it by the sword; but I was seeking the last, the least things in your creation and left you behind; I was earth going into the earth.* If I had been forbidden to read those works, I would have grieved to be unable to read what made me grieve. This is the insanity of considering such literary training more respectable and more fertile than the training by which I learned to read and write.

22. So now let my God shout in my soul, and let your truth say to me, "That isn't better training! It isn't!" Absolutely better is the primary schooling. Just take me, for example: I'm far more apt to forget the wanderings of Aeneas and everything else of the kind than to forget to read and write.

Yes, curtains hang in the doorways of literary classrooms, but they stand less for prestigious exclusivity than for the obscuring of wandering error. People I'm not afraid of any longer may as well not yell at me, as I testify to *you* now, in the manner my soul desires, my God, and as a means to love your good paths I second your censure of the evil paths I took.

The hawkers of literary studies—and the customers as well— might as well not yell at me, because if I challenge them by asking whether it's true what the poet said, that Aeneas came to Carthage way back when, those who are less well educated will answer that they don't know, while those who are better educated will say that it isn't true. But if I ask how Aeneas's name is spelled, everybody who's learned to spell it will tell me the truth, according to the generally accepted human compact established for the use of those symbols.

* Genesis 3:19.

Likewise, if I were to ask which it would be a greater drawback in this life of ours for any given person to forget, reading and writing or those poetic fairy tales, who (unless he'd forgotten his own existence, i.e., was brain-dead) wouldn't see what the answer needed to be?

I sinned, when I was small, by placing my passion for these idiocies before more useful resources—or rather I reviled the latter and was enamored with the former. At the time "One plus one equals two, two plus two equals four" was a revolting singsong to me, but I found adorable that extravaganza of emptiness, the wooden horse full of armed warriors and the conflagration of Troy and—just imagine!—the ghost of Creusa.*

23. Why, then, did I despise the Greek curriculum, when it warbled comparable material? Homer, too, is an expert in spinning little yarns of a similar kind, and his works comprise excessively sweet nothingness. Yet he was distasteful to me as a boy.

I believe that it's the same for Vergil with Greek boys, when they're forced to learn him the way I was forced to learn Homer. Plainly, it was the difficulty, it was nothing but the difficulty of learning a foreign language thoroughly, that sprinkled a sort of gall all over the savors of fictive storytelling in Greek.

I didn't know any of those words, yet savage threats and violent punishments loomed over me to *make* me know. At one point in the past, of course, as a baby, I hadn't known any Latin words, either, but I took note and learned them without any terror or torture, amid the sweet talk of my nurses and the jokes of people who were chuckling to me and the pleasure I shared with

* See book 2 of Vergil's *Aeneid*.

people who played with me. Really, I learned without any penal burden from instructors pressing down on me, since my own heart pressed me forward into giving birth to the things it conceived. This couldn't have happened unless I learned some words not from teachers but from mere talkers, in whose hearing even I could begin to labor in bringing forth whatever was in my mind.

From this, it's clear enough that free inquisitiveness has a greater power for learning than timorousness under compulsion. But the latter chokes off the flow of the former according to your laws, God, your laws that reach from teachers' switches clear to the ordeals of the martyrs; your laws that have the power to blend wholesome bitterness into our life and call us back to you from the noxious pleasure through which we have withdrawn from you.

24. Listen to my supplication, Master, so that my soul doesn't stagger under your instruction, so that I don't stumble in testifying to your mercies, by which you tore me away from all my ruinous pathways. Thus you'll grow sweet to me beyond all that led me wrong, in my willingness to follow it. Thus I'll love you most mightily, and grasp your hand with all the strength of my inmost being. Thus you'll tear me away from every trial, clear to the end.*

Here you are, Master, my king and my God. May whatever useful thing I learned as a boy be your slave, may whatever I speak and write and read and count serve you, because when I learned frivolity, you gave me your instruction, and you forgave the sins

* 1 Corinthians 1:8.

of my frivolous enjoyments. In the course of my studies I did learn many useful words—but they can also be learned in serious study, and that path is the safe one for boys to walk.

25. Oh, you woeful river of human ways! Who's going to stand against you? How long will you flow without drying up? How long will you go on sweeping the sons of Eve into the vast and fearsome sea, barely to be crossed by those who have embarked on that piece of wood, the cross?

Didn't I read, among your works, that Jupiter both caused the thunder and committed adultery? Certainly, he couldn't do both, but the story set out was such that real-life adultery would have the sanction to imitate him, with fictional thunder playing the pimp.

Who among the professors in their hooded gowns gives a serious hearing even to someone in their same arena who's loudly declaiming, "Homer made these things up and was giving human traits to the gods; I'd rather he'd given divine traits to us"? But it's more true to say that, yes, Homer made these things up, but his method was to attribute divine traits to mortals behaving outrageously, so that outrages wouldn't be considered outrages, and so that whoever committed them would seem to be imitating not abandoned human beings but the gods in heaven.

26. And yet, you river of the underworld, the sons of humankind are tossed into you, and their fare along with them, so that they can learn these things; and it's a great business when a transaction of this nature is enacted in the public square, before the

faces of the magistrates who decide the teaching stipend to be granted on top of the private fees. You, the river, clash your boulders with a crash, intoning, "Hence words are learned, hence eloquence is acquired, and they are eminently necessary for effecting persuasion and elucidating opinions."

Does it really follow that we wouldn't understand the words "rain of gold" and "bosom" and "sham" and "heaven's precincts," and other words that are written in the passage, unless Terence brought onto the scene a worthless young man using Jupiter as a justification for rape, while he contemplates some picture or other, painted on a partition, this wall-painting depicting "the manner in which, as they say, Jupiter made a golden rain run into Danae's bosom, once upon a time—a sham through which he managed to impose upon a woman"? Just look at how the young man lashes himself on in his lust, as if according to a heavenly precept:

> Oh, what a god! (quoth he). At the sky's summit he thunders, with a wrenching, a roiling of heaven's precincts!
> And I, a petty mortal, wouldn't do it? No, I did it, and quite gladly.˙

These words aren't in the least more opportunely learned through this indecency; in fact, through these words, indecency of that stripe is more boldly practiced. I'm not blaming the words; they're like choice, costly containers;† but the wine of wrongheadedness in them was used by drunken educators to

---

˙ In the comedy of Terence entitled *The Eunuch* (of which several lines are quoted here), a young man gains access to a young girl by trickery and rapes her.
† Proverbs 20:15.

start us on a round ourselves, and unless we drank, we were beaten up, and we weren't allowed to call in an arbitrator who was sober. Nevertheless, my God—under whose gaze my recollection is now carefree—I was actually glad to learn these things, and I enjoyed my ordeal, and for this reason I was called a promising boy.

27. My God, let me say something about my mind, your gift to me, and about the delusions by which it was worn down. A job was assigned to me, and it proved quite a source of disturbance for my soul, as I might be rewarded with praise, yet I was in terror of disgrace or a whipping: I was to give a speech of Juno in her aggrieved rage at being unable to keep the king of the Trojans from coming to Italy*—a speech that, as I had heard, Juno never gave. But we were forced, in our wanderings, to follow in the steps of poetic fabrications, and to express something in prose approximating what the poet had expressed in verse. And the boy who earned more praise for speaking was the one whose emoting stood out as more like aggrieved rage, as befit the worthiness of the character he was sketching, with the words clothing the sentiments in an appropriate manner.

But what should it have mattered to me, you true life, my God, that I was applauded for my performance, more than the rest of the large class, my fellow scholars of the same age? Wasn't all of this only smoke and wind? Wasn't there, then, any other possible exercise for my mind and my tongue? Your praise, Master, your praise as read in the scriptures would have been a stake to hold up the vine-shoot that was my heart, so that futile triviality wouldn't leave it a despicable prey to the birds of the air. There's

* Vergil, *Aeneid*, 1.37ff.

more than one way to make a sacrifice to those angels who've changed their allegiance.*

28. Why was it amazing that I was whisked off into empty places, leaving your home, my God? The men who were set before me to imitate were devastated if scolded for divulging, *with some foreign impropriety in pronunciation or a mistake in grammar,* any innocent actions of theirs; but if they *told* of their lustful indulgences *faultlessly*, with pure and flowing diction, eloquently and elaborately, they would preen with the flattery accorded them.

You see this, Master, yet stay silent, long-suffering and with so much mercy in your heart, and speaking the truth yourself. You won't always be silent, will you? Even now you pluck from this monstrous abyss† the soul that seeks you and thirsts for your delights,‡ the soul saying to you from the heart, "I have sought your face."§

Let me seek your face again, Master: a long way from your face is a life in the murk of emotion. And it isn't on foot and over a physical distance that a person goes away from you or returns to you; nor, in reality, did that younger son in your scripture seek out horses or chariots or ships, and he didn't fly away on wings for everyone to see, or even stir a step in his journey, in order to live in a faraway country and extravagantly waste what you gave him when he set off; you were a kind father in conferring it on him, but an even kinder one when he returned to you needy.¶ To

* I.e., rebellious angels are demonic. See 1 Corinthians 10:20 about pagans sacrificing to demons.
† Psalms 86:13.
‡ Psalms 42:2, 63:1.
§ Psalms 27:8.
¶ The prodigal son (Luke 15:11–32).

live in the emotion of desire, therefore, is to live in the murk of emotion, and this is to live a long way from your face.

29. Look, God the Master, and look with forbearance (as in fact you do), on how carefully the sons of men mind the rules of spellings and syllables handed down to them from speakers in the past, but disregard the eternal and unending laws of their rescue handed down to them by you.

If someone who upholds and teaches those ancient tenets should, against the rules of the language, pronounce the word *homo,* or "human being," without an aspiration in the first syllable, as '*omo,* he would offend other human beings more than if, in violation of *your* decrees, he hated a member of the humanity to which he belongs. It's as if he experienced that any enemy in the world could be more ruinous to him than the hatred that incites him against his enemy; or that anyone could wreak more grievous devastation on another person by hounding him than on his own heart by making an enemy. But surely, the art of letters isn't closer to his heart than what's written on his conscience,* which says that he's doing to someone else what he wouldn't want done to himself.†

How far apart from us you are, living on high and in silence, God who alone are great, you who in accordance with your tireless law strew cases of blindness—penalties in themselves— over cravings that aren't allowed: such as when a human being, hot on the trail of a reputation for eloquence, in front of a human judge, and with a human crowd standing all around him,

* Romans 2:15.
† The Golden Rule: see Tobit 4:15, Matthew 7:12, Luke 6:31.

lights into his enemy with the most brutal hatred, yet stays on absolutely unflagging guard against his *tongue* making a mistake and saying "among we human beings" (that is, with the wrong grammatical case), while, in his lunacy, he doesn't guard against removing a human being *from* among humankind (with the right case to go with that preposition).

30. As a mere boy, I sprawled like a forlorn lover on the threshold of such ethics. In this arena, on this wrestling floor, I was more wary of making a mistake in pronunciation than of envying people who didn't make one when I did.

I tell you, I testify to you, my God, about the things I was praised for by people whose approval meant a respectable life for me. I didn't have a view of the vortex of disgrace into which I'd been hurled out of your sight.* In your sight, what was more disgusting than myself at this point, when even people like that disapproved of me for fobbing off with innumerable lies the slave who was in charge of me, and my teachers and parents, out of my infatuation with playing, and my passion to be a spectator of twaddle, and my acting-up mimicry of comic nonsense?

I made thieving raids on my parents' storeroom and their table, whether under the incessant commands of my greedy gullet, or for the wherewithal to buy participation in games from boys who in fact enjoyed them just as much as I did.

In games themselves, I often laid traps to catch cheating victories, out of a brainless lust for superiority. And what was I less willing to endure, what did I so pitilessly prosecute, if I detected it, than the same thing I was doing to the other boys? But

* Psalms 31:22.

if I was detected and prosecuted, I preferred to go on the attack rather than give ground. Is *that* childhood innocence? It isn't, Master, it isn't.

But I beseech you, God, and I beseech you because these are exactly the sins that make the transition, from babysitting attendants and teachers, nuts and marbles to play with, and sparrows as pets, to governors and kings, gold, landed estates, slaves; these are in every respect the sins that make the transition as we grow greater and one stage of our life follows another; and accordingly, punishments grow greater following teachers' canings. You, *our* king, accordingly commended childhood's slight stature as a token of lowliness, when you said, "To such belongs the kingdom of heaven."*

31. Notwithstanding, Master, to you as the absolutely superior and the perfect originator and regulator of everything that is, to you as our God thanks are due—even had it been your will that I be nothing beyond a boy.

Even at that early stage, I existed, I lived and was conscious, and I was concerned with my body's soundness, which was a trace of that most secret oneness from which my being came; I guarded my physical senses, keeping them inviolable through an inward sensibility, and I delighted in the truth even in my small meditations about small matters. I didn't like to be misled, I had a strong memory, I was on the way to being equipped with articulate speech, I was soothed by friendship, I avoided pain, humiliation, empty-headedness.

* Matthew 19:14.

In a living being like me, what shouldn't have amazed, shouldn't have evoked praise? But all those things, such as they are, are gifts from my God. I didn't give them to myself, but they are good gifts, and all of them make up myself. Therefore the one who made me is good, and he himself is my good, and in his name I rejoice in all the good things that comprised me, even as a boy.

My sin was that I sought not in God himself, but in things he had created—in myself and the rest of his creation—delights, heights, and perceptions of what was true and right, and in this way I collapsed into sufferings, embarrassments, and erring ways.

Thanks be to you, my sweetness and my honor and my faithfulness, my God, thanks be to you for your gifts; but you must preserve them for me, and by doing this you will preserve me, and what you have given me will grow and come to fulfillment, and I will be with you, because it was your gift that I exist at all.

BOOK 2

1. I want to be mindful of the ugliness I engaged in back then, and the dissolution my body wreaked on my soul—not because I'm in love with any of that, but rather, my God, for the purpose of loving you.

I do this out of love for the love I have for you; I recollect the paths of my depravity in the bitterness of my inspection of myself, so that you grow sweet to me, with a sweetness, a charm that's not deceitful but blessed and safe, binding me together against the scattering force that ripped me to pieces as long as I turned my back on your singularity and disappeared into multiplicity.

At one time, you see, in my youth, I caught the flame of desire to glut myself on the pit of hell, and recklessly grew a whole grove of shady love affairs, several species of them. Any beauty in me ran to ruin, and in your eyes I rotted from the inside out while I approved of myself so much, and yearned for approval in human eyes.

2. What used to delight me other than "loving" and "being loved"? But the limit did not hold, the limit that reaches merely from mind to mind, between which lies the well-lit boundary-land of friendship. No, mine were the putrid fumes rising from scummy bodily lust and the diseased eruption of puberty, befouling and befuddling my heart with their smoke, so that there was no telling the unclouded sky of affection from the thick murk of carnality.

I didn't know which was which—they blended in my seething senses and dragged me, at this spineless age, off sheer cliffs of desires and sank me in a whirlpool of depravity. Your anger exercised its power over me, but I didn't know it. The screeching chain of my deathly nature, the punishment for my soul's arrogance, had deafened me, and I made my way farther and farther from you, and you let me.

I was storm-tossed, gushing out, running every which way, frothing into thin air in my filthy affairs—and you said nothing.* Oh, you my joy were long in coming! You said nothing back then, and on I went, far away from you, sowing more and more seed that grew nothing but grief. This was the insolence of my humiliation and the restlessness of my slacking.

3. Who could have attuned my torment to temperance, turned to good use the fugitive beauties of these least things, which run

* Isaiah 42:14.

last in the race? Who could have set a turning post in front of their blandishments, so that the surf of my youth would have broken on the shore of marriage?

If, for me, a contented (or at least contained) tranquillity could not have been found within boundaries of a state whose purpose is to beget children—as this is what your law prescribes,* Master, you who craft an actual graft on our death, putting your puissant hand to gentle work in holding back the thorns shut out of your paradise, because your power over everything isn't far off from us, even when we're far off from you—I could at least have been more alert to the thunderous voice from your clouds:

"Those in this state will have much to endure in the body's life; I, however, want to spare you," and "It is good for a person not to touch a woman," and "Whoever is without a wife thinks of the things that belong to God, but whoever is joined in marriage thinks of the things that belong to this world, namely how to please his wife."† I might, in short, have been wider awake and caught these words, and as a "eunuch for the kingdom of heaven's sake,"‡ I would have been happier waiting for *your* embrace.

4. But I boiled over in my torment, following my own flowing momentum and abandoning you. I went over all your lawful limits, and I didn't escape the blows of your lash—what mortal, after all, can do this? You were always there, savaging me in your pity, scattering the most acrid upsets on everything illicit that that I enjoyed, and you did this to make me look for enjoyment

---

* Genesis 1:28.
† These three quotations are from 1 Corinthians 7, verses 28, 1, and 32–33, respectively.
‡ Matthew 19:12.

without any upset and be unable to find it in anything but you, Master, in anything but you, who fashion pain as a lesson and lambaste us to heal us* and kill us so that we don't die away from you.

Where on earth was I? And how far away was my exile from the pleasures of your house† in that fifteenth year of my body's life?‡ That was when a lunatic lust—which humankind licenses to our disgrace, but which your laws do not allow—had come to lord it over me, after I made a complete surrender. My family was not concerned to scoop me up into marriage as I slid into ruin; their sole preoccupation was for me to learn the most estimable style of speech making possible, and persuasion through the arrangement of words.

5. But during that year, in fact, came a gap in my studies. I was brought back from Madauros, the town in our district where I had already started to live away from home for the sake of imbibing literature and oratory. The money to pay for a sojourn farther away, in Carthage, was being arranged—more through the sheer enthusiasm of my father than his actual means: he was a citizen of Thagaste with property that was hardly substantial.

To whom am I telling this story? It isn't of course to you, my God, but in your presence I'm telling it to my race, the human race, however minute a snippet out of that might stumble on my

* Hosea 6:1–2.
† Luke 15:13.
‡ The ancients counted age and similar lengths of time with "inclusive reckoning," taking the first and last units of time as full ones, and so the sums commonly come out one unit ahead of ours. The length of human gestation, for example, is called "ten months." I therefore subtract one year from Augustine's age whenever he records it—which I hope explains discrepancies with most translations and with some historical accounts.

writing, such as it is. And what's the story's purpose? Obviously, it's so that I and whoever reads this can contemplate from what depths we must cry out to you.* But what's closer to your ears, if the heart humbles itself in confession and the life is lived in faith?

But whose praises, at the time, didn't raise on high a mere human being, my father, because he taxed the family property beyond its strength, spending whatever it took for his son to study, even when that meant living quite far from home? Many citizens, far wealthier than he was, went to no such trouble for their children's sake; but at the same time, the father who was showing them up made no fuss about how I was growing up in your judgment, and how pure I was, as long as my oratorical skill developed, even if I was a devastated land and nothing was developed in me by you, God, who are the one true and good owner, or master, of your field, my heart.†

6. But when during that fifteenth year of mine,‡ that interval of leisure due to the family's financial straits, I began in my parents' house a holiday from schooling of any kind, the thorn bushes of desire grew higher than my head, and no hand was there to tear them up by the roots. Just the opposite: when, in the baths, my father saw I was growing the hair that's the clothing of restless young manhood, he was practically over the moon, even at this early date, about the grandchildren this development was supposed to promise, and in his glee he told my mother—it was the sort of tipsy glee in which this sorry world

* Psalms 130:1.
† 1 Corinthians 3:9.
‡ See note on chapter 4 above.

has forgotten you, its creator, and fallen in love instead with something you've created;* it's from the unseen wine of a self-willfulness distorted and tipped down into the depths.

But in my mother's breast you'd already started to build your temple, laying the foundations of your holy dwelling-place,† whereas he was still a convert under instruction before baptism,‡ and a recent convert besides. It was therefore she who endured a violent spasm of reverent, tremulous trepidation, and though I hadn't yet committed myself to the faith, she nevertheless feared the crooked paths walked by those who show you their backs and not their faces.§

7. Oh, the state of me! Do I actually dare to say that *you* were silent, my God, when *I* went farther away from you? But were you truly silent to me at the time? Whose words were those if not yours, the words you chanted in my ears through my mother, who was devoted to you? But from that source nothing made its way down into my heart to make me obey.

At that period she didn't want me—and I remember how she took me aside and warned me with huge agitation—to engage in sexual immorality, and absolutely not to debauch anyone's wife. These seemed to be nothing but the sort of warnings women typically give, so complying would have been mortifying.

* Romans 1:25.
† 1 Corinthians 3:10–17.
‡ A catechumen; a person could spend many years at this stage, as Augustine himself was to do.
§ Jeremiah 2:27. See book 1, chapters 17–18 above: Monica held the common view that sin was graver when committed by a full, baptized member of the Christian community.

But they were *your* warnings, and I didn't know. I thought you were silent and she was speaking, though it was through her that you *weren't* silent. In the form of her, you were held in contempt by me, her son, the son of your female slave, which made me your male slave.*

But I didn't know this, and I was going straight downhill in such thorough blindness that among boys my age I was embarrassed at having disgraced myself less than they had, since I heard them tossing around stories of their crimes and preening more intensely the more disgusting these were; and I felt like doing the thing not only because I craved it, but also because of the plaudits that went with it.

What deserves to be reviled, if not vile behavior? But to avoid reprobation, I made myself a worse reprobate, and when I had no basis for confessing to compete with those depraved people, I pretended to have done what I hadn't, so that I wouldn't seem more despicable the less I was to blame, and worth less the purer I kept myself.

8. So there they were, the comrades with whom I pursued my course through the streets of Babylon,† and I rolled in the mud as if it were cinnamon and expensive perfumes. And to keep me stuck more tightly to the city's umbilical cord, the unseen enemy trod on me and led me astray, prone to straying as I was.

The mother of my life in the body—who had by this time fled from Babylon's downtown‡ but was still strolling in other

* Psalms 116:16. Augustine's logic also follows Roman law.
† Babylon was the emblematic place of pagan exile because of the sixth-century B.C. Babylonian Captivity of the Jewish elite.
‡ Jeremiah 51:6.

districts—didn't follow through on her warning in favor of chastity; she didn't take steps to confine within the boundary markers of married attachment (if she couldn't cut it to the bone) what she'd heard about from her husband concerning me and understood to be already a ravaging disease, one that could prove quite dangerous for the days to come.

She didn't take these steps for fear of shackling my otherwise hopeful future with a wife. I don't mean the hope my mother had in you for the life to come, but the hope of an education, which both parents were overly eager for me to obtain, he because his thinking about you was practically nonexistent, while about me it was frivolous; whereas for her part she considered that the traditional curriculum would mean not only no impediment but actually a certain advancement on my way toward you.

This is what I conclude, at any rate, when I recall as well as I can my parents' attitudes. The reins were actually slackened to let me caper around at will, to an extent beyond a mere compromise of strictness, and to a point where my disposition broke down in a number of ways, and in all these things there was a fog shutting me off, my God, from the clear sky of your truth, and it was as if I was fattened up and bursting with iniquity.*

9. Stealing—for certain, the law you wrote punishes it,† Master; as does the law written in human hearts,‡ which not even iniquity itself can erase. What kind of thief, however well provided, would stomach the depredations of another thief, however poor

---

* Psalms 73:7.
† The Sixth Commandment (Exodus 20:15, Deuteronomy 5:19).
‡ Romans 2:14–15.

that one's provisions? But I wanted to commit this crime, and commit it I did, though destitution didn't drive me to it—unless I was starving for what was right but turning my nose up at it anyway, and at the same time stuffed and swollen with my own sinfulness:* so I stole a thing I had a better sort of in lush supply already; and I didn't want to enjoy the thing my hand grasped for—the actual stealing, the transgression, was going to be my treat.

There was a pear tree in the neighborhood of our vineyard, but the fruit weighing it down offered no draw either in its look or its taste. After playing in vacant lots clear till the dead of night— that was the behavior we visited on the town as our habit—we young men, full of our endless mischief, proceeded to this tree to shake it down and haul away the goods. We filched immense loads, not for our own feasting but for slinging away to swine, if you can believe it. But in fact, we did devour some pears; our only proviso was the potential for liking what was illicit.

Look at my heart, God, look at my heart, which you took pity on at the very bottom of the abyss. Let it tell you now, this heart you see, what it was looking for there, let it tell you how I was evil entirely on the house, and how there was no cause for my viciousness except viciousness. She was ugly, and I loved her, I loved my own demise, I loved my failing—not the thing for the sake of which I failed, but the failing itself, as in the hideousness of my soul I plunged down from your steady structure that held me up, into utter annihilation; I wasn't looking for what I could get from infamy, but looking for infamy.

* Psalms 73:7.

10. There is in fact an impressiveness in lovely material things—gold and silver and everything, and in contact with the flesh an accord between it and what it touches has huge appeal; and each of the other senses, too, has a specially arranged accommodation with objects. Worldly honor and the power to give orders and maintain the upper hand have their own kind of attraction, from which also the hunger for retribution rises.

When it comes down to it, in getting all these things a person must not depart from you, Master, or turn aside from the path of your law. The life we live here has its own enticement, because of a certain measure of charm that belongs to it and the attunement to all these beautiful things of the lowest order. Friendship between human beings is sweet in its cherished bond, because it creates a unity out of many separate souls.

Because of all these things, and other worldly things as well, sin is committed when an unchecked leaning toward these, given that they are the lowest order of good things, causes a desertion of the better and the highest, namely you, God our Master, and your truth and your law. These lowest things do have their delights, but not in comparison to you, my God, who made everything. The just person delights in God's self, and God himself is the delight of those with righteous hearts.*

11. When, therefore, people investigate a crime and why it was committed, it's usual for no one to believe the explanation unless it's based on evidence of a drive for getting one of these good things we've just called the lowest, or else a fear of losing

* Psalms 64:10.

one. They're beautiful and worthy of esteem, after all, though in comparison with the good things that are higher and make a person truly happy, they're debased and lie in the dirt.

A man's committed a murder. Why did he do it? He fell in love with his victim's wife or his land, or he wanted to live off the proceeds of a violent robbery, or he was afraid of losing something in these categories at the victim's hands, or he'd been wronged and was on fire for revenge. A person doesn't commit a murder for no reason, just for the fun of it, does he? Who would believe that?

One psychotic, sadistic man is supposed to have been brutally evil for its own sake, yet the reason's made quite clear: "so that his hand and his mind," the author states, "wouldn't lose their aptitude from lack of work." You can ask a further question: "Why did he act that way?" Plainly it was because if he'd been able, through his active proficiency in crime, to seize control of the city, he would have attained high public offices, the command of armies, and wealth—and fear of the law wouldn't have been a factor for him; likewise any material hardship he was experiencing due to the "reduced circumstances of his household and his bad conscience from his outrages." Not even Catiline himself, it follows, loved his crimes; without a doubt, it was something else he loved that caused him to commit crimes.*

12. What did I, pathetic dupe that I was, love in you, theft of mine, nighttime crime of mine committed during the fifteenth

---

* The references are to the historian Sallust's *Catiline,* an account of an attempt during the Republican era to overthrow the Roman state.

year of my life?* You weren't beautiful, since you were, well, theft. But were you actually anything, to justify my speaking to you now? That fruit we stole was beautiful, because you created it, you, the most beautiful of all things, creator of all things, the good God, God the highest good and my true good. That fruit was beautiful, but my pathetic soul didn't yearn for it in itself. I had plenty of better fruit, but I picked this in order to steal, as once I'd picked it, I threw it away, and the banquet I had from it was only my own evil-mindedness—*that* I enjoyed with glee. If any of that fruit actually entered my mouth, my crime was the flavoring on it.

And now, God my Master, I want to know what it was that gave me pleasure in that theft, and here's the answer: there was in fact nothing attractive about it. I'm of course talking not about the attractiveness of probity or good judgment, but also not of human intelligence or memory or the senses, or living energy; nor am I talking about the attractiveness such as we find in the heavenly bodies, stately in their spheres, or on the earth or in the sea, full of their young born to take the place of those departing; and I don't mean even that faulty attractiveness shadowed over by the failings that delude us.

13. Prideful human exaltation, for its part, only mimics transcendence, since *you're* the one exalted over everything, the transcendent God. What does ambition seek but honors and glory?—whereas you're the one to be honored before all, and full of glory into eternity. The brutality of power wishes to be feared, but who should be feared but God alone? And what can

* See note on chapter 4 above.

be seized or purloined from his power? When, or where, or through what, or by whom? Lewd people's sweet talk shows a wish to be desired, but nothing is sweeter than your loving care; and there's no desire more wholesome and sweeter than for *her*, the most shapely and shining of all things, your truth.

Curiosity seems like a mere pretense for the pursuit of knowledge, when *you* know everything to the highest degree. Even ignorance itself, even stupidity hides under the name of simplicity and innocence—a sham, because nothing can be found that's simpler than you. What is more innocent than you?— whereas to wicked people even their own acts are their enemies. Laziness makes as if it's striving for repose, but what secure repose is there except in the Master? Overindulgence longs to be called "having enough" and "living the good life." But you are fullness and abundance of pleasure that never goes off or runs short. Overspending tries to take on the cover of generosity, but the most profuse spendthrift of all good things is you.

Greed wants to own a lot: you own everything. Envy makes a formal case against the greatest merit: what has more merit than you? Anger seeks to inflict punishment: Who punishes more justly than you do? Fear shakes in its shoes at unfamiliar and sudden things, which oppose what it loves, and is paranoid in advance of events. To you, what is unfamiliar? What happens suddenly? Who separates you from the object of your care?* And where is solid safety except in your presence? Grief wastes away when it loses what amused its acquisitive passion; it doesn't want anything taken away from it—as in fact nothing can be taken away from you.

---

* Romans 8:35.

14. In these ways the soul goes whoring, when it turns away from you* and seeks beyond you those things it can't find in clean and clear forms, unless it returns to you. It's the kind of backward imitation of you performed by all the people who place themselves far from you and try to exalt themselves at your expense. But even by imitating you in this way, they disclose that you're the creator of all the natural world, and that therefore there is, in every sense, nowhere for anyone to draw back from you.

What, then, did I care for in that theft of mine, through what did I imitate my Master in that vicious and twisted way? Did I like to break the law because I could at least do it sneakily, as no great endowment of power allowed me to act, and I was a sort of maimed prisoner trying to achieve a one-handed liberty by going unpunished for doing what was forbidden, in the shady guise of omnipotence? Here's that slave we all know about, running away from his master and chasing the shadows. The putrefaction of it, the abomination of life and the depths of death! Could I have liked what wasn't allowed for no reason other than that it wasn't allowed?

15. How shall I pay back my Master for letting my memory go over those things without feeling any fear from them? I will love you, Master, and give thanks and testimony to your name, since you pardoned me from such terrible wrongdoings, from such unspeakable things that were my work. To your grace I give the credit, and to your mercy, that you've melted my sins like ice.† And to your grace I impute it that I didn't do other evil things, whatever they would have been.

* Psalms 73:27, with erotic wording in the Latin Bible.
† Sirach 3:15.

What was I not capable of doing, since I actually loved crime for its own sake? I profess that I was released from everything, both what I did of my own free will and what, with your guidance, I didn't do. But who on earth is there who, taking account of his weakness, dares ascribe his purity and harmlessness to his own strength? The result would be that he loves you less, as if he had less need of your pity, through which you write off the sins of those who've turned to you.

Whoever's been called by you and has followed your voice, so as to avoid these things—things he's reading the recollection and admission of in my own case—shouldn't laugh at me because I was healed, when I was sick, by that same doctor who saw to it that he didn't get sick in the first place, or rather that he got less sick than I did. On the contrary, he ought to love you just as much, and in fact more, for that very reason: he sees me shedding the overwhelming diseases of my sins by virtue of that same being who allowed him to escape such an entanglement.

16. For me as a pathetic youngster, what was, in the end, the harvest my behavior yielded, behavior the recollection of which makes me turn red*—especially that theft? I loved doing it for the fact of the theft itself, nothing else, since in itself it was nothing, and this made me that much more pathetic.

If I'd been alone, I wouldn't have done it (this is how I remember my disposition then)—alone, there's no way I would have done it. So in this instance I also loved the company of those with whom I did it. So didn't I love something besides the theft?

* Romans 6:21.

No, I loved nothing else, because such company itself is also nothing.

What is all this in reality? Who is there who can instruct me, unless it's the one who shines a light in my heart and makes its shadows known? What else could have led my mind to inquire into and discuss and contemplate this matter?

If, you see, I'd been in love with the fruit I stole and longed to enjoy it, I could have done alone what I did. If the pleasure I was after had been a sufficient rationale for committing that crime, I wouldn't have needed to rub up against accomplices' minds to set alight my itching concupiscence. But since there was no pleasure for me in that fruit, the pleasure was in the crime itself, committed simultaneously by an association of sinners.

17. What was that attitude in my mind? It couldn't be clearer that it was revolting in the extreme, and I'm one sorry person for having harbored it. And yet what was it? Who understands his own misconduct?*

We laughed, it tickled our hearts, because we'd fooled those who didn't think we'd be doing this, and who would have strongly opposed it. Why, then, did I take pleasure in not doing it alone? Was it because no one finds it easy to laugh alone? That's true, but it does happen once in a while, to people keeping their own company, when no one else is around, that a laugh gets the upper hand if something overly absurd presents itself to their senses or their mind. But I wouldn't have done what I did alone, absolutely wouldn't have done it alone.

* Psalms 19:12.

Here, before your eyes, my God, is the living retrospection of my soul. Alone, I wouldn't have committed that theft, from which there was no pleasure in what I stole but rather in the act of stealing. What would have given me absolutely no pleasure to do alone, I wouldn't have done alone.

Oh, you friendship that couldn't be more unfriendly! You led my mind astray on paths I couldn't trace; you were a playful, joking greed for doing harm, an avarice for somebody else's loss, absent any appetite for my own profit, or for reprisal. Instead, at the words "Come on, let's do it," there's shame in not being shameless.

18. Who can disentangle that wretched immensity of distortions and contortions and knottedness? It's a grotesque creature. I don't want to pay any attention to her, don't want to look at her. *You're* the one I want, justice and innocence so beautiful and graceful; I want to enjoy you with honorable eyes and a satisfaction I can't get enough of. Rest is with you, lavishly, and a life without distress. The one who enters into you enters into the joy of his Master,* and he won't fear, and he'll do unsurpassably well in the one who's unsurpassed. I flowed abruptly downward from you and wandered off, my God; in my young manhood I went on an awfully erratic course away from your steadfastness, and I turned myself into a famished land I had to live in.†

* Matthew 25:21.
† Luke 15:14.

Book 3

1. I came to Carthage, to the center of a skillet where outrageous love affairs hissed all around me. I wasn't in love yet, but I was in love with the prospect of being in love, and in my more latent need, I hated myself because that need wasn't greater. I looked for something to love, lover of loving that I was, and I hated my safety and my path free of mousetraps, since my real hunger was inside me, and was for a more inward food—it was for you, my God.

But I didn't feel that starving need; I didn't desire that nourishment that wouldn't rot—not because I was full of that, but because the emptier I was, the pickier I was. Therefore, my soul was in bad shape and hurled itself, festering sores and all, out in public, wretchedly insatiable in scratching up against objects of the physical senses.

But if these didn't have a soul, they wouldn't do as objects for love. To love and to be loved was sweet to me, and more so if I could enjoy the body of someone who loved me. That meant I was in the habit of polluting the shared channel of friendship with putrid rutting, and clouding its pale purity with a lust from hell.

Though I was revolting and degraded, I nevertheless yearned—in my overflowing inane emptiness—to be fashionable and sophisticated. I swooped recklessly into love, only panting to be its prisoner. You my God, who are my mercy, with how much gall did you sprinkle that sweet taste, and how good you were to do it—because I was loved in turn, and on the sly I made my way to the shackles of gratification, and was gleefully trussed up in those afflicting bonds, so that I could be flogged with the fiery iron rods of jealousy and bouts of paranoia and anxieties and rages and brawls.

2. Theater productions ravished me, brimming as they were with depictions of my own miseries, and with kindling for my own fire. What does a human being want with the pain he feels when he watches scenes of mournful tragedy, notwithstanding he wouldn't want to suffer such things personally? Just the same, the spectator wants to suffer anguish from these things, and the anguish itself is his pleasure.

What is this if not an amazing madness? In fact, an individual is moved more by theatrics the sicker he is himself with the sort of feelings he sees displayed—though when he suffers them alone, it's called misery, whereas when he suffers them along with others, it's called having a heart for misery.

But what kind of empathy is it at the end of the day, where made-up events on the stage are concerned? The listener isn't hearing a call to come help, but is only being invited to feel pain, and the more pain he feels, the more he applauds the one who acts out these apparitions. And if human disasters—ancient or invented as they might be—are acted out in such a way that someone in the audience fails to feel pain, he withdraws with his nose in the air, complaining. If, on the other hand, he does feel pain, he stays, transfixed, and weeps and enjoys himself no end.

3. Thus even distress is an object of affection. No doubt every human being wants to enjoy himself. Nobody finds it nice to be wretched, but it's nevertheless nice to have a heart for wretchedness; yet this feeling can't exist aside from pain; so is distress loved for these sole reasons?

This, too, comes from the channel of friendship I mentioned above. But where does it head? Where does it flow? Why does it run down into a scalding torrent of bubbling pitch, an immense seething mass of hideous libidinousness? This is what, of its own will, it merges into and transforms itself into, in its twisted and fallen route away from the clear heavenly vault.

Is sympathy, then, to be rejected? By no means. Let suffering be beloved on occasion, but watch out for uncleanliness, my soul, and against it let my God be the protector, the God of our fathers who is to be praised, who is to be raised on high above all things, from age to age forever: watch out for uncleanliness.

No, I'm not empty of pity, to this day. But back then in the theaters I was gratified along with a couple when they enjoyed each other in indecent acts, although they did these as a pretense, as entertainment for an audience. When the couple was separated, I was sad along with them, as if from tenderheartedness—either situation delighted me regardless.

Now, in contrast, I pity more the man who enjoys himself in indecency than the one who endures hardships in the curtailment of an indulgence that destroys him, and in the loss of his lamentable "happiness." This latter is for certain the truer pity, but here there's no feeling of fun in the pain. A person is esteemed for pitying someone in a dismal state, because it's love's duty to pity him. But the person who pities like a true brother would naturally prefer that there be nothing for him to pity.

If there were such a thing as malevolent benevolence—which there couldn't be—then the person who truly, sincerely pitied might desire others to be miserable so that he could commiserate with them. Hence there's a certain amount of suffering that's commendable, but none that anyone ought to love. The very reason, in fact, that you, God the Master, lover of our souls, far and away more purely, more sincerely pity than we do is that no pain is ever inflicted on you. Who among us has the wherewithal for pitying that God does?

4. As for me, in my sorry state at that time, I just loved to suffer, and I looked around for some cause or other for suffering. That was when, in the experience of someone else's excruciation—artificial little dance that this was—I was allured all the more intensely by an actor's interpretation when it forced me to tears.

But what was amazing, after all, when as a poor animal wandering away from your herd, intolerant of your tending, I was marred by disgusting mange? That was the source of my love affair with sorrow—not sorrow that would penetrate me deeply (as I had no love for enduring the kind of thing I loved to watch), but made-up sorrow that would graze my top layer, so to speak, as I listened to it. However, as from scratching fingernails, a seething, swelling putrefaction and revolting pus resulted. Such as my life was then, my God, was it any kind of life at all?

5. Your mercy, faithful from a distance, was hovering above me. But how great were the wrongdoings into which I rotted away, as I pursued them with desecrating curiosity! This induced me to desert you and sink to the lowest depths, to faithless, cheating service to the demons, to whom I offered up my offenses.*

But in everything, you were lashing me. I even had the gall, during the celebration for your rites, within the walls of your church, to fall in lust and transact the business of purchasing a harvest of death.† Hence you whipped me severely as a punishment, but not to the full extent of my guilt, my God, my preeminent mercy, my refuge from the terrifying criminals among whom I wandered. Placing altogether too much faith in my own stiff-necked will made me retreat far from you, because I loved my paths and not yours, because I was in love with the "freedom" of a runaway slave.

6. Those studies I wrote of, which were styled "a gentleman's education," looked toward the goal of the lawsuit-happy public

---

* 1 Corinthians 10:20, probably quoting Deuteronomy 32:17.
† Romans 7:5.

square; there I was supposed to excel more, and be more praise-worthy, the more skillful a scam artist I was. That's how terrible human blindness is, with the human beings actually boasting of their blindness.

To make it worse, I surpassed the others in my school of rhetoric, and I exultantly preened myself on my superiority and was full of diseased pride. I was, however, far more sedate than the rest, as you know, Master, and had nothing whatsoever to do with the work of the demonic "demolition men" (a rascally title reminiscent of the devil's name in Greek,* and one they wore like a badge of smart-aleck rank). But I lived *among* them in a sort of brazen propriety, given that I wasn't one *of* them. But I was *with* them, and from time to time I enjoyed their friendship, though I was always repulsed by what they did—meaning the violent pranks by which they preyed impudently on students new to the scene, playing on their shyness to drive them into utter panic for the sheer fun of it, just to nurture their own vicious glee.

No activity resembles theirs more than the demons' own. What adds veracity to their being called "demolition men" is that they themselves, transparently, were first turned upside down and distorted out of all decency. The demons who pull their pranks unseen laugh at them while leading them by the nose—which is the exact way they love to treat their own victims.

---

* The most literal meaning (the common, figurative meaning is "slanderous") of the Greek word (*diabolos*) from which we have "diabolic" and "devil" is "throwing every which way" or "destroying." Accordingly in Latin, these young men are "those who turn [things] upside down," or *eversores*.

7. Among these persons I was, at my impressionable age, study-ing books about oratory, an art in which I longed to be promi-nent, with the execrable goal of producing a lot of hot air for the delectation of human fatuity. At one point in the traditional curriculum, I encountered a book by—in case you haven't heard of him—Cicero, whose tongue almost everyone admires; but what was in his bosom, not so much.*

In any case, in this book of his, entitled *Hortensius*, he urgently commends the study of philosophy. That work did renovate my attitude; it changed my pleas, directing them to you, Master, and altered my aspirations and desires. Suddenly all my empty ambition was deeply discounted, and with an unbelievable seething of my heart I longed for everlasting wisdom. I began to pick myself up so that I could return to you.† It wasn't to sharp-ening my tongue—though this was my purported purpose, for which the tuition financed by my mother went at this time, when I was eighteen,‡ my father having died three years before—it wasn't, I repeat, to sharpening my tongue that I ap-plied that book; and it wasn't the style in which it spoke, but what it said that persuaded me.

8. How I burned, my God, how I burned to fly back from these earthly places to you, even though I didn't know what you would do with me! But wisdom is with you.§ The Greek name

---

* This preeminent Roman Republican orator would of course have been central in Augus-tine's education; I read this reference to him as dismissive, if not downright sarcastic.
† Luke 15:18, 20: Augustine is probably playing on the repeated "arise and go" wording of the prodigal son's return home.
‡ See note on book 2, chapter 4.
§ Job 12:13 and 16.

philosophia means "love of wisdom," and this love set me on fire through Cicero's treatise.

There are those who debauch others through "philosophy," using that great and persuasive and respectable word to gloss over and whitewash whatever they do wrong; and in this book are singled out and censured nearly all those who, in Cicero's time and before, were in this category. This book lays out that rescuing instruction from your Spirit through your dutiful and reverent slave, Paul: "Look out for anyone who wants to trick you through philosophy and lead you meaninglessly astray, according to received human wisdom, and according to this material universe, and not according to Christ, because in him there lives the entire fullness of what is holy, in physical form."*

At that time—as you know, light of my heart—I had no knowledge yet of this passage from the apostles' writings; yet I was delighted by *one* thing in Cicero's urgings: I was supposed to conceive an affection for and seek out and grasp and hold and embrace, for all I was worth, not this or that system but philosophy herself, whatever *she* was; that's why his words instilled such a thrill in me, why such a flame flared up.

And there was only a single thing to repel this great conflagration: Christ's name wasn't in the work. This name, according to your mercy, Master, this name of my Savior, your son, had been in my mother's milk itself; my infant heart had reverently drunk that name in and kept it deep within me, and without it, whatever I read—however studied and polished it was, and however much of the truth it told otherwise—couldn't ravish me altogether.

---

* The "slave" is Paul of Tarsus; Colossians 2:8–9.

9. Therefore I undertook to consider the sacred texts and get a sense of them. And lo and behold, the subject matter wasn't "factual" in pretentious people's opinion, or laid straightforwardly bare for children's eyes, either, but lowly when I stepped toward her, of lofty dignity when I came up close, and veiled in mysteries. But back then, I wasn't the sort of person who could enter into her, or bend my neck submissively to follow her own strides.

The tone I take now, you see, doesn't show the way I felt when first turning to these writings, which seemed not even worth comparing to the excellence of Cicero. My swollen-headed opinion of my own taste recoiled from their mediocre manner, and my critical eye couldn't pierce into the qualities behind that. In actual fact, this writing is just the sort to grow up alongside small children, but I wasn't going to stoop to being a small child.* I was bloated with conceit and seemed—to myself, anyway—quite grown up.

10. Accordingly, I fell in among people who were insanely arrogant, living for their bodies and their blather, in whose speech lurked the devil's bird-snares,† smeared with a glue concocted from a commingling of the mere syllables of your name and the name of Jesus Christ, and the name of our advocate and comforter, the Holy Spirit.‡ These words never retreated from their mouths, but never advanced farther than the squawky racket of their tongues; their hearts were hollow. They used to intone "Truth, truth," and many times they intoned this to me, but the

---

* Matthew 18:4.
† 1 Timothy 3:7, 2 Timothy 2:26.
‡ The Manichaeans were a sect with a version of the Trinity sharply distinct from that of the mainstream Christian church.

truth wasn't in them. They discoursed in lies, and not only about you, who are truly the truth, but even about the poor material components of this world, your creation.

Concerning *this*, I should have skipped over even the philosophers, who *were* telling the truth. I should have skipped over them for the sake of your love, since you're the highest good, and the beauty of all beautiful things. You, the truth, the truth! How the very inmost core of my consciousness sighed for you, while those people noised at me often and endlessly, conveying nothing but the sound of their voices and their large collection of hulking books. Those were so many trays on which, as I sat starving for you, the sun and moon were conveyed to me instead. These are your beautiful works, yet they're only your works. They're not you—and they themselves don't come first in importance among your works; your works of the spirit come before those petty material things, the shininess and heavenliness of these aside.

Yet it wasn't your works of the spirit but you yourself—you the truth, in which there's no change and no shadowing over from movement*—for which I was starved and parched. But on and on, those platters were set in front of me, heaped with flashy apparitions, and it would actually have been better for me to be in love with that sun of ours—it's at least the truth to these wretched eyes—than to be in love with those lies, and to have my mind hoodwinked by my eyes. And yet, since I thought that what I was getting was you, I ate it—not gluttonously, for sure, because I didn't taste you in my mouth the way you really are (and in fact you *weren't* those empty inventions)—but I didn't

* James 1:17.

draw any nourishment from it; instead, I was more thoroughly drained than before.

Food eaten in dreams is very much like food eaten when people are awake—except that those sleeping aren't being fed; that's because they're sleeping. But those things were in no way at all like you, you as the truth that has now spoken to me, because they were mere phantasms, phony versions of material things.

More reliable than these are material objects, which we (in company with farm animals and birds) see with the sight of the flesh, whether these objects are in the sky or on the earth, and the objects are more real than the pictures we have of them in our heads. However, we picture them more clearly than we can use them to postulate other things on a larger, in fact over-whelming scale, things that absolutely don't exist. It was such nullities that I was being fed on then, but I wasn't being fed.

But you, my love, into whom I collapse so that I can be strong,* you're *not* the material things we see in the sky, and you're not those we don't see there, either, because you originated both; nor do you rank them highest among the things you originated.

That's how far you are from those apparitions of mine, appari-tions of objects that never existed in the first place! Images of objects that do exist are more real than them, and the objects themselves are more real still—but they still aren't what you are. Nor are you a soul, which is the life of objects (meaning the higher life of objects, a life more real than the objects them-selves are)—no, you're the life of souls, the life of lives, living

* 2 Corinthians 12:10.

through yourself alone, and you don't change—you, the life of my soul.*

11. Given that, where were you then, in relation to where I was, and how far away from me were you? But I took a long foreign journey away from you, and I was barred even from the chaff on which I fed the pigs.†

How much better the fairy tales of the scholars and poets than those contemptible booby traps in which I found myself! Verses and poetical works and Medea airborne‡ are at any rate more useful than five elements in various tinges because they're in five different dusky caves,§ elements that in no wise exist and are death for the person who believes in them.

Poetry and tragedy I can transform into true entrées; furthermore, although I recited Medea's flight, I didn't vouch for it. Though I heard it recited, I didn't credit its occurrence. But I believed what my new mentors told me—and too bad it was for me, led step by step down to the lowest depths of the pit, struggling and sweltering as I was for want of the truth. This was while I sought you, my God (I place this confession of it before you, who had pity on me even before I placed my faith in you), while I sought you not with the mind's understanding, by which you willed me to excel wild animals, but according to my flesh's

---

* Here I must credit my amanuensis Samuel Loncar: "[This chapter] clearly [alludes] to the Platonic critique of art based on the theory of *mimesis*. Augustine has in view the Platonic set of concentric circles of reality: God/being, the forms, then material objects, then representations of those objects, then representations of representations."
† As pictured in the parable of the prodigal son, Luke 15:16; ordinary pagan literature is a form of refuse compared to scripture.
‡ Medea, in her eponymous tragedy by Euripides, escapes on a magical chariot after committing a series of murders.
§ These elements are basic to Manichaean physics and biology.

perceptions. You, however, were deeper inside me than my deepest depths and higher than my greatest heights.

I encountered that allegorical shameless woman in Solomon's writings, who's short on any thought for the future and sits on a chair in her doorway, saying, "Eat bread on the sly—you'll enjoy it; and steal water to drink—it'll taste so good."* She seduced me, because she found me living homeless, i.e., under the eyes of my body alone, and in my mind chewing the cud from the sort of things I'd been able to gobble down through that eyesight.

12. I didn't know, you see, another reality, which exists in truth. Instead, under the pretense of being oh-so-precise, I got shifted into partisanship with those idiot confidence men when they asked me what the source of evil was, and whether God was limited by a physical form and had hair and fingernails, and whether we should consider righteous the men who had many wives at the same time, and killed people, and performed animal sacrifices.

This line of questioning bothered me, as I didn't know anything about its background; and while I was withdrawing from the truth, I imagined myself moving toward it. I didn't know that evil doesn't exist except as the absence of good up to the point of annihilation. (How was I going to have such an insight when the sight of my eyes didn't extend past the material world, and the sight of my mind went only as far as illusions?) I didn't know that God is a spirit,† with no body having any length or breadth,

* Proverbs 9:13–17.
† John 4:24.

and with no mass. The mass of anything is less in one part than it is in the whole; and if the mass is infinite, then it's less in any part that's set off within a definite space than in its full, boundless extent. It's not whole everywhere, like a spirit, like God. I had no idea whatsoever as to what could be within us to make it possible for us to be, and to be correctly described in scripture, as made in the image of God.*

13. And I didn't know about true inward justice, which judges not on the basis of mere habit, but on the basis of the faultlessly correct law of the all-powerful God. This law shapes customs to be appropriate to different times and places, but in itself it's everywhere and eternal; it doesn't vary from place to place or behave differently on different occasions. It was this law according to which Abraham and Isaac and Jacob and Moses and David were righteous, and according to which they all had praise from God's mouth. But I heard them condemned as wicked by people who didn't know what they were talking about, when these people judged by the standard of human time and measured the customs of the whole human race by the portion of custom that happened to be their own.

It was as if someone who knew nothing about which piece of armor fits which part of the body were to try covering his head with a greave or wearing a helmet like a shoe, and were to grumble that it was a bad fit; or if, on a single day when a public holiday has been decreed for the afternoon hours, somebody were to work himself into a lather because he isn't allowed to display something for sale that he was allowed to display in the morning; or if in a given private household someone were to see

* Genesis 1:27.

something handled by a given slave, whereas the slave who waited at the table wasn't permitted to handle it; or were to see something happening behind the stables that was prohibited in the dining room, and were to complain, since it's just one small set of living quarters and one household, that everybody wasn't allowed to do the same anywhere.

That's the level of reasoning in those who complain when they've heard that something was permitted to righteous people in that past age but not permitted to the righteous of this one; and that God commanded those people to do one thing, and these here to do another, for reasons that are circumstantial, although both groups were bound to serve the same righteousness. But the complainers do see that in the case of a single person in a single day and in a single house, different things are fitting for different parts of the body; and that a thing that's been permitted for some considerable time isn't permitted an hour afterward; and that something may be allowed or even commanded in one spot but in a spot right next to it is forbidden and punished.

Righteousness itself isn't different in each case, is it? And it can't change, can it? But specific times, over which it presides, don't proceed side by side. That's because they're time. Human beings, for their part, whose life on earth is short, lack the perceptive power to link together causalities of earlier ages and other races—causalities of which they have no experience—with causalities here and now, of which they do; but they can easily see in one body, or in one day, or in one home, what's fitting for what part, and at what stages, and for which groups or individuals. Where past ages are concerned, they're upset, but in the here and now they're submissive adherents.

14. These were things that I didn't know or pay any attention to at the time; they were battering against my eyes everywhere, but I didn't see. Yet I composed poetry, and I wasn't allowed to put any old foot in any old spot but had to reserve different ones for different meters, and in a single given line I couldn't put the same foot everywhere. The art of poetry itself, my basis for composition, didn't vary in its rules: they all applied at the same time.

But I did not perceive the capacity of righteousness, to which good and holy people are slaves, for comprising—far more excellently and loftily—at the same time everything it ordains and never differing in any particular, while nevertheless at different times allotting and ordaining what is fitting to each, instead of everything at once.

And in my blindness I found fault with the reverent patriarchs, not only in that, as God commanded and inspired them to do, they based their behavior on contemporary circumstances, but also in that they prophesied the future as God revealed it to them.

15. It can't be, can it, wrong at any time or at any place to love God with all your heart and with all your soul and with all your mind, and to love your neighbor as yourself?* In the same way, shameful acts that are contrary to nature—such as those committed by the people of Sodom†—are reviled and punished everywhere and always. If all nations did these things, they would all be arraigned for the same crime by the divine law, which

---

* Matthew 22:37 and 39, Mark 12:30, 33, Luke 10:27, 1 John 4:7, all echoing Deuteronomy 6:5 and Leviticus 19:18. The combined commandments are sometimes called the Great Law.
† Genesis 18:20–21, 19:4–5.

didn't create humankind to have intercourse in this way. This is because the critical bond that ought to be between us and God is outraged when the human nature of which he's the source is sullied by this twisted libidinousness.

But as for those acts that are shameful according to human custom, they're to be avoided in accordance with the whole variety of customs, so that the social compact established by the city or the nation's usual practice or its law won't be outraged by any citizen's or sojourner's lust. Any part that doesn't fit into its proper whole is disgraceful.

When, on the other hand, God orders something that's contrary to the custom or the compact of any people you might cite, the thing *must* be done, even though it was never done there; and if it's been left off, it must be taken up again; and if not established up to this time, then it must be established now.

If, after all, a king is permitted, in the city over which he rules, to order something that no one prior to himself nor even he himself either ever ordered, and obedience wouldn't be contrary to the city's covenant—and in fact disobedience would be contrary to the city's covenant (as human society generally agrees in complying with kings' orders)—how much more should we, without any hesitation, submit to God, the ruler of the universe, which is his own creation? As with the hierarchy of human society, where greater power is placed above less and is to be obeyed, so God is placed above everyone.

16. It's likewise with crimes, wherever there's an appetite for doing harm, either verbally or physically. In either case, the reason may be revenge, as when one enemy attacks another; or the

desire to gain something good, in the absence of any right to it, as when a bandit attacks a traveler on the road; or the desire to avoid something bad, as in cases where the perpetrator fears the victim; or envy, as when someone who's worse off attacks someone better off, or when someone who's succeeded in some enterprise goes after someone he fears will match him, or is resentful toward someone matching him already; or the reason could be nothing but the pleasure of someone else's suffering, which is the way the spectators at a gladiatorial show feel, or those who make fun of or play pranks on other people of any sort.

In any event, these are the principal pustules of evil that break out from a penchant for primacy, or for ogling, or for physical sensations—one or two of these, or all three together,* and it's a bad life in defiance of that sum of three and seven, your harp with ten chords, the Ten Commandments given by you,† God, the highest and sweetest being.

But what shameful acts can be inflicted on you, who can't be tainted? Or what crimes can be committed against you, who can't be harmed? Nonetheless, you punish the wrong that human beings do to themselves; when they sin against you, they treat their own souls with irreverence, and their wickedness deceives them.‡ They taint or twist their own nature, which you made and regulated; either they make excessive use of things allowed them, or their passions burn their way into things that aren't allowed, into usage contrary to nature.§ Either they're

---

* 1 John 2:16.
† The first three concern the relationship with God, the final seven the treatment of other human beings.
‡ Psalms 27:12 (but the modern English Bible does not indicate self-deception here).
§ Romans 1:26.

held liable for lashing out against you in their minds and in their words and kicking against the goads,* or they shatter the confines of human society and impudently delight in their own little cliques and feuds, according to whether any particular thing thrills them or gets in their way.

These things happen when they leave you, the flowing spring of life, you who are the one true creator and regulator of the universe; when, in a fragmented manner and out of a private pride, they value a false oneness. The return to you is through humble reverence. You wash out our accustomed evil ways, and you're indulgent toward the sins of those who confess them. You lend your ear to the groans of those in shackles,† and you free us from the chains we've made for ourselves, if we no longer butt at you with the horns of a fictional liberty, in our greed for more and more, though it loses us everything, and in our greater love for what belongs to us personally than for you, who are the good that belongs to everyone.

17. But in addition to outrages and offenses and any number of other wrongdoings, there are the transgressions of those who are, nevertheless, making some progress in their behavior. When people of sound judgment see these acts, they both criticize them, applying the standard of perfection, and praise them in the hope of a harvest, in the way green sprouts are praised because of the ripe grain to come.

And there are also certain acts that look like outrages or offenses but aren't sins, because they aren't committed against

* Acts 9:5, 26:14.
† Psalms 102:20.

you, Master, our God, nor against the community and its fellowship. One example would be that someone procures goods of one kind or another to serve a practical use in his life; they may be suitable for his particular situation, but it still might not be clear whether his motive isn't the sheer craving to procure them. Another example is that people are punished by duly vested powers that evince zeal for correcting behavior, but it's unclear whether the motivation isn't the craving to do harm.

Furthermore, many acts are approved according to your testimony but wouldn't find approval among human beings, and many things are praised by human beings that are, once you're called as a witness, condemned: often the appearance of an act is different from the intentions of the person who performed it at a particular juncture, which an outsider can know nothing about.

But suppose you, God, suddenly issue an unprecedented and unexpected order, although you've forbidden the same thing at some point in the past. Although for a time you hide the reason for your order, and although it's against the agreed-on law of a given human society, who would doubt that the order must be carried out? The society that is your slave is a just one.

But it's blessed individuals who know that you've given the order: everything, of course, that's done by your slaves is either for the purpose of demonstrating what's needed in the present, or for proclaiming what will be needed in the future.

18. In my ignorance of all this, I ridiculed those holy slaves and prophets belonging to you. But what was I doing in ridiculing them, if not making myself an object of ridicule to you as, grad-

ually and by tiny degrees, I was drawn into that Manichaean twaddle I wrote of above, into believing that a fig weeps when it's plucked, and that its mother the tree sheds lacteous tears? And there's more: that if some "saint" gobbled the fig—provided that plucking it was somebody else's crime, not the saint's!—he could then exhale the angels he'd concocted in his guts—no, wait: it would be little crumbs of a god coming out whenever he groaned or belched in prayer. The selfsame tiny morsels of the true god on high would have been tied up helpless in that piece of fruit unless released by the grinders and the belly of the chosen saint. I had the misfortune to believe that greater pity must be on hand for the earth's produce than for the human beings because of whom the produce came into existence. If a starving person asked for some, and he didn't happen to be a Manichaean, then you were supposed to be condemning to capital punishment whatever you gave him to munch on.

19. But you extended your hand from on high and snatched my soul from that deep murk,* at a time when my mother, your committed Christian, was weeping in your presence for me more than mothers weep for the death of their children's bodies. Through the faith and the spirit she possessed from you, she saw my death, and you gave ear to her pleas, Master; you listened to her and didn't look down on her tears. When in every place she prayed the water gushing out of her eyes drenched the ground, you listened.

What else could have been the source of that dream with which you consoled her, so that she submitted to living with me and sharing the same table in the house? (She was on the verge of

* Psalms 144:7.

unwillingness, in her disgust and loathing for the blasphemies inherent in my delusion.)

In this dream, she saw herself standing on a sort of wooden ruler, while there approached a luminous young man, smiling at her in joy, though she was in mourning, and actually exhausted from it. The young man asked her the reasons for her sadness and her daily tears; in the customary way, the inquiry was meant not to learn but to teach. She answered that she was beating her breast over my ruin. Then, to free her from any worry, he ordered her urgently to look and see: where she was, I was, too. When she looked, she saw me standing beside her on the same ruler. How could this happen, unless it was because you lent your ears to her heart, you, the good and the all-powerful, who care for each one of us as if your cared for him alone, and who care for all of us the same way you care for us one by one?

20. And what was the source of what happened next? When she told me of her vision, and I was trying to force on it the meaning that she shouldn't lose hope of being where *I* was, right away and without any hesitation she said, "No, no—what was said to me wasn't 'Where he is, you are, too,' but 'Where you are, he is, too.'"[*]

I offer as testimony to you, Master, my memory as best I can retrieve it (and I've often spoken of this scene): I was more impressed by your answer through my mother while she was awake. Though my wrong interpretation was just adjacent to the truth, she wasn't distressed by it, and saw so quickly what

---

[*] Monica's dream alludes to but gender-reverses the traditional Roman marriage vows, in which the bride pledges to be wherever her husband is.

needed to be seen (which I, for sure, hadn't seen before she said it). Her answer, then, impressed me more than the dream itself, through which, to comfort her in the anxiety she suffered at this period, a joy that was to come so long afterward was foretold so far ahead of time to this reverent woman.

Around eight years* followed during which I rolled around in the mud of that deep pit and in the darkness of that lie, often trying to rise out of it but always taking a more forceful plunge back in. She, meanwhile a chaste, pious, and sober widow, such as you love, was already more lighthearted with hope, but she didn't slack in weeping and groaning; she didn't cease, in all the hours of her prayers, to beat her breast before you, and her pleas were granted an audience with you;† and yet you left me to wallow and be swallowed in that darkness.

21. But during that time, you gave a second answer that I recall. I do pass by many things, and the reason is that I'm hurrying to those that drive me more strongly to make my testimony to you; and there are also many things I don't remember. But you gave a second answer through your priest, a certain bishop fostered in your church and deeply learned in your books.

The woman asked him to be so good as to speak with me and refute my mistaken notions, to teach the bad things out of me and the good things into me. (He used to do this, in fact, for people he happened to find suitable.) He was, however, unwilling; quite shrewdly so, as I realized later. He answered that I was still unteachable, as I was full of hot air due to the heresy's ex-

---

citing novelty and had hounded many uneducated people with trivial conundrums—as she'd just told him.

"Let him alone with it," he said. "Only entreat the Master on his behalf. On his own, through reading, he'll discover the nature of his wrongheadedness and the extent of his wickedness."

During this same interview, he told her that as a small boy he'd been turned over to the Manichaeans by his mother, whom they'd led astray, and that he'd not only read nearly all their books but also scribbled his heart out reproducing them; and it had become clear to him, with no one arguing with him or confuting him, that he had to get away from this cult; so he'd gotten away.

When he said this but still found her unwilling to give the matter a rest, but instead assailing him even more with her begging and her gushing tears, to try to make him meet with me and have a discussion, he became sick of it, and rather annoyed. "Get out of here," he said. "Just go on living this way. It's impossible that the son of these tears of yours will perish." In her conversations with me, she often recollected that she had experienced this like thunder from heaven.

Book 4

1. Throughout that same time, which was nine years, from the eighteenth year of my life clear up to the twenty-seventh,* we were led and leading astray in turn,† our various passions serving as so many confidence tricks played on us and by us. This happened openly through the studies they call "fit for a free man"‡ and secretly through a counterfeit religion.§

We were conceited as to the former, gullible as to the latter, and fatuously full of ourselves whatever we did. On the one side, we ran after the inanity of public acclaim, and we went for nothing less than applause in the theater, for wrangling over poetry

---

* See note on book 2, chapter 4 above.
† 2 Timothy 3:13.
‡ That is, a "liberal" education, whose subjects at the time were literature, rhetoric, philosophy, mathematics, and music.
§ Again, Manichaeism, a heretical Gnostic sect forbidden by the Roman state.

prizes, for literary Olympiads at which you might be crowned with grass clippings, and pageants of pure folderol, and itches and cravings without end.

On the other side, we burned for a way to clear all this nasty stuff out of our systems, and we brought goodies to those who styled themselves "saints" and "chosen ones," so that in the workshops of their paunches they could craft "angels" and "gods" who would set us free. I enacted all this garbage with my friends, who were fooled by me and right along with me.

They can go ahead and laugh at me, all those insolent people not yet flattened to the earth and smashed to pieces in wholesome fashion by you, my God, but for my part I want to plead to my humiliations because they glorify you. I beg you, let me, through today's memories, tour the detours of my bygone wrongheadedness and slaughter for you a victim, which is the gift of my rejoicing.* For what was my self to my self without you, if not a guide over the edge of the chasm? Or what am I, doing well, but a suckling of your milk, enjoying you, the food that doesn't go bad?† And who is a human being, anyone at all, as long as he's just a human being as such? Robust, powerful personages can laugh at us in our weakness and poverty; we will testify to you.

2. During those years, I taught the science of rhetoric and, subjugated by my own greed, I kept my garrulity—though it was designed to subjugate others—on the auction block. As you know, Master, I did prefer to have good-solid-respectable

---

* Psalms 27:6.
† John 6:27.

students—the kind that are called good-solid-respectable, at any rate—and with complete scrupulousness I instructed them in the scams; not, I mean, equipping them to put the innocent on trial for their lives, but just to advocate for the guilty once in a while.

God, you saw me from far off, slipping on that slick surface. You saw, through thick smoke, my good faith sparking; even though, in fact, in working as a teacher, I displayed it for the approval of those showing a dutiful attachment to idiotic self-regard and making an energetic quest for mendacity—in this I was their confederate.

In those years I had one woman—not that I had acquired carnal knowledge of her in what's called a lawful union, but rather, my roving heat, with no good sense to its name, had tracked her down. But there was only one woman, and I stayed loyal to her bed. In her case, I certainly found out, on the evidence of my own experience, what a gap there is between the sanctioned scope of marriage, a bond contracted for the purpose of producing children, and a deal arising from lustful infatuation, from which progeny is born *against* the parents' fervent wishes—though once it's born, it forces them to love it.

3. I also recollect that when I had decided to enter a contest for a poetic work to be performed in the theater, some soothsayer or other sent me a message to find out what kind of fee I would pay him to make sure I won. I replied that I execrated and loathed the disgusting rites to which he alluded, and that I wouldn't let a fly be slaughtered for the sake of my victory, even if the garland were made of gold unwithering for eternity. He

was, you see, going to put to death creatures with the breath of life in them, and it appeared that by these gifts of honor he meant to solicit demons' votes for me.

But I didn't decline this evil act because of the purity you impart, God of my heart. This is because I didn't know—I who knew nothing but how to muse about the flashes of mere material things—how to love you. If any soul sighs for such fabrications, doesn't it whore around on you, isn't it faithful to what's imaginary, isn't it grazing a flock of winds?* Of course, I said no to a sacrifice to demons to benefit myself, but I sacrificed myself to those demons through the Manichaean superstition. What is grazing the winds if not grazing demons themselves—by which I mean being so wrong that they can find plenty of entertainment making fun of you?

4. Accordingly, I clearly wasn't going to stop consulting, openly and in the clear light of day, those clairvoyant con men called astrologers, because they made more or less no sacrifices and sent no prayers to any supernatural being for the sake of divination. But genuine Christian reverence does repudiate and condemn the practice.

It's good to confess to you, Master,† and to say, "Have pity on me: heal my soul, since I have sinned against you"‡—and not to use your leniency as a license to sin, but instead to remember the words of my Master: "See, you are made whole; do not sin now, in case something worse should happen to you."§

---

* Hosea 12:1.
† Psalms 92:1 (though the modern Bible has "to give thanks" instead of "to confess").
‡ Psalms 41:4.
§ John 5:14.

But the astrologers try to kill this principle in all its wholesomeness by saying: "You have, straight from the heavens, a reason for sinning that you can't avoid," or "The planet Venus did this, or Saturn, or Mars did it—not you," apparently as if there were no fault in a human being, who is flesh and blood and arrogant putrefaction; as if, on the contrary, the one who creates and regulates the heavens and the stars is to blame. And who is this if not our God, the sweet source of justice, who gives each and every person what he is owed for his works* and does not scorn a broken and humbled heart?†

5. At that time there was an astute man, with a profound knowledge of medical science and great distinction in that field. When he held the office of provincial governor, he placed with his own hands on my unhealthy head that crown for which I'd contended—though he didn't do it (of course) in the capacity of a physician.

You, rather, who stand against the arrogant but grant your favor to the weak,‡ are the healer of the disease I suffered from then. But you didn't—did you?—fail me or fall off in treating my soul even through that old man. I'd become something of an intimate of his, and I sat rooted and stuck like a nail to his conversation (which, though unpolished in its manner, was appealing and commanding of respect because of the strong-minded opinions displayed in it). When he found out, in dialogue with me, that I was a devotee of the horoscope-casters' books, he advised me in a kind and fatherly manner to throw them away and

* Romans 2:6.
† Psalms 51:17.
‡ James 4:6 and 1 Peter 5:5, both quoting Proverbs 3:34.

not waste on that poppycock the trouble and attention that were needed for useful things.

He said that during his early youth, he'd studied such books so eagerly that he'd conceived a wish to carry on this calling as his livelihood and life's work; and he thought that if he'd understood Hippocrates,* he certainly must be able to understand these writings, too. Yet he abandoned them later and pursued medicine, precisely because he'd come to recognize that they were deceptive in the extreme, and as a man with self-respect he was unwilling to make his living by deceiving people.

"But you," he said, "can sustain yourself in the community through the profession of rhetoric that you maintain, and yet you run after this chicanery as a pastime, voluntarily, and not because your household is hard up. You should trust me all the more when I tell you this, in that I took great pains to learn this stuff through and through, as I meant it to be my sole livelihood."

I asked him what the reason was, then, that many pronouncements from this source turned out to be true. He answered that as far as he could see, the power of fortune's lottery, spread everywhere throughout the universe, made for this result. If, for example, it often happens that a poet—any poet at all—is consulted at random, and a line emerges that's amazingly in harmony with the reason for consulting him, though the poet was writing about and meaning something far different, it isn't all that amazing that in astrology a chord might be struck—not through science but by chance—that resonates exactly with

---

* The name under which a famous and voluminous corpus of medical literature circulated.

concerns and actions of the person consulting the astrologer; the human soul can in fact strike such a chord through some higher prompting and without even an awareness of what that prompting is about.

6. Truly, this was provident care you took of me from this source or through this channel, and you traced the outline in my memory for what I could look into on my own later. At the time, however, neither he nor even Nebridius, a good and very pure young man of whom I was extremely fond, and who ridiculed the whole field of prognostication, could persuade me to discard its claims, since it was more the prestige of those who penned them that motivated me, and up to this time I hadn't found the certain proof I was seeking, to show me beyond any doubt that the true things these people said when consulted were said at random or by the raw luck of the draw and not by the science of those who scrutinize the stars.

7. During those years, the period when I was first starting to teach in the town in which I was born, I acquired a friend who, because of our shared interests, was incredibly dear to me. He was my age, and flourished with me in the flower of young manhood. As a boy, he'd grown up with me, and we'd gone to school side by side, and side by side we'd played. But he wasn't then the friend he was later on, and even later on he wasn't a true friend; true friendship is what you glue together between those who cling to you when love floods our hearts through the Holy Spirit, which is given to us.*

* Romans 5:5.

But it was an excessively sweet friendship, cooked up as it was in the heat of our similar pursuits—*excessively* sweet because I turned him away from the true faith, which as a youth he didn't have in his blood, as part of his deeper self. I led him into those superstitious, malignant Manichaean fairy tales that made my mother mourn for me. My friend was, in his mind, lost along with me, and my soul couldn't be without him.

But there you were, breathing down the neck of your runaways, God of retributions* and flowing spring of mercies, who turns us back around toward you in marvelous ways; there you were, taking that person out of this life when he had scarcely rounded out a year in my friendship, which was sweet beyond all the sweet things in my life then.

8. What individual could tally up your merits—only the ones he's experienced individually?† What did you do at that time, my God, and how untraceable are the depths of your judgments?‡ When he was suffering with a fever, he lay a long time unaware of what happened around him, and in a death sweat. When there was deemed to be no hope for him, he was baptized without knowing it. I thought nothing of it and presumed that his soul kept what it had gotten from me, not what happened to his body while he was unconscious.

It turned out far different, however. He recovered, escaping the danger to his life, and as soon as I could speak to him (which I could do as soon as he could speak, since I didn't leave him the

* Psalms 94:1.
† Psalms 106:2.
‡ Romans 11:33, Psalms 36:6.

whole time—we were so excessively attached to each other), I tried to laugh it off with him, assuming he was going to join me in laughing at the rite he'd received when his consciousness and physical senses were completely unreachable.

He had, however, already learned that he'd received it, and he shrank back from me as if I were his deadly enemy, and with immediate and startling frankness he warned me that if I wanted to be his friend, I should stop saying such things. I was stunned and distressed and put off telling him my reactions until he convalesced and was suitably strong and healthy, so that I could deal with him however I liked. But he was snatched away from my madness, to be kept with you for my comfort. After a few days, when I wasn't there, he was again attacked by fever and passed away.

9. The sorrow of this overshadowed my heart, and whatever I looked at was death. My hometown was an agonizing punishment for me, and my father's house a place of bizarre misery, and all the activities I'd shared with him turned, without him, into a monstrous torture. My eyes searched everywhere eagerly for him, but he wasn't presented to them. I hated everything, because nothing had him in it, and nothing could now say to me, "Look, he's coming," as things did while he lived and wasn't in my company. I became my own elaborate investigation, and I grilled my soul as to why it was sad, and why it threw me into such terrible distress, but it didn't have any answer for me. If I tried saying to it "Hope in God," it was right in not obeying me, because the man it had loved devotedly and lost was more real and better than the figment in which it was commanded to hope.

Only weeping was pleasant to me, and that had taken my friend's place as my heart's delight.

10. But now, Master, those things have passed away, and time has soothed my wound. Am I able to hear something from you—who are the truth? Can I move my heart's ear to your mouth, so that you can tell me why weeping is pleasant for those in misery? Or have you, though you're present everywhere, thrown our misery far away from you, so that you remain in yourself,* whereas we are rolled along in our trials? And yet if we didn't wail for your ears to hear it, there would be nothing left of our hope.

Why, then, is sweet fruit plucked from life's bitterness, from groaning and weeping and sighing and lamenting? Does the sweetness in it consist of our hope that you'll listen? That's the case where prayers are concerned, because they include the desire to reach you. But that couldn't be the case in sorrow for a loss, and mourning—feelings in which I was buried back then—could it? I neither hoped that he would come back to life, nor begged for it with my tears; I simply suffered and wept. In my misery I missed what had been my joy. Is weeping essentially a bitter thing, gratifying us because we turn up our noses at the things we enjoyed before, and shrink back from them afterward?

11. But why am I discussing these things? Now is not the occasion for an inquiry, but for giving my testimony to you. I was wretched, and every mind is wretched when chained to friend-

* Wisdom of Solomon 7:27.

ship with things bound to die, and is torn to shreds when it loses them; that's when it *feels* the anguish that actually afflicts it long before it loses them.

That's how it was with me at that period, and I cried very bitterly and rested in my bitterness. Thus, I was in anguish, but I held my actual anguished life dearer than that friend of mine, because though I would have liked to change my life, I was less willing to lose it than to lose him. Well, maybe I would have been willing, if it was actually for him—as in the tradition about Orestes and Pylades (if it's not just made up),* who were willing to die, one in place of the other, or at one and the same time, because it was worse for them not both to be alive at once.

But no: in me had arisen a certain feeling as different from theirs as it could be: I was weighed insufferably down with weariness from being alive, but I dreaded death. I believed that the more I loved him, the more I feared and hated death, which had taken him away from me, as if it were a savagely cruel enemy. I thought death would suddenly devour all of humankind, since death was able to do that to him. That's the state I was in, all told, as I remember it.

My God, here's my heart; here's my inner being. See it, because I remember it, you my hope, who cleanse me from the uncleanliness of feelings like these, guiding my eyes to you and plucking the snare from my feet.† I was amazed that other mortals were alive, because he, whom I loved as if he were never going to die, was dead. I was even more amazed that I was alive while

---

* The most famous depiction of the two was in the fifth-century B.C. tragedy *The Libation Bearers* of Aeschylus. Naturally Augustine considered the pagan story "made up."
† Psalms 25:15.

he wasn't, because I was his counterpart: him, but another one of him.

The author was exactly right who called his friend "half of my own soul."* I felt that my soul and the soul of the other had been a single one in two bodies,† and for that reason life was pure horror to me, because I didn't want to live as a half; and conceivably for the same reason, I dreaded death: I didn't want the one I had loved so much to die in his entirety when I died.

12. What an insanity of ignorance, the inability to keep human affections on a human scale! And how a human being bungles in bearing human fate intemperately! That was what I was at the time: so I seethed, I sighed, I sobbed, I turned myself inside out, and I had neither rest nor access to reason. I hauled around with me a gouged and gory soul, which itself had had quite enough of this, but I couldn't find a place to put it down: not in scenic groves, not in sports and music, not in fragrant spots, not in well-appointed dinner parties, and not in the sensuality of the bed and the couch, and not, would you believe it, in books and poetry. Everything repelled me, even daylight itself, and everything with a being apart from him was obnoxious and offensive— except for groaning and tears: in these alone was a scintilla of rest.

But whenever my soul was shifted from there, it was loaded down with a big sack of misery. I knew my soul needed to be lifted up to you and thus relieved,‡ but I had neither the wish

* Horace, *Odes,* 1.3.8.
† Ovid, *Tristia,* 4.4.72.
‡ Psalms 25:1.

nor the push in me; and even less so in that *you* weren't any kind of solid or steady resource when I contemplated you; you weren't you, but an empty apparition, and my god was my mistake. If I tried to put my wretchedness there so that it could rest, it fell through the empty space and crashed down on top of me again, and there I was stuck, a cursed spot for myself, where I couldn't remain and from which I couldn't retreat. To where could my heart run away from my heart? Where could I run away from myself? Where could I not pursue me? Yet I did run from my hometown. My eyes were going to look for him less in a place where they weren't used to seeing him, and I left the town of Thagaste for Carthage.

13. Time doesn't take any time off, doesn't roll idly through our perceptions. Instead, it does astonishing work in the mind. There it was, coming and going from day to day, and in coming and going it planted in me new hopes and new memories, and little by little it mended me through old kinds of pleasures, to which that grief of mine gave way. Taking its place were not other immediate sorrows, but attachments that would lead to other sorrows.

But how had that first sorrow been able so effortlessly to pierce me to the core, unless it was because I had already bled my soul out onto the sandy floor of the arena by feeling affection for a mortal being as if he were immortal?

To a great extent, naturally, the solaces felt through other friends restored and revived me; it was in their company that I loved what I loved instead of you. But this was a giant fiction and an interminable lie; rubbing against it adulterously, our minds were infected, with the itch coming in through our ears.*

But that fiction didn't die if one of my friends died. Among the ones who remained, things other than this issue were more arresting to my mind. We had conversation, we shared jokes, made obliging exchanges of favors, read beguiling books together, were silly together and serious together, were at odds from time to time but without resentment, as a person might be at odds with himself—we actually spiced up a plethora of shared opinions with just a sprinkling of differences. We exchanged teaching and learning, felt put upon when missing those who weren't there, and were elated in having them back.

We made full use of these tokens and others of the same sort—which come from the hearts of those who love and who love in return, and which issue forth through the face, the tongue, the eyes, and through a thousand delightful gestures—as a sort of kindling in igniting our minds and melting many of us into one.

14. This is what's loved in friends, and it's loved in such a way that human conscience arraigns itself if it doesn't return love for love (no matter who began it), seeking nothing from the object of that love beyond signs of goodwill. Hence there's grief if someone dies, and the darkness of sorrow; and a heart overcome with tears once sweetness turns into bitterness; and living deaths due to lost lives.

But it's a happy person who loves *you*, God, and in you loves his friend, and loves his enemy because of you.† The only one who

* 2 Timothy 4:3–4.
† Matthew 5:44, Luke 6:27.

never loses anyone dear to him is the one to whom everyone is dear through him who can't be lost.

And who is that if not our God, who has made heaven and earth and fills them, because by filling them he has made them? No one loses you unless he leaves you, and in leaving, where does he go, where does he run away,* if not from your favor and to your anger? Where does he not find your law in the form of his own punishment? Your law is the truth,† and the truth is you.‡

15. God of the armies of heaven, turn us around to you and show your face, and we will be saved.§ In whatever direction the soul of a human being turns, it is stuck to sorrow in any place but in you, even though it's fastened to beautiful things outside you and outside itself.

There would, however, be no such beautiful things unless they came from you. They rise and set, and in rising it's as if they begin their existence, and they grow and come into the fullness of their being, and once in the fullness of their being, they grow old and perish; or not all grow old, but all do die.

Therefore, while they arise and strive to be, the more swiftly they grow into being, the more they hurry toward not being. This is their limitation. This much you gave to them, because they are parts of the universe; not all parts are there at once, but in ceding and succeeding to each other, they carry out the whole, of which they are separate parts.

---

* Psalms 139:7.
† Psalms 119:142.
‡ John 14:6.
§ Psalms 80:7.

And, you see, this is the way that our speech is carried out from beginning to end, through vocal signals. It wouldn't be complete speech if one word didn't cede, once the parts of it had made their sounds, so that another word could succeed it.

Let my soul praise you for these things, God, creator of all things. But don't let me be glued firmly to them through the love the physical senses generate. These things go where they were already going when they began, so that they won't exist, and they tear the soul apart with noxious longings, since it wants to exist, and loves to rest, in the things it loves, whereas in these things there's no place to do this, as they don't stand in one place; they run away, and who can follow them with the body's perception? And who can grasp them, even when they're at hand? The body's perception is slow, because it's the body's perception: this is *its* limitation. It's enough for one purpose, for which it was created, but it's not enough for another, which is to hold on to fleeting things from their due beginning to their due ending. In your Word, through which they're created, they hear, "From here to here you will go, and no farther."*

16. Don't be empty air, my soul. Do not let your heart grow hard of hearing in the racket of your emptiness. You, too, must listen: the Word itself shouts for you to return, and there lies a place of calm that will never know any uproar, where love is not abandoned unless it abandons. See how the things I've been writing about depart so that new ones can take their part, so that the universe here at its foundation can be made up of all its components.

* Job 38:11.

"I'm not leaving for anywhere, am I?" says the Word of God. Imbed your home in him,* place in safekeeping with him whatever you have from him, my soul—if only because you're worn out by lies. Place in safekeeping *with* the truth whatever you possess *from* the truth, and you won't lose anything. The things that have rotted in you will flower again, and all the afflictions that make you sluggish will be healed,† and the things that are slack will be remade and renewed and hold together with you. They won't drop you in the depths (where they themselves go), but will stand steady at your side and hold their ground in the presence of God, who also stands steady and holds his ground.

17. Why, my soul, do you twist yourself around to follow your body? It should follow *you* now that you've turned to God. Whatever you perceive through the body, you perceive in part, and you don't know the whole, of which these things are parts—but they delight you nevertheless. But if your body's perception were adequate for grasping the whole, and if it hadn't, as your punishment, been justly limited to a part of the whole, you'd wish for whatever exists in the present to pass away, so that everything, all of it together, could give you more enjoyment.

For example, whatever we say you hear with that same physical perception, and you certainly don't want the syllables to stand still but to fly past, so that more can come and you can hear the whole. It's always this way with all the things of which any single larger thing consists (given that all the things of which that one thing consists don't exist simultaneously). All of them together give more delight than they do individually, if only they

* John 14:23.
† Matthew 4:23, which may quote Psalms 103:3.

can all be perceived. But far better than them is the one who made everything, and he's our God, and he doesn't leave, and no one comes to relieve him.

18. If material things please you, praise God for them, and turn back toward their maker the course of your love for them, so that the sources of your pleasure don't make you yourself an object of displeasure. If souls meet with your approval, let them be loved in God, because in themselves they're changeable, whereas in him they're attached to a firm foundation: otherwise they would go, they would run to their ruin. So let them be loved in him, and however many you can, carry them off—along with yourself—for God, telling them the following:

"He is the one we must love. He made these things, and he is not far away.* He didn't make them and take his leave, but rather they come out of him and exist in him as well. Just look: he's there, wherever you can taste the truth. He's in the inmost part of the heart, but the heart has wandered away from him. Return to the heart, you double-crossers,† and cling to the one who made you. Stand with him, and you'll stand indeed. Rest in him, and restfulness will be yours.

"Where are you going on that steep, rough road? Where are you going? The good that you love is *from* him, but only inasmuch as it's directed back *toward* him is it good and sweet. Otherwise it will turn bitter, and rightly so, because it's not right to love whatever is *in him* while abandoning *him*. With what destination in mind are you walking, endlessly, endlessly, on those hard

---

* Acts 17:27.

† Isaiah 46:8 (but the Latin scripture this follows closely is quite unlike the Hebrew or its modern English translations).

paths of suffering?* There's no rest where you're looking for it. Look for what you're looking for—but it's not there where you're looking. You're seeking a happy life in a land of death. It's not there. How can there be a happy life where there isn't even life?

19. "Our life, in person, came down here, and took on our death, and killed it with his own overflowing life, and he spoke like a thunderclap, shouting for us to return to him from here, and enter that secret place from which he came forth to us, coming first into the virgin womb itself, where the creation that was humankind became his bride, so that the dying body wouldn't always have to die. From there he came forth like a bridegroom out of the bedroom, and he was thrilled like a giant with a race to run.† He lost no time, but ran with shouts of words, acts, death, life, descent, ascent,‡ all the time shouting for us to return to him. He departed from our sight§ so that we would return to the heart and find him. He parted from us, and look, here he is. He was unwilling to be with us long, but he didn't leave us. He withdrew to a place from which he never drew back, because the universe was made by him, and he was in this universe,¶ and he came into this universe to save sinners.** To him my soul confesses, and he heals it, since it sinned against him.†† Sons of men, how long will you be heavyhearted?‡‡ Even after the descent of life, would you be unwilling to ascend and live? But where do

---

* Wisdom of Solomon 5:7.
† Psalms 19:5.
‡ Ephesians 4:9.
§ Luke 24:51, Acts 1:9.
¶ John 1:3, 10.
** 1 Timothy 1:15.
†† Psalms 41:4.
‡‡ Psalms 4:2.

you have to climb to, since you've already exalted yourselves and set your loud mouths up sky high?* Come down, so that you can go up, and you can go up to God. You fell by climbing up to try to challenge God."

Tell them this, so that they wail in the valley of wailing,† and carry them off—along with yourself—to God, because you say these things to them out of his Spirit, if in speaking you burn with the fire of selfless love.

20. At the time, I did not know these things, and I was infatuated with the lower beauties and was heading toward the depths. I used to say to my friends, "We don't love anything unless it's beautiful, do we? But then what's beautiful? And what's beauty? What is it that draws us and endears us to the things we love? Unless there were some seemliness and attractiveness in them, there would be no way they could pull us toward themselves."

Well, I set my mind to it, and I began to see that there inhered in material objects one quality that's a sort of whole, which is beautiful for that reason; and that there's another quality that's attractive because it's well adapted to fit something else, like a part of the body in its relation to the whole body, or a piece of footwear in relation to the foot, and so on with other examples.

And this contemplation of mine burbled up in my mind from the inmost recesses of my heart, and I wrote some volumes entitled "On the Beautiful and the Fitting." I think there were two

* Psalms 73:8; the Latin Bible is much closer than ours to Augustine here.
† Psalms 84:6 (but just forget about the English Bible here).

or three of them—you know, God, but I forget. We haven't got them any more; they've wandered away from us somehow.

21. But what was it, my God and Master, that impelled me to dedicate those books to Hierius, an orator in the city of Rome? I'd never met this person face-to-face, but I'd fallen in love with him because of his reputed learning, for which he was in fact celebrated—plus, I'd heard certain quotations from him, which I liked; but my stronger reason for liking him was that other people liked him and praised him to the skies, as they were amazed that somebody from Syria, who'd initially been trained only in Greek oratory, had later on turned out to be a marvelous speaker in Latin, and also deeply learned in questions connected to philosophical studies.

A person is praised and loved, though he's not present. Does this love enter from the mouth of the one praising him into the heart of the one who hears? Nonsense! Instead, one lover sets another on fire. Hence it comes about that the object of praise becomes the object of love, as long as he's not thought to be publicized by someone whose praise originates in a deceitful heart—that is, someone who truly loves him must praise him.

22. This was how I loved human beings at the time, on the basis of human judgment, not on the basis of your judgment, my God, in whom no one is deceived. Yet why didn't I praise Hierius the way you'd praise a widely acclaimed chariot racer, or a wild beast hunter in the arena, but rather much differently, more seriously, the way I'd want to be praised myself? I wouldn't

have wanted to be praised and loved as actors are, though I myself praised and loved them; I would have chosen to skulk below public notice rather than to be well known for the reasons actors are; I would even have preferred to be hated than to be loved on those grounds.*

On which side is each of the various and contrasting loves set to be weighed in the scale of a single soul? How can it be that I love in another person what I hate in myself?—and I do hate it, as otherwise I wouldn't reject it and curse it; yet either of us is, after all, a human being. It's not the same with a fine horse, loved by someone who wouldn't want to be a horse even if he could, as with an actor, who's our partner in humankind. Does this mean that I love in another human being what I would hate to be, although I'm a human being too, or because I'm a human being too?†

But a human being as such is a huge abyss. You know the number of hairs on his head, Master, and in you there's no subtraction from that number;‡ but it's easier to count his hairs than his moods or the workings of his heart.

23. But that orator was the sort with whom I was so infatuated that I wanted to be just like him. I was blown off course by the storm of my own arrogance and hauled around by every wind that hit me;§ you were my helmsman, but not openly enough my helmsman.

---

* Public entertainers were not a respectable class; many were slaves, freed slaves, or convicted criminals.
† The Latin is ambiguous as to the meaning "although" or "because."
‡ Matthew 10:30.
§ Ephesians 4:14.

So how do I know, and why am I confident in testifying to you that I was passionate about him more because of the passion of those who praised him than because of the things he was praised for? Well, if the same men hadn't praised him but instead decisively disparaged him, and told me the exact same story about him, except in the mode of reviling and rejecting him, I wouldn't have been inflamed or aroused. The facts, anyway, would have been just the same, and so would the man; only the attitude of those telling about him would have been different.

Here's the ground on which a weak soul lies, not yet clinging to truth's solidity: whatever breezes blow, delivered by human tongues out of the bosom of humanity's various views, they can carry that soul round and about, twist it inside out, while the light is clouded over and the truth not perceived—but it's right there in front of us.

It would have been a momentous thing for me if that gentleman had familiarized himself with that discourse of mine, and with my endeavors in general. If he'd approved, I would have been on fire even more; if he'd disapproved, I would have been stabbed through my hollow heart, which was empty of your substantiality.

Nonetheless, I enjoyed composing something for him on "The Beautiful and the Fitting"; I liked turning the thing over in my mind and viewing it in my imagination. Having nobody to join me in praise, I admired the work myself.

24. But I didn't yet see that the pivot of such an important matter is in your artistry, All-Powerful One, since on your own you

make wonders.* My mind went off among material forms, and I defined and distinguished the beautiful as being something fine in itself and the fitting as being fine when adapted to something else, and I supported this with material examples.

I did turn my attention to the mind's character, but the mistaken view I had of spiritual things didn't allow me to discern the truth. The very vigor of truth crashed into my sight, and I averted my heart-thudding understanding from unembodied being to shapes and colors and objects in ever so gross and swollen sizes,† and because I couldn't see these in mind, I thought I couldn't see mind at all.

And as I loved the peace that's in virtue and hated the dissension that's in vice, in the first I identified unity, and in the second a sort of division. In that unity there appeared to me to be reasoning thought and the essence of truth and of the highest good; in that division of mine was some substance or other of unreasoning life and the essence of the deepest evil; and not just a substance, but genuine life; and yet it wasn't from you, my God, from whom everything comes. Such, anyway, was my woefully inadequate estimation.

I called the first the "monad," as being, like thought, without gender, and the second I called the "dyad," such as anger in faction fighting, and lust in depraved acts—though I had no idea what I was talking about. I didn't know, I hadn't learned that evil isn't any substance whatsoever; or that our mind, in itself, isn't the highest good, or an unchangeable one.

* Psalms 72:18, 136:4.
† Probably a sarcastic reference to the Manichaean cosmology and mythology, which echoed pagan conceptions of more important gods having a greater physical weight.

25. It's much the same: crimes come about if the mind's activity partakes of the wrong impulse and flaunts arrogantly and recklessly; and disgraceful acts happen if the disposition of the soul for gulping down pleasures of the body isn't kept within bounds. And delusions and wrongheaded opinions pollute a life if reasoning thought itself is wrong, as it was in me then.

I didn't know that my thought had to be elucidated with a light from outside it, in order to make it a sharer in the truth, because my mind itself *isn't* the essence of truth; but rather you, Master, will light my lamp. My God, you will light my darkness,* and from your abundance we all have received;† for you're the true light that gives light to every person coming into this world,‡ because in you there is no change, and no shadow cast by any movement.§

26. I was struggling toward you, but at the same time being thrown back, with the taste of death in my mouth, since you take a stand against the insolent.¶ What could be more insolent than for me to insist, with bizarre lunacy, that I was, in my very nature, what you are?

I could in fact change, and that was proved by the very fact that I was certainly keen to be wise, which meant becoming better after having been worse; but I preferred that even you be subject to change, rather than that I not be what you are.

* Psalms 18:28.
† John 1:16.
‡ John 1:9.
§ James 1:17.
¶ James 4:6, 1 Peter 5:5.

So I was thrown back, and you held your ground against me, stiff-necked bag of wind that I was. I kept making mental pictures out of material forms, and I kept indicting the flesh, in spite of being flesh myself. I was wind, breath, spirit out for a stroll and not yet returning to you,* and my strolling for the mere sake of strolling took me into things that don't exist, either in you or in me or in the material world at all, and they weren't created for me out of your truth, but rather my empty-headedness fantasized them out of that material world.

And I used to say to your lowly, innocent believers, citizens from whose country I was an exile without even knowing it, I used to say to them, like the blabbering fool I was, "So why does the soul that God created go wrong?"

I didn't want to hear in response, "You mean why does *God* go wrong?" But I did contend that the immutable substance in you is *compelled* to go wrong,† and I did so in preference to professing that the quite mutable substance in me had gone off the path of its own free will and was wandering around as a punishment.

27. I was maybe twenty-five or twenty-six years old‡ when I filled those scrolls, rolling around in my mind inventions about materiality that were dinning in my heart's ears, though I was intent on hearing the inner melody of you, my sweet truth; I thought about the beautiful and the fitting, and I yearned to stand still and listen to you, and to rejoice beyond all rejoicing in the voice of my betrothed§—but I couldn't do any of this,

---

* See Psalms 78:39, Proverbs 2:19.
† A Manichaean doctrine concerning the god of light.
‡ See footnote to book 2, chapter 4.
§ John 3:29.

because the voices of my wrongheadedness seized me and carried me off outside, and I toppled into the lowest depths, pulled down by the weight of my own uppitiness. You didn't grant joy and delight to my hearing, and my bones didn't leap into the air for joy, as they hadn't been brought down to the ground.*

28. What good did it do me that when I was around nineteen,† I could read on my own and understand a treatise of Aristotle called *The Ten Categories*,‡ once I'd obtained a copy? When the city rhetorician at Carthage, who was my teacher (his jaws flapping in a gale of pretension), and other men with a reputation for learning had described this work, the title itself made me acutely keen and avid, as if for something magnificent and holy.

But when I discussed the treatise with other students—who said they'd scarcely been able to understand it with the help of the best-educated teachers, who not only described it but also drew a lot of diagrams in the dust—they couldn't tell me any more about it than I'd learned on my own, all by myself.

It appeared to me pretty much self-evident that the treatise was about "substances," such as humanity, and what comprises them. For example, there's the shape of a human being, whatever it happens to be; and the height, or number of feet; and family relationship, as in whose brother he is; or where he's located, or when he was born, or whether he's standing or sitting, or wearing shoes or maybe battle gear, whether he's doing something or having it done to him—and countless other things of all kinds

* Psalms 51:8.
† See footnote to book 2, chapter 4.
‡ This is now known under the title *Categories*. It is the first work of Aristotle's *Organon*, a collection of writings on logic.

that are found in these nine categories, or in the tenth category, which is "substance" itself.

29. But what good did this system do me? It even got in my way! Thinking that whatever existed at all was included in these ten "predicates," I tried to understand even you, my God, miraculously unitary and unchangeable, as if you were "subject" to your magnitude or to your beauty; that is, as if they were attached to you (like predicates to a grammatical subject) and you were their "subject," as properties are predicated on material objects—whereas in reality your magnitude and your beauty are you yourself.

A body, in contrast, isn't large or beautiful by virtue of being a body, because even if it's less big or less beautiful, it's still a body. It was a lie that I was cogitating about you, and not truth. It was the feeble imaginings of my misery, not the buttress of your bliss. You'd given the command, and it was realized in my case, that the earth would grow thorns and thistles for me, and that only toil would bring me bread.*

30. And what good did it do me, utterly worthless slave of nasty lusts as I was then, that I read and understood all the books of the arts they call "liberal" (or worthy of a free man)†—or at least whichever of these books I could get hold of? I was delighted with them, but without any idea where anything true and reliable in them came from. This was because I had my back to the light and my face to the things lighted up; the result being that

---

* Genesis 3:18.
† See book 4, chapter 1, and the note.

my face, from which I saw what was lighted up, wasn't exposed to the light.

Anything in the science of speaking and debating, in geometry and music and mathematics, I understood without great difficulty, and nobody in the world needed to convey it to me. You know this, God my Master, because both speed in understanding and sharpness of discernment are gifts from you.

But I didn't employ them to make offerings to you, and that's why they had more capacity to doom me than to be of any use, because I meddled in trying to keep such a good part of my own substance, my property, in my own possession, and I didn't keep my strength in stock for you, but I left you and traveled to a distant country, to waste that strength on the whores that were my desires.* How could I benefit from a good thing if I didn't use it in a good way?

I didn't perceive that these sciences are hugely difficult even for the hardworking and talented to understand, until I tried to explain the same material to such students myself, and the most outstanding of them proved to be merely the one who followed my explanation less slowly than the others.

31. But what good did this do me, given that I thought you—Master, God, Truth—were an enormous, shiny material object, and that I was a hunk of that object? Outrageous twistedness! But that's how I was, and I don't blush, my God, to testify to you about your mercies and to call on you; after all, I didn't blush back then to profess my blasphemies to human beings and to yap away at you.

* The comparison is to the parable of the prodigal son (Luke 15:11–32).

So what good to me then was the brilliant mind that could prance right through all those branches of learning? What good was the unknotting of so many of the knottiest books without any human teaching to help me jimmy it all apart? What good was that when, with shameful, with unsightly indecency, I went astray when I should have been taught reverence?

And what was the great disadvantage for your lowly children with their much slower minds? They didn't place themselves at a great distance from you, but grew their feathers safely in the church's nest and nurtured their wings of love on the food of healthy faith.

Oh, Master, our God, we must find our hope in the shelter of your wings: cover us over and carry us. You'll carry us even as lowly children, and you'll carry us until our hair is white, because when you are our firm support, then we truly have that; when the "firm support" is our own, it's weakness.*

Our good lives forever in your presence; because we've turned our backs on you, we're turned inside out. Let's return now, Master, so that we're not overturned, because in your presence our good lives without ever failing, because you *are* that good, and we aren't afraid that there'll be no place for us to go back because we rushed ruinously from it. No, in our absence, our house, your eternity, doesn't fall into ruin.

---

* 2 Corinthians 12:9.

Book 5

1. Accept the sacrifice that is my testimony, from the writing hand that's here my speaking tongue,* the hand you formed and filled with its energy, so that it could testify in your name; and heal all my bones,† so that they can say, "Master, who is like you?"‡ But whoever testifies to you is hardly instructing you as to what happens inside him, because the heart that's locked up hardly locks out your eyes, nor does people's hard surface fend off your hand, but you melt that barrier whenever you want, either in pity or in punishment, and no one can hide from your heat.§

---

* Proverbs 18:21; the Vulgate: "Death and Life in the Hand [= power] of the Tongue."
† Psalms 6:2.
‡ Exodus 15:11, Psalms 35:10.
§ Psalms 19:6.

But let my soul praise you so that it loves you, and let it testify to you about your mercies so that it praises you.* The whole of your creation never leaves off, never lets your praise fall silent: every mouth that breathes is turned toward you in praise;† not excepting every beast with the breath of life, and every object without it,‡ as these are heard through the mouths of those contemplating you. Let all this raise our soul out of its weariness and into you, let our soul lean on the things you made, and let it pass over to you, who wondrously made them. And in that place is our restoration and our true strength.

2. Let the restless unrighteous go, let them run from you. But you see them, you split the shadows apart—and look, everything around them is beautiful, but they themselves are ugly. But how have they ever hurt you? What have they ever done to discredit your dominion, which is just and unsullied from the sky all the way down to the lowest part of the world?

Where in fact have they fled to, when they've fled from your face? And where won't you find them?§ They've turned tail and so didn't see you seeing them, and in their blind rush they ran into you—because you don't abandon anything you've created; the unrighteous ran into you and were rightly harried as they ducked away from your clemency, colliding with your justice and falling into your severity.¶

Plainly, they don't know that you're everywhere, as no place confines you within its boundaries; that you alone are near at

---

* Psalms 107:8.
† Psalms 150:6.
‡ Psalms 148.
§ Psalms 139:7–8.
¶ Romans 11:8–9.

hand for those who make as if to distance themselves from you. Let them turn around, then, and look for you, because you haven't abandoned what you've created the way they've abandoned you: they're the ones who must turn around.

And see: there you are in their hearts, in the hearts of those who testify to you and cast themselves on you and cry in your arms, since they've come to you by such trying paths. And you obligingly dry their tears,* and they weep all the more and rejoice in their weeping, since you, Master, aren't some human being or other, flesh and blood; you, Master, who made them, remake them and comfort them.

And where was I myself, when I was looking for you? You were right in front of me, but I had left myself and couldn't find me. How much less was I able to find *you*!

3. In the sight of my God, I will speak openly about the twenty-eighth year of my life.† There had come to Carthage a certain prelate of the Manichaean sect, whose name was Faustus. He was a great snare in the devil's service, and many people were baited by his tasty eloquence and became entangled with him.

From the first, I praised that eloquence, but I nevertheless distinguished it from the truth of the matters I was keen to learn about; I wasn't scrutinizing what kind of half-adequate dinnerware his style was, but what knowledge this Faustus—such a famous name among those people!—would serve up in it for me to devour. The preliminary remarks of rumor held him to be

---

* Isaiah 25:8, quoted in Revelation 7:17, 21:4.
† See note on book 2, chapter 4 above.

thoroughly expert in every prestigious field, but he was supposed to be an especially polished adept in the liberal arts.

Since I'd read many works of the philosophers and still retained what I'd learned, I now proceeded to compare selected material from this source with those long, fanciful stories of the Manichaeans, and I found more plausible the statements of those with only an aptitude for evaluating the material world—notwithstanding that the Master of it was hardly among their discoveries.*

This is because you are great, Master, yet you have regard for lowly things, while you recognize overexalted things from far off;† and you don't approach any people but those trampled down at heart;‡ and you aren't discovered by the high and proud,§ not even if, in their painstaking expertise, they can count the stars and the grains of sand and measure the tracts full of heavenly bodies and track down the stars on their trails.

4. They sought all this out using their minds, and using the talent you gave them, and they discovered many things. Many years ahead of time they predicted eclipses of those illuminations, the sun and the moon: on which day they would happen, in which hour, and how much would be obscured; and their calculations didn't deceive them. The eclipses came about just as predicted, and the predictors wrote up the principles they'd hunted down, which are read even today, and on them are based new predictions of the year, the month of the year, the day of

* Wisdom of Solomon 13:9, Romans 1:19–22.
† Psalms 138:6.
‡ Psalms 34:18.
§ James 4:6 and 1 Peter 5:5, both quoting Proverbs 3:34.

the month, and the hour of the day when an eclipse will happen, and of the portion of its light the moon or the sun will lose. And it's going to happen just as it's predicted.

And people who don't know anything about this just marvel, they're stunned, and those who do know shoot up in their own estimation and are praised to the skies. Through their irreverent uppitiness they recede from you and suffer an eclipse of your light. They can see a future eclipse so far ahead of time, but they don't see their own eclipse right now (for they don't reverently investigate the source of their genius for making these investigations of theirs), and even when they do discover that you made them, they don't hand themselves over to you, so that you can preserve what you made; they don't immolate themselves (in the character in which they've created themselves) as a gift to you; they don't slaughter, like fluttering birds, the lofty flights of their self-regard; they don't slaughter, like fish of the sea, their prying inquiries, the rounds they make of mysterious byways in the abyss; they don't slaughter their self-indulgences that make them like beasts of the field, so that you, God, a voracious fire,* can consume these dead preoccupations and create their owners anew in everlasting life.

5. But they don't know the way, your Word, through which you made those things they enumerate, and through which you made their very selves who make these calculations, along with the perception through which they discern the things they enumerate, and the mind that lets them do that; but there is no calculating your wisdom.†

* Deuteronomy 4:24, quoted in Hebrews 12:29.
† Psalms 147:5.

He himself, the only-begotten, was created to be wisdom and justice and holiness for us,* and he was counted among us, and he paid the reckoning, the tribute to Caesar.† They don't know the way to come down to him from themselves, and to go up *to* him *through* him.

They don't know this road, and they think they're up there shining on high with the stars, but look how they've crashed down into the ground,‡ and their heart, empty of wisdom, is darkened over.§ They do say many true things about what has been created, but the Truth itself, the artisan of creation, they don't reverently seek, and therefore they don't find him.

Or if they do find him and recognize him as God, they don't honor him as God or give him thanks, and in all their ideas they fade away to nothing; and they claim to be wise, attributing to themselves qualities that are yours; and in doing so they strive, in their depraved blindness, actually to attribute to you what belongs to them, plainly imputing lies to you, who are the truth, and transforming the glory of God, who can't perish, into a simulacrum of a human being who's going to rot, and of birds and four-footed animals and snakes; and they turn your truth into a lie, and they worship and serve the creation rather than the creator.¶

6. Nevertheless, I retained in my mind many true statements of the philosophers based on the created natural world, and I kept

* 1 Corinthians 1:30.
† The crucifixion at the hands of the Imperial Romans; but see Matthew 22:15–22 and Mark 12:13–17 on "rendering [taxes] unto Caesar."
‡ Isaiah 14:12–15.
§ Romans 1:21, Ephesians 4:18.
¶ The passage depends heavily on Romans 1:18–25.

seeing that the logic behind these statements coincided with mathematics, the divisions of the year following in a fixed order, and the visible evidence of the stars. I compared all this with the statements of Mani in his copious and most verbosely raving writings on the subject, and no solid rationale met me there for solstices or equinoxes or eclipses of illuminating heavenly bodies, or anything else of the kind that I'd learned in books of this immediate universe's science. In Manichaean literature, I was ordered to believe, yet there was no coincidence with any logic that had been put to the test with calculations and with my own eyes—the two sets of claims were very widely separated.

7. Master, God of truth, is it really possible that whoever knows that sort of thing ipso facto pleases you? No, because even anyone knowing all of that, but not knowing you, is an unfortunate person. It's a happy one, on the other hand, who knows you, even if he doesn't know any natural philosophy.

In fact, the one who knows both you and science isn't any happier on account of the science: he's happy because of you alone, if in recognizing you he glorifies you as God and gives you thanks, and doesn't fade away into nothingness amid all his speculations.

A person who knows that he possesses a tree and thanks you for the use of it, even though he doesn't know how many cubits high it is, or how far it stretches from side to side, is better off than the person who measures it and counts all its branches but doesn't possess it or know or love its creator. In the same way, just say a person is committed and faithful, and thus a whole universe of riches belongs to him, and though he has nothing it's as if he possessed everything* because he's a part of you, to whom everything is enslaved. It's idiotic to doubt that a person actually unaware of the Great Bear orbit is better off in every sense than the person who can measure the sky and count the stars and weigh up the components of the universe but leaves aside you, who've placed everything in order through measure and number and weight.†

8. Anyway, who asked Mani (whoever that was) to write about all this as well, when without any expertise in it at all a person can pursue a knowledge of reverence? You've said to human-kind, "Look here: awe before divinity *is* wisdom."‡ Mani might of course not have known anything about *that*, even if he knew the other stuff flawlessly; but inasmuch as he *didn't* know the latter, yet had the shameless gall to set up as a teacher of it, he couldn't in the least have known what it means to feel awe.

Professing science is as good as doing nothing; awe means confessing to you. Hence, the only result of that renegade's so copiously addressing scientific topics was his confutation and condemnation by those who had actually mastered these topics, making it red-handedly evident how little his understanding must be worth in matters even more arcane. And in fact, in order to boost his prestige he was at pains to persuade people that the Holy Spirit, which consoles§ and enriches your faithful followers, had manifested its very self, with its full authority, in himself.

---

* 2 Corinthians 6:10.
† Wisdom of Solomon 11:20.
‡ Job 28:28.
§ John 14:16, 26.

Therefore, when he was caught in false statements about the sky and the stars and the movements of the sun and moon, his blasphemous recklessness was easy enough to spot—even though the subject had nothing to do with religious teaching. He spoke not only ignorantly but even deceptively, and with psychotic self-regard, bragging about nothing, to the point where he aspired to ascribe his statements to divine personhood in his own person.

9. When I listen to a Christian brother who doesn't know about natural philosophy and gets something wrong, I look on him and his views with forbearance, as long as he doesn't believe anything inappropriate about you, Master, the creator of everything. I don't consider it a problem for him if by chance he lacks knowledge about the distribution and disposition of an object in your creation. It *is* a problem, however, if he thinks what he says belongs to the essential structure of religious instruction, or if he obstinately and audaciously asserts something about which he knows nothing.

But Love, our mother, puts up even with a weakness of this sort in faith's infancy, until the newcomer rises to maturity and can't be blown around by every pedagogical wind.*

In contrast, as a teacher, an author, a leader and authority to those he won over to his opinions, Mani had the gall to make his followers think they were following not a human being like any other, but your own Holy Spirit: So who wouldn't see fit to curse his monstrous senselessness and send it packing out of our

---

* Ephesians 4:14.

midst, if in any particular instance he'd been found guilty of telling lies?

Nevertheless, at that early point I hadn't determined transparently whether the changes from longer to shorter days and nights and back again throughout the year, and even the alteration between night and day, as well as eclipses of the sun and moon, and whatever else along these lines I'd read about in non-Manichaean books, could be explained according to Mani's formulations as well. So as long as I thought that this might be the case, I remained unsure on which side the truth lay; but because of the holiness so confidently attributed to the man, I placed his authority in charge of my faith.

10. So for the nearly nine years of my life I spent as an "auditor" of the sect (and as a wandering derelict in my intellect), I awaited with unhealthily strained longing for this Faustus person. Other adherents whom I chanced to meet with, and who lacked the wherewithal to parry my queries, kept promising me this man: when he arrived, and conferred himself on conferences with me, he would effortlessly deal with these questions and even any more momentous ones I happened to have, disentangling them and freeing them from the slightest knottiness.

When he did come, I found him a pleasant, well-spoken man, who nattered on more agreeably than the others, but on the very same subjects. Yet what good was the handsomest waiter when I was thirty for costlier vintages? My ears had already had their fill of the kind of things he was saying, and these didn't seem better because they were being said better; and they didn't seem true just because they were skillfully expressed; and his soul didn't seem wise just because his face suggested wisdom and he spoke with proper diction. However, the people who'd promised him to me all that time weren't competent critics, and he seemed to them shrewd and wise simply because his speaking gave them pleasure.

I understood, at any rate, that another class of people regards even the truth with suspicion and refuses to agree to it if it's presented in an elegant and inventive style. Me, however, you had already educated, in your wondrous and mysterious ways (and I believe what *you* taught me, since it is true; and no one but you is a teacher of the truth, whatever the immediate place in which or the immediate source from which it shines forth), and I had thus already learned from you that a statement shouldn't seem true just because it's eloquently stated, nor false, just because the symbols sounding forth from the lips are clumsy; on the other hand, I'd learned that a statement isn't true for the sole reason that its expression is unrefined, or false merely because its style is superb. I'd learned that wisdom and dull-wittedness are like nutritious and worthless food, and either can be served up in either fancy or plain words, as either kind of food can be served in tableware characterized by either urban sophistication or rustic simplicity.

11. Thus, the ardent appetite with which I'd waited for him during that long period was indeed sated to the point of delight by his gestures and his expressiveness in argument, and by the fitting words that came so easily to him, as clothing, so to speak, for his views. I was delighted, really, and along with many people, and even more than many people, I praised him to the skies; but I was irritated that as part of his crowded audience I wasn't

allowed to force myself on his notice and share intimately with him, in a conversational exchange, the questions that were bothering me. But in time I had a chance, and along with some intimates of mine I proceeded to take command of his ears on an occasion when back-and-forth discussion wasn't inappropriate, and I put before him certain matters that concerned me.

I found straight off that this was a person with no knowledge of the liberal arts, except for literary studies, and even there he was only at an ordinary level. He had read some speeches of Cicero, and just a few of Seneca's books, and a certain number of the poets' works, and whatever tomes from his sect were in Latin, and well written; and he also had daily practice in conversation. These things contributed to his speaking ability, which was more pleasing and enticing due to the careful use of his intelligence within its limits, as well as a certain natural charm.

Do I remember it right, Master, my God, you who are the judge of my conscience? My heart's core is before you, and so is my recollection.* It was you who at that time led me along, in the mystery of your providence remote from my sight, and you were already turning my sordid mistakes around and placing them before my face, so that I would see them and hate them.

12. After it became sufficiently clear that he had no knowledge of the liberal-arts fields in which I'd believed he excelled, I began to lose hope that he could open up and extricate the difficulties that concerned me. Though ignorant in these fields, he could still have possessed truth in the form of reverence—had

* Numbers 10:9.

he not been a Manichaean. Their books, you see, are full of interminable tales of the sky and the stars and the sun and the moon.

Already I was starting to think that he couldn't do for me what I really longed for, which was to compare the numerical explanations that I'd read elsewhere, work out all the fine points, and disentangle whether the Manichaean books were correct on these points, or at least whether they gave an equally persuasive account.

Nevertheless, I set before him these things to consider and discuss, and he quite sensibly and self-deprecatingly didn't dare take that load on his shoulders. He knew he didn't know this stuff, and he wasn't ashamed to admit it. He didn't belong to that tribe of loudmouths I'd endured in great numbers, who tried to teach me while telling me not a thing.

That guy genuinely had a heart, and though it wasn't facing you straight on, it showed a decent degree of carefulness about himself. He wasn't altogether inexpert in his lack of expertise, and he didn't want to engage recklessly in a disquisition by which he might well jam himself into a place he couldn't get through at all, or easily back out of, either; and when I found this out, I actually liked him more. The self-restraint of a mind that testifies to its own weakness is more beautiful than the things I was hot to know. And that's in fact how I found him to be, when all the harder and more intricate questions were before him.

13. The interest that I'd had in Manichaean writings was now in a shambles. I had even less hope about the other teachers among

them, since in many things that preoccupied me the man with such a great reputation gave me the impression I've just described.

But I began an intimate association with him on the basis of his interests instead. He was excited about the literature I was teaching to young men as a rhetorician at Carthage at the time. I set about reading with him both things that he'd heard of and had a hankering for, and things I thought were suitable for his intellect.

However, once I got to know this man, any effort or resolve on my part to advance in that sect fell into oblivion—but not so that I cut myself off from them altogether; rather, the upshot was more or less that, not finding anything better, I'd decided to be content for the time being with where (never mind how) I'd rushed in headlong—unless some preferable beacon should happen to beckon me. In this way Faustus, who proved a fatal snare for many, now started to loosen the snare in which I myself was caught, though he didn't intend it or know it.

Your powerful hand, my God, in the hidden manner of your providence, didn't discard my soul. Blood wrung from my mother's heart through her tears was sacrificed to you night and day, and miraculous was what you brought about for me. It was you who brought it about, my God, for by the Master a mortal's steps are directed, and his way shall be the Master's will.* What will take charge of his rescue except your hand, remaking what you made?

* Psalms 37:23.

14. You brought it about for me that I was persuaded to proceed to Rome and by preference to teach there what I'd been teaching at Carthage. And I won't bypass my testimony to you concerning the source of that persuasion, since even in matters such as these the most remote depths of your mystery, along with your most immanent mercy, must be considered and proclaimed.

My reason for going on to Rome wasn't the greater earning power or the greater prestige promised me by the friends who were recommending the move—though that sort of thing, at the time, also had a hold on my mind; rather, the biggest reason, and almost the only one, was that I kept hearing that there the young men pursued their education more peacefully and were kept in check by a better regulated, more restrictive mode of instruction. They weren't allowed to charge, at random and without the slightest restraint, into the classroom of a teacher they didn't actually employ; and they weren't let in at all without his permission.

At Carthage, in contrast, so-called scholars show a disgusting, riotous wildness. They shamelessly shove their way in, and—almost giving the impression that they're insane—they overthrow whatever system each teacher has set up to allow his students to advance. With a stunningly brain-dead attitude, they commit many acts of violence that would be punished by law if common practice in that city didn't function as their influential protector.

This plainly makes their wretchedness greater: they're doing right now what seems to be allowed yet according to your eternal law will never be allowed; and they think they're acting with impunity, whereas through the blindness of their actions they're being punished, and they suffer more severely, with incomparably more pain than they inflict. In this way, I was forced to put up, as a teacher, with behavior I was unwilling to adopt when I was a student.

Hence it seemed preferable to go where every informed person assured me such things didn't happen. But in fact you, my hope and the share given me in the land of the living,* acted in my decision to move to a foreign land, and this was for the saving of my soul. You applied at Carthage the sharp prod needed to separate me from the place, and you set before me at Rome the enticements needed to draw me there; you acted through people who are fond of this life of death—some of them behaving like raving lunatics, others promising advantages of no real importance—and you used their misguided ways and mine to put my feet on the right path.

Those who wrecked my peace of mind were blinded by a revolting mania, and those who urged me toward something else had a taste for earthly things, which was the taste of earth in my mouth,† whereas I, who loathed true misery here, went on the hunt there for happiness that didn't exist anywhere.

15. You knew why I needed to leave Carthage and go to Rome, but you didn't reveal the reason to me or my mother, who beat her breast quite brutally over my departure, and who trailed me all the way to the sea. But I tricked her, as she was hanging onto

* Psalms 142:5.
† Philippians 3:19 (but the English Bible does not give an idea of Augustine's punning).

me coercively, trying to either stop my journey or come along with me on it. I made up a story that I didn't want to walk out on a friend before the wind picked up and he set sail; I lied to my mother, a mother such as I've described.

I got away, and got away with it—because in your mercy you remitted even this sin, and saved me from the seawater, though I was full of abominable filth, and kept me safe until I reached the baptizing water of your grace. When I was washed in that, the rivers would dry up that flowed from my mother's eyes, rivers she addressed to you daily for my sake, irrigating the ground under her face.

Anyway, she refused to return home without me, and I barely persuaded her to stay that night at a spot right near our ship, a shrine commemorating the blessed Cyprian;* and during that night I slunk off and began my journey, which she didn't share. She stayed behind, praying and weeping.

What was she seeking from you, my God, with all those tears, but for you to keep me from setting sail? But your deliberations were profound, and you could hear what the hinge of her longing actually turned on. You didn't attend to what she was seeking then, and your purpose was to make me into what she was always seeking. The wind blew and filled our sails, and from our sight the shore withdrew, the shore on which in the morning she lost her mind with grief and filled your ears with groaning, querulous laments.

But you disregarded all that, since you were snatching me away through my desires in order to put an end to those very desires;

* The Latin church father Cyprian was bishop of Carthage and a prolific and influential author who was martyred in 258, in the reign of Emperor Valerian.

and her longing, which was physical, was taking a beating from the justified whip of sorrows. She had a passion for my presence, which is the way mothers are, but with her it was far more the case than with most, and she didn't know the kind of joy you were going to create for her out of my absence; but she didn't know, and therefore she wept and howled, and these tortures revealed the vestiges of Eve she had within her, as with groans she searched for what she had given birth to with groans.* However, after indicting me for trickery and cruelty, she turned back to praying to you for me and returned to the home she was used to, while I went to Rome.

16. But there I was in Rome, taking the full force of—or rather, taken under the protection of—the lashes of physical sickness, and was heading for the underworld with the load of all the evil I'd done, to you and myself and others, a great many heavy crimes to carry—besides the shackle of original sin, by which all of us die in the person of Adam. You hadn't let me off through Christ,† nor had he dissolved and resolved, by his crucifixion, any of the vendettas‡ I had provoked against you through my sins. How could he settle them by being crucified as a mere apparition,§ which is what I believed about him?

The death of my soul was as real as the death of his body seemed illusory to me, and the death of his body was as much a fact as

---

* Genesis 3:16.
† 1 Corinthians 15:22.
‡ Ephesians 2:14.
§ Docetism (from the Greek *dokesis,* "appearance, seeming, semblance") was a tenet of the Manichaean sect, as well as other heretical groups; the denial that Jesus possessed a material body was rooted in the abased status of matter in Gnostic thinking.

the life of my soul—which didn't believe that fact—was a sham. The rounds of fever became more and more oppressive, and I was passing on, passing away. And what would I have been passing *to*, if I had passed out of this world then, if not to the fire and the torments I deserved for what I'd done, according to the truth inherent in your dispensation?

My mother didn't know this, and yet she prayed for me in my absence; you, for your part, who are present everywhere, heard her where she was. And where I was, you had mercy on me, so that I recovered my body's health, though, given my blasphemous heart, I was still mentally unsound.

Though I had been in such extreme peril, I didn't yearn then for your baptism; in fact I had been better off as a boy, when I demanded the rite in the name of my mother's piety, as I've already narrated and testified. I'd now grown into increasing disgrace, and because I was off my head I laughed at your medical advice, though you didn't let me die in such a state—and die again, as it would have been.

If such a wound had struck my mother's heart, it never would have healed. I haven't given a full enough account of the feeling she had for me; I haven't expressed how much more stress she suffered giving birth to me in the Spirit than she had in the flesh.

17. That's why I don't see how she could have healed, if my death in such a state had impaled the innermost being of her love. Where would that have left those powerful prayers, so constant—never stopping, no less? They would have been nowhere but with you.

But would you really, God of mercies, have scorned the heart, broken and cast to the ground,* of a sober, chaste widow, busy with almsgiving, deferring to and slaving for your holy ones,† not missing a day in making an offering at your altar, going twice a day to your church, morning and evening unceasingly, not for pointless gossip and old women's chatter, but so as to hear you in your own discourses, and to be heard by you in her prayers? How could you have disdained and rebuffed her tears, refusing your help, when with them she wasn't seeking from you gold and silver, or any other benefit liable to totter or wobble, but her son's salvation? How could you, *you*, when her character was your gift?

You absolutely couldn't, Master; and in point of fact you came to her aid and heard her prayers and proceeded to act in the sequence of time you'd ordained beforehand for your actions. Unthinkable that you would trick her in her visions and the answers you gave her—the ones I've already mentioned, and the ones I haven't—which she cherished in her faithful heart, and always in her prayers kept thrusting on you like signed promissory notes. You see fit, since your mercy has no end,‡ actually to become a debtor and issue guarantees to those whose debts you've completely remitted.§

18. Thus you restored me out of that sickness, giving safety to your slave's son¶—at the time, in the meantime, as far as his body was concerned—so that he could become the person you

* Psalms 51:17.
† See the strictures about widows in 1 Timothy 5:9–10.
‡ Psalms 118:1.
§ Colossians 2:14.
¶ Psalms 86:16, 116:16.

could give a better and surer safekeeping. But even then I was connected at Rome with those deceived and deceiving "holy ones," not only those who were "auditors" (a group including the man in whose house I'd been sick and recuperated), but also those they call "the chosen."

I still was convinced that it wasn't we who sinned, but some alien property within us, and it tickled my feelings of superiority to think I was outside the sphere of blame; it tickled me, when I'd done something evil, not to testify truthfully that I had done it, so that you could heal my soul, as I had sinned against you. I was infatuated with excusing myself and accusing some other thing that was with me but wasn't *me.* *

Of course it *was* me, me entirely, but my lack of reverence had factionalized me against myself,† and mine was a form of sin harder to heal in that I didn't consider myself to be the sinner; and it was a damnable wickedness that I preferred for you, the all-powerful God, to be defeated within me, for my own destruction, than for me to be defeated by you for my salvation.

You hadn't yet posted sentries in front of my mouth, or a fortress entryway of restraint around my lips,‡ to keep my heart from swerving into evil words pleading those pleas while sinning with people whose work was iniquity. The upshot was that I was still associating with their "chosen ones"; nevertheless, by this time I no longer had any hope of increasing my proficiency in their phony teaching, and I now relaxed my hold and became

---

* The Manichaean system of ethics was fragmented by Manichaean theology and its view of good and evil as both sharply dualistic and controllable through human knowledge and agency.
† Matthew 12:26, Romans 7:15–16, James 1:8.
‡ Psalms 141:3.

less committed to the stuff I'd decided to settle for—if I couldn't find anything better.

19. Along these lines, the thought occurred to me that the philosophers they call the Academics had been shrewder than all the others, because they'd expressed the view that everything should be doubted, and they'd determined that no part of truth could be grasped by humankind. This seemed to me plainly to be their judgment—it was their judgment as popularly reported, at any rate; I didn't actually understand yet what their point was.*

I was quite open in discouraging my host, whom I mentioned above, from the excessive credulity I judged him to evince concerning the fabricated matter that crams the Manichaean books. However, I had more intimate friendships with the Manichaeans than with people outside this heretical sect. I didn't defend the sect with my original ardor, but still my intimacy with them (Rome conceals large numbers†) made me sluggish in seeking out anything else, particularly because, Master of the sky and the earth, creator of all things visible and invisible,‡ I had no hope of being able to discover the truth in your church.

The Manichaeans put me off that, and I recoiled strongly from believing that you have the shape of human physical existence and limits like those outlining the parts that make up our

---

* Critical to the development of the Academy—the philosophic school descending from Plato—over a certain period was the defense of Platonic metaphysics against the quasi-scientific assertions of Stoics and Epicureans; it was these assertions that Augustine, later in his life, identified the Academics as resisting, and not the possibility per se of perceiving truth.

† The sect was banned by the state.

‡ Colossians 1:16.

body.* When I tried to think about my God, I didn't know how to think about anything but a mass of material embodiments (as it seemed to me that nothing existed that wasn't material). This was the greatest, and almost the sole, reason for my wrongheadedness—a wrongheadedness I couldn't get away from.

20. Accordingly, I used to believe that evil was a sort of substance along those lines: it had a characteristic mass; and it was either vile and repulsive and viscous, referred to among the Manichaeans by the term "earth," or thin and delicate, like the physical form of air, which they picture as a malicious mind crawling through that earth. My religious sense (such as it was) forced me into faith that a good God couldn't have created any property that was evil, so I posited two masses, both infinite, but the evil one more restricted, and the good one on a larger scale, and from this noxious beginning other abominations came to dog me.

When my mind tried to return to the catholic or "universal" faith, I was thrown back, because catholic faith wasn't what I thought it was. If I believed that you, my God (to whom your own mercies testify,† out of my mouth) were infinite in all *other* directions, even though I was obliged to admit that you were finite on the side where the mass of evil blocked you, I had the impression that I was more reverent than if I held the view that in all directions you were limited by the form of a human body. It seemed to me not as bad to believe that you'd created nothing evil (as evil, in my ignorant estimation, was not just some sort of substance, but an actual material substance, given that I didn't

---

* There is superficial scriptural authority for this, especially in Genesis 1:27.
† Psalms 107:8 (but with broad differences from the modern English version).

know how to regard mind except as being a tenuous material object—which, however, permeated physical space) as to believe that the particular property of evil—such as I posited it to be—came from you.

Our actual Savior, your only begotten son, I thought of as a sort of extension, for our salvation, from that lump, that superlucent mass that was you—the result being that I didn't believe anything else about him except what I could invent in the void of my own head. It followed that I didn't think his nature, being such, could be born of the Virgin Mary unless he became intermeshed in the flesh. And how such a thing as I'd represented to myself could become intermeshed without becoming besmirched, I couldn't see. I was thus terrified to believe that he'd been born in the flesh, in case I should be forced to believe that he'd been made filthy from the flesh. Today, those who share in your Holy Spirit will gently and lovingly laugh at me, if they read these testimonies—but in any event, that's the way I was.

21. In addition, I didn't think that there was any defense against the Manichaeans' censures of your scriptures, but from time to time I grew keen to meet with someone among them who was an expert on these books, to debate given passages and explore what he thought about them.

The dialogues of a certain Elpidius, who in person addressed and debated these same Manichaeans, had begun to intrigue me even when I was still in Carthage, as he'd made some points about the scriptures that couldn't easily be refuted. Their response seemed feeble to me, and they'd in fact resisted publishing it but instead offered it to us on the quiet. In this document, they claimed that the writings of the New Testament had been tampered with by unnamed persons who wanted to foist Jewish law on the Christian faith—yet the Manichaeans didn't produce any uncorrupted copies as evidence.

But the worst during this period was that while I meditated about materiality, those great bulks managed to crush me, and I was trapped and choking; beneath them, I gasped for the clear, unadulterated air of your truth but couldn't breathe it.

22. Anyway, I took up diligently the business for which I'd come, which was to teach the art of rhetoric at Rome. The first thing I did was to assemble at home some persons with whom I started to establish a reputation, and who started to spread it. And wouldn't you know: I learned that certain abuses take place at Rome that I hadn't been a victim of in Africa.

It was true that those rampages by out-of-control young men, which I mentioned above, didn't happen in Rome—that was quite clear to me. But I was told, "Instead, a lot of the youngsters put their heads together and, to avoid paying the teacher their tuition, they enroll with another teacher; they turn tail on their word, and for them money's all they value, while fairness goes dirt cheap."

My heart hated the boys though not with a mature hatred.* It may well be that I hated them more for what I was going to suffer at their hands than because they treated anyone else wrongly. Nevertheless, there's no question that such people behave shamefully, and they cheat on you, God,† in their passion for

---

* Psalms 139:22.
† Psalms 73:27; again, the Latin scripture has sexual wording that modern versions lack.

playthings of the present age, which flutter away quite fast, and for money, though it's smeared with muck that dirties the grasping hand.* They throw their arms around a world that's making a getaway, and they reject you, though you remain and call them home and forgive the prostitute human soul when it returns to you.

Even now, I hate crooked, twisted people like that, although I can feel affection for them as people to be corrected, to the end that they'll value the instruction that enlightens them more than they value money; and more than money, you, God, who are the truth, and an extravagant supply of goods that can't be taken away, and peace free from any vice. But back then I was unwilling to endure those wicked people because of myself, as opposed to wanting them to become good because of you.

23. A message arrived from Milan for the city prefect at Rome, requesting him to provide a head rhetoric teacher for that community, and stipulating transport there via the Imperial courier system as an added benefit. I secured the influence of those same Manichaeans (who were drunk on their own emptyheadedness, and whom I was to get rid of by leaving, though neither party knew this at the time), so that once I passed the test set for me, a sample speech, Symmachus, who was then the prefect at Rome, sent me along.

I came to Milan, where the bishop was Ambrose, known throughout the world for his rare excellence, and a reverent worshipper of yours. At this period, his sermons tirelessly

---

* 1 Peter 5:2.

served up your toothsome grain and merry oil* and soberly ine-
briating wine† to your people. I was brought to him by you,
though I was oblivious of it, so that through him I could be
brought knowingly to you. That man of God took me up as a
father takes a newborn baby in his arms, and in the best tradition of bishops, he prized me as a foreign sojourner.

I fell in love with him, as it were, not at first as a teacher of the
truth—as I had no hope for that whatsoever in your church—
but simply as a person who was kind to me. I began to listen to
him eagerly as he preached in public, though I didn't have the
focus I should have had and was in effect scouting out his eloquence to see whether it matched its reputation, or whether the
praise of it I'd heard proclaimed fell short of or flattered its actual fluency. I hung on his words with great concentration, but I
had no interest in the subject matter; in this regard I was a
standoffish scoffer. I was delighted with his appealing discourse,
more learned than that of Faustus, but less cheering and charm-
ing as far as style is concerned. But there was no comparing the
topics themselves. Faustus rambled off among the Manichaean
con games, whereas Ambrose taught salvation in a most salutary
manner. But salvation is far off from sinners,‡ such as I was then
in my approach; and yet I drew near, little by little and uncon-
sciously.

24. Though I wasn't exactly in a flurry to be informed by him as
he held forth—but only to hear *how* he held forth, as this fatuous preoccupation was all that remained for me now that I de-

---

* These phrases echo repeated terms in the Vulgate's Latin, which are hard to pin down in
English but do indicate lavish abundance.
† A phrase quoted from one of Ambrose's own hymns.
‡ Psalms 119:155.

spaired of the road to you being open to a human being—there
entered my mind, together with the words I prized, the actual
subject matter that I was disregarding, as I wasn't able to separate the two. While I was opening my heart to take in how ex-
pressively he spoke, there came in at the same time, merely step
by step, a sense of how truly he spoke.

First of all, it began to seem to me that the things he said actually admitted of a defense, and I now reckoned that a person
could claim universal faith without embarrassment, though
previously I'd thought no discourse could be launched against
the Manichaeans' assaults. I felt this way most strongly after I'd
heard a couple, in fact a number of obscurities in the Old Testament cleared up, riddling matters that, when I took them literally, used to take my life.*

Once I'd heard quite a few passages in those books expounded
in the Holy Spirit, I started to find fault with my despair, or at
any rate the despair that went with my belief that there was
absolutely no possibility of opposing those who cursed and ridiculed the law and the prophets. However, I didn't yet feel I
should continue down the universal or catholic road, merely
because this faith did have its learned champions, who could
repel, fluently and rather credibly, what was thrown against it;
and I didn't think I should pass judgment against what I was
professing at the time, just because the two sides were a match
in defending themselves against each other. Thus the universal
way didn't seem to me to be defeated, but it hadn't yet emerged
victorious, either.

---

* 2 Corinthians 3:6 ("for the letter kills, but the Spirit gives life").

25. Then at last I determinedly turned my mind to finding some kind of clear evidence that would convict the Manichaeans of fraud. If I could just figure out what the substance was of which the Spirit consists, then instantly all of their artifices would come to pieces and could be thrown out of my mind; but I *couldn't* figure it out. Nonetheless, concerning the material being of this world, and every property that physical perception can contact, as I more and more carefully contemplated and compared explanations, I came to judge that the opinions of most philosophers were much more plausible.

Thus, in the tradition of the Academics (or what passes for it*), I held all the possibilities in doubt and bobbed around among them all, but at least I decided to leave the Manichaeans; I didn't think, even during what was a period of doubt for me, that I should stay in a sect I already felt was inferior to the teachings of many philosophers. Yet I absolutely refused to entrust the treatment of my soul's malady to the philosophers, since the health-giving name of Christ was missing from their works. So I decided that for the time being I would continue as a catechumen† in the universal church, an institution my parents had commended to me, until some sort of reliable illumination should shine forth to direct my further course.

---

* See above, book 4, chapter 19, and the note.
† A person undergoing instruction prior to baptism.

Book 6

1. You, my hope from the time of my youth,* where were you for me, and to what place had you drawn away?† Hadn't you made me, and made me different from the four-footed beasts and wiser than the flying ones?‡ But I walked through darkness and on a slippery path, and I looked for you outside myself and couldn't find the God of my heart. I had come down to the sea's depths,§ and I lost any trust in, any hope for detecting the truth.

And now my mother had come, strong in her faith, following me on land and sea, serene in you through all her dangers. In

---

* Psalms 71:5.
† Psalms 10:1.
‡ Job 35:11.
§ Psalms 68:22.

the maritime perils she actually reassured the sailors, by whom novice voyagers on the great abyss are usually reassured when they're in a panic. She gave her word for a safe arrival, because you'd given yours to her in the form of a vision.

She found me, in fact, in a gravely dangerous despair of tracking down the truth. But when I informed her that I at least wasn't a Manichaean any more (but wasn't a universal Christian, either), she didn't jump for joy, as if she'd heard anything unexpected. She was already serene in one respect about my pathetic state: that though she was bewailing me, before you, as dead, you must bring me back to life.

She presented me to you, in her mind, as lying on a bier, so that you would say to this widow's son, "Young man, I command you, rise!" And he would come back to life and start to speak, and you would hand him over to his mother.*

Therefore, no stormy, boisterous joy shook her heart when she heard that the purpose of her daily breast-beating in your presence had already been achieved to such a large extent that, though I hadn't yet attached myself to the truth, I was snatched away from falsehood. On the contrary, because she was positive that you who'd promised the whole would give what remained, she responded, in profound tranquillity and with a heart replete with faith, that she trusted, through Christ, in seeing me made faithfully catholic or universal before she took leave of this life. That's in fact what she said to me.

For you, however, my flowing spring of mercies, there were more or less uninterrupted tears and prayers to get you to send

* Luke 7:12–15.

your succor more swiftly* and light up my darkness.† More eagerly now, she would run to the church and listen rapturously to Ambrose, whose words were a fountain leaping up into eternal life.‡

She was attached to that man as if he were an angel of God, because she'd found out that it was he who'd brought me to this present back-and-forth vacillation—and she took it completely for granted that this was to be my passage from sickness to health—though in the course of it would come a more dire peril, like the spike in fever that doctors call the crisis.

2. She once brought to the shrines of the holy ones—as she'd done in Africa many times—porridge and bread and unmixed wine and was stopped by the doorkeeper. When she found out that the bishop had forbidden these offerings, she so dutifully and obediently embraced the change that I myself marveled at how easily she was turned into a prosecutor of her own habit rather than a protester against the prohibition.

It hadn't been that tipsiness besieged her spirit, nor that love of wine goaded her into hatred of the truth, as is the case with many, male and female alike, who heave at the sound of sober hymn-singing the way soused people do when presented with diluted wine. She'd only been used to bringing a basket full of festival foods to nibble herself and then generously share; and she set out only one small cup of wine, watered down to suit her quite sober taste, from which she would sip as an act of respect.

---

* Psalms 70:1.
† Psalms 18:28.
‡ John 4:14.

If there were many shrines of the dead she meant to honor in this way, she would take around that same single cup and set it down everywhere, and pretty soon the stuff, watery to begin with, would become the quintessence of lukewarm as well while she shared it out by tiny swallows among those who were there with her; this was because she was aiming for reverence, not pleasure, in these sanctuaries.

Therefore, when she heard that Ambrose, that very popular preacher and exponent of piety, was the source of the rule against such rituals, even when carried out in a sober manner—the point being not to give drunkards an occasion for guzzling, and also that these virtual ancestor offerings looked a great deal like pagan superstition—she was most happy to refrain, and instead of a basket filled with the earth's produce, she learned to bring to the martyrs' shrines a mind full of even purer prayers. Hence she gave whatever she could afford to the poor, and this act celebrated in that place the sharing of the Master's body, in imitation of whose suffering the martyrs were immolated and won their victory garlands.

Nevertheless, it seems to me, my Master and God (and this is my heart's witness, in your sight, about the matter), that perhaps my mother wouldn't have yielded so easily in pruning away this habit if the prohibition had come from someone she had less affection for than Ambrose. It was the prospect of my salvation that most endeared him to her, and he in turn was fond of her because of her habitual conduct, which was God-fearing to a very high degree. With a spirit burning for good works, she resorted unceasingly to the church—so much so that when he saw me, he would often impetuously praise her, felicitating me for having a mother like that. He didn't know that she had a son like me, who was uncommitted about all these matters and hugely uncertain whether the way leading to life could ever be located.

3. I hadn't started to groan in my prayers for you to come to my aid; but my mind was keen on inquiry and impatient for debate. And Ambrose was one person I considered happy by the standards of this world, because so many influential people showed him respect. His celibacy was the only thing about him that seemed a hardship.

I had no experience of a life like his and couldn't guess at what hopes he cherished, what struggles he had against the temptations his preeminence brought, and what consolation he enjoyed when things went against him; I didn't know his secret mouth, which was in his heart, or how savory the joys were that he ruminated in the form of your bread.

He in his turn didn't know my turmoil or the pit into which I was in danger of toppling. I couldn't ask him the questions I wished to, in the circumstances I wished for asking them, as I was blocked off from getting his ear, or getting a word from him, by the swarms of people bringing him their business, people to whose weaknesses he was a slave.

When he wasn't with them—and this would be only for some exceedingly short time—he was refreshing either his body with the essential small means of keeping it alive, or his mind with reading. When he read, his eyes moved over the pages, and his understanding ferreted out the sense, but his voice, his tongue, was inactive.*

---

* This passage is an important indication that silent reading was an anomaly in the ancient world.

Often when we were with him (as he didn't prevent anyone from coming in—nor was it his habit to have visitors announced), we saw him reading this way, and never any other way. We would sit in prolonged silence (because who was going to dare bother someone concentrating that hard?) and then go away. We figured that in the short time he could get for reinvigorating his mind, when he had a little leisure from the din of other people's problems, he didn't want to be distracted and was perhaps avoiding having someone listening to him with eager intensity, which would mean that if the book he was reading made any sort of puzzling assertion, he would have to explain it as well as read, or deal with some even harder questions: and if he spent time on these tasks, he would get through fewer books than he wanted to. But saving his voice, which could easily get hoarse from all the punishment it took, was perhaps a sounder reason for reading silently. Whatever his intention was in doing it, the gentleman certainly had a good intention.

4. But in any event, no opportunity was given me to interrogate, as I longed to, the very holy oracular shrine that was his inner self—or not unless I had something to say that took only a short time for him to hear. The swelling billows I was experiencing, however, powerfully demanded that he be fully at leisure when they poured out over him, but they never found him in such a state.

I did hear him in public every Sunday, treating the scriptures' words of truth in just the right terms,* and more and more it was established in my eyes that all the twisty, wily knots of slander that those Manichaean deceivers of ours had devised against

* 2 Timothy 2:15.

the holy books could be undone. I ascertained that "man being made in your image"* wasn't understood by your sons in the Spirit—to whom you gave a second birth, through the free gift of grace from their mother the universal church—in such a way that they believe or conceive that you're limited by the shape of a human body; and though I couldn't form any idea, not even a flimsy and still baffling one,† about the qualities of "spiritual substance,"‡ yet I was joyful in blushing with shame that for so many years I'd been yapping not at the universal church but at fabricated cogitations about mere materiality.

I'd been more reckless and irreverent in that I simply expressed my thinking as an indictment, when I ought to have imbibed opinion through inquiry. But you, who are the highest and the most near, the most remote but the most present, having no separate parts to you, some bigger and some smaller, but instead existing everywhere in your wholeness and yet in no particular place: you're certainly not that petty physical body I'd been positing; *yet* you made humankind in your image and—look!— there he is, from head to foot existing in space.

5. So since, back then, I didn't know how this "image" of you could exist, I should have rapped on the door§ and presented my difficulty, asking how this claim might be believed, instead of just jumping in and making a scoffing objection, as if the prevailing belief were in fact what I presumed it was.

---

* Genesis 1:27.
† 1 Corinthians 13:12. Ancient mirrors were liable to distort images.
‡ I have construed this clause not parenthetically, as O'Donnell's Latin text shows it, but as the start of a new line of thought; this appears to be the more traditional reading.
§ Matthew 7:7.

As a result now, in proportion to the even sharper anxiety chewing at my deepest feelings concerning what I could hang onto as certain, I was all the more ashamed that for so long I'd been made a fool of, misled by a mere promise of certainty, and that in the childish sassiness of my wrongheadedness I'd blathered about so many things I couldn't know, as if they were facts.

It became brilliantly clear to me afterward that these Manichaean assertions were wrong. But at this earlier period it was already certain that they were dubious, and that I'd nevertheless taken them as factual when denouncing your universal church in my obtuse disputes. Though now I hadn't yet verified that the church was teaching the truth, it was plainly not teaching what I'd so obnoxiously accused it of teaching.

I was deeply embarrassed and began an about-face,* and I rejoiced, my God, that the one church, the body of your only son,† on whose authority the name of Christ was put on me as a baby, didn't smack of such babyish absurdity and didn't, in her own wholesome teachings, cram you into a physical space that, high and broad as it might be, nevertheless had on all sides the boundaries of a human body's shape.

6. I rejoiced also because the ancient writings of the law and the prophets were no longer presented to me for reading with the kind of gaze that had made them look ridiculous before, when I'd accused your holy followers of holding opinions that in fact they didn't hold. I was happy in hearing Ambrose say often in

* Psalms 6:10.
† Colossians 1:18, 24.

his public sermons, as if he were recommending this very carefully as a basic principle, "The letter kills, but the Spirit gives life."*

He was removing the ritual covering, as it were, from the deeper meaning, to disclose the spiritual sense of things that, when taken literally, seemed to teach what was untenable. He didn't say anything I found troublesome, but he did say things I hadn't yet learned how to distinguish as true or false. I was, you see, holding my heart back from any admission of the truth, as I feared the sheer drop into it; but hanging (myself) in the air above it was more like killing myself.

I wanted to be as certain about the things I *couldn't* see as I was certain that seven plus three makes ten. I wasn't such a lunatic as to think that not even this could be grasped, but I really wanted other things to be the way this was, whether they were material things that weren't face-to-face, as it were, with my physical senses; or spiritual things I didn't have the means to contemplate, unless I treated them as material.

I could have been healed by believing, so that my mind's eyesight, to some degree purged of its infections, might somehow have been directed at your truth, which remains the same forever and falls short in nothing. But what usually happens happened with me: when someone's suffered at the hands of a bad doctor, he's afraid to trust his care even to a good one, and this was the case with my soul's health: it certainly couldn't be healed without belief, but for fear of believing something false, it refused to be treated, withstanding your hands†—yours,

* 2 Corinthians 3:6.
† Daniel 4:35.

though you've compounded the medicines of faith and sprinkled them over the world's ailments and endowed them with so much power.

7. For this reason as well, however, I began to favor universal teaching. I saw more restraint, and the least room for dishonesty, in the command to believe what couldn't be proved (whether just not to some people, or not at all) than in acting the way the Manichaeans did: they gave reckless promises of knowledge that made a joke of their recruits' trustfulness, and then commanded them to accept on faith—because they couldn't be proved!—all those totally outrageous, hypermythic assertions.

Next, Master, you gradually caressed and calmed my heart with a very tender, very compassionate touch: I considered that there were things beyond counting that I believed without seeing them, or having been there when they were happening. Examples were innumerable in world history, and concerned lands and cities I'd never seen; and there were innumerable things that we had to take on faith from our friends, and from doctors, and from other people of all kinds, or we couldn't deal with anything in this life. Finally, I considered how fixed and unshakable my faith was about which parents I'd come from, a fact it was impossible for me to know except by believing it after hearing about it.

You persuaded me that the blame shouldn't be on the people who believe in your books—which you've set down, with such great authority, as a foundation in nearly all nations—but on those who don't; and that none of these should be given a hearing if they happened to say to me, "How do you know that the

Spirit of the one true God, who speaks the truth without exception, provided those books to the human race?"

This, then, was the very thing I most needed to believe, because no belligerent, vexatious interrogations, found anywhere in all the works of the feuding philosophers I'd read, had in the end been able to wrench away from me my belief that you were whatever you were—not that I knew what that was—or that the governance of human affairs belonged to you.

8. Sometimes my belief in this was sturdier, and sometimes more scrawny; but I nonetheless always believed that you existed and took care of us, even if I didn't know, for instance, what opinion I should hold about your substance, or what road led to you, or back to you. Thus, as we were too feeble to find the truth by some transparent rationale of our own, and because of this feebleness needed the authority of sacred literature, I'd already started to believe that there was no way you could have set out to grant such preeminent authority to this writing throughout the world unless you'd wanted belief in you and the search for you to come about through this very means.

Now that I'd heard plausible explanations for many passages, I proceeded to attribute to the depth of the mysteries there the apparent lack of sense that used to put me off this literature. Its authority appeared to me more worthy of reverence and more deserving of an inviolable trust in that it was within everybody's reach for reading, but it preserved its impressive mystery within hidden significance. It offered itself to everybody with extremely simple words in the most colloquial style, but also required serious minds to exert themselves with concentration.

The result was that it could take everyone in its arms, like true popular writing, and let a few through to you through narrow apertures*—many more, though, than it could if it didn't loom on such a high peak of authority and at the same time draw whole masses of people into the lap of its pure-hearted humility.

I thought all this through, and you were with me; I sighed, and you heard me; the waves tossed me, and you steered; I walked on the worldly wide road,† and you didn't abandon me.

9. I had an openmouthed fixation on professional distinctions, moneymaking, and marriage, and you were laughing at me the whole time. I experienced very bitter difficulties in the pursuit of what I desired—and you were more provident the less you let what wasn't you grow sweet to me. Look at my heart, Master, since you wanted me to remember this and render it as testimony to you.

Let my soul now stick to you, since you stripped from her the glue of death's bird-trap. How terrible her anguish was! And you poked at her wound where it was most sore, so that she would leave everything else and turn to you, who are above everything, you without whom everything would be nothing; so that she would turn to you and be healed.‡

How miserable that made me! And how you drove me to feel my misery on the actual day when I was preparing to deliver an encomium to the emperor, to include any number of lies, so

---

* Matthew 7:13–14.
† Ibid.
‡ Matthew 13:15, quoting Isaiah 6:10.

that in the act of lying I could win the approval of those well aware of what I was doing. My heart was issuing furnace-blasts anxiety over this assignment, and seething with the fever of the obsessive thoughts disintegrating me from within, as I passed down a street in Milan and noticed a destitute beggar; it wasn't late in the day, but he'd had quite a few, it looked to me, and he was humorous and enjoying himself.

To the friends who were with me, I moaned in speaking of the many sufferings of our own insanity. In all our kinds of effort, like the effort straining me so badly now—when my longings sharply prodded me to drag along a load of my own unhappiness that was heaped up higher with the exhaustion of dragging it—we didn't want anything but to reach a state of carefree enjoyment; that beggar had beaten us to it, and perhaps we were never going to arrive. Toward what he'd achieved already—which was evidently the enjoyment of a strictly time-bound happiness—with just a tiny handful of small change he'd panhandled, I was taking a woefully winding course, advancing myself by paths that circled back on themselves. He didn't have true joy, but I with all my bids for advancement was in quest of something much less real. He was enjoying himself, no doubt about it, while I was in distress; he was carefree, while I was shaking in my shoes.

And if anyone had asked me whether I preferred dancing for joy or feeling terrified, I would have answered, "Dancing for joy." If, on the other hand, someone had asked me whether I preferred to be a person like him, or a person such as I was then, I would have chosen to be myself, with all the worries and fears that overwhelmed me—but was that only because of my pertinacity? My answer couldn't have been based on veracity, could it? I shouldn't, after all, have preferred myself to him because I had a better education, as that wasn't a source of joy to me. I was seeking to use my education to please other people—not to teach them, but just to please them. Because of this, you took the rod *you* use for instruction and battered my bones to pieces.*

10. So I want to warn away from my soul the people who tell it, "It makes a difference where someone gets his joy. That beggar found his in tipsiness, whereas you were longing for the joy of glory."

In what glory could I have found joy, Master, if not in the glory that's in you?† Just as the beggar's joy wasn't real joy, so the glory I was after wasn't real—but it did more to turn my mind upside down. On that very night, he was going to sleep off his drunkenness. Just think how many nights and days I'd slept and gotten up, and was going to go on sleeping and getting up, with mine.

It *does* make a difference where someone gets his joy, I know, and the joy of faithful hope is incomparably far from that fatuous ambition of mine. But even at the time that beggar was far ahead of me—hardly surprising, as he was happier, and not only in that he was flooded with cheerfulness, whereas I had anxieties tearing at my insides: through a few polite words of well-wishing, he'd obtained his wine, while with my lying I was still seeking swollen-headed self-delusion.

At this period I said a lot in accordance with this sentiment to those close to me, and I often noticed that it was the same for them as for me. I found my condition awful, and in my pain over

* Psalms 2:9, 53:5.
† 1 Corinthians 1:31. Latin vocabulary conflates the ideas of glory and boasting.

it, I doubled that awfulness. If some good fortune smiled on me, I had no interest in laying hold of it, because practically before I could take it in my hands, it would fly away.

11. Those of us who were living together as friends used to unite in lamenting over these things, and I discussed them most often and most intimately with Alypius and Nebridius. Alypius came from the same town as I did, and his parents were highly placed among its citizens. He was younger than I was, and in fact he had studied under me when I first started to teach in our town, and then later in Carthage. He was very attached to me, because he thought I was an upstanding person and had a good education. For my part, I was attached to him because of his natural tendency to do right, which was quite striking in a boy so young.

However, the vortex that was the Carthaginian scene, bubbling with time-wasting public entertainments, had sucked him into the mania for the games put on in the circus. At the period when he was dismally wrapped up in those, I was a teacher of rhetoric using a public lecture hall; but he wasn't yet in my class because of a quarrel that had arisen between me and his father.

But it had come to my attention that he had a self-destructive infatuation with the games, and I was deeply distressed, because it seemed to me that he was going to waste his considerable potential, or had already wasted it. But I had no chance to advise him or dissuade him, or any means of restraining him, either through friendship's kindness or the authority of my position as a teacher. I thought he had the same feelings about me as his father did, but in fact he wasn't like that; so he discounted his father's wishes as to his schooling and began to come into my classroom, greet me, listen to part of a lecture, and then leave.

12. But by that time I'd lost track of my resolution to have a talk with him and try to prevent a blind plunge into the distraction of pointless games from being the death of his outstanding talent. But *you*, Master, who stand at the helm of everything you've created, hadn't forgotten that he was destined to be the official in charge of your rite among your sons.* So that his change of course for the better would be, without any doubt, attributed to you, it was through my unconscious intervention that you engineered it, though you did in fact engineer it through me.

One day when I was sitting in my classroom as usual, with my students in front of me, he came in, greeted me, sat down, and turned his attention to what was going on. It happened that, while lecturing on the text I had in my hands, it occurred to me that an analogy to the games would be an apt one to apply, merely as a more appealing and clearer way to work my point in: I should sardonically deride people held captive to a crazed obsession with this pastime.

You know, our God, that at the time I had no notion of curing Alypius of this disease. But he seized on my words and assumed that he was the sole target. What another student would have taken as a reason for flaring up in anger at me, this fine young man took as a reason to flare up at himself and conceive a warmer affection for me.

---

* The Eucharist, or celebration of the Lord's Supper; Alypius would be bishop of Thagaste.

You yourself said long ago, and wove it into your writings: "Find fault with a wise man, and he'll love you."* I hadn't found fault with him, but you use everyone, those who know it and those who don't, in an orderly plan that's within *your* knowledge, and that plan is just. From my heart and my tongue you crafted burning coals with which to cauterize and heal that promising mind when it was being eaten away by this infection.

Anyone who doesn't contemplate your merits can just be quiet; but from *my* inmost being they testify to you. The fact is that after hearing what I said, he tore himself out of that ditch, deep as it was, in which he was willingly sinking and losing his sight with bizarre enjoyment. With a valiant resolve, he shook his mind clean, all the muck of the games spattered off him, and he never went to the circus again.

Next, he won out against his father's resistance and made me his regular teacher; his father gave up and gave in. But when Alypius began to attend my lectures again, he got caught up in the Manichaeans' superstition along with me, as he was in love with their show of moral purity—he thought it was real, sincere purity. On the contrary, it was depraved and led others astray, angling for precious souls† who didn't yet know how to reach the lofty place of virtue and who were easy to trick with the surface appearance of a "virtue" that was a counterfeit and a sham.

13. But at any rate Alypius didn't leave the worldly pathway whose praises his parents sang to him hypnotically, and he went to Rome before I did, to study law. There, to an incredible ex-

* Proverbs 9:8.
† Proverbs 6:25–26.

tent, he was carried off by an incredible fascination with gladiatorial shows. Though he was first repelled by them and reviled
them, certain friends and fellow students of his happened to run
into him on their way back from lunch during the days set aside
for these sadistic and murderous sports, and took him to the
amphitheater. He violently resisted and fought back, but they
dragged him with the kind of force a man's intimates might use.

He said, "Even if you haul my body to that place and sit me
down there, you can't aim my mind and my eyes at the show,
can you? Though I'm there, I *won't* be there, and that's how I'll
be the victor over what's going on, and over you, too." When
they heard this, they took him along just the same, now maybe
with the added motivation of testing whether he could achieve
what he'd said he would.

They arrived and took their places in the seats available, and
everything was seething with the most barbaric kinds of entertainment. He closed the doors of his eyes and forbade his mind
to go outside into such terrible wickedness. If only he'd plugged
his ears! One of the combatants fell, and a booming shout from
the whole crowd struck him forcefully. Curiosity overcame him,
and on the pretext that he was ready to condemn and overcome
whatever he saw, he opened his eyes.

He was run through with a wound in his soul more lethal than
the physical wounding he'd longed to look at, and he fell more
pitifully than the one whose fall the shouting was about. The
yells came in through his ears and unlocked his eyes, so there
was access for assaulting and bringing down a mind that was
daring but not yet strong, and was weaker in that it relied on
itself when it should have relied on you. When he saw the blood,

he guzzled the cruelty at the same time. He didn't turn away but instead riveted his gaze there; he gulped down the demons of rage, though he didn't know it. He was delighted at the criminal contest and got drunk on the gory diversion. He was no longer the person he'd been when he came, but now actually part of the mob he'd come to, and he was a true confederate of those who'd brought him along.

No need for a long narrative! He watched, shouted, got fired up, took away with him an insanity that prodded him sharply to come back—not only in the company of those who'd dragged him there, but even in advance of them, and even dragging others with him. With your overwhelmingly powerful, overwhelmingly merciful hand you snatched him out of there, and taught him to have faith not in himself but in you*—but that was much later.

14. Already, however, he stored this episode in his memory, as medicine to be taken a future date. But there was something else worth remembering that happened to him in his student days, while he was still attending my lectures at Carthage.

Once at midday he was in the town square thinking out a speech he was going to recite—an ordinary exercise for students of rhetoric—and you let him be arrested by security guards as a thief. I don't think you, our God, would have allowed it for any other reason than that, as he was to be such a powerful man, you wanted him to start early with a lesson in the caution needed in judicial investigations, to keep one person from being found guilty on the evidence of another because of an official's thoughtless credulity.

* Proverbs 3:5, Isaiah 57:12.

He was walking back and forth with a pen and notebook in front of the magistrates' platform in the law courts, when here comes a young man, a student from the school of rhetoric and the real thief, carrying an ax under his clothes. This student approached the lead bars above a block of silversmiths' workshops without Alypius noticing, and started to hack through the lead. When they heard the sound of the ax, the silversmiths who were underneath started to mutter under their breath, and they sent out people to apprehend whomever they might find. Hearing the voices of his pursuers, the thief dropped his tool and made off in fear of being caught with it.

Alypius, who hadn't seen him come into the forum, did notice him leaving. Watching him exit with speed, he wanted to know why; he went up to the spot where the young man had been, found the ax, and was standing there looking it over, puzzled, when those the silversmiths had sent there happened on him alone, hefting in his hand the very weapon whose sound had served to rouse and summon them thither. They seized him and dragged him away, and to the denizens of the forum who flocked around them they bragged that they'd caught a thief red-handed. He was led off from there to be turned over to the judicial authorities.[*]

15. But this was the end point of Alypius's lesson. Immediately, Master, you came to aid the innocent man, for whom you were the sole witness. When he was being led away, either to prison

---

[*] This all probably took place at the time of the general afternoon nap, which explains why the law court is idle, Alypius is composing (until this point) undisturbed, and the silversmiths and their henchmen (the security guards mentioned near the start of the chapter?) are roused only by the loud noise of the ax.

or to physical punishment, the crowd met on their way a master builder who was the chief supervisor of public edifices.

They were delighted to run into him, of all people, as they'd habitually incurred his suspicion of their filching things that went missing in the public square: he was now finally to know who was responsible! However, the master builder had often, when making regular calls to pay his respects, seen Alypius in the house of a certain senator. He now recognized him instantly, took him by the arm, and drew him aside from the crowd. He asked how such a disaster had come about, and heard what had happened. He then ordered the whole crowd, which was making a commotion and rumbling with threats, to come with him, and they all went to the house of the young man who'd committed the act.

In front of the gate was a slave boy, so young that he would easily give all the evidence needed without any fear of consequences for his master. He'd been his master's attendant in the town square; Alypius recognized him and relayed the fact to the master builder. This man then showed the boy the ax and asked whose it was. He instantly said, "Ours." Then, when he was questioned, he revealed the rest.

The case was redirected against that household, and the mob that had already started to exult over Alypius's fall was thoroughly embarrassed. And the future steward of your Word and a weigher up of many cases in your church emerged with valuable new experience and direction.

16. This was the man I now found at Rome, and he became attached to me with a very strong bond. He moved to Milan with

me, both to stay loyally with me and to make some use of his legal training, though he had acquired this more from his parents' wish than his own.

Already, he'd served three times as an assessor,* with a conscientiousness that had been amazing to others, whereas he was more amazed at people who placed gold ahead of their integrity. His own character was in fact put to the test not only by the lure of greed but also by the sharp goad of fear.

At Rome, he was an assessor to the Imperial official in charge of public finances for Italy. At that period, there was a certain extremely influential senator who'd put many people under heavy obligation with his favors, and cowed many with the threat of retaliation. He wanted permission to do something that wasn't allowed under the law, but that he was accustomed to doing because of his power. Alypius stood up to him. A bribe was promised; he laughed at it bravely. Threats were made; he stamped them into the dirt, while everyone marveled over this extraordinary soul, that didn't want such a powerful man as a friend or fear him as an enemy, though he was renowned far and wide for his innumerable means of helping and hurting.

The judge for whom Alypius was an adviser didn't himself want to give the senator the exemption he sought, but he still didn't refuse openly; rather, he foisted the matter onto Alypius, who he claimed wouldn't let him settle things the way he himself wished; whereas in reality if he'd done so, Alypius would have resigned.

There was, however, one thing that came close to enticing Alypius into doing something wrong, but only because of his pas-

* In the late Imperial legal system, a sort of apprentice judge.

sion for literature: the chance to order copies of books at the reduced prices available to the Imperial administration. Giving thought to equity, he weighed up the matter and changed his mind for the better, judging that the sense of fairness that held him back was more serviceable to him than the power that allowed him to go ahead.

This is a small thing, but the person faithful in a small thing will be faithful in a big thing, too, and what issued from the mouth of your truth will in no way prove meaningless: "If you haven't been faithful in the handling of wrongly acquired riches, who'll give you true riches? If you haven't been faithful in the handling of others' riches, who'll give you your own?"*

This is what Alypius was like at the time, when he was tightly attached to me; and along with me he wobbled with uncertainty in planning what way of life we would commit ourselves to.

17. Nebridius, for his part, had left his family's district near Carthage—and had left Carthage, where he had spent more time. He'd left behind his father's splendid rural property, and his home, and his mother, who wasn't about to follow him. He, too, had come to Milan for no reason except to live with me in the blazing pursuit of truth and wisdom. He sighed by my side and by my side was tossed on waves of uncertainty; he had a burning determination to get the facts on what a happy life was, and he rooted relentlessly through the most difficult issues.

So here were three hungry beaks, gasping to each other in their helpless need and waiting for you to give them their food at the

---

* Luke 16:10–12.

right time.* In all the bitterness that—through your mercy—
followed our worldly pursuits, we tried to see what point there
could be in our enduring all this, but darkness got in the way.
We used to turn away, groaning, and ask, "How long will this go
on?" We said it constantly, but though we said it, we didn't give
up what we were enduring, because nothing definite had shone
out of that darkness for us to seize on, if we abandoned the rest.

18. But I myself was the most perplexed, feeling quite overwhelmed and recalling how long it had been since I was eighteen years old† and started to seethe with enthusiasm for
wisdom; I'd been determined that once I found it, I would give
up all my trifling hopes based on my trivial desires, and all my
illusory insanities. But here I was, making my way through
my twenty-ninth year,‡ and I was stuck in the same mud, in my
greed for enjoying things of the moment—which ran away from
me, rending me to pieces as they went.

I said, "Tomorrow I'll find it. It's going to appear right in front
of me, plain as day, and I'll take it in my hands ... Faustus will
come, he'll be right here and explain it all ... Oh, you eminent
Academic philosophers! Nothing definite can be grasped about
how to lead our lives ... No, wait, let's make a careful search and
not give up hope.

"And here's something: the passages in the church's books that
seemed nonsensical don't seem so any more: they can be construed differently, and make solid sense. Let me stand with

steady feet on the stairstep where my parents placed me,* until the transparent truth is found.

"But where should I look for it? And *when* can I look for it? There's no time to visit Ambrose, no time to read. Where do we find the books, anyway? Where's the time and money to buy them? Who are the people we can borrow them from? There should be assigned times, the hours should be scheduled for different purposes—for my soul's welfare.

"There's a great hope that's turned up; the universal faith doesn't teach what we thought it did, and what we accused it of teaching—we were idiotic in that. Its educated adherents think it's blasphemous to believe that God has the limits of a human body's shape. So are we hesitating to knock, and have the rest opened up to us?†

"But students take up the morning hours. What are we doing with the rest of the day? Why don't we get down to business? But then when do I go pay my respects to powerful patrons, whose recommendations I need? When can I prepare the lessons for my students to buy from me? When can I simply take the time off I need, and give my mind a break from the stress of its worries?

19. "To hell with all of this! We've had enough of this empty, worthless stuff. We need to devote ourselves solely to investigating the truth. Life is wretched, and we don't know when death is coming. It can creep up suddenly. In what condition

---

* This is probably the stage of the catechumen, or person receiving instruction before baptism.
† Matthew 7:7–8.

will we go out of this place? Where is it that we'll have to learn what we should have done when we were here? And, what's more, will there be penalties to pay for not doing it?

"But what if death actually cuts off and puts an end to all our concerns, together with our physical senses?* This is a possibility worth looking into. But no, that couldn't be—how could we think that! It's *not* meaningless, *not* humbug that the towering height of Christian authority's faith extends over the whole world. Such things, and such great things, could never be done by divine agency on our behalf if the soul's life were reduced to nothing by the death of the body.

"So then why do we hesitate to abandon all hope in this world and devote ourselves wholly to seeking God and a happy life? But wait: this stuff itself is pleasant; it's got quite a bit of its own sweetness. It's not a straightforward thing to cut off our pursuits in that direction; it would be very embarrassing to go back to them.

"And just think how much progress there's been already toward an appointment to some high public office. What more is there to wish for in this world? Plenty of powerful friends are backing us; provided that we pour our effort—a lot of effort—into one thing, we could even be granted a lower-ranking governorship. A wife has to be acquired, one with a certain amount of money, so that the expenses of officeholding aren't troublesome†—and there's the whole extent of what's desired. Many great men, highly deserving of emulation, have been dedicated to the study of wisdom while they were married."

---

* This is an outline of the Epicurean theory of death, often adduced in late antiquity.
† The holder of any important public office was obliged to spend lavishly in his private capacity on public entertainments, handouts to the poor, and other social obligations.

20. Even while I was talking to myself, and these different winds blew and pushed my heart in opposite directions, time was in transit; but I was slow in turning to the Master. Day after day, I put off living in you,* but I didn't put off dying every day in myself. I loved the happy life, but I didn't love her in the place where she presides. I ran away from her and looked for her at the same time.

I thought I would be excessively miserable if I couldn't have a woman's arms around me, and I had no notion of your mercy's medicine for healing this infirmity. I hadn't tried that medicine, and I believed chastity was about an individual's strength, strength such as I'd never been aware of having. I was idiot enough not to know that as it's written, nobody can be chaste unless you grant this.† You would certainly have granted it to me if I'd battered your ears with groans from deep inside me and, out of a firm faith, thrown the burden of my distress off onto you.‡

21. Alypius did hold me back from getting married, dinning it into me that if I did, there was no way we could live together in peaceful retirement and our passion for wisdom—as had been our desire for a long time now. Even back then, he himself, in the domain of sex, was extremely pure—to an amazing extent, because in early youth he'd actually had the experience of sleeping with a woman. But he hadn't taken to it; instead, he'd found it unpleasant and disdained it, and from then on lived in

* Sirach 5:7.
† Wisdom of Solomon 8:21. There is some coincidence between the vocabulary for chastity and for mental acuity in Greek, and this Greek verse of the Old Testament may have been misunderstood and quoted out of context. See also 1 Corinthians 7:7, concerning chastity as a particular gift.
‡ Psalms 55:22, Matthew 11:28–29, and other verses.

perfect chastity. However, I argued against him, citing men who, while married, had cultivated wisdom, served God meritoriously, and faithfully kept and cherished their friends.

I, of course, was a long way off from their souls' nobility. I had the deadly-sweet disease of carnality fastened on me and kept dragging my chain along. I was afraid to have it unlocked, and the hand that would have done that—by which I mean his words of good advice—felt as if it were striking against a wound, and I pushed that hand away. Besides that, the snake* even used me to speak to Alypius and was getting him bound up, too; through my tongue, it tossed attractive snares in his path to entangle his honorable and unencumbered feet.†

22. He was amazed that I, for whom he had a substantial respect, was so stuck in the glue of that pleasure's snare that whenever the issue came up for discussion between us, I insisted that there was no possible way I could lead a life of celibacy. When I saw how amazed he was, I defended myself by saying there was a great difference between his hurried, furtive experience, which he could hardly remember any more and therefore could easily write off, without its bothering him, and the delights of my established relationship with a woman; if the respectable name of marriage were added to this relationship, he shouldn't find anything amazing in the reasons for my inability to disdain this way of life.

He himself then started to long for marriage—certainly not because he was overcome by lust for the kind of pleasure I had, but because of curiosity's lust. He kept saying that he yearned to

* Genesis 3:1.
† Psalms 142:3.

know what on earth this thing was without which I would have felt that my life, which he approved of as it was, wasn't a life but a punishment. His mind, free of that chain, was stupefied at my slavery, and this stupefaction led him into a desire to investigate the phenomenon. He was on the brink of carrying out an actual test, a test that might have toppled him into the very slavery he was stupefied about. He was willing to contract a pact with death.* Whoever loves danger is going to fall into it.†

But if there's any dignity in the partnership, in the duties of directing a marriage and raising children, it wasn't more than a weak draw for either of us. For me, the major factor was a relationship as a habit, the habit of (temporarily) satiating an (in the long term) insatiable lasciviousness—and the habit held me violently captive and tortured me. Luring Alypius into captivity, in contrast, was his sheer astonishment. That's how it was with us, until you, the Highest, not deserting the dirt we're made of,‡ had mercy on our misery and came to our aid in marvelous and mysterious ways.

23. But there was energetic pressure put on me to take a wife. In no time, I was a suitor, and in no time, a bride was promised. But my mother took the most trouble in this, with the idea that once I was married, the salutary baptism would wash me clean;§ so she was overjoyed that day by day I was becoming more suitable for it; and she was seeing her prayers and your promises fulfilled by my faith.

---

* Wisdom of Solomon 1:16, Isaiah 28:18.
† Sirach 3:26.
‡ Genesis 2:7.
§ Her notions on this point—namely that baptism should be timed conveniently in relation to desires converts were unwilling or unable to control—represent a strain of popular Christianity that Augustine would grow to deplore. See above, book 1, chapter 18.

But to be sure, though at my request and by her own desire she prayed daily, with dinning shouts from within her heart, for you to grant her some vision concerning the coming marriage, you were never willing. She saw certain insubstantial, ghostly things, but that was only what she was driven to by the momentum of a human spirit fussing over this business.

She didn't tell me about these visions with the confidence she habitually showed when you yourself gave her a sign; instead, she brushed off the things she saw. She said she could tell by some kind of flavor, which she couldn't put into words, the difference between you making a revelation to her, and her own consciousness dreaming. However, the pressure was kept up, and parents were approached about a girl; the girl was almost two years under marriageable age, but because she met with approval, the wait was acceptable.

24. But in fact many of us friends were in a ferment of thought and discussion. We despised the uproarious annoyances of human life and were on the brink of resolving to live in retired leisure away from the mob. We were going to engineer this leisure by placing everything we could lay our hands on into a joint holding and thus create a single combined household estate. In the integrity of friendship, we would see that things didn't belong to us individually, but instead, what came from the entire community would be unified, and this whole would belong to each of us, and each item to everybody.

We thought we could form an association of ten or so people; some who were extremely wealthy would be included, most notably Romanianus, a citizen of my hometown. At the time, serious business troubles had brought him to the Imperial court at Rome; but I'd been very close to him from my earliest youth. He was the most enthusiastic about this project, and his arguments in its favor had a great influence, because his abundant wealth outdid ours by so much.

We decided that two of us each year, like regular magistrates, would take care of all necessary business, leaving the others undistracted. But then came the question of whether the little women would allow these arrangements; some of us were married already, and others (including me) wanted to be. At this point the whole enterprise, which we'd given such a satisfactory shape, exploded in our hands, and was ruined and thrown away. Subsequently there was deep sighing, and steps toward following the wide, well-worn worldly roads.*

Our heart has any number of ideas, but your plan is for all time.† With your plan in mind, you had a good laugh at all of ours and prepared for us to do what you intended. You were going to bring us our food at the right time,‡ opening your hand and filling our souls with blessings.

25. Meanwhile, the number of my sins was growing. The woman I'd been accustomed to sleeping with was torn from my side, because she was supposed to be an obstacle to my marriage. My heart, which had fused with hers, was mutilated by the wound, and I limped along trailing blood. She went back to Africa, vowing to you that she would never know another man, and leaving with me the illegitimate son she'd given birth to.

---

* Matthew 7:13–14.
† Psalms 33:11, Proverbs 19:21.
‡ Psalms 104:27, 145:15–16.

I was wretched, but I couldn't even manage to emulate a woman. Instead, I itched at delay, as it was two years before I could have the girl I was arranging to marry. I was no lover of marriage but instead a slave to my lust, so I secured another woman—but not a wife, to be sure. It was as if I wanted my soul's disease to be maintained unimpaired, or maybe even augmented, and conveyed into the realm of lawful wedlock, and I needed a sustained relationship to serve as a sort of escort on this journey. But that wound of mine made by hacking off the woman I'd had before wasn't healing; on the contrary, after excruciating inflammation and pain came putrefaction and a growing numbness and hopelessness.

26. You're the one to be praised, you're the one to be glorified, fountain of mercies! I was growing more wretched, and you were growing nearer. Your right hand was almost—almost!—there to pluck me out of the slime and wash me clean, but I didn't know that.

Nothing but the fear of death and your judgment after it held me back from a deeper whirlpool of bodily pleasures; this fear never left my heart no matter how many different views I held about the nature of things. I used to have arguments with my friends Alypius and Nebridius about what the ultimate good and evil might be.* In my *mind,* I would have given the prize to Epicurus for figuring this out,† had I not believed that the *soul's*

* These are the same Latin words as the title of a treatise by Cicero, *De finibus bonorum et malorum* (literally, "about the ends/aims/fulfillments of good things and bad things"), whose controlling idea goes back to Aristotle's *telos,* which signifies both purpose and full development.

† Augustine probably means the value Epicureanism placed on inner peace and ordinary pleasures (particularly those of friendship). Epicureanism is discussed in Cicero's *De finibus.*

life survived death and that we would then be dealt with as we deserved, whereas Epicurus refused to believe this.

But I used to ask why, if we could live *forever* in unending *physical* pleasure without any cause for fear, we wouldn't be happy and not ask for anything else. I didn't know that this very line of speculation was characteristic of my immense misery: I was so deeply submerged and blinded that I couldn't conceive of the light of virtue, the light of a beauty that can be embraced for free, which the body's eyes can't see—which is seen from a person's inmost being.

Nor, in my dismal state, did I reflect on the channel from which flowed the possibility of having pleasant discussions—though on these actual sordid topics—with my friends. Yet I couldn't be happy without friends—not even according to my understanding of happiness at the time—no matter how sumptuous my physical pleasures might be. My affection for my friends, at least, was a free gift, and I felt that theirs for me was the same.

Oh, the twisted roads I walked! Woe to my outrageous soul, that hoped for something better if it withdrew from you! The soul rolls back and forth, onto its back, onto one side and then another, onto its stomach, but every surface is hard, and you're the only rest. But look, you're here, freeing us from our unhappy wandering, setting us firmly on your track,* comforting us and saying, "Run the race! *I'll* carry you! *I'll* carry you clear to the end, and even at the end, *I'll* carry you."†

* Psalms 32:8, 86:11.
† 1 Corinthians 9:24, Isaiah 46:4.

Book 7

1. Now my evil youth, really too evil to speak of, was dead, and I proceeded into young manhood.* But I'd advanced in shameful frivolity as far as in age, because I couldn't think of any kind of substance except what I was used to seeing with my own eyes. It wasn't that I thought of you, God, in the shape of a human body. From the time I began to hear anything about philosophy, I always ran from this notion, and now I rejoiced to find the spiritual faith of our mother, the universal church, running from it too.

But no other way of thinking of you entered my head. *I* was a human being—the one I've described, alas; as such, I tried to

---

* By Roman reckoning, male "youth" extended to the age of about thirty (the ordinary age of a first marriage), and "young manhood" into middle age.

think of *you* as the supreme and true and only God,* and my inmost being was permeated by the belief that you weren't subject
to decay or damage or change. I hadn't worked out the how or
why, but I could plainly see, and I was positive, that what could
decay was inferior to what couldn't. I didn't hesitate a second in
preferring what could not be harmed to what could, and I saw
that what never endures change is better than what does.

My heart cried out savagely against all my ghosts, and I tried to
drive away the swarming mob of filthy beings from my mind's
eye. They were hardly scattered when—in the blink of an
eye†—there they were, teeming back again, swooping into my
sight and clouding it over, so that I was compelled to contemplate, not the form of a human body, but nevertheless something material existing in space, whether *in*fused in the world or
*dif*fused outside the world through infinity.

This was supposed to be that very being not subject to decay or
harm or change, the being I preferred to what *was* subject. If I
denied it locations such as these in which it could exist, it appeared to me to be nothing, and I mean nothing at all, not even
a void. If an object were removed from a place, and that place
remained, though emptied of every object (whether made of
earth, moisture, air, or heavenly fire‡), that empty space would
still exist, as an expanse of nothing, so to speak.

2. So this was me, with my mind so calcified§ that I couldn't get
a good look even at myself. I thought anything that wasn't

---

* John 17:3.
† 1 Corinthians 15:52.
‡ The "four elements" in ancient scientific-philosophical thought.
§ Matthew 13:15, Acts 28:27, both quoting Isaiah 6:10.

stretched—or poured—or balled up—or swollen out over some measure of space—or that didn't contain something like that—or *couldn't* contain something like that—didn't exist at all. My mind moved over images corresponding to the forms my eyes were used to moving over, but I didn't see that the mental effort with which I formed these images wasn't the same kind of thing as eyesight, and that only something momentous could form these images for me in the first place.

I thought of even you, life of my life, as a huge being, penetrating the infinity of space, the whole mass of the world and beyond that in all directions through the measureless void without any boundary, so that earth partook of you, and sky partook of you—everything partook of you and found its limits in you, but you found your limits nowhere.

Just as the material of air, this air that's above the earth, doesn't prevent the sun's light from penetrating and crossing through it, doesn't break it apart or destroy it but still fills it completely, I thought that not only sky and air and sea, but even earth was material you could pass through, and that in all its components, from the smallest to the largest, it could be penetrated to contain your presence, which works from inside and outside with hidden power to govern everything you've created.

This is what I speculated, because I couldn't come up with anything else. In fact, I was wrong. In this schema, a larger part of the earth would partake of a larger part of you, and a smaller part would partake of a smaller part, and everything would be filled with you in such a way that an elephant's body would contain more of you than a sparrow's, inasmuch as the first is bigger and takes up more space, and so on and so forth: with everything chopped into pieces, you'd make large pieces of yourself present in large parts of the world, and small pieces in small parts. No, it's not like that, but you hadn't yet lighted my darkness* to show how it is.

3. In fact, Master, I had on hand plenty with which to counter the Manichaeans, those misled misleaders and blathering mutes (since no sound of your Word came from their mouths): what Nebridius used to posit long before at Carthage—and all of us who heard it were shaken to the core—would do fine:

What would that mysterious tribe of darkness that the Manichaeans in their stories customarily deploy against you, God, from its huge defensive mound of contrasting substance, have done to you had you refused to fight?

If anyone answered that this tribe would have hurt you, that would mean you were vulnerable and perishable. If, however, the assertion was that the enemy had no power to hurt, then no reason could be adduced for fighting, much less fighting in such a way that some portion of you, some part of your body, or the offspring of your substance, would be interlocked with the opposing powers—not with properties created by you—and would be polluted and changed for the worse by them to such a degree as to turn from bliss to misery, and would need reinforcement to rescue and cleanse it.

This being in question, to whom this would be happening, would have to be the soul, to whose aid your Word comes— freedom coming to the aid of slavery, purity to defilement,

* Psalms 18:28.

wholeness to dissolution. But—oops!—your Word would have to be subject to the same dissolution, since it's one and the same substance as the soul.

Therefore, if the Manichaeans said that you, God—that is, the substance through which you exist—weren't perishable, then their whole theory was an outrageous lie. But if they said you *were* perishable, that in itself is a lie, to be denounced with loathing as soon as they opened their mouths.

So, Nebridius's formulation did fine against the Manichaeans, whom I needed to vomit up any way I could. I was sick to my stomach with them, because they had no way around a grisly sacrilege of their hearts and tongues, as long as they perceived and described you like this.

4. But even now I had a difficulty. Though I stated, and solidly understood, that our God—the true God, who made not only our souls but our bodies, and not only our souls and bodies, but all people and all things—couldn't be defiled or displaced or changed in any respect, I had no grasp of the cause of evil: it wasn't disentangled for me, it didn't have the knots picked out of it. But whatever that cause might be, I saw that it needed to be investigated in such a way as not to force me to believe that the unchangeable God is changeable. That would turn me into the evil I was investigating!

As a result, I confidently set about investigating the cause, certain that the Manichaeans, whom I ran from with unwavering determination, weren't stating the truth. I was certain because I saw that their inquiry into the source of evil had filled them

with evil-mindedness: on this disposition was based their view
that your substance could be affected by evil, rather than that
theirs could do evil.*

5. I set my mind to sorting out what I kept hearing, which
was that the free exercise of the will is the reason we do evil,
and that your just judgment is the reason we suffer the
consequences—but I didn't have the power to perceive all this
clearly. Thus, though I was trying to drag my mind's eye out of
the depths, I went under again; ceaselessly I tried, and monoto-
nously I went back under.

What lifted me out into your light was the knowledge that I do
have a will; that was as sure as the knowledge that I was alive. It
followed that when I wanted or didn't want something, I could
be absolutely certain that nothing but myself was doing that
wanting or not wanting. And I gradually became aware that in
this responsibility lay the cause of my sin.

I saw, conversely, that what I did unwillingly I endured rather
than did, and I judged these actions to be not my fault but rather
my punishment—but I was quick to admit, when I thought
about it, that you, being just, weren't inflicting an unjust chas-
tisement on me.

But I went back to saying, "Who made me? Wasn't it my God,
who's not only good but goodness itself? Then how does it come
about that I will evil and don't will good? Is it to give me a basis
for paying a just penalty? Who set out in me this seedbed of

---

* For Augustine, the necessary first step in an inquiry into the nature of evil was to deter-
mine its location; the Manichaeans, he felt, had theorized evil in the divine realm to avoid
acknowledging it in themselves, despite the dangers of a self-deceiving egotism that this
premise entailed.

bitterness,* and who sowed it for me, when all of me comes from my God, who's the ultimate sweetness? If the devil is responsible, then where does the devil come from? If, out of wrong-headed willfulness, he changed from an angel into the devil, how did there come to exist in him the will that turned him into the devil, when he was made, in his entirety, as an angel by the perfect creator?"

I was weighed down and suffocating under these thoughts, but I wasn't sucked clear into that underworld of delusion where no one confesses to you, as he thinks that you have evil things imposed on you rather than that a human being does them.

6. I made an effort to investigate the rest of the matter, having already found that the imperishable is better than the perishable, and on that basis acknowledged that you, whatever you are, are imperishable: no soul was ever able, or ever will be able, to conceive of anything better than you, who are the highest and the most excellent good. Given that in the truest, most definite sense, the imperishable must be preferred to the perishable (as I was in fact already preferring it), I would have been able to speculate about something better than my God—but only if you weren't imperishable.

Therefore, the place where I needed to seek you was in the realization that the imperishable is to be preferred to the perishable; and from there I needed to turn my attention to the question of where evil was; that is, what the source was for an act of spoiling something—but an act that could in no way sully *your* substance.

* Hebrews 12:15.

No, in no way whatsoever can any such act sully our God—not by anyone's will, or by any necessity, or by any unexpected chance. God is God, and what he wills for himself is good, and he himself is that same good; and to deteriorate is *not* good.

You're not forced, against your will, into anything, because there's no inequality between your will and your power. The will might be greater, if you yourself were greater than yourself, but the will and the power of God *are* God himself. And what's unexpected to you, who know everything? There is no inherent potentiality that you don't know. Why should we be long-winded in this explanation? A perishable substance can't be God, because if it were perishable, it wouldn't be God.

7. So I was asking about the origin of wrong, and I was asking in the wrong way, yet I didn't see anything wrong in my inquiry. I erected within sight of my spirit a structure for the whole cre-ated universe, whatever in it we can perceive—such as land, sea, air, stars, trees, and mortal creatures—and whatever we can't see—such as the support for the sky above, and all the angels and other spiritual entities there; my imagination arranged even these neatly, in various places, as if they were material objects.

I made your creation an enormous lump, divided internally into different kinds of objects, actual material ones on the one hand, and on the other spiritual beings whose forms I had made up in my head. My lump was not the right size, of course, because there was no way I could tell, but the size I felt like making it, and at any rate finite in all directions. I made you surround and infuse every part of it, but *you were infinite* in every direction. It

was as if a sea were everywhere, and on all sides, through measureless infinity, there were nothing *but* sea, and it had within it
a sponge of some large size (pick any!), but finite, and every last
part of this sponge was absolutely full of this limitless sea. Thus
I posited your finite creation to be full of an infinite you. And I
declared:

"Here's God, and here are the things God created, and he's a
good God, and overwhelmingly, to the absolutely greatest extent, superior to these things; and yet, being good, he created
good things,* and look how he surrounds and fills them.

"So then where does evil come from, and by what route did it
crawl in? What is its root, and what is its seed? Or doesn't it exist
at all? But then why do we fear and avoid what doesn't exist? But
if our fear is baseless, then for sure that fear, at least, is evil, because it jabs and tortures the heart for no purpose; and it's a
more oppressive evil inasmuch as nothing exists for us to fear,
yet we do fear. On these grounds, either the thing we fear is evil,
or it's evil because we fear it.

"Where does evil come from, then, since a good God made all
these good things? The greater and the highest good did make
lesser good things, but nevertheless both the creator and all created things are good. So where does evil come from? Was there
some evil matter from which he made those things, and did he
shape and arrange that but leave something in it that he didn't
turn into good? But why would he do that? Didn't he have the
power to change or replace it, so that nothing evil remained,
given that he's all-powerful?

* Genesis 1:31.

"But now it comes down to the question of why he would have wanted to make something out of that substance. Why didn't he, using the same omnipotence, act so that the substance didn't exist at all? Would it really have been able to come into existence against his will in the first place? If, alternatively, it were eternal, why did he allow it to exist for so long, from clear back through the endless ages of time, and why did he, so long afterward, decide to make something out of it? Or at that point, if he wanted to do something all of a sudden, why didn't he instead— since he's all-powerful—act so that this substance didn't exist and he was left alone as the entire, true, highest, and limitless good?

"Or if it weren't a good way of acting, for the God who was good, not accordingly to work with and establish something good, couldn't he have first done away with and reduced to nothing the substance that was evil, and then brought into being some good substance from which to create everything? He wouldn't be omnipotent if he were unable to create something good without the help of some substance he hadn't created himself."

These were the kinds of things I was turning over in my mind, weighted down as it was with viciously gnawing anxieties, from the fear of death and from the truth I hadn't found. But there remained firmly fused to my heart, through your universal church, my faith in your Christ, our Master and rescuer. It's true that this faith was still in many respects shapeless, and bobbing along on streams outside standard instruction; and yet over time my mind didn't abandon it, but rather absorbed it more every day.

8. By this time I'd also thrown off the sham prognostications and irreverent ravings of the astrologers. On this account, too, let your own mercies testify to you, my God, out of the inmost, most intimate recesses of my soul!* You, and no one but you—for who else calls us back from every one of death's delusions, if not the life that doesn't know how to die, and the wisdom that lights up intellects in need, and that doesn't stand in any need of light itself, because it governs the universe, down to the trees' fluttering leaves?—you took care of the cantankerousness with which I struggled against Vindicianus, that shrewd old man, and Nebridius, that young man with his amazing inspiration.

The former fiercely insisted, and the latter stated constantly, though with some hesitation, that the so-called art of predicting the future didn't exist; rather, they said, the guesses people made often turned out to be impressive because of sheer chance, and by a whole lot of talk, people can ensure that a fair amount of it comes true: when they emit it, they have no idea, but they stumble on future events, so to speak, by dint of never shutting up.

Anyway, you took care of my curmudgeonly resistance to these two by providing me with a further friend who was in fact energetic in consulting the astrologers yet not an old hand at their writings; he was instead, as I said, keen in consulting them; but he was nevertheless apprised of something that he used to say he'd heard from his father—though he didn't know how much weight it might have for reversing his opinion of this "field of expertise."

* Psalms 107:8.

This friend was a gentleman named Firminus, who had a liberal education and was very accomplished in rhetoric. Because I was very close to him, he consulted me about what his so-called stars meant for a certain set of concerns that had given rise to some overblown worldly hopes in him. I had already started to lean toward Nebridius's view of astrology, but I didn't actually refuse to speculate and say what came into my mind—though I was wavering. But I added that I was very nearly persuaded that the claims of astrology were absurd and meaningless.

At that point, he told me that his father had been quite deeply occupied with these books, and had a friend who at the same period was an equally strong enthusiast. Identically keen, and putting their heads together, they blew on the flames of each other's passion for this twaddle, to the point that even when animals were going to litter in their households, they watched for the time the young would be born and took note of the constellations' positions, so that they could assemble evidence, as it were, about astrology.

Firminus said that, accordingly, he'd heard from his father that when his mother was pregnant with himself (as his father told him), a female slave of his father's friend was at the same stage of pregnancy. She couldn't hide it from her master, who made extremely careful observations to learn about even his bitches' whelping. And it turned out that, with one man counting for his wife, the other for his housemaid, the days, the hours, and the smaller divisions of hours with the most minute scrutiny, the two women went into labor at the same time. The result was that the two friends were forced to cast the same horoscope, down to the smallest detail, for both newborns, a son and a little slave. When, in fact, the two women started the process of giving birth, each man let the other know what was happening in his own house, and they got messengers ready to send, as soon as a baby was born, with news of the labor's conclusion. The men had, each in his virtual kingdom, each easily worked it out that the message would be sent immediately.

And Firminus used to say that the messengers were sent by both men at the exact same time, so that they met at the halfway point between the two houses. Since this was the case, neither of the friends had a basis for writing down a different position of the constellations—even a miniscule, momentary difference. But Firminus, born into a distinguished family, ran back and forth on the world's thoroughfares as a matter of course, and was magnified with wealth and lofted up to public offices, whereas the slave served his masters, and the yoke of his rank was by no means loosened on his shoulders. Firminus, who knew him, told me this.

9. So once I'd heard this story—and felt I could rely on it, because the man who told it was so reliable—I completely gave up the tussle, relaxed, and tumbled to the floor. And the next thing I did was try to reclaim Firminus himself from his preoccupation with astrology.

I told him that in order to make a factual statement after inspecting the positions of the constellations at his birth, I would certainly have had to claim I saw there parents of the highest standing in their community and a family distinguished in its own commonwealth. I would have had to say I saw he was freeborn, that he had a gentleman's upbringing and a liberal education.

If, on the other hand, the slave he'd told me about had consulted me concerning this collection of stars—because the slave's was exactly the same—then in order to make a true assessment for him, too, I would have had, in contrast, to see a family in the most degraded position, a state of slavery, and in all other respects a life extremely different from Firminus's and extremely remote from it.

So here was the situation from which I had to reason: I was looking at the same stars but would have to say opposite things about the two lives they were supposed to represent, if I were to say the truth; if, on the other hand, I said the same things about the two lives, I would be lying. On this evidence I definitively deduced that true statements made from observations of the constellations were the result not of science but of pure chance; and that the false statements made on this basis, for their part, were not due to ignorance of the science, but to the mendacity of chance, as it were.

10. Once I'd gained this special access to the matter, I chewed privately over things along the same lines. I longed every moment to attack, ridicule, and rebut those who were deliriously cultivating this profitable trade of astrology, and I felt I had to prevent any of them from putting up a fight by claiming that Firminus had told me a made-up story, or that his father had told one to him; so I turned to thinking about those born as twins.

Most are expelled from the womb in such quick succession that the short gap in time—however great a power people argue it makes in the workings of the universe—can't be computed through human observation, and has no capacity whatsoever for being represented in a written form, which an astrologer can later examine as a basis for true statements about the twins' lives.

But statements about twins just *won't* be true. For example, a person who examined the astrological records—which would have been the same—of Jacob and Esau's birth would have had to make the same predictions about the lives of both, but the same things didn't happen to both. The astrologer would therefore have been saying what wasn't true, or, if he'd spoken the truth, it wouldn't have been the same for both—but he would have been examining the same account. It follows that he'd be speaking the truth not through science but chance.

You, Master, most just regulator of the whole world—though neither those who consult astrologers nor the astrologers who are consulted know it—you act with hidden inspiration. The result is that when anyone asks about fate, he may hear from the bottomless chasm of your judgment everything he ought to hear, based on what various souls, in their hidden inwardness, deserve. A human being must not say to you, "What is it?" or "Why is it this way?" He must not, must not say this, because he's a human being.

11. So you, my helper, had released me from those chains. However, I kept trying to find the source of evil, and there was no way out of the obsession. But you didn't allow any waves of speculation to carry me away from the faith through which I

believed that you exist, that your substance is unchangeable, that you take care of human beings and pass judgment on them, and that in Jesus Christ, your son and our Master, and in the holy scriptures that the authority of your universal church commends to us, you have laid a road for the rescue of humankind, a road leading to the life that is to be after our earthly death.

But though these beliefs were safe and unshakably ironclad in my mind, I was still feverishly trying to find where evil comes from. What tortures my heart went through as it gave birth, what groans it emitted, my God! But your ears were there to hear, though I didn't know it. When in silence I searched energetically, the unspoken grindings of my mind were words shouted to your mercy. You knew what I suffered—you, and nobody among the human race.

How little it was, after all, that could be dispersed from my mind through my tongue and into the ears of my most intimate friends. It couldn't possibly be, could it, that the whole uproar of my soul dinned at them, when neither the time I had on hand nor all the powers of my mouth would have been enough for that? Yet all the roaring noise from my groaning heart reached your hearing, and my desire was in your presence, but the light of my own eyes wasn't with me.*

It was inside, whereas I myself was outdoors—but really it wasn't in any place at all. Yet I was concentrating on things that are contained in spaces, and there I couldn't find any place to rest. Those things didn't take me in, so that I could say, "It's enough, and it's good." But the things also didn't let me go,

---

* Psalms 38:9–10.

didn't let me return to a place that actually would have been good enough for me.

I'm above all that stuff, but I'm below you, and you are my true joy when I'm placed under you, and you've placed under me what you created below me. Accepting this was the right moderation and the middle ground for my rescue, so as simply to stay in your image, and in acting as your slave, to be master of my body. But when in my insolence I rose up against you and charged my Master with the dense shield of my stubbornness upheld before me,* even the lowest things there were shifted to a place above me and weighed me down, and I had no room to move and couldn't breathe. These things piled onto me profusely from all sides and packed into my perception, and as I pondered them, the mere images of material objects placed themselves in the path along which I needed to return, opposing me, as if a voice were saying, "Where are you going, you worthless, dirty person?"

These experiences grew out of my wound, because you'd struck me to the ground like a blusterer who's cut down. I was divided from you by my swollen-headed conceit, and I was puffed up so grossly out of proportion to a human face that it closed off my eyesight.

12. But you, Master, remain into eternity†—but you won't be angry with us into eternity,‡ since you've had pity on dirt and ashes.§ You resolved to restore my malformations, and with in-

* Job 15:26.
† Psalms 102:12.
‡ Psalms 85:5, 103:9.
§ Job 42:6, Sirach 17:32.

ward goads you roused me and made me restless until you were indisputably there before my inward sight. My swelling settled down under your unseen medicinal hand, and the disordered and darkened eyesight of my mind, when the stinging salve of wholesome sufferings was applied,* was healing day by day.

13. At first, you wished to demonstrate to me how you hold out against the arrogant but grant grace for free to the humble;† and with how much compassion the road of humility has been pointed out to humankind, as your Word was made flesh and lived among them;‡ thus you obtained for me (through a certain person bloated with the most giant grandiosity imaginable§) certain books by Platonists translated from Greek into Latin,¶ and there I read—not in these exact words, but it was the same thesis entirely, put forward with many arguments of many kinds:

"In the beginning was the Word, and the Word was with God, and God was the Word. This one was in the beginning with God. All things were made through him, and without him nothing was made. What was made in him is life, and the life was the light of humankind. And the light shines in the darkness, and the darkness did not grasp it."

And I read that the soul of a human being, though it "gives testimony to the light," is nevertheless not itself the light; instead, the Word was God, "the true light, which lights every person who comes into the world." And I read that "he was in this

* Revelation 3:18.
† Proverbs 3:34, James 4:6, 1 Peter 5:5.
‡ John 1:14.
§ Probably the pagan Neoplatonist Manlius Theodorus.
¶ Plotinus and Porphyry; the translator was Marius Victorinus.

world, and the world was made through him, but the world did not know him."*

But that "he came into what was his own, yet his own people did not accept him; but to however many accepted him and believed in his name, he gave the power to become sons of God"—this part I didn't read in the books given to me.†

14. Likewise I read there that the Word, God, was born not from the body, not from blood, not by the will of a man or the body's will, but from God; yet that the Word became a body and lived among us—this part I didn't read in the books given to me.‡

I did track down in these writings—though it was stated otherwise in a number of ways—that because the son was in the form of the father, he didn't think that his equality with God was a sort of plunder, as this equality was his very nature.

However, he made himself empty and took on the form of a slave, assuming the likeness of humankind. Encountered as someone human in his appearance, he debased himself to the point of death—and no less than a death on the cross—through his obedience. Because of this, God lifted him up on high from among the dead, and granted him a name above every other name, so that at the name of Jesus every knee—of heavenly, earthly, and infernal beings—must bend, and every tongue

---

* John 1:1–10. Thus far, the pagan philosophical principle of transcendent reasoning (in Greek, *logos,* very roughly translated into Latin as *verbum* and much later into English as the "Word") prevails, but without the orthodox Christian insistence on human existence of the Word as Jesus, an insistence to follow in the next verses quoted. John the Baptist is the "soul" who must not be confused with Jesus.

† John 1:11–12.

‡ John 1:13–14. Again, Augustine distinguishes between the transcendent Word congenial to the Platonists and its fulfillment in Jesus' human existence.

must testify that the Master Jesus is in the glory of God the Father*—those books didn't have any of this in them.

Before all time and above all time, your only begotten son remains and cannot change, as he is eternal along with you, and souls receive their enrichment, their blessedness, out of his abundance,† and are renewed so as to grow wise when they become sharers in the Wisdom that remains in herself.‡ This was in the books given to me.

However, when it was time, he died for the wicked, and you didn't spare your own only son, but for the sake of us all you handed him over.§ That wasn't there in the books.

You hid away these things from clever people, and you unveiled them to little children,¶ so that with their toil and burdens they would come to him, and he would relieve them, since he is gentle and humble at heart;** and with his judgments of what's right he will guide those who are gentle,†† and he teaches the meek to walk in his ways, as he sees our lowliness and our toil and forgives all our sins.‡‡

But those who are raised high in the air, as if by the stage boots of a loftier teaching, the platform boots of actors supposed to represent divinities, don't hear Jesus saying, "Learn from me, since I am gentle and humble at heart, and you will find rest for

* Philippians 2:6–11.
† John 1:16.
‡ Wisdom of Solomon 7:27.
§ Romans 5:6, 8:32.
¶ Matthew 11:25, Luke 10:21.
** Matthew 11:28–29.
†† Psalms 25:9.
‡‡ Psalms 25:18.

your souls."* Although these characters recognize God, they
don't glorify him and give him thanks as if he were in fact God;
they fade away in their speculations, and their foolish hearts are
overshadowed. By claiming to be wise, they have become dolts.†

15. And accordingly I also read there, in the philosophical
books, that your imperishable glory had been transfigured into
idols, with a whole array of representations—of perishable humanity, and birds, and four-footed animals, and snakes.‡ This
was clearly the Egyptian food by which Esau lost his rights as
the eldest son,§ since the firstborn people, the Jews, worshipped
the head of a quadruped in your place:¶ in their hearts they
made an about-face toward Egypt,** and they bent down your
image—their soul—before the image of a yearling calf that
munches hay.†† I found such an attitude there in the philosophical books, but I didn't munch on it.

You resolved, Master, to remove from Jacob his degradation as
the younger brother, and to make the elder serve the younger,‡‡
and thus you called the gentiles to take up your inheritance. I
myself had come to you from the gentiles, and I set my sight on
the gold that you willed your people the Jews to carry out of
Egypt,§§ since the gold was yours, wherever it was.

---

* Matthew 11:29.
† Romans 1:21–22.
‡ Romans 1:23.
§ Genesis 25:33–34.
¶ Exodus 32:1–6.
** Acts 7:39–40.
†† Exodus 32:1–6, Psalms 106:20.
‡‡ Genesis 25:23, Romans 9:12.
§§ Exodus 3:21–22, 12:35–36.

And you said to the Athenians through your apostle Paul that in you we "live and move and have our being,"* as certain of the Athenians also said, and in any case Athens is the source of those philosophical books. But I didn't set my sight on the idols of the Egyptians, which they served by drawing from your gold†—and these were the same people who made the truth of God into a lie, and worshipped and served the creation rather than the creator.‡

16. By these books, then, I was prompted to return into myself, and I entered my inmost core under your guidance—and I was able to do that because you became my helper. I entered, and I saw, with some sort of eye belonging to my soul, something above that same eye, and above my mind: an unchangeable light. It wasn't the ordinary light that's visible to any being with a body—nor was it anything like that same kind of light, except bigger, as if the ordinary light shone many times brighter, and with its sheer abundance took possession of all that is.

The light wasn't this but something else, a powerfully different thing from everything of that sort. It wasn't above my mind the

---

* Acts 17:28, in which Paul is shown addressing the Athenian Areopagus, or religious court, in his own defense and quoting the astronomical poet Aratus in these quintessential philosophical terms.

† Exodus 32:2–4.

‡ This last quotation is from Romans 1:25. By the allegories in this passage, Augustine has been making a wide-ranging argument about intellectual and religious integrity. Esau thought so little of his rights as the eldest son that he traded them to his brother, Jacob, for a stew made with lentils, which Augustine labels as "Egyptian food" and associates with the regret of the Israelites after escaping from Egypt and its paganism, shown most strikingly in their worship of the golden calf. The argument about plundering the Egyptians holds that as the Israelites were given license to appropriate the Egyptians' precious goods to take along with them into the wilderness on the way to Canaan, so Christians were allowed to use for their own ends the philosophical wealth of pagan authors. Folded into the argument there appears to be a collateral claim that Christians have replaced Jews as God's inheritors.

way oil is above water, or the way the sky is above the earth; it was higher in that it made me, and I was lower in that I was made by it. Whoever knows the truth knows this light, and whoever knows this light knows eternity. Selfless love knows it.

Oh, eternal truth and true love and beloved eternity, you are my God, for you I sigh day and night! And when I first came to know you, you took me up where I could see that there was something for me to see, but that I wasn't yet the person who could see it. And you beat back the weakness of my sight, sending your fierce rays of light onto me, and I shook with passionate desire and abject fear.

And I found that I was far away from you, in a land wholly unlike yours, as if I heard your voice from on high: "I am the food of grown-ups. Grow, and you will take me in.* But you won't change me into yourself, like the food of your physical being; instead, you will be changed into me."

And I recognized how you'd disciplined this human being due to his wrongdoing; you made my soul shrivel up like a spider,† and I said, "The truth can't be nothing, can it?—because it's spread out neither in finite nor in infinite space?" But you shouted from far away, "No! In very truth, I am who I am!"‡ And I heard, the way something is heard in the heart, and there was now absolutely no way I could doubt; I could more easily doubt that I was alive than that the truth existed—the truth that is understood and discerned through the things that have been made.§

---

* 1 Corinthians 3:2.
† Psalms 39:11. The image makes its way through biblical languages with some variation.
‡ Exodus 3:14.
§ Romans 1:20.

17. And I gazed at the other things under you, and I saw that they neither altogether exist nor altogether fail to exist; they do in fact exist, in that they're from you; but they fail to exist, in that they aren't what you are. Only that thing that unchangeably remains truly exists. For me, then, it is good to cling to God,* because if I don't remain in him, I won't be able to remain in myself, either. But he, for his part, by remaining in himself, renews all things.† And you are my Master, since you don't need any good things that belong to me.

18. And it was made evident to me that things that perish are good. They couldn't perish either if they were the highest good or if they weren't good. If they were the highest good, they would be imperishable, but if they weren't good at all, there wouldn't be anything in them to perish. Perishing is (of course) a form of harm, and unless it lessened what is good, it wouldn't do any harm. Therefore, either perishing doesn't do any harm—which is an impossibility—or—and this is an absolute certainty—all things that perish are deprived of something good.

If they're going to be deprived of *everything* good, they're not going to exist at all. If they go on existing and are actually unable to perish, they will be better than the things that are merely good, because they will remain imperishable through all time. What's more outrageous than to say that things become better once they lose everything that's good about them?

Hence, if things are deprived of everything good, then they'll no longer exist at all: so as long as they exist, they're good, and

* Psalms 63:8, 73:28.
† Wisdom of Solomon 7:27, Matthew 19:28, Romans 21:5.

that evil for whose source I was searching is not a substance, because if it were one, it would be a good thing. It would either be an imperishable substance, and certainly a great good, or it would be a perishable substance, which could not perish unless it were good.

Thus I saw, and it was made evident to me, that you made all things good, and that there are absolutely no substances that you didn't make; and since you have not made all things equal, all things are good in that individually they are good; and all things together are very good, since our God made all things very good.*

19. To you, evil does not exist at all—but this is the case not only for you but for the whole of your creation, because there is nothing outside that can break in and break up the order that you have placed over this creation. In parts of it there are certain things that, because they don't fit in with certain other things, are considered evil; but these same things do fit in with still other things, and thus are good—and they are good in themselves. But all these things that don't fit in with each other do fit in with the lower part of the universe, which we call the earth, which has its own cloudy and windy sky suitable to itself.

It would be unthinkable for me now to say, "I wish this stuff didn't exist." If I looked at it on its own, I might in fact long for more, but even on the basis of this alone I ought to praise you. Showing that you must be praised are the earth's sea monsters and all its fathomless chasms, fire, hail, snow, ice, the spirited breathings of the storms, all of which carry out your Word, the

* Genesis 1:31.

mountains and all the hills, the fruit trees and all the cedars, the wild animals and all the animals of the herd, the crawling creatures and the flying, winged ones. Let the kings of the earth and all its nations, the rulers and all the judges of the earth, youths and unmarried girls, and older along with younger people praise your name. Let them praise you, our God, since even from the sky you are praised. In the heights let all your angels, all your heavenly armies, the sun and moon, all the stars and the daylight, the heaven above all heavens, and the waters above heaven praise your name.*

I no longer yearned for anything better, because I contemplated everything, and, with a more balanced judgment, I assessed the higher things as better than the lower things—that was a given— but also the whole as better than the higher things on their own.

20. People aren't right in the head when they decide they don't like some part of your creation†—as I wasn't right in the head when I turned against many things that you made. And since my soul didn't dare to be unhappy with my God, it was unwilling for anything it was unhappy with to belong to you.

From this position, it moved to the view that there were two substances, but it couldn't find rest there, speaking other people's words. Coming back from this position, my soul made for itself a god distributed through the infinity of physical space, and considered that this god was you, and housed this god in its heart,‡ and thus became once again the shrine—hateful to you—of an idol to itself.

* Psalms 148:1–13.
† Psalms 38:3.
‡ Ezekiel 14:7.

But later, you nursed my head (though I didn't know it at the time) and lulled my eyes shut, so that they couldn't look at illusions. I had a little pause from myself, and my lunacy was put to sleep. I woke up in you and saw that you're endless in another way—and this vision wasn't drawn from my physical existence.

21. And I regarded other things, and I saw that they owe their existence to you, and that in you all things find their boundaries—but differently than it would be in physical space; rather, you hold all things in the hand of truth, and all things are true to the extent that they exist, and untruth isn't anything, unless it's the notion that something exists that doesn't.

And I saw that each thing fits not only into its proper place but also into its proper time; whereas you, who alone are eternal, didn't begin to do your work after countless stretches of time, because all stretches of time, both those that have passed by and those that will pass by, couldn't go or come unless *you* were at work and unshakably remaining.

22. By having the experience myself, I could tell it was no wonder that even bread that's sweet to a healthy person's sense of taste is a punishment to a sick one's, and that to ailing eyes the light that clear eyes love is abhorrent. And the wicked dislike your justice, to say nothing of a poisonous snake or a maggot, which are good things you created, suitable for the lower parts of your creation—for which the wicked themselves are suitable to the extent that they're unlike you; but they're suitable for the higher parts of creation to the extent that they become like you.

Asking what wickedness was, I didn't find any substance, but instead a twisting of the will, a wrenching of it down into the lowest things from the highest substance, which is you, God. The will to wickedness is what casts out the innermost part of itself and swells beyond its own walls.

23. I marveled that now I loved you, and not an apparition in place of you. But I didn't stand still to enjoy my God. I was ravished into your presence by your beauty, yet soon torn away from you by the weight of myself, and I smashed down with a groan into those lower things I've been writing of. The habits of my body comprised that weight.

But the memory of you remained with me, and in no way did I doubt that you were the one I should cling to; but I also couldn't doubt that I wasn't yet one who could cling to you, as the body, breaking down and perishing as it does, weighs on the soul, and the business of living on earth presses down on the understanding as it considers so many things;* yet I was absolutely sure that since the founding of the universe, the unseen things that belong to you have been seen and comprehended through the things that are made, and your eternal power and divinity are seen and comprehended along with them.†

I was asking, you see, what the source was of the approval I gave to the beauty of material objects, whether these were on earth or in the sky, and what was at hand to assist me when I spoke with sound judgment about things that change and said, "This should be this way," or "That shouldn't be this way"—I was, in

* Wisdom of Solomon 9:15.
† Romans 1:20.

short, asking what my source of judgment was when I judged this way, and I had found an unchangeable and true eternity of truth above my changeable mind.

Thus, step by step, I moved from material objects to the soul that perceives through what is material, and from there to the inward power to which physical perception sends messages of things outside—and thus far, animals have the same abilities—and hence again to the reasoning capacity to which something received from the physical senses is referred for judgment.

This capacity for reasoning also ascertained itself to be changeable in me, and so it raised itself up to the level of its own potential for understanding and led its thinking away from the habitual, withdrawing itself from the contesting swarms of apparitions, so that it could discover the light that could spread out onto it.

Then, without any hesitation, reasoning shouted that the unchangeable must be preferred to the changeable; and that on this basis it could know the unchangeable thing itself (which, unless it were somehow known, couldn't with certainty be preferred to the changeable). Thus, in one flash of sight that trembled with excitement, reasoning came to that which is. Then truly I gazed on the unseen things that belong to you and are understood through the things that have been made.* But I didn't have the power to keep my eye on them. My weakness was repelled, and I returned to what I was used to and took nothing along with me but a memory, which loved and, so to speak, craved what I had smelled but wasn't yet able to eat.

* Romans 1:20.

24. So I looked for a way to obtain the reinforcement necessary for enjoying you, but I didn't find it until I took in my arms the mediator between God and human beings, the human Jesus Christ,* who is God above all things, and blessed into eternity.† He calls, saying, "I am the way, the truth, and the life."‡ He mixes with his flesh the food that I wasn't strong enough to take, since through him the Word was made into a body.§ Thus your wisdom, God, through which you created everything that exists, could be the nursing mother of our infancy. But I didn't take hold of Jesus as my God, the way a lowly being takes hold of another lowly being; I didn't know what that instructress, his weakness,¶ had to teach me.

It was this: your Word, the eternal truth, towering above the higher parts of your creation, causes to rise to herself those who are placed below in subjection; but in those lower parts she has built for herself a lowly house out of the mud we're made of,** and in this house she could bring down from themselves those who must accept subjection, and bring them across to herself, healing their swelling excess and nurturing their passionate love, so that they wouldn't go too far forward in reliance in themselves. Rather, they were to grow weak and see at their feet the holy being in her weakness, as she shares the pitiful human hide that clothes us;†† in their exhaustion, they could throw themselves on her, and as she rose, she could lift them along with her.

---

* 1 Timothy 2:5.
† Romans 9:5.
‡ John 14:6.
§ John 1:14.
¶ 1 Corinthians 1:25.
** Genesis 2:7.
†† Genesis 3:21.

25. But as for me, I used to think otherwise, and my understanding of the Anointed, my Master, was limited to the following: that he was a man of outstanding wisdom, and that no one could be his equal—especially in that he was miraculously born of a virgin, to demonstrate that the things of this world should be scorned for the sake of gaining immortality: thus, through his holy care for us, he seemed to have earned so momentous an authority in giving instruction.

But what kind of divine mystery the "Word made into a body"* partook of, I couldn't even guess at. I only knew, from the writings that are handed down about him, that because he ate and drank, slept, walked, felt joy, felt gloom, and conversed, his body wasn't fused to your Word unless a human soul and mind were there in him as well.

Everybody who knows that your Word is unchangeable knows this, too; I knew it at this point, to the extent that I could know it, and I had no doubt about it whatsoever. But the fact is, to put parts of the body in motion as an act of will sometimes, but at other times not to move, to feel some feeling at one moment but not at another, to express considered opinions symbolically sometimes but at others to be silent, are characteristic of a soul and mind that can change.

But if what's written about Jesus along these lines is untrue, then everything else risks being a lie, and in those writings there wouldn't remain any salvation through faith for the human race. Since, therefore, these things were written truthfully, I recognized in Christ a full human being, not just a human body, or a body with a consciousness but not a mind, but an actual human

* John 1:14.

being. I thought that he was superior to other human beings not as a mask of the truth, but because he had some sort of great excellence in human character and partook more completely in wisdom.

Alypius, in contrast, thought that members of the universal church believed Jesus was simply God clothed in a body, meaning that in the Anointed there was nothing but God and a body; he reckoned preachers held that there was no human soul or mind in him. But since Alypius was substantially firm in his conviction that the traditional accounts of Jesus show acts characteristic strictly of a living, reasoning created being, his movement toward the actual Christian faith was more sluggish.

Afterward, however, when he recognized that this was a mistake of the heretics following Apollinaris,* he tempered his drink to take part in the joyful feast of universal faith. As for me, I admit it was some time later that I learned how, in the matter of the Word being made flesh, the universal church's truth is split off from Photinus's deception.† No matter: the discrediting of heretics raises to prominence what your church understands and what wholesome teaching contains.‡ It's been useful for there to be heresies, so that creditable people came to be unmistakable among the susceptible.§

26. But at that earlier point, I read the Platonists' books, and after I was prompted by them to look for truth that was beyond the physical, I could gaze on and understand, through the things

---

* A heretical bishop of Laodicea.
† A heretical bishop of Sirmium.
‡ 1 Timothy 1:10, Titus 1:9.
§ 1 Corinthians 11:19. Paul, however, was probably writing of social, political, and ritual "factions" (the Greek word is *haireseis*) rather than differences in theology.

that are made, the unseen things that belong to you.* Though I
was pushed back, I still got a look at what the darkness of my
soul didn't allow me to contemplate. I was certain that you were
infinite, and yet not spread out through places either finite or
infinite; and that you truly existed, being the same, yourself always, with no part or movement making you another being, or
making you exist in a different way; and I was certain that all
other things draw their existence from you†—on the single but
absolutely solid proof that they do exist.

I was at least sure of all that, but I was too weak to enjoy you. I
could rattle everything off as if I had my lessons all done, but
unless I'd sought your path in Christ, our Savior, I would have
been not done but done for. Now, you see, I'd started to want to
look wise—puffed up as I was with what was in fact my punishment. I didn't weep, and worse than that, I was swollen with
self-satisfied scholarship. Where was that thing the scriptures
call love,‡ which builds from a foundation of humility, which is
Jesus Christ?§ When were those philosophical books going to
teach me that?

I believe, though, that you wanted me to have recourse to those
books before I considered your scriptures, so that the way they
made me feel would be imprinted on my memory; and so that
afterward, when I was gentled by your books and my wounds
were handled by your doctoring fingers, I could discern and distinguish the difference between assumptions and testimony;
and between those who know where the journey must lead but

* Romans 1:20.
† Romans 11:36.
‡ 1 Corinthians 8:1–3, 1 Corinthians 13.
§ 1 Corinthians 3:11.

not how to get there, and the actual road that leads not only to glimpsing but to living in the blessed homeland.

If from the first I'd been shaped by your holy writings, and through my intimacy with them you had become sweet to me, and I had stumbled on those philosophical scrolls afterward, they might have torn me away from the solid foundation of reverence; or, alternatively, if I could have maintained the wholesome feeling I'd absorbed, I might have thought that the feeling could be inspired also by the philosophical books, if everybody read them exclusively.

27. Thus, it was with great greed that I grabbed the revered writings of your Spirit, and especially those of the apostle Paul.* The conundrums disappeared from the passages in which at one time he had seemed to contradict himself, and in which the text of his discourse seemed to clash with the testimonies of the law and the prophets.† Those pure verbal expressions now seemed to me to come from a single face, and I learned to thrill to the point of trembling.

I started out, and I discovered that whatever true thing I had read in the philosophical works was stated here along with an appreciation of your grace, your favor. This is to keep anyone who sees from boasting, as if he hadn't been given not only what he sees, but the ability to see as well. (What does he have, after all, that he didn't receive as a gift?‡) This is not only to prompt him to see you, who are always the same,§ but also to have him

---

* The author of a number of books of the New Testament.
† Matthew 5:17, 7:12, Luke 16:16–17.
‡ 1 Corinthians 4:7.
§ Psalms 102:27, quoted in Hebrews 1:12.

healed and able to hold on to you; and the one who can't see from a distance is nonetheless to walk the road by which he can come to you and see you and hold on to you; for though a human being, in keeping with his more inward humanity, delights in God's law, what will he do about the other law, in his body, which is at war with the law of his mind and leads him captive under the law of sin?*

You are just, Master, whereas we have sinned, we have done wrong, we have behaved godlessly, your hand has weighed down on us,† and we have been justly handed over to that primordial sinner, the commander of death,‡ because he won over our will to resemble his own, by which he failed to stand fast in your truth.§

What will a wretched human being do? Who will free him from the body of this death,¶ unless it's your free gift through Jesus Christ our Master, whom you begot as a sharer of your eternity and created at the beginning of your pathways;** in whom a ruler of this world found nothing worthy of death, yet whom he killed?†† The writ by which our life was forfeit was nullified.‡‡

Nothing of this is in those philosophical writings. Those pages don't have the face of this reverence, the tears of confession, your sacrifice, the crushed and broken spirit, the heart worn down to the dust,§§ the rescue of your people, the city to be mar-

---

* Romans 7:22–23.
† Psalms 32:4.
‡ Hebrews 2:14.
§ John 8:44.
¶ Romans 7:24.
** Proverbs 8:22.
†† Luke 23:14–25.
‡‡ Colossians 2:14.
§§ Psalms 51:17.

ried to you,* the earnest money of the Holy Spirit,† the cup of our ransom.‡

No one in those other books sings, "Will my soul not be subject to God? From him comes my salvation. He is indeed my God and my Savior, my protector. I will stand fast from now on."§ No one there hears someone calling, "Come to me, all you who toil." Those books won't stoop to learn from him, because he is gentle and humble at heart.¶ You've hidden these things away from the clever and the shrewd, and unveiled them to little children.**

It's one thing to see from a wooded mountaintop the country of peace, but not to find a way there, and to struggle hopelessly through a trackless wilderness, while blocked and attacked and stalked from all sides by deserters on the run, with their leader the lion and the dragon.†† It's quite another to stay on the road to that country when that road is carefully guarded by the heavenly general, and there are no bandit raids by deserters from the heavenly army. They avoid that road as if it were torture.

All these things became marvelously part of my inmost being when I read the least of your apostles.‡‡ I had contemplated your works and trembled.§§

---

* Revelation 21:2.
† 2 Corinthians 1:22, 5:5.
‡ Matthew 26:39, Luke 22:42.
§ Psalms 62:1–2.
¶ Matthew 11:28–29.
** Matthew 11:25.
†† Psalms 91:13.
‡‡ Paul of Tarsus; 1 Corinthians 15:9.
§§ Habakkuk 3:2.

Book 8

1. My God, let me remember in giving you thanks, and let me testify to your mercies for me. Let your love wash through my bones, and let them say, "Master, who is like you?"* You have broken apart my chains: I will offer up to you a sacrifice of praise.†

I will tell the story of how you broke those chains; let all those who worship you say, when they hear the story, "Praise be to the Master in heaven and on earth; great and wonderful is his name."

Your words had fused into my heart, and on all sides you had set up ramparts.‡ I was sure about eternal life in you, though I had

---

* Exodus 15:11, Psalms 35:10.
† Psalms 116:16–17, quoted in Hebrews 13:15.
‡ Isaiah 29:2.

seen it only in a riddling form, as if in a mirror.* But any doubt
about an imperishable substance—since every other substance
must be derived from it—was removed from me, and I couldn't
wish to be more firmly convinced about you—only more steadfast. But in my life in time, everything was tottering, and my
heart needed the old yeast of yesterday, my worldly yearnings,
cleaned out of it.† Though I was happy with the Way, the Savior
himself, I was still irked at having to squeeze painfully through
its narrow defiles.‡

But you put it into my mind, and in my own view it looked like
a good thing, to go and visit Simplicianus,§ who appeared to me
a good slave of yours, with your favor shining in him. I had even
heard that from his youth, he had lived in absolute dedication to
you. At the period I'm writing of, however, he was an old man,
and from the long years he'd spent in such virtuous zeal, sedu-
lously pursuing a life in you, it seemed that he must be abun-
dantly experienced and thoroughly capable; and that's truly
what he was. I wanted to confide in him about my turmoil so
that he could reveal to me, bringing out the supplies of his
experience,¶ the right way for someone with my disposition to
walk in your path.

2. I saw that the church was full of people going their various
ways, but I was unhappy with what I was doing in the world of

* 1 Corinthians 13:12.
† The Passover celebration requires thorough housecleaning beforehand to remove every trace of forbidden yeast. There is probably a pun on *mundare* ("to clean or purify") and *mundus*, which would here mean the material world.
‡ Matthew 7:13–14.
§ Simplicianus was to be bishop of Milan after Ambrose.
¶ Matthew 13:52.

time, and it was a great burden to me. I was no longer on fire with the avarice that had been usual for me, when the hope for officeholding and money made me willing to endure the quite heavy servitude I've described. Those enticements no longer held any delight for me in comparison to your sweetness and the seemliness of your house, to which I was greatly attached.

But I was still firmly tied up by a woman. The apostle didn't forbid me to marry, although he urged me to do better, quite decidedly wishing for all people to be like himself.* But I was weaker and chose a softer spot to rest in, and in that alone I was thrashing around; but I was drooping and pining everywhere else from the anxieties that sapped me, because in other things that I was reluctant to tolerate, I was, by necessity, adapting to life in a household partnership; and in my commitment to that I was under a binding obligation.

I had heard from the mouth of truth that there are eunuchs who have castrated themselves for the kingdom of heaven, but, well, "whoever can get this life, let him get it."† For sure, all people who lack the knowledge of God are empty-headed, and among the things that *seem* good, they haven't been able to find the one who *is*.‡ I had already climbed above that empty-headedness, and, on the corroborating testimony of the whole of creation, I had found you, our creator and your Word, who is God in your presence, and is the one God along with you—the Word through which you created all things.§

---

* 1 Corinthians 7:1–7.
† Matthew 19:12.
‡ Wisdom of Solomon 13:1.
§ John 1:1–3.

But there's another kind of godless people, who though they recognized God didn't glorify him as God or give him thanks.* I'd fallen in with these people, too, but your right hand caught me up, took me away from there, and set me down where I could regain my strength—because you said to mankind, "Look, reverent dread is wisdom,"† and "Don't wish to seem wise, since those who claimed to be wise became idiotic."‡ I had now discovered the precious pearl, and I needed to sell everything I had to buy it;§ but I held back.

3. Thus I made my way to Simplicianus, who had acted as a father to Ambrose (who was now bishop), leading him to accept God's favor, and Ambrose truly loved him like a father. I told Simplicianus about all my roundabout wanderings, but when I mentioned that I'd read certain books of the Platonists, translated by Victorinus—at one time the city of Rome's rhetorician, who I'd heard had died a Christian—he expressed his pleasure that I hadn't come by the writings of other philosophers, which were full of shams and hoaxes in line with the principles of this immediate world;¶ in the Platonic books, on the other hand, God and his word were worked in by every possible means.

Next, in order to urge me toward the lowliness of Christ, which is hidden from clever people but unveiled to little children,** he gave me an account of Victorinus himself, whom he'd known

* Romans 1:21.
† Job 28:28.
‡ Romans 1:22, probably quoting Proverbs 26:5.
§ Matthew 13:45–46.
¶ Colossians 2:8.
** Matthew 11:25.

very intimately when he was at Rome, and I won't pass over in silence the story he told me about the man, as it's a reason for great praise of your favor, praise to be rendered as testimony to you.

The venerable Victorinus was extremely learned and deeply accomplished in all liberal studies. He had read so many philosophical writings, of which he was a judicious critic, and he was an instructor of so many distinguished senators, that as public recognition for his outstanding teaching, he was actually rewarded with a statue in the Roman forum—the citizens of this world think there's nothing more special.

Up to an advanced age, he was a worshipper of idols and took part in "sacred" rites that were in fact sacrilegious, a disease from which practically the entire Roman nobility was blasted, bloated, and exhaling a stench [ ]:*

> *Abominable gods of all races, like the yapping Anubis,*
> *Who had once against Neptune and Venus and Minerva*
> *Wielded their spears.*

Rome, having conquered these gods, now propitiated them.†

The old man Victorinus had in all those years never stopped defending them with his voice like a terrible thunderclap, but now he didn't blush to become a little child of Christ and a baby fathered by your baptismal font, placing his neck under the

---

* The square brackets represent a *locus desperatus* or "hopeless place" in the (probably corrupt) text; there is a Latin word (*popiliosiam*) no one has managed to interpret convincingly in this context.

† Vergil, *Aeneid*, 8.698–700. The conquest of Egypt in 31 B.C. marked the end of the Roman Republican civil wars and the beginning of a long period of stable Imperial rule, during which several exotic gods came to be worshipped alongside the Roman pantheon.

yoke of lowliness* and subjugating his forehead to be marked with the sign of the shameful cross.†

4. Oh, Master, Master, who bent the sky downward and descended, touched the mountains and they smoked,‡ what were the means by which you worked yourself into Victorinus's heart? According to Simplicianus, this man was reading the holy scriptures and searching every corner of Christian writings with great enthusiasm, and he used to say—not in public, but more or less confidingly, as is characteristic of a close friendship—to Simplicianus, "You know that I'm already a Christian." But the other answered, "I'm not going to believe that, or count you among Christians, unless I see you in Christ's church." Victorinus would laugh, asking, "So it's walls that make Christians?"

This happened often: Victorinus saying that he was already a Christian, Simplicianus responding in the same way, and the joke about the walls being repeated by Victorinus. He was dismayed, of course, at the prospect of offending his friends, who were arrogant worshippers of demons; he thought that from the peak of their self-important folly—as bad as that of Babylon, and as lofty as the cedars of Lebanon before the Master broke them down§—vendettas would come crashing heavily down on him.

---

* Matthew 11:29.
† Galatians 5:11.
‡ Psalms 144:5.
§ Psalms 29:5. The cedars of Lebanon, the highest and sturdiest trees in the region, were used to build Solomon's Temple. Their height is here associated with the imperial Babylonians, who destroyed the Temple in 586 B.C. but were themselves conquered by the Persians shortly afterward.

But in a while, through his reading and his avid assimilation of the means to stand firm, he came to fear that Christ in the presence of the holy angels would deny knowing him if he himself were afraid to acknowledge Christ in the presence of humankind;* he felt he was guilty of a great crime in blushing at the rites of your Word brought low but not blushing at the sacrilegious "sacraments" of shameless demons, rites that he, as the demons' shameless imitator, had accepted as satisfactory. He now was utterly ashamed at his pretentious, trifling mentality and abashed at truth's reality. All of a sudden, and to the complete surprise of Simplicianus (as he himself told me), he said, "Let's go to the church; I want to be a Christian."

Simplicanus was beside himself for joy, and went with him. Victorinus was initiated by the first ceremonies, which began his period of instruction, and not long afterward submitted his name in order to be born again through baptism, to the amazement of Rome and the rejoicing of the church. Arrogant people watched and raged, gnashing their teeth and wasting away.† But as for your slave, God the Master was his hope, and he didn't look back at pretentious trifling and delirious lies.‡

5. At last came the hour for his profession of faith. At Rome, it is usual for those about to be admitted into your favoring grace to memorize this profession in a set form and deliver it from a raised platform before the assembly of your committed followers. Simplicianus said the priests had offered Victorinus the chance to make his profession with less publicity, which was

* Mark 8:38, Luke 12:9.
† Psalms 112:10.
‡ Psalms 40:4.

customary in the case of some people who seemed liable to be frightened, due their modesty. But it was in the sight of the sanctified congregation that Victorinus chose to testify to his salvation.

It wasn't salvation that he'd been teaching in his capacity as rhetorician, but rhetoric had been his public profession. How much less reason for fear must he have had in proclaiming your Word in front of your tame flock? He hadn't, after all, had any anxiety in addressing his own words to mobs who were off their heads.

Thus, when he mounted the platform to make the profession, everyone murmured his name audibly to each other, in a muttered clatter of appreciation drawn from their individual knowledge of him—and who was there who *didn't* know him? From their collective mouths the low sound of common delight resounded: "It's Victorinus, it's Victorinus." Quickly they grew noisy with the thrill of seeing him, and quickly they fell silent with attention, so that they could hear him. And he declared his confidence in the true faith with outstanding confidence, and everyone wished to ravish him in their hearts—and they did that through their passionate love and their rejoicing: those were the hands they used to ravish him.

6. My good God, what happens in a human being to make him rejoice more when a soul he's given up hope for is saved and freed from a greater danger, than if he'd always had hope and the danger had been less? In fact, you also, tenderhearted father, rejoice more in the one who repents than in the ninety-nine righteous who don't need to repent. We listen with great plea-

sure when the lesson is about the jubilation the shepherd feels in his shoulders when he carries home the sheep that's strayed.*

The drachma is returned to your treasury while the neighbors celebrate with the woman who found it.† We weep for the festival joy of your house, when in that house is read the story of your younger son, and how "he was dead, but now he lives again; he was lost, but now he has been found."‡ You certainly rejoice in us and in your angels, made holy by holy love—for you are always the same, and you always know in the same way all those things that don't always exist, and all those that don't always exist in the same way.

7. So what's happening in the soul to make it delight more in beloved things that are obtained or returned than in those it has always possessed? Other things corroborate this, and the whole world is full of evidence shouting "This is how it is." The victorious general celebrates a triumph,§ but he wouldn't have won if he hadn't fought, and his joy in the triumph is proportional to the danger there was in the battle. A storm tosses voyagers and threatens to shipwreck them; all of them are white with the fear of impending death. The sky and sea grow calm, and they're excessively thrilled because they were excessively terrified just now. A loved one is sick, and his pulse gives gloomy news: all the people who long for him to be well are sick along with him in their hearts. But there's a recovery, and though he no longer

---

* Luke 15:3–7.
† Luke 15:8–10, the parable of the lost coin.
‡ In Luke 15:11–32, the parable of the prodigal son.
§ The greatest honor in Roman public life, a military triumph, included a procession with captives and extravagant festivities.

walks with his previous vigor, there's a far more intense joy than before, when he was well and sturdy on his feet.

Human beings obtain their lives' pleasures, as such, in contrast not merely to irritations that rush in unexpectedly and against their will, but also to established and willingly accepted irritations. Eating and drinking has no pleasure in it unless the irritation of being hungry and thirsty comes first. Drunkards gobble up salty snacks to create an irritating, scorching desire that guzzling quenches, causing delight. The custom is not to turn a bride over right away, though she's already promised; this is to prevent her husband from undervaluing her once she's given to him, because he hasn't sighed, as her betrothed, over the delay in possessing her.

8. It's the same for morally shameful and deplorable rejoicing, and for rejoicing that's allowed and lawful, and for friendship of the most genuine integrity—and for the young man who had been dead but then lived again, had been lost but then was found.* Everywhere, greater joy is preceded by greater trouble.

Why is this, God my Master, given that you, in yourself, are eternal joy for yourself; and that certain creatures, gathered around you, always rejoice in you? Why is it that this other part of the universe goes alternately forward and backward, by repulsions and attractions? Or is this simply the measure of these things, and your allotment for them, as from the highest heaven to the lowest place on earth, from the beginning to the end of the ages, from an angel to a tiny worm, from the first movement

* Luke 15:11–32, the parable of the prodigal son.

of material being to the last, you've set in their individual proper places and activated at their individual proper times all kinds of good things and all of your righteous works?

Ah, when I think how high you are in the heights, and how deep in the depths! You never recede, but we struggle to return to you.

9. Come, Master, and act, rouse us and call us back, set us alight and ravish us; blaze for us, grow sweet to us. Let us love you passionately, let us run to you.

But wait—don't many people from a lower region of hellish, blinding darkness than Victorinus had inhabited come back to you and come near to you? Aren't *they* illuminated with the light they take in?* And if they take it in, they take on from you the power to become your sons.†

Yes, but if they're publicly less conspicuous, even those people who do know them rejoice over them less. When many rejoice, the joy is richer in individuals, too, because they ignite and incandesce from one another. Besides, those known to many influence many to seek salvation, and when the well known go in advance, many are going to follow them. Even those who've gone ahead of them are happy, because they're not happy only for these present, individual converts.

But in your tabernacle rich characters must not be welcomed in preference to poor people, or the distinguished in preference to

---

* Psalms 34:5. The modern English wording differs markedly from the Latin.
† John 1:9, 12.

the obscure;* since you, in contrast, chose the weak things of this world so that you could put to shame the strong ones; and you chose the obscure and despised of this world, and you chose the things that don't exist, just as if they did, so that you could do away with the things that exist.†

Nevertheless, that very man, the least of your apostles,‡ through whose tongue you made those words heard, when fighting in your service subdued the high and mighty provincial governor Paulus and sent him under the gentle yoke of your Christ, and made him a mere provincial subject of the Great King; and after that the apostle loved to be called Paul (and not Saul, as before), as a mark of honor for such a great victory.§ Our enemy is more soundly vanquished in the person of someone whom he controls more, and through whom he controls more people. The devil has a firmer hold on the high and mighty by virtue of their prominence, and by virtue of their influence has a hold over more people.

Victorinus's heart, therefore, was reckoned more welcome in that the devil had occupied it as an unconquerable stronghold; and your sons were entitled to revel more extravagantly over Victorinus's tongue, that sizable, sharp weapon with which he had done away with many of them. Our king had tied up the strong man;¶ and the people saw his utensils snatched away from

---

* James 2:1–5.

† Romans 4:17, 1 Corinthians 1:26–28.

‡ Paul of Tarsus, who deprecates himself in this way in 1 Corinthians 15:9.

§ The official was Sergius Paulus, based at Cyprus, who according to Acts 13:7–12 was converted by seeing the miracle of Paul of Tarsus's blinding a local wizard. The story as an explanation for Saul's name change is not biblical, though "also known as Paul" is mentioned for the first time in this passage (verse 9).

¶ Matthew 12:29, in a passage about casting out demons: only through the power of God can a demon, like an able homeowner guarding his goods, be overcome.

him, cleaned, and made suitable to honor you, and useful to the Master for every good work.*

10. After your man Simplicianus told me this story about Victorinus, I was on fire for emulation—and that's of course why he told the story. Afterward, in fact, he added another episode. In the time of the emperor Julian, when there was a law passed banning Christians from teaching literature and public speaking,† Victorinus embraced the law and preferred to abandon the gabbling schoolroom than abandon your Word, through which you make even the tongues of speechless infants eloquent.

To me, he seemed not so much brave as lucky, because he'd found an opportunity of taking time off for you, which was the thing I myself was sighing to do. But I was bound not by anybody else's irons, but by my own iron will. The enemy possessed *my* wanting, and from it he had constructed a chain for me and constricted me in it. Inordinate desire arises from a twisting of the will; and in the course of slavery to this desire, habit forms; and through lack of resistance to this desire, a certain inevitability emerges. With these links, as it were, interconnected (and that's why I've called this a chain), a harsh slavery held me tightly in check.

The new will that had started to exist in me, for worshipping you for no material reward, and *wanting* to enjoy you, God, the only sure pleasure, wasn't yet adequate for overcoming my earlier will, which was reinforced by my long-standing way of life.

* 2 Timothy 2:21. The analogy there is to a household's best tableware. Even outside ritual contexts, the cleanliness of implements that touched food and drink, which had moral implications, was a preoccupation.
† Julian the Apostate (who reigned from 361 to 363) attempted to reestablish traditional paganism and to marginalize Christianity.

Thus my two wills, one old and one new, one of the body and the other of the spirit, clashed with each other* and in their combat were devastating my soul.

11. In this way I understood through actual experience what I had read: how the body's desire is against the Spirit, and the Spirit's desire against the body.† I in fact found myself on both of these sides, but more on the one I approved of in myself than on the one I disapproved of. I was no longer on this latter side to such a great degree, because in large part I was enduring the condition unwillingly rather than creating it willingly.‡

Nevertheless, habit had grown more combative against me, because I'd made a willing journey to where I now didn't want to be. And anyway, who has any right to object when a righteous punishment ensues after his sins? And I no longer had the excuse I was accustomed to, the reason I used to give myself for not yet despising the world and serving you, namely, that my understanding of the truth was unsure: that understanding already *was* sure. It was I myself, still tied down to the earth, who was declining to join your army,§ and my fear of shedding all my heavy gear in order to be ready for action should have been my fear of being hindered by that gear.

12. Thus, as often happens in sleep, I was pleasantly oppressed by the world's weighty load, and my thoughts that reflected on

---

* Ephesians 4:22–24, Colossians 3:9–10.
† Galatians 5:17.
‡ Romans 7:16–17.
§ 2 Timothy 2:3–4.

you* were like the efforts of those who want to wake up but are nevertheless overcome by the depth of their drowsiness and pulled back under.

There's no one who'd like to sleep forever, and everyone with unimpaired judgment prefers being awake, yet a person still generally puts off rousing himself while a heavy sluggishness lingers in his body, and he'd rather grasp at dozing—though by now he disapproves of it—in spite of its being time to get up. In the same way, I was quite convinced that it was preferable to give myself over to your loving care than to give in to my own inordinate desire, but whereas what won out in my mind proved better, the whim was my fetter.

I had no answer when you said to me, "Get up, sleeper, and rise from the dead, and Christ will be your light."† All around me, you demonstrated that what you were saying was true, but though I was proved wrong by the truth, I had no kind of answer at all, except a few slow-witted and slow-waking words: "In a minute," and "Hey, in a minute," and "Let me alone a little while." That "minute" was hardly minute, and that "little while" went on longer and longer.

It did me no good to be delighted with your law, according to the person I was within, when in my own body a different law was at war with my spirit's law and led me off as a captive under the law of sin—the one in my body.‡ The law of sin is the lawless force of habit, by which even the unwilling mind is dragged away and confined—and this is justified in that the mind will-

* Psalms 63:6.
† Ephesians 5:14.
‡ Romans 7:22–23.

ingly fell into the habit. Who was going to set my wretched self free from the body that was death, unless your grace through our Master, Jesus Christ, could do it?*

13. How you set me free from the chains—which held me very tautly—of yearning for sex, and from the slavery of worldly business, I will narrate as testimony to your name, Master, my rescuer, who bought my freedom.

I was going about my usual activities with growing distress, and every day I sighed for you. I did go to your church, as often as I had time off from the business under the weight of which I was groaning.

Alypius was staying with me; he had a break from his work in legal consultation after his third appointment as an assessor, and he was waiting for clients to whom he could sell his advice now, just as I sold my verbal ability—if to any extent that *can* be furnished through teaching.

Nebridius, for his part, had done us a special favor, for the sake of our friendship, by teaching as an assistant to Verecundus, who was very close to all of us. He was a citizen of Milan and a teacher of literature there who'd very urgently requested—in fact, demanded as a privilege of our intimacy—reliable assistance from someone in our group, because he had a pressing need for it. Nebridius wasn't drawn to the work by a desire for material advantages (he could have accomplished more on the basis of his literary knowledge had he wanted to); instead, he was unwilling to reject our entreaty and refuse to do a kind service, as he was a very gracious and tender friend. He carried out

* Romans 7:24–25.

the job, however, with an extremely low profile, so as to avoid becoming known to people of worldly importance; he meant to shun any mental agitation from their company. He wanted to keep his mind free and at leisure for as many hours as possible so that he could seek out whatever was worth reading or listening to concerning wisdom.

14. So then one day (and Nebridius wasn't there—but I don't recall why), a man called Ponticianus came to see Alypius and me at our house. He was a countryman of ours—or at least he was African, and he was serving with great distinction in the emperor's palace. He wanted something or other from us. We sat down and were talking, and by chance on the game table in front of us he noticed a bound book. He picked it up, opened it, and found—quite unexpectedly—that it was the apostle Paul's letters. He'd thought it was one of those books I was being worn down by teaching professionally.

Then he smiled and looked at me with appreciation, surprised to find right away that I'd just been reading this book, and this book only. He was a Christian himself, a committed one, and he often prostrated himself before you, our God, in the church with constant and prolonged prayers.

Once I'd told him that I devoted a great deal of attention to the scriptures, the subject changed to the monk Antony of Egypt, with Ponticianus himself telling us about him. Antony had an outstanding, glorious name among your slaves, but until that very hour, the name was unknown to us. When Ponticianus became aware of this, he lingered over his story and made us well acquainted—not without expressing his amazement at our ignorance—with the great man of whom we were ignorant. We ourselves were stunned when we heard such a recent account—almost from our own generation—of your extremely well attested miracles, performed in the legitimate faith and in the universal church. We were all amazed—the two of us because these were such great miracles, and Ponticianus because we'd never heard of them.

15. Then his talk turned to the flocks in the monasteries, those fertile deserts of the wilderness, with their way of life that's the sweet odor of an offering rising to you. We knew nothing about any of this. There was even a Milan monastery, full of good brothers, outside the city walls, and Ambrose fostered it, but we had no idea.

Ponticianus persisted, talking on, and we paid quiet, close attention. Then he happened to say that at one point he and three of his fellow soldiers in the emperor's service had been—at Trier, I'm pretty sure. While the emperor was occupied by a morning show of the games, the four men went for a walk in the gardens right outside the city walls, and it happened that they were strolling in separate pairs, Ponticianus with one of his colleagues, and the other two also straying off together.

This latter pair, in their wanderings, happened on a hut where there lived some slaves of yours, paupers in the Spirit, the kind to whom the kingdom of heaven belongs,* and there they found a book in which the life of Antony was written up. One of the pair began to read it, and in his fresh amazement he caught the spark: while he was still reading, he conceived a plan to lay hold

* Matthew 5:3.

of a life like Antony's for himself, leaving the world's army and placing himself under you.

The two men were among those called administrators at large.* But at this moment he was filled with holy passion, sober shame, and anger at himself. He turned his eyes to his friend and said to him, "Tell me, please, in all these hard efforts of ours, where do we mean for all the rounds of glad-handing to take us? What are we looking for? In what cause are we on the march? Could there be any greater hope for us in the palace than to become 'friends of the emperor'?† But is there anything about that position that's not breakable and bursting with hazards? How many risks does it take to reach an even bigger risk? And when will that happen? But if I want to, I can become a friend of God‡ this very second." He spoke in the agitation of giving birth to a new life, and returned his eyes to the pages.

He read, and he was altered within, where *you* can see, and his soul stripped off the world, as immediately became plain: while he read, churning his heart's waves of disturbance, he bellowed at intervals, and in his mind there was a division of possibilities and a decision for the better ones. He already belonged to you, and he said to his friend, "I've now torn myself away from that ambition of ours and decided to serve God, and that's my mission from this hour and in this spot. If you don't like the idea of doing as I do, at least don't oppose me."

The other answered that he was sticking to him as a comrade in so great an enlistment for such great pay. And presently both,

* This was an office that, under a general and innocuous title, literally "those doing in the things," combined the functions of courier, auditor, and intelligence gatherer.
† An inner circle of distinguished advisers.
‡ Judith 8:26 (the Latin version has the idea of friendship with God added), James 2:23. (Both quote Genesis 15:6.)

belonging to your force, proceeded to build a redoubt at the reasonable expense of leaving everything they had and following you.*

In the meantime Ponticianus and his companion were walking around elsewhere in the garden, looking for the other two. Now they arrived at the hut, found the men, and told them it was time to come back, because the day was getting late; but these told them what they'd decided and determined to do, and how their inclination had arisen and been strengthened, and they asked their colleagues, if they weren't willing to join in, at least not to make trouble.

The two who heard this weren't altered in the least from the way they'd been before—yet they wept for themselves, as Ponticianus told us, and dutifully expressed good wishes to the others, and asked for their prayers. Dragging their hearts through the dirt, they returned to the palace, while their former colleagues fastened their hearts to heaven and stayed in the hut. Both of them had brides promised to them, and after the girls heard what had happened, they themselves, too, dedicated their virginity to you.

16. This was the story Ponticianus told us. But while he was speaking, you, Master, twisted me back to yourself, catching me from behind,† where I'd taken up a position in my unwillingness to pay any attention to what I was. You stood me firmly in front of my own face, so that I could see how ugly I was, how deformed and dirty, blotched with rashes and sores. I saw, and I

* Matthew 4:19–20 *et passim.*
† Jeremiah 2:27.

shuddered with disgust, but I had nowhere to make off to. If I so much as tried to turn my gaze away from myself, there Ponticianus was, telling that story of his, and you again confronted me with myself and forced me to look, so that I would find my sin and hate it.* I knew it, but I tried to pretend I didn't; I tried to squelch any awareness of it, and to forget.

17. At the time, the more ardent my affection for those wholesome characters I used to hear about, who'd turned themselves entirely over to you for a cure, the more I loathed myself as abominable, compared to them. So many years (maybe eleven) had drained out of my life—and I had drained out with them— since I was eighteen† and read Cicero's *Hortensius*. I'd been roused then by my enthusiasm for wisdom, but I'd put off rejecting earthly happiness and taking the time to track wisdom down. Yet merely hunting for it—let alone finding it—now was more important for me than buried treasure uncovered, or the kingdoms of this world, or a flood of physical pleasures at my beck and call.‡

But I was an excessively wretched young man, clear from the prelude to my youth, when I actually begged you for chastity by saying, "Give me chastity and self-restraint, but don't do it just yet." I was afraid that you'd hear my prayer quickly and quickly cure me of the disease of lust, which I preferred to have satisfied rather than nullified. And I'd also gone down crooked paths in that godless cult of Manichaeism, not from any assurance that its assertions were true, but merely preferring it to other beliefs—

* Psalms 36:2.
† See note on book 2, chapter 4.
‡ A fragment of Cicero's *Hortensius* itself is cited in connection with this sentence.

and these I didn't reverently pursue, but instead attacked like an enemy on the battlefield.

18. I had thought the reason I delayed from day to day the abandonment of any worldly hope in order to follow you was that nothing definite showed up for me by which I could set my course. Yet now the day had come in which I was naked in front of myself and my conscience was scolding me: "Nothing to say for yourself? You used to say—remember?—that it was only because the truth was unclear that you didn't want to throw away your big load of nothing. Well, here the truth is, clear now, and that thing on your back is still weighing you down. Other people are getting wings for shoulders less like those of a slave—and not by getting worn down in a quest like this, or by a decade or more of contemplating this drivel."

Thus I was gnawed away inside, and violently, dreadfully confounded by shame while Ponticianus gave his own account. But then his discourse reached its end, and so did the errand on which he'd come. He went away, and I went away again to what I was.

What did I spare saying against myself? With what assaults of my own judgments did I not scourge my soul, trying to make it follow me in my efforts to go where you led? It fought back, and it talked back, but it had no justification. All its arguments were exhausted and exploded. There was nothing left in my soul but speechless quaking. It had a deathly dread of having the diseased discharge of its habits repressed, the discharge from which it was in fact wasting to death.

19. Then, in the course of that big brawl in the most intimate recesses of my house, the brawl with my soul that I'd violently provoked in our bedroom, my heart—I attacked Alypius. I was as wildly disturbed in my face as in my mind, and I yelled, "What's happening to us? What's this? What have you heard about it? Uneducated people are rising up and seizing heaven,* and here we are with all our heartless learning, wallowing in flesh and blood! Because those people have gone ahead of us, are we ashamed to be their followers? If we're ashamed of nothing else, aren't we ashamed that we're *not* their followers?"

I said some stuff like that, but then my brain fever sent me tearing away from him, and he stared after me in stunned silence. These weren't in fact normal noises coming out of me. And more than the words I was issuing, my forehead, my cheeks, the shade my skin had turned, and my tone of voice spoke my mind.

There was a small garden belonging to the place we were staying in, a garden we were enjoying as we did the entire house: our host, the owner, wasn't living there at the time. The uproar in my heart drove me out there, where no one would get in the way of this flaming lawsuit with myself that I was pursuing, insisting on a result—and you knew what that result would be, but I didn't: I was only wholesomely off my head and dying so that I could live, aware of how evil I was but unaware of how good I would be in a little while.

I made off into the garden, with Alypius close behind. Though he was with me there, I still had my privacy. If he hadn't been there, he would have been abandoning me in that extreme dis-

* Matthew 11:12.

tress, and when would he ever have done a thing like that? We found a place to sit as far as possible from the house. I was groaning noisily in spirit,* aggrieved with a devastating grievance because I wasn't coming into an accord and covenant with you, my God—an accord and covenant that all my bones were shouting that I should come into and were praising to the skies.

But the journey there couldn't be by ships or chariots or on foot—yet the journey wasn't even as far as I had come from the house to this spot where we were sitting. The act not only of making my way onward, but of coming clear to the end, consisted of nothing but to want to make my way—but that meant wanting powerfully and soundly, instead of rolling to this side and that side and throwing to the floor a will that was half-impaired, with part of it rising and part of it toppling as it wrestled against me.

20. At last, with my hesitation boiling over, I made all those physical movements that people sometimes want to make but can't, whether it's because they're missing the actual parts of the body at issue, or because these parts are bound up in chains or enervated by disease or immobilized in some other way. If I tore out my hair or struck my forehead or joined my fists together and hugged a knee to my chest, I did it because I *wanted* to do it; *but* I could have wanted to do it but not done it, if parts of my body hadn't obeyed me by moving.

This means that, as to all those things I physically did, the will and the ability were not identical. But I *didn't* do what I was re-

* John 11:33.

solving incomparably more passionately to do—yet I could have done *that* the moment I wanted to, because the moment I wanted to, I would have *wanted* without any qualification. In that respect, the ability *is* the will, and to want and to do are one and the same. Yet this wasn't coming about for me, and my body more easily obeyed the flimsiest whim of my soul (with the result that parts of my body moved at any inclination of mine) than my soul would begin to obey itself for the purpose of achieving its own great act of will, strictly out of free will.

21. Where does this bizarre phenomenon come from? Let your mercy light my way, and I'll inquire, in case by any chance the lurking punishments inflicted on mankind and the shadowy griefs of the sons of Adam might by any chance be able to give me an answer.

So—where does this bizarre phenomenon come from? And how? The mind commands the body, and there's instant obedience. The mind commands itself, and there's resistance. The mind commands the hand to move, and there's such a great readiness that a person can hardly tell the order from the servile compliance. But the mind is the mind, and the hand is part of the body. The mind commands the mind to be willing, and the mind isn't a different thing from itself—yet it doesn't become willing. Where does this bizarre phenomenon come from?

And I want to know how the following happens: the mind gives itself an order to want something—which is not an order it could give unless it wanted to—and yet it doesn't do what it orders. The answer is that it doesn't wholly will the act, and so doesn't wholly order it. It gives an order only to the same extent that it wills what it's ordering, and what it's ordering fails to come about to the same extent that it *doesn't* will it, since the will orders that there *be* a will—not different from itself, but exactly the same.

This means that it's not the full will doing the ordering, and so the will isn't the same as what it commands. If it were the full will, it wouldn't be ordering itself into existence, because it would already exist. It follows that to be willing in part and in part unwilling isn't a bizarre phenomenon but a sickness of the mind, because the mind, being top-heavy with habit, doesn't stand up wholly straight in the truth. For this reason, there are two wills, because neither of them is complete, and what's present in the one is missing from the other.

22. Let these "two wills" vanish into nothingness from before your face, God, just as those vacuously chattering debauchers of the mind vanish into nothingness.* When they weigh matters up, they notice that there are two wills, and on this basis they claim that there are two natures, one good and the other bad, belonging to two minds. In actual fact, they themselves are bad in holding that bad opinion, but the very same people will be good if they hold true opinions and agree to the truths they hear.

Then your apostle Paul can say to them, "Once you were darkness, but now you are light in the Master."† They want to become light not in the Master but in themselves, and they think

---

* Psalms 68:2, Titus 1:10.
† Ephesians 5:8.

that their soul's nature is the same as God; by this means they become thicker darkness, since their grisly insolence makes them withdraw farther from you, even though you're the true light that lights every person coming into this world.* All of you, pay attention to what you're saying and blush for shame; draw near to him and be filled with light—then your faces won't be blushing.†

I myself, when I was weighing whether to serve God my Master (as I had decided to do long before), I was the person who wanted that and the person who didn't want that: it was simply me. I didn't fully want it or fully not want it. Thus I was inwardly at war and being laid waste by myself; yet this devastation was happening against my will. Nevertheless, this didn't characterize a mind as a thing apart; rather, it showed the punishment of my own mind. That meant it was no longer myself producing that punishment: the sin living in me‡ did that. And this punishment was for a sin committed by a freer choice, as I was a son of Adam.§

23. If as many opposing natures as wills were withstanding each other, there will of course not be two but many. If someone were weighing whether to go to a gathering of the Manichaeans or to the theater, those guys would be shouting, "There they are, two natures, one that's good and leads here, and another that's bad and leads back there. Otherwise, what would be the source

* John 1:9.
† Psalms 34:5.
‡ Romans 7:17, 20.
§ This passage is informed by Augustine's idiosyncratic theory of original sin: the first sin in the Garden of Eden was committed with maximal free will to choose the good, and once it was committed, it deprived the rest of humankind of the same range of choice.

of that hesitation between impulses counteracting each other?" I, however, call both those impulses bad, the one that leads to the Manichaeans and the one that leads back to the theater again, whereas they don't believe that the one leading to them is anything but good.

So what if one of our church members were weighing up— were storm-tossed on two impulses wrangling back and forth between themselves, that is—whether to go to the theater or to our church? Wouldn't the Manichaeans, too, be bobbing violently up and down, in their case with doubt about how to explain this? Either they're going to admit, against their will, that it's a good impulse that takes a person to our church—the way people go there and remain engaged after being initiated into its sacraments—or they're going to think that two evil minds are clashing in a single person, so that what they're used to saying about one mind being good and the other evil will prove untrue; or they'll turn to the truth and not deny that when anyone's weighing alternatives, his single soul is merely hurled around on waves of divergent wills.

24. So they'd better not say any longer, when they perceive two wills opposing each other in a single person, that two opposite minds made of two opposite substances and with two opposite origins are contending—good on the one side, and bad on the other. It's you, truthful God, who repudiate these people, prove them wrong, and find them at fault.

Take, for example, a *pair* of evil impulses: someone's deliberating whether to do away with a person by poisoning or stabbing him; or whether to seize one plot or another of land he has no right to (in a situation where he can't seize both); or whether to spend extravagantly on sensual enjoyments or hoard his money stingily; or whether to go to the games or the theater, when there's a show at both places on the same day. I can even add a third option for occupying the time: whether to rob someone's home, if the chance arises; and I can add a fourth as well: whether to commit adultery, if an opportunity simultaneously presents itself for that. If all these possibilities arise together, and they're all equally desirable but can't all be pursued at once, they tear apart the consciousness with four mutually opposing impulses or even more—however large the supply of alluring activities. Nevertheless, the Manichaeans aren't accustomed to saying that there's such a great mob of divergent *substances* in human beings.

The same goes for good impulses. Say I ask the Manichaeans whether it would be a good thing to revel in reading the apostle Paul; or to have a sober celebration of psalm singing; or to discuss the Gospels. They'd answer about each option, "That would be good." So what if they're all equally attractive at the very same time? Aren't these incompatible impulses spreadeagling the human heart, as long as we ponder which possibility to pounce on? They're all good, yet they're all contending with one another until one is chosen as the direction for a single, unified will, which was split into many parts before this.

Thus, even while eternity offers a higher thrill, the pleasure of what is good in this world of time maintains its lower grip; it's the same soul, wanting one thing or the other, but neither with the whole will, and that's why the soul is pulled to pieces with harsh distress while it puts first what it knows is the truth, but still doesn't put away what it knows congenially.

25. So I was sick and suffering horrendously, accusing myself more fiercely (or excessively more fiercely) than usual and turning and churning in my chain until the last tiny trace of it still holding me could be entirely torn off; but for now it held me nevertheless. And within my secret self you stood over me, Master, with your cruel mercy, stepping up the lashing of terror and shame, so that I wouldn't stop trying. If I did stop, that single tiny, wispy chain that remained wouldn't be broken; instead, its soundness would be renewed, and it would bind me more sturdily.

I was saying to myself inwardly, "Okay, right now, I'm letting it happen, right now I'm letting it happen." Even as I spoke I was already starting to enter into the resolve. I was already—almost—acting, and yet I *wasn't* acting. However, I didn't fall back into my former state, but was standing firm, right on the edge, and catching my breath. And once again I tried, and I was a little closer to being there, and then a little closer still, and I was almost—almost—touching and grasping it; but I *wasn't* there, and I *wasn't* touching and grasping it.

I was hanging back from dying to death and living for life. For me, what was worse was stronger, because it was deeply inculcated, than what was better, because I wasn't habituated to the latter. The nearer to me that moment moved at which I was to become something different, the more it struck terror into my heart. But it didn't strike me back or turn me to the side; it just left me dangling there.

26. Time wasting and empty-headedness in their ultimate, exalted forms*—those age-old friends of mine—held me back.
They tugged underhandedly at the cloak that was my flesh, and
murmured in undertones to me, "Are you really going to show
us the door?"

They said to me, "The moment you do that, and for all time, we
won't be any further company for you." They said, "From that
moment, you won't be allowed to do such and such, ever again,
for eternity." What they reminded me of, which I've just called
"such and such"—what they mentioned, may your mercy spare
your slave's soul from it! What muck they called to my mind,
what a lot of degradation!

Far less than half of me was now listening to them, because they
weren't, so to speak, forthrightly meeting me face-to-face and
telling me I was wrong, but more or less muttering behind my
back and making sneaky potshots to try to get me to look back
at them as I was walking away. But they did manage to slow me
down, as I hesitated to tear myself away from them, shake them
off me, and leap across to where I was being called. My ruth-
lessly impinging habits kept asking me, "Do you imagine you
can make it without those guys?"

27. But at the moment they were saying this to me with utter luke-
warmth, there appeared from the direction where I'd turned my
face, but trembled to traverse, Self-Restraint in her pure decorum.

She was calm, and not lax in her lightheartedness. She honor-
ably sweet-talked me, telling me to come and not delay, and she

---

* The Latin wording replicates the repeated phrase in Ecclesiastes traditionally translated
as "vanitiy of vanities."

extended reverent arms to lift me up and embrace me. She already held whole flocks of people who could teach me by example: no end of boys and girls were there, and many people in early adulthood—but every age was represented, including serious-minded widows and elderly virgins, and among all these people, Self-Restraint was anything but barren: she was a fruitful mother whose sons were joys begotten from you, Master, her lawful husband.

She laughed at me, but it was encouraging laughter, suggesting the question "You won't be able to do what all these mere males—and females!—have done? Do you really think they achieved it through themselves, and not through God, their Master? Their Master and God gave me to them. Why are you trying to stand on your own—so that you fail to stand? Throw yourself forward onto him! Don't be afraid. He won't back away and let you fall. Fling yourself forward and don't worry about it! He'll catch you, he'll take you up under his care and heal you."

I blushed like fire, because I was still hearing the muttering of my frivolities; I kept delaying and was up in the air. Again Self-Restraint seemed to speak: "Deafen yourself to those dirty parts of your body that live on this earth, so that they're killed off.* They tell you stories of delights, but the law of the Master your God has more about delights to tell you."†

This dispute going on in my heart was nothing other than myself versus myself. Alypius, meanwhile, remained immovably at my side, waiting in silence to see how this strange upset of mine would turn out.

* Colossians 3:5.
† Echoes the Latin version of Psalms 119:85.

28. But when this profound pondering drew up all my misery from the bottom of the mysterious abyss and heaped it up where my heart would see it, there arose a tremendous tempest bringing a colossal downfall of tears. So that I could pour it all out, and the words that went with it, I got up from beside Alypius (as solitude appeared to me more suitable for the business of weeping), and I went off on my own to a distance great enough that even his innocuous presence couldn't weigh on me. That's the condition I was in at the time, and he could tell. I'd said something, I believe, in which the tone of my voice was clearly already pregnant with weeping, and with those words I was up and gone; so he stayed where we'd been sitting, in a mood beyond shock.

Hardly knowing where I was or what I was doing, I sprawled under a fig tree and gave my tears free rein. Rivers of them burst out of my eyes—an acceptable sacrifice for you*—and I spoke to you at length, not in these exact words, but in this general sense: "But you, Master—how long? How long, Master, before your anger reaches its end?† Don't cling to the memory of our old wrongdoings."‡ I felt I was in the grip of these. With abandon, I uttered pitiful words: "How long, how long will it be 'Tomorrow! No, the *next* tomorrow!'? Why not *now*? Why can't *this* hour be the end of the disgusting state I'm in?"

* Psalms 51:17.
† Psalms 79:5. The likely meaning of the Hebrew verse is "How long, Lord? Will you be angry forever?" As the Latin sentence is punctuated in the O'Donnell text of the *Confessions* (which indicates how the modern editor thought Augustine meant it in quoting the Latin scripture faithfully), it is difficult to construe; but "How long, O Lord, will you be angry forever?" (which is a standard translation) seems unworkable.
‡ Psalms 79:8. The Hebrew seems to read differently: "Don't remember to *our* disadvantage the wrongdoings of our ancestors."

29. I was saying these things and weeping, with agonizing anguish in my heart,* and then I heard a voice from the household next door, the voice of someone—a little boy or girl, I don't know which—incessantly and insistently chanting, "Pick it up! Read it! Pick it up! Read it!"

Immediately, my mood changed, and I started considering, with great concentration, whether children were accustomed to chanting something like that in any kind of game. I couldn't remember that I'd heard anything like it anywhere. I got control over the onslaught of my tears and got up, construing the chant as a straightforward divine command to open a book and read the chapter I first found there. I had heard that Antony had been admonished by a reading of the Gospel that he had walked in on by chance; what was being read seemed to be speaking to him personally: "Go, sell everything you have and give it to the poor, and you will have treasure in heaven; and come, follow me."† Moved by this omen, he turned to you in no time.

Excited, I returned to the spot where Alypius was sitting: I'd put down a book of the apostle Paul's letters there when I got up. I grabbed it and opened it, and I read in silence the passage on which my eyes first fell: "Don't clothe yourself in raucous dinner parties and drunkenness, not in the immorality of sleeping around, not in feuds and competition; but clothe yourself in the Master, Jesus Christ, and do not make provision for the body in its inordinate desires."‡

I didn't want to read further, and there was no need. The instant I finished this sentence, my heart was virtually flooded with a

* Psalms 51:17.
† Matthew 19:21.
‡ Romans 13:13–14.

light of relief and certitude, and all the darkness of my hesitation scattered away.

30. Then I put my finger or some other placeholder in the book, closed it, and with a calm expression on my face told Alypius what had happened. And he, for his part, told me what was happening in himself (which I didn't know about). He asked to see what I had read. I showed him, but he looked beyond the sentence I had read; I wasn't aware what followed. It turned out to be "But accept in faith the one who is weak."* He thought it referred to himself, and he disclosed that to me. He was encouraged by instruction of this kind, and without any disturbed dilatoriness he joined me in a good resolve and plan—which was very suitable to his own way of life, far different from and very much better than mine from far back.

Then we went indoors to my mother, and told her: she was overjoyed. We told her how it had happened; she was thrilled and exultant and blessed you, who in your power do more than we ask for or understand.† She saw that you had granted her so much more, in me, than she had been used to asking for in her wretched, tearful groaning. You had turned me to you, so that I would pursue neither a wife nor any other hope in this world, but would stand on that measuring rod of faith, as in the vision you had given her so many years before.‡ You had turned her mourning into a joy§ much more fertile than she had wished for, and much more precious and pure than she had sought from grandchildren of my body.

* Romans 14:1.
† Ephesians 3:20.
‡ See above, book 3, chapters 19–20.
§ Psalms 30:11.

BOOK 9

1. Master, I am your slave, I am your slave and the son of your female slave. But you have torn my chains apart; I will offer up a sacrifice, the praise of you.* Let my heart and my tongue praise you, and let all my bones say, "Master, who is like you?"† Let them say it, and you, answer me and say to my soul, "I am your rescue."‡

But who am *I*, and what sort of person? What evil has been absent from the things I've done? And if not from the things I've done, then from the things I've said? And if not from the things I've said, then from my inclinations?

---

* Psalms 116:16–17.
† Exodus 15:11, Psalms 35:10.
‡ Psalms 35:3.

Yet you, God, are good and compassionate. With your right hand, you explored the depths of my death, and from the floor of my heart you drained out the sea of rot. But the whole of what brought this about was that I stopped wanting what *I* had been wanting, and instead wanted what *you* wanted.*

But where was your right hand in that stretch of time so weighed down with its years? From what deep, what deepest, hidden place was my free choice in an instant called out—the choice to place my neck under your yoke, and my shoulders under your light load,† the load that was yours, Jesus Christ, my helper, who bought me out of slavery?‡

How delectably it happened, all of a sudden: all of those inane delectations weren't there any longer; I'd been terrified of losing them, but now I was delighted to turn them loose. You, my true, my highest sweetness, threw that nonsense out of me—threw it out and entered in its place; sweeter than any pleasure, though not felt in the body and the blood; brighter than any light, but more inward than any intimate retreat; loftier than any achievement that wins recognition—but those with a lofty self-regard can't know this.

Now my mind was free from the gnawing anguish around advancing myself toward everything I itched for, and acquiring it, and wallowing in it, and scraping off the scabs. I prattled to you, my glory, my riches, my rescue, my Master and God.

* Matthew 26:39, Mark 14:36.
† Matthew 11:30.
‡ Psalms 19:14.

2. So I decided, within your sight—not to tear off in an uproarious manner, but to gently withdraw my tongue's services from
those hawkers' fairs of chatter. I was no longer going to let
boys—who rehearse not your law, not your peace, but crazed
lying and wars in the forum—buy out of my mouth the weap-
ons to use in their lunacy. Conveniently, there were very few
days left before the vintage-season vacation, and I chose to endure those days and remove myself with all the proper formali-
ties. Then, my freedom being purchased by you, I would never
again return to the auction block.

My plan was thus witnessed by you, but not by any human beings except those in our intimate circle. We had agreed not to
let the plan flow out promiscuously in public—although, in
fact, as we now climbed upward through the valley of wailing*
and sang a Song of Steps,† you had already given us sharp arrows and burning coals of devastation to use against the cunning tongue.‡ This offers confutation under the pretext of good
counsel, and it can consume a person like food, and in the same
way, through "loving" it.

3. You, in contrast, had shot up our heart with your devotion,
and we carried around with us your words like arrows impaling
our guts. The examples of your slaves, whom you changed from
black to white and from dead to living, stuffed full the pouch of
our pondering, burned there, and reduced our heavy sluggish-

---

* Psalms 84:6. Standard modern English versions are irreconcilable.
† This is the Latin translation of the heading to certain psalms (such as the one Augustine
is about to quote); some standard English translations have "A Song of Ascents." The image
prevailing in Latin seems to be that of a step-by-step climb; the Hebrew may refer instead
to the "ascent" of sacrificial smoke to heaven.
‡ Psalms 120:2–4.

ness to ashes, so that we wouldn't slope down into the bottom of the abyss. In fact, your words set us powerfully alight, so that every blast of opposition from a cunning tongue could only blow us into a fiercer blaze, rather than snuff us out.

Notwithstanding all that, because of your name, which you've made holy throughout the world,* our fervent wish and resolution would still find people to praise it. We bore this in mind, and so it would have seemed to us like bragging if we didn't wait for the time of the vacation—which was so close—but before that left a career that was a public trust, on display to the whole population. In that case, everybody would be riveted on what I was doing; they would be scrutinizing how near at hand the first day of the vintage holiday was that I nevertheless wanted to get the jump on; there would, consequently, be a great deal of comment to the effect that I was eager to look like a mover and shaker. What would have been the point of that for me, to have all that imputed and disputed about my intention, and to have the good that we'd obtained so irreverently traduced?†

4. Besides that, during this very summer my excessive scholastic toil started to get the better of my lungs, which now had actual trouble drawing breath; the pain in my chest gave evidence that they were damaged, and they balked at giving louder and more drawn-out speeches. At first, this was a source of distress, suggesting that I would be practically forced to lay down for good the load of teaching I had on me—granted that treatment and recovery were possibilities—or at least take a break.

* Ezekiel 36:23.
† Romans 14:16.

But once there arose and solidified in me a will to do nothing and simply see that you are the Master,* then—and you know this, my God—I found myself thrilled that here in reserve was an honest excuse to mollify people's bad feeling about my choice: for the sake of their freeborn children, you see, they didn't want me ever to have my freedom.

Thrilled, then, by this, I endured that stretch of time; it was twenty days, maybe—I'm not sure. Anyway, I endured it with a strong will; the greed had retreated that habitually carried its share of teaching's heavy business; in staying on for a while I would have been crushed flat had not patience taken greed's place.

Perhaps someone or other among your slaves, who are my brothers, might say I sinned in remaining this long: being wholeheartedly bound to serve you as a soldier, I shouldn't have allowed myself to sit even an hour in the prestigious, comfortable chair of falsehood.† And I wouldn't argue the point. But you, Master, with your endless mercies: Didn't you take this sin, too, along with others that were downright revolting and deathly, and forgive it and let it go in the holy waters?

5. Verecundus was growing thin with fretful envy of our great blessing. Because of his chains, which clung so closely to him, he saw himself being abandoned by our group. He was not yet a Christian, whereas his wife was a committed one—but she herself was a more constricting shackle than the others keeping him back from the journey on which we'd set out. He kept saying that he didn't want to be a Christian in any other way than

---

* Psalms 46:10.
† See Psalms 1:1. The *cathedra* is a special armchair, sometimes associated with teaching.

the one that was impossible.* Nevertheless, he kindly offered us hospitality for as long as we wanted to stay.

You'll repay him, Master, in the resurrection of the righteous;† in fact, you already gave him that portion at the time. In our absence (because we were at Rome‡) he was seized with a physical illness and during it became a committed Christian before sojourning out of this life. In this way, you had pity not only on him but on us: in thinking of his sympathy toward us, which showed him to be someone far out of the common herd, his friends didn't have the torture of overwhelming grief because we couldn't count him among *your* herd.

Thanks be to you, our God! We are yours; your encouragements and your comforts make this known. You are faithful in your promises; you render to Verecundus, in exchange for his rural estate at Cassiciacum where we rested up in you after the heat of worldly life, the pleasant landscape of your eternally green garden, your paradise.§ You have sent away his earthly sins on the mountain of Cassiciacum's choice cheese, your mountain, a fertile mountain.¶

6. At that earlier time (as I was saying), Verecundus was tormented, whereas Nebridius shared my joy. He also, when not

---

* I.e., he wished to be celibate, the spiritually advantageous state (1 Corinthians 7:1, 8), but for Christians, marriage was considered binding, and they were specifically instructed not to leave their spouses after converting (1 Corinthians 7:12–14).
† Luke 14:14.
‡ Before the departure of the group for Africa.
§ When the word is taken in itself, without context, there is no difference between the Latin *paradisus*, the garden, and *paradisus*, paradise; here, in the context of Verecundus's rural estate and his reward in paradise for its use, both translations at once are appropriate.
¶ The Old Latin version of the Psalms 68:16 contains a word that suggests coagulated milk, and "Cassiciacum" suggests the Latin word for cheese. There is probably a play on the theme of "a land flowing with milk and honey," as in Exodus 3:8.

yet a Christian, had fallen into that ditch of irredeemably deadly wrongheadedness, Manichaeism,* so that he believed the living body of your son, who is the truth, to be imaginary. He now emerged from that ditch in an interim condition, not yet dyed† with any of your church's rites, yet tirelessly aflame in investigating the truth. Not long after our own turning and my rebirth through your baptism, and when Nebridius became a committed member of the universal church himself. You set him free from his body. He was slaving for you in faultless chastity and self-restraint in Africa among his own people, and had made his entire household Christian.

Now he lives in Abraham's bosom‡—whatever's meant by the word "bosom"; my Nebridius, my sweet friend, but your adoptive son, who was your freedman, lives there. What other place could there be for a soul like that? He lives there, in the place he asked so many questions about—asked me, a joke of a person who didn't know a thing about it.

Now he doesn't put his ear to my lips; instead, he puts his lips of the spirit to your spring, and he drinks all he can hold, wisdom in proportion to his thirst for it, in an ecstasy without end. And I don't think he gets so drunk that he forgets about me—since you, Master, whom he's guzzling, remember us.

So that was how we were. We comforted Verecundus in his dejection, and our friendship was preserved in spite of my momentous turning. We urged him toward a religious commitment suitable to the condition in which he found himself, married

---

* The biblical reference may be to the blind leading the blind, so that they both fall into a ditch: Matthew 15:14 and Luke 6:39; but Psalms 7:15 may instead or also have been the source.

† The Greek from which our word for "baptize" comes could also mean "dye."

‡ Luke 16:22.

life. Nebridius, on the other hand, we were waiting for, anticipating the time when he would come along and join us. He was within very near reach of it, and he was just about to do it, when my last days of teaching finally rounded their full course.

They did seem long and numerous to me, in my passionate longing for leisurely freedom in which to sing out of my innermost being: "To you my heart spoke, 'I have sought your face; your face, Master, I will seek.'"*

7. Now the day came when, by what I actually did, I would be set free from my career as a teacher of rhetoric; in what I thought, I was already free. And it was done: you rescued my tongue from that activity from which you'd already rescued my heart, and in my rejoicing I blessed you and set out for the country house with everyone who belonged to me.

The writing I did there—it did in fact now serve you, but still panted with classroom pretension—taking a breather, if you will. This is witnessed by the books I wrote, both the ones argued out among the people with me, and those argued out with myself alone in your presence. The things I discussed with Nebridius, who wasn't there, my letters witness.

But when would I ever have enough time to go over all your great blessings of that time? That's particularly because I'm rushing onward toward other, greater blessings in my account here. But my recollection does call me back; it grows sweet to me, Master, to testify to the inward goads you used to tame me thoroughly; to testify to the way you leveled me out, bringing the mountains and hills of my thinking down to lowliness,

---

* Psalms 27:8.

straightening my twisted ways and smoothing the rough spots;* and to testify how you subdued Alypius as well, my heart's brother, to the name of your only begotten son, our Master and Savior Jesus Christ, a name he at first snubbed—he didn't want it in our writings. He wanted these to smell like the high cedars of the Greek philosophical schools, which the Master has now broken to pieces,† rather than like your church's healthy herbs, effective against snake venom.

8. The words I poured out to you, my God, when I read the Psalms of David, those faithful songs, the sounds of godliness that shut out the spirit that's full of itself! I was then unschooled in true passion for you. I was a candidate for baptism, on vacation in a rural estate along with my fellow candidate Alypius. My mother clung closely to us, with a woman's demeanor, a man's loyalty, an old woman's assurance, a mother's love, and a Christian's devotion.

But what words I poured out to you as I read those psalms! And how I caught the spark from them and kindled in you and burned to read them out, if only I could, to the entire earth to denounce swollen-headed humanity! But they *are* sung throughout the earth, and there's no one who can hide from your burning heat.‡

With what savage, biting acrimony I raged against the Manichaeans; but then I would turn around and pity them, because they didn't know those rites, those medicines, and were manically set against the remedy that could have healed them. I

* Isaiah 40:4, quoted in Luke 3:4–5.
† The metaphor is three-dimensional: the cedars of Lebanon (representing previously foreign wealth) were cut to build Solomon's Temple (see Isaiah 10:34); the loftiness of Greek learning was brought low to serve the Christian church.
‡ Psalms 19:6.

wished they could be somewhere nearby at this time and, without my knowing it, could get a good look at my face and hear my words as I read the fourth psalm in the leisure you had given me: "When I called, the God of my righteousness listened to me; I was trapped, and you released me. Have pity, Master: hear and grant my prayer."*

I wanted them to hear—without any awareness on my part whether they were hearing or not—what that psalm made out of me. Then they couldn't think it was because of them that I said what I said when I read those words. And in reality, I wouldn't have said those things—or wouldn't have said them in the same way—if I had perceived those people hearing or seeing me; and if I did say those things, those people still wouldn't have acknowledged how it was inside me, and in my own sight—that intimate feeling in my soul.

9. I shuddered with fear, and in the same instant I came to a boil through hoping and exulting in your mercy, Father.† All of these realizations manifested in my words and my tears when I read how your good Spirit, turning to us, says to us, "Sons of men, how long will your hearts be heavy? Why this dutiful affection for inanity and this quest for falsehood?"‡ *I* had had a dutiful affection for inanity and had conducted a quest for falsehood.

But you, Master, had already exalted your holy one,§ raising him from the dead, placing him at your right hand, from where on high he could send his promise,¶ the protector, the Spirit of

* Psalms 4:1.
† Psalms 31:7.
‡ Psalms 4:2.
§ Psalms 4:3.
¶ Luke 24:49.

truth.* He had already sent him, but I didn't know. He had already sent him, because he was exalted, rising again from the dead and ascending into heaven. But before that, the Spirit was not given, because Jesus was not yet glorified.† But the prophet cries, "How long will your hearts be heavy? Why do you love inanity and seek falsehood? You are to know that the Master has exalted his holy one."‡ The prophet cries, "How long?" and "You are to know"—yet for all that time, not knowing, I loved inanity and sought falsehood.

That's why I now heard and trembled, since those words are addressed to those who are the way I remembered being. In illusions that I had taken for the truth were inanity and falsehood.

I cried out again and again, vehemently, loudly, in the pain of my recollection. I wish that the people with an enduring affection for inanity and a continuing quest for falsehood could have heard me. Perhaps they would have been shaken up and vomited out that way of thinking, and you would listen to them when they shouted to you,§ because it was a real death in the body that the one who intercedes for us died for us.¶

10. I used to read, "Be angry, all of you, but do not sin."** How strongly I was moved by that, my God! I had now learned to be

* John 14:16–17. The idea of the "advocate," "comforter," "helper," or "paraclete" has been important in forming the theology of the Holy Spirit, the third person of the Trinity or Three in One divinity, but the reference in the original text of the Gospel is somewhat unclear.
† John 7:39. This is another of the very few Gospel references (see immediately previous note) that have supported the idea of the Holy Spirit.
‡ Psalms 4:2–3.
§ Psalms 4:3.
¶ Romans 8:34.
** Psalms 4:4.

angry with myself about my past sins, so that in the future I wouldn't sin. And it was a just anger, since it was no alien element, belonging to a race of darkness, that had sinned with respect to me. That's what the Manichaeans say: they *don't* spend their anger on themselves, which means that they lay up treasure for themselves, which is anger in the day of anger, the day of your just judgment's unveiling.*

No longer were my goods outside me, nor were they sought with my body's eyes under this paltry sun. Those who want their joys on the outside melt easily away and flow out into the visible things that depend on time†—such people only slobber, with famished thinking, over the mere images of such things.

If only they got exhausted with starvation and said, "Who will show us good things?"‡ Then we would say, and they would hear, "The light of your countenance is set on us like a seal, Master."§ We ourselves aren't the light that illuminates every human being;¶ rather, we are illuminated by you, so that we who were once darkness may be light in you.**

If only they could see the internal eternal! Because I'd tasted it, I gnashed my teeth, as I couldn't show it to them if they brought me their heart contained in their eyes, turned outward from you, and said, "Who will show us good things?"

There in my bed where I was angry with myself,†† where I'd been stung deeply, where I'd made an offering, slaughtering my old

---

* Romans 2:5.
† 2 Corinthians 4:18.
‡ Psalms 4:6.
§ Ibid.
¶ John 1:9.
** Ephesians 5:8.
†† Psalms 4:4. The standard English version is somewhat different.

way of life* and hoping in you with the rudimentary contemplation of my renewal;† there you had started to grow sweet to me
and had given me gladness in my heart.‡ And I shouted out,
reading these things outwardly and recognizing them inwardly.
I didn't want to be enriched with multiples of earthly goods,
gulping down time and gulped down by it in turn, when I had,
in the oneness of eternity, other grain and wine and oil.§

11. And at the next line, I shouted, with a shout that echoed deep
in my heart, "Oh, in peace! Oh, toward what is, in itself!" Oh,
what did the author say? "I will fall asleep and take my rest"¶—
because who will struggle against us, when that saying written
in the scriptures is realized: "Death is swallowed up in victory"?**

And you are very much what is, in itself, you who do not change,
and in you is the rest that forgets all kinds of work, since there
is no other with you, and you did not constitute me to acquire
many other things that aren't you; rather, you established me in
a oneness of hope.

I read, and I burned, but I didn't find what I should do for the
deaf and the dead, from whom I had come. I had been a plague,
a bitter, yapping dog, and blind toward the writings dunked in
heavenly honey and lit up with your light.†† I was shriveling away
in my upset about the scripture's enemies.

---

* Ephesians 4:22, Colossians 3:9.
† Romans 12:2.
‡ Psalms 4:7.
§ Ibid.
¶ Psalms 4:8.
** 1 Corinthians 15:54, which quotes Isaiah 25:8.
†† Psalms 119:103, 105.

12. When will I retrieve all the memories of those days away from work? But I haven't forgotten, and I won't pass over in silence, the cut of your whip and the amazing speed of your mercy.

At that time, you tortured me with toothache, and when it grew so severe that I couldn't speak, it occurred to my heart to tell all my friends and relatives who were there with me to pray for me to you, the God of every kind of rescue and well-being.

I wrote this request on a wax tablet and gave it to them to read. As soon as we knelt in devoted and humble pleading, the pain vanished. But what pain? Or if it was real, how did it disappear?

I was terrified, my Master, my God, I admit: from my earliest childhood, I'd never felt anything like it. Yet your will was conveyed to the depths of my being. Rejoicing in faith, I praised your name, but that faith didn't allow me any feeling of safety in regard to my past sins, which had not yet been forgiven through my baptism.

13. Once the vintage vacation was over, I gave notice to the citizens of Milan that they would need to get another peddler of palaver for their students, because I'd chosen instead to serve you, and was not up to the profession I'd been in, because of my difficulty in breathing and my chest pain.

I communicated by letter to Ambrose your bishop, that godly gentleman, my past mistakes and my present earnest desire, and asked him to advise me which in particular of your books I should read to make myself readier and more suited for receiving such a great gift and grace as baptism. He told me to read the prophet Isaiah; I believe it was because he's more open than the other prophets in proclaiming in advance the good news and the calling of the gentiles. But I didn't understand the first part I read, and thinking it was all like that, I put off taking the book up again until I was more practiced in the Master's way of speaking.

14. Next, when the proper time came for me to put my name down for baptism, we left the countryside and returned to Milan. Alypius decided to be born again in you together with me. He was already clothed in a lowliness* suitable to your rites, and was a very stalwart vanquisher of his body, to the point where he used to walk barefoot on the icy Italian ground, quite an unusual venture. We made the boy Adeodatus† our partner in baptism as well. He was born from me in the flesh, from my sin.

You made him well. He was around fourteen years old then,‡ and his mind excelled those of many serious and learned men. I testify to you about your own gifts, my Master and God, maker of all things and very powerful in shaping what is misshapen in us. I had no part in the boy except for my wrongdoing. As for his being brought up by us in your moral training, you, and no other, breathed into us the will to do that. I testify to you about your own gifts.

There's a book of mine entitled *The Teacher,* and in it my son himself converses with me. You know that all of his own thoughts are represented there through the character of my partner in

---

* Colossians 3:12.
† "Given by God."
‡ See note to book 2, chapter 4.

this dialogue, when he was fifteen years old.* In other respects as well, I found him to be astonishing: his mind actually made me shudder. But who except you is the craftsman behind such wonders? You quickly removed his life from the earth, and I'm more carefree in the memory of him, not fearing any danger to him in boyhood or in youth—fearing nothing at all for that person.

We included him in your gift of baptism, so that being born again with us, he was the same spiritual age, to be raised in your training. So then we were baptized, and anxiety over our past life vanished. In those days of marvelous sweetness, I couldn't get enough of contemplating the profundity of your plan for the salvation of humankind. How often I wept at your hymns and canticles, when I was painfully shaken by the voices of your melodious church! Those voices ran into my ears, and the truth dripped down into my heart. Reverent feeling then seethed up, and my tears flowed, and it was well with me when I cried this way.

15. The church at Milan had quite recently started a comforting and encouraging practice of this sort, with the brothers very enthusiastically harmonizing in their voices and their hearts. It had been—I think—just a year before, or not much longer, when Justina, the mother of Valentinianus the boy emperor, persecuted your man Ambrose on account of her heresy, as the Arians had led her astray.†

---

* See note to book 2, chapter 4.

† Arianism held that Christ was a created being, and so not coeternal and one with God the Father. As a heresy favored in outlying yet strategic parts of the Roman Empire, Arianism (adopted by the Goths and Vandals) was subject to serial reemergence partly because struggles for control of the Empire had always been military and were increasingly tribal. The episode referred to here was a power struggle between Ambrose and the regent empress, resulting in a mass sit-in to prevent the military from enforcing her decree that churches be handed over to the Arians.

The God-fearing common people camped out, on guard in the churches, prepared to die along with Ambrose, your slave. There my mother, your slave woman, took the leading role in all the anxious effort, including keeping watch all night, and survived on prayers. We ourselves, still chilly and untouched by the heat of your Spirit, were nonetheless stirred up amid the shocked and agitated city.

At the time, the custom was established of singing in the Eastern mode, to keep the people from wasting away under the unmitigated stress of their despondency. Since then—to this day, in fact—they've maintained the custom, and many—or nearly all—of your other flocks elsewhere in the world imitate it.

16. At the time, to that same bishop you revealed through a vision the place the bodies of your martyrs Protasius and Gervasius‡ were hidden. You had laid them up and preserved them all those years in your secluded treasure house so that at the right moment you could bring them out to repress the frenzy—of a mere woman, but a royal woman.

The bodies, divulged and excavated, were moved, with the honor worthy of them, to Ambrose's church building. Then not only were those tormented by evil spirits healed, with the actual demons admitting openly what they were doing; there was also a certain man, a citizen quite conspicuous in that commonwealth, who had been blind for a number of years, and when he asked, and was told, why the people were in a commotion of rejoicing, he jumped up and demanded that his guide take him

‡ These twins are the patron saints of Milan; their historical dates and the other facts are quite uncertain, but they would have lived centuries before Ambrose and Augustine.

to the bodies. Once led there, he gained access that enabled him to touch with his handkerchief the bier of your holy ones whose death is precious in your sight.* After that, he applied the handkerchief to his eyes, and they were instantly opened.

The story spread quickly in all directions; then praise of you was feverish and far-flashing; then the mind of that hostile woman, though not brought to wholesome belief, was nonetheless restrained from persecutorial lunacy.

Thanks be to you, my God! But from where, and to where, have you led my recollections, so that I testify to you of these things as well? They are momentous, but in my forgetfulness I was going to omit them.

However, at that time of crisis, when the smell of your perfumes was so enticing, we didn't run after you.† That's why, later, I wept more amid the songs of your praise. For so long, I had sighed for you, and now I caught my breath—to the extent that there's fresh air in this house of straw that is our body in this life.‡

17. You, who inspire the harmonious sharing of a house,§ joined to our company Evodius, a young man from our hometown.¶ He'd been enlisted as an Imperial adminstrator at large**—but then turned to you before we did. He was baptized, abandoned worldly campaigning, and equipped himself to serve in your

---

* Psalms 116:15.
† Song of Solomon 1:3–4.
‡ Psalms 103:15, Isaiah 40:6.
§ Psalms 68:6, 133:1.
¶ This traveling companion later became a fellow bishop and important correspondent of Augustine.
** See book 8, chapter 15, and the note on this position.

army. We were now together, with the intention of living together according to our holy resolve.

Seeking the kind of place that could make better use of us in our servitude to you, we were returning to Africa as a group. But when we were staying in the port city of Ostia, at the mouth of the Tiber River, my mother expired.

I pass over a great deal in my account, as I'm in a great hurry. Accept my testimony and my expressions of thanks, my God, even though about countless things they remain silent. But I'm not going to pass over anything my soul gives birth to about her, your servant, who gave birth to me both in the flesh, into the light of this world in time; and in her heart, so that I could be born into eternal light.

I won't speak of her gifts, but instead of your gifts to her, as she didn't make herself or bring herself up. You created her (and neither her father nor her mother knew what she, coming from them, would be like), and she was trained in the fear of you by the disciplining switch of your Christ,* the guidance of your only son, in a committed Christian household, a sound part of your church's body.

As for her moral instruction, she was accustomed edifyingly to praise, to a greater extent than her mother's care, the care of a certain broken-down old serving woman, who had carried her father around as a baby, in the way little ones are commonly carried on the backs of girls just a tad bigger than they themselves are. In grateful remembrance of this, and because of her age and her outstandingly virtuous life, she was held in quite substantial respect by her owners in this Christian household.

* Psalms 23:4.

This was how she came actually to have charge of her owners' daughters, a charge she carried out conscientiously. When the need arose, she would control them with a fiercely God-fearing harshness, and in teaching them she showed a sober foresight. Except for those hours when they were nourished with extreme restraint at their parents' table, she wouldn't as much as let them drink water, even if they were desperately thirsty. This was her way of heading off a bad habit, and she gave this wholesome explanation, too: "Now you drink water, as you have no access to wine. But when you've entered your husbands' houses and become owners of the storehouses and wine cellars, water will look like dirt to you—yet the habit of guzzling's going to win out." With this methodical way of teaching, and with this authority for commanding, she reined in the greed natural at that susceptible age and actually shaped the girls' thirst to a decent proportion, so that they already wouldn't even have liked to do what it wasn't proper to do.

18. Yet there did creep in—as your servant told me, her son—yes, there did creep in a weakness for wine. In the usual way for a soberly behaved girl, she was dispatched by her parents to dispense wine from the cask. After she lowered the cup down through the opening at the top, but before she poured the unmixed wine into the bottle, she'd take a little sip with just the edge of her lips—she couldn't do more without recoiling at the taste.

It wasn't any desire to get tipsy that made her do this, but only a degree of high spirits ordinarily spurting out of bounds and overflowing in the young; playful impulses that bubble over in childish minds and are usually repressed by the weightiness of

older people. In any case, she added small portions day by day to that first small portion—since the person who pays no attention to small matters gradually falls away*—and fell into the routine of greedily gulping down small but nearly full cups of undiluted wine.

Where was the shrewd old woman then, with her fierce prohibition? Was anything going to win out over this lurking disease, Master, if your doctoring didn't keep watch over us? With her father and mother and other minders gone, you were present, you who created us, who call us, and who also do something good to save our souls through people put in charge of us. What did you do then, my God? How did you care for her? How did you heal her? Didn't you draw a hard, sharp insult out of another soul, like a surgical knife from among the things you'd provided for in secret, and with one stroke slice off that festering flesh?

A slave girl, with whom she used to go to the cask, was having a dispute with her young mistress in the ordinary way, and when they were all alone, hurled a name-calling accusation as a vicious taunt: "You're a little lush!" Stung to the heart, the other took a look at her own ugly behavior and instantly rejected and shed it.

In parallel to flattering friends bending us out of shape, enemies calling us to account generally straighten us out. But you pay them their due, not for the correction you achieve merely by their unwitting agency, but for the hurt they intend. That slave girl was angry, and keen to send her young mistress into a rage, not to heal her. That's why she insulted her in secret—either

* Sirach 19:1.

because this just happened to be the time and place of this dispute; or because she was afraid of her own liability, having waited so long to point out this wrongdoing.

But you, Master, who govern beings both in heaven and on earth, wrench into your uses the waters hurtling through the depths, so that the ages flow onward in an orderly turmoil. Even from the sickness of one soul, you've on occasion been able to heal another; so let no one, to whom this becomes apparent, give credit to his own power if a word of his straightens out someone he wants straightened out.

19. Raised in this chaste and sober way, and made submissive to her parents by you rather than to you by her parents, when she reached a ripe age for marriage and was turned over to a man, she served him as her master and took a lot of trouble with him for you. She spoke to him of you through her behavior,* by which you made her beautiful and an object of reverent love and admiration to him. Accordingly, she endured the insults of her husband's infidelities and never quarreled with him over that situation. She simply awaited your mercy for him, when belief in you would render him chaste.†

In addition to his infidelities, he could be as exceptionally hot-tempered as he was kind at other times. But she knew not to stand up to her husband—not physically, of course, but also not even verbally—when he was angry. At a point when she saw that his mood had changed and he was calm and approachable, then she would give him an account of what she'd done, if it

* 1 Peter 3:1–2.
† 1 John 3:3.

happened that he'd become worked up without adequate deliberation.

The upshot was a great contrast. Many other married ladies whose husbands were gentler carried around the marks of blows, which did discredit to their faces. In conversation among friends they would make cases against their husbands' conduct, but she would make one against their mouthiness. By way of a joke she would give them serious advice, to the effect that from the moment they had heard what's called the marriage contract read, they should have classed it as the bill of sale by which they became slaves; hence, they should keep in mind their place in life, in which it was wrong to act insolently toward their owners.*

They knew that she bore with a ferocious spouse, and they were amazed that there had never been a word about Patricius beating his wife, or any other evidence to show he'd done so, or that the two of them had ever fallen out in a domestic squabble for even a single day. When in intimate conversation they asked why this was, she explained her established method, which I've described above. Those who listened to her and tried it commended her; those who didn't listen were ground down and tormented.

20. Her mother-in-law was at first provoked against her by the whispers of evil-minded female slaves, but my mother got the better of her through sheer subservience, holding out with fortitude and gentleness. In the end, the mother-in-law, on her

* Technically, this form of marriage (prevailing at the time) placed the wife in the legal position of a daughter to her husband; a daughter's life was differentiated from a slave's more by security and prestige than by freedom. See the footnote to chapter 22 below.

own, turned these servants in to her son as mischievously chattering go-betweens who had upset the domestic peace between her and her daughter-in-law, and she demanded that there be punishment.

Once he'd heard this, he yielded to his mother's wishes, cultivated good order in his household, and provided for harmony in his family: he disciplined with a whipping the slaves who'd been brought to his attention as troublemakers—the whipping being the choice of the woman who'd brought them there. She vouched that any one of them should, in the future, expect the same reward at her own hands for saying anything bad about her daughter-in-law, with a view to getting in good with herself. None of them dared any longer, and they all lived in exemplary mutual goodwill and affability.

21. You granted also to your good chattel—in whose womb you, my God, my mercy, created me—this considerable gift: between souls in disagreement and discord, she offered herself (whenever she could) as an outstanding peacemaker. Though she'd heard many extremely bitter statements from either party about the other—the sort of thing that the bloated backup of an unassimilated dissension tends to send retching up, when acid confabs let undigested resentments of an enemy who's not there belch out at a friend who is—she never revealed across the divide anything she'd heard except what had the power to reconcile.

This talent she was given might seem to me to be a small matter if I didn't, unhappily, know countless hordes (suffering from some ghastly plague spreading into incredibly wide prevalence) who not only divulge statements *of* enraged enemies *to* enraged enemies, but even add statements that weren't made.

In contrast, in the eyes of a humane human being, the absolute minimum obligation would be not to stir up other people's feuds, and not to make them worse by bad-mouthing; that is, if he doesn't actually put effort into calming them by speaking soothingly. My mother was the kind of person to do that, and her lessons were from you, her teacher at the core of her being, in the school of her heart.

22. Lastly, she even won for you her husband, at the end of his life on earth; and now that he was committed to you, she didn't beat her breast over the infidelities she'd put up with when he wasn't yet committed.

She behaved like an actual slave of your other slaves. Whoever among them knew her praised and loved and honored you by praising much that was in her, because he could sense your presence in her heart, according to the testimony of her blameless conduct.*

She had been the wife of only one husband her whole life, she had done her duty by her parents in return for her upbringing, she had run her house devotedly, and she had given witness by good works. She had tended to her sons, suffering birth pangs,† so to speak, again every time she saw them leave the true path and move away from you.

---

* See Galatians 5:22–26.
† Galatians 4:19.

Last of all—and by your gift, Master, you allow me to speak—
she cared for all your slaves who, before she went to sleep in
you, had attained the favor of your baptism and lived in unity
because of you. She cared for us as if she'd given birth to us all,
and she served us as if she'd been born from all of us.*

23. Then the day on which she was to leave this life was looming
(the day you knew about but we didn't). It happened—because,
I'm convinced, you arranged for it through your mysterious
means—that she and I were standing alone together in the
house where we were staying, leaning on the sill of a window
that looked out to the garden. This was in Ostia on the Tiber
River, and we had withdrawn from the crowds after the hardships of a long land journey, and were resting up for our voyage.

Therefore we conversed together alone, very gently. Forgetting
the past as we stretched out to what was before us,† we sought,
in the presence of truth in person, which is you,‡ what the eternal life to come would be like for the holy ones, the life that
neither the eye has seen nor the ear heard, nor has it entered
into the human heart.§ But with that mind's mouth, we panted
for the streams of your spring on high, the spring of life, which
is where you are.¶ We wanted, as far as we could sustain them, to
have a few drops of that water splattered on us so that we could
contemplate such a mighty thing.

---

* Augustine's praise of Monica is consonant with Roman family law: children as their fathers' property shared certain conditions of slaves, such as the expectation of absolute
obedience.
† Philippians 3:13.
‡ John 14:6, 2 Peter 1:12.
§ 1 Corinthians 2:9, quoting Isaiah 64:4.
¶ Psalms 36:9.

24. Our conversation was brought clear to the conclusion that any degree of delight in the physical senses, under however much material light, didn't seem worthy of comparison or even of mention in relation to the bliss of that eternal life.

Stretching upward with a more fiery emotion toward that thing itself, we walked around, step by step, all material objects and even the sky, from which the sun and moon and stars shine over the earth. And still we climbed up inwardly as we thought of and spoke of and wondered at your works. We came into our own minds and climbed up beyond them, to reach the land of abundance that never fails, where you graze Israel forever on the fodder* that is truth.

In that place is found the life that is wisdom, through which all these things around us are made,† both those that were and those that will be. Wisdom itself is not made, but is what it has always been, and it will always be that. In actual fact, there is no "was" or "will be" in it, but only being, since it is eternal: "to have been" and "to be about to be" are not eternal. But while we were speaking and panting for it, with a thrust that required all the heart's strength, we brushed against it slightly.

Then we sighed and left behind us, adhering up there, the first fruits of the Spirit,‡ and made our way back down to the racket of our mouths, where a word has both a beginning and an ending. What in that is like your Word, which is our Master, remaining forever in himself without growing old, but making all things new?§

---

* Ezekiel 34:14, Psalms 80:1.
† Proverbs 8:23–31.
‡ Romans 8:23.
§ Wisdom of Solomon 7:27.

25. So we said, "Suppose a person were to experience that the uproar of the body becomes silent, and the illusions of the land and water and air become silent, and the whole extent of the sky is silent, and his very soul is silent to itself and passes beyond itself by not thinking of itself; and dreams and revelations full of images are silent, along with every kind of language and signal; and suppose that a person were to experience the absolute silence of whatever comes into being through passing away.

"If anyone hears, all these things do say, 'We did not make ourselves, but rather the one who remains into eternity made us.'* But suppose that once they've said this, they fall silent. They've made the ear prick up toward him who made them, but he himself alone speaks, not through them but through himself, so that we hear his Word, not through the body's tongue or through the voice of an angel, or through a thundering cloud or a riddling analogy,† but instead we hear himself, whom we love in the form of these things, but we hear him without these things— just as, right now, we're stretching forward‡ and with quick thought reaching the eternal wisdom that remains above all things.

"Suppose this were to be prolonged, and other visions of a far lesser kind were to be taken away, and this single vision would ravish and draw in and hide in its inward joys the one who sees it, so that life without end would be like this moment of understanding was, for which we've sighed. Isn't this what's described by 'Enter into the joy of your Master'?§ And when will this

* Psalms 100:3.
† Numbers 12:8, 1 Corinthians 13:12.
‡ Philippians 3:13.
§ Matthew 25:21.

happen? Is it when 'we all rise again, but we will not all be changed'?"*

26. I said things like this, though not in that kind of style or in those exact words. But you, Master, do know that on that day, when we were saying things like this, and when this material world, with all its delights, was looking tawdry to us as we talked, she then said, "My son, as far as I'm concerned, nothing in this life delights me. What I should do after this, and why I'm here, I have no idea. My hopes for this earthly existence are reduced to nothing. There was one thing for the sake of which I wanted to remain somewhat longer in this life, and that was to see you a universal Christian before I died. My God has fulfilled this wish—filled it to overflowing, as I actually see that you're his slave, scorning earthly happiness. So what am I doing here?"

27. I don't have a clear memory of my answer to her. In any case, it was barely five days later (or it couldn't have been much more than that) that she took to her bed with a fever. Some days into her illness, she had a blackout and for a short while lost any awareness of her surroundings. We rushed to her; but soon she regained consciousness and looked at my brother and me as we stood by her bed, and she said in a confused manner, "Where was I?"

Next, as, stunned with grief, we gazed at her, she said, "You're burying your mother here." I was silent and controlled my cry-

---

* 1 Corinthians 15:51; the standard English version reads "We will not all die, but we will all be changed."

ing; my brother, in contrast, said something about hoping she would pass away not in a foreign country but in her own native one, as this would be happier for her.

When she heard this, her face became strained, and she scolded him with her eyes for that level of thinking. Then she turned her gaze to me and said, "Just listen to what he's saying."

Soon afterward she said to both of us, "Bury this body anywhere you like. Don't be troubled or perturbed about it. All that I'm asking of you is to remember me at the altar of the Master, wherever you are." When she'd made this sentiment clear to us, with the words she could manage, she fell silent and was tormented by her intensifying illness.

28. Unseen God, as I thought about your gifts, which you plant in the hearts of your faithful followers, and from which marvelous harvests come forth, I was thrilled and gave thanks to you: I recalled what I knew about the considerable anxiety that had continually agitated her about the tomb she'd provided and prepared for herself next to her husband's corpse. They'd had a very harmonious home together, and so—since the human mind can't fully take in heavenly things—she'd wanted this also to be added to that happiness and remembered among humankind: that after her sojourn across the seas, it had been granted that mingled earth should cover over the earthy matter of both married partners' bodies.

I didn't know at what point this frivolity began—through the abundance of your goodness—to disappear from her heart. But I rejoiced, amazed at the change revealed in the way I've just described. (However, in our conversation at the window, when she said, "What am I doing here now?" it didn't in fact appear that she longed to die in her native country.)

I also heard afterward that one day after we'd arrived in Ostia, she was talking in motherly confidence with certain friends of mine, when I wasn't there, about disdain for the world and the blessing of death. They were astounded at the woman's manly fortitude (which you gave her), and asked whether she didn't dread leaving her body behind so far away from her own commonwealth, and she said, "Nothing is far from God, and there's no reason to fear that when the world ends, he won't know the place from which to resurrect me."

On the eighth day of her illness, when she was fifty-five years old and I was thirty-two,* that reverent and devoted soul was set free of its body.

29. I closed her eyes, and into my heart there flowed together an immense sorrowfulness, which seeped through into tears; at the same time, on a forceful command from my mind, my eyes choked back the spring that was gushing out of them, to the point that it dried up; the fight this required put me in a really awful state.

But then, at the moment when she breathed her last, the boy Adeodatus shouted in grief, was hushed by all of us, and became quiet. In parallel, something childish, even in me, which was slipping into weeping, was hushed by a youthful voice in my heart and held its peace.

* See the note on book 2, chapter 4.

We didn't think that these funeral observances should include tearful lamentations and groans. This is the common and customary way to bewail some wretched state people are in when they die, or to suggest that they've been annihilated in every sense. She, however, died neither wretchedly nor completely. We held this to be a fact, by deducing it confidently from the proofs her conduct offered, and from her faith that was no counterfeit.*

30. So what caused me such severe inward pain, unless it was the fresh wound from the sudden tearing asunder of our close day-by-day relationship, a very pleasant and loving one? I was in fact gratified by her avowals: at the actual crisis of her illness, she had sweet things to say to me while I waited on her. She called me a dutiful son, and with a burst of fond feeling recalled that from my mouth she'd never heard a hard, insulting expression launched at her.

And yet, my God who made us, how could the respect I paid her possibly be compared to her servitude to me? Because I was abandoned by such a tremendous solace, my soul had a deep wound, and my life was as good as dismembered—because her life and mine had become one.

31. When we'd prevented the boy from weeping any more, Evodius snatched up a book containing the Psalms and began to sing one of them, and the whole household sang it back to him: "I will sing to you of mercy and judgment, Master."†

* 1 Timothy 1:5.
† Psalms 101:1.

When they heard what was going on, many brothers and devout women gathered. While those whose duty this was prepared the body in the customary way,* I (in a part of the house where I could properly do this) discoursed suitably to the occasion with people who didn't think I should be left alone, and with this salve of truth I softened the torment that you knew about. They didn't know about it, and though they listened closely to me, they thought I wasn't experiencing any pain.

But for your ears, in a place when none of them could hear me, I scolded myself for the weakness of my emotional state and restrained the onrush of my sorrow. For a little while, it submitted to me; then it was carried forward on its own violent momentum again—not to the point where I burst into tears, or even to where my expression changed; but I was aware of what I held down in my heart. I was keenly displeased that these things, humankind experiences, had so much power over me, experiences that have to happen, according to the due order of things and the lot assigned to us; I felt the sting of a second kind of suffering and was afflicted with a double sadness.

32. So now, when the corpse was carried out, we went with it, and we returned without tears. At the tomb itself, when her body was set down before being lowered in (as this is customary in that locale), we poured out prayers to you as we offered, on her behalf, the sacrifice—the price in body and blood paid for us;† but even during those prayers I didn't cry.

---

* I.e., the women washed it and dressed it in grave clothes.
† The Communion or Eucharist of bread and wine.

No, that whole day I mourned intensely but secretly, and in mental turmoil I asked you—to the extent I could manage to ask—to heal my grief. You wouldn't, and I think it was because you were committing to my memory, by this single piece of evidence (if nothing else), the chain that every established relationship constitutes, even on a mind that's no longer feeding on false discourse.

I even decided to go bathe, because I'd heard that the bathhouse got its name in Latin (*balneum*) because the Greeks named it *balaneion*, for its power to cast (*ballein*) grief (*ania*) out of the mind. So, true father of bereaved children,* here I am, testifying to your mercy about this, too: I bathed, and I was exactly the same as before I'd bathed: the bitterness of sorrow hadn't been sweated out of my heart.

But then I slept and woke up, and I found my suffering in substantial measure relieved. Alone in my bed there, I remembered your Ambrose's lines, which don't lie: you are

> *God, the maker of all things*
> *Ruler of the skies, who clothes*
> *The day in lovely light,*
> *The night in welcome sleep:*
> *Then rest can ease the body and send*
> *It back to useful work,*
> *And relieve exhausted minds,*
> *And free from mourning the distressed.*

33. Then, gradually, I recovered my previous sense of your slave, and her devout life in you, and her—in godly ways—sweet and indulgent behavior toward us, which I was abruptly deprived of.

* Psalms 68:5.

I felt like crying in your sight, about her and for her, about my-self and for myself. I let go the tears I'd held in, letting them run out as freely as they wanted, and out of them I made a bed for my heart. And it rested on those tears, since there only you could hear, and not any human being who would put some con-temptuous meaning on my wailing.

But now, Master, I testify to you in writing: whoever wants to can read it, and let him put whatever meaning he wants on it. If he finds it a sin that I wept for my mother for just a fraction of an hour, the mother who for the time being was dead in my eyes, but who'd spent many years crying for me to live in your eyes—then he shouldn't laugh at me but rather, if he has ample love, he should weep for my sins himself in the presence of you, the father of all us brothers of your Christ.

34. For my part, though, now that my heart is healed of that wound—which provided plenty of evidence to convict me of emotions with a mere physical basis—I pour out to you, our God, tears of a much different kind for your servant. They flow from a spirit assaulted by assessing the perils of every soul that dies in Adam.

My mother was given life in Christ* even before her release from her body, and she lived in such a way that her faith and her conduct still give rise to praise of your name. Notwithstanding all that, I wouldn't dare to say that from the time when she was born again through your baptism,† no word against your com-mands came out of her mouth.‡ But it was said by your son, who

---

* 1 Corinthians 15:22, Ephesians 2:5.
† Titus 3:5.
‡ Matthew 12:36–37.

is the truth, "If anyone says to his brother, 'You fool!' he will be liable for punishment by hell's fire."*

Woe to even an exemplary human life, if you conduct its trial in the absence of your mercy!† Because in fact you don't inquire aggressively into wrongdoings, we faithfully hope for some kind of place in your home. But if anybody recites to you a list of his genuine good deeds, what's he giving you if not a list of your good gifts to him? If only human beings would recognize themselves as human beings, and if only the person who boasts would boast of the Master!‡

35. God of my heart, whom I praise and in whom I live, hear me: setting aside for a little while her good works—for which I give joyful thanks to you—I now entreat you to forgive my mother's sins. Hear me, I ask in the name of our wounds' cure, who hung on a piece of wood§ and intercedes for us as he sits at your right hand.¶

I know my mother busied herself with works of mercy, and that from her heart she forgave her debtors their debts.** You, too, forgive *her* debts, if she incurred any more in all those years after the cleansing water of her salvation. Forgive them, Master, forgive them, I beg you, and don't put her on trial.†† May your mercy triumph over judgment, since your words are true and you promised mercy to the merciful.‡‡ Merciful is what you

* Matthew 5:22.
† Psalms 130:3.
‡ 1 Corinthians 1:31, 2 Corinthians 10:17.
§ Galatians 3:13. Standard English versions carry the sense of "curse," not "remedy."
¶ Romans 8:34.
** From the Lord's Prayer, the version in Matthew 6:9–13.
†† Psalms 143:2.
‡‡ Matthew 5:7, James 2:13.

granted them the chance to be, as it's you who "will have mercy on whomever you have mercy, and will be tenderhearted to whomever you're tenderhearted."*

36. I believe you already did what I ask, but sanction these free-will offerings from my mouth, Master.† As the day on which she would be released loomed close,‡ she didn't contemplate having her corpse expensively clothed or preserved with perfumes; she didn't covet a choice monument, or care about a tomb in her homeland. She didn't give us any instructions of that kind, but merely asked that we remember her at your altar. And she had served there without missing a single day; and she knew that your sacrificial victim was shared out from there—the victim who erased the record of the debt we owed.§

That sacrifice triumphed over the enemy who counted up our wrongdoings and looked for whatever he could charge us with—but he found nothing in the one through whom we won out. Who will pour his blameless blood back into him?¶ Who will pay him back the price for which he bought us and take us away from him?

To the rite of that price paid for us, your slave bound her soul with a chain of faith. No one could tear her away from your sheltering care; neither the lion nor the dragon could get in her way, not by confronting her with force and not by ambushing her.** She won't plead that she owes nothing—that way, she

* Exodus 33:19, quoted in Romans 9:15.
† Psalms 119:108.
‡ 2 Timothy 4:6.
§ Colossians 2:14. The central rite of the early church was the Lord's Supper.
¶ Matthew 27:4.
** See Psalms 91:13.

would lose the case and be turned over to the wily plaintiff; instead, she will plead that her debts were paid by the one nobody can pay back: he wasn't a debtor, yet he settled our debts.*

37. So let her be at peace with her husband, before whom and after whom she was married to no man. She slaved for him, bestowing a harvest on you through her endurance,† so that she acquired him for you as an additional profit.

And breathe your Spirit, my Master, my God, breathe it into your slaves—my brothers—your sons—my masters, those whom I serve with my heart and my voice and my writing: so that all of them who read my account remember at your altar your servant Monica, along with Patricius, who was at one time her husband. Through their bodies they brought me into this life—how, I don't know.‡

Let them remember with dutiful fondness those who were my parents in this passing light; and let them remember my brothers under you, our father, in our mother the universal church; and let them remember my fellow citizens in the everlasting Jerusalem, for which your people in their sojourn here on earth sigh from the time they go out until they return. Thus, through my testimonies here, more richly than through my prayers alone, what she asked of me at the end will be granted to her, in the form of many people's prayers.

---

* The analogy is to the poor borrowing money with their own persons as collateral, which makes them liable to slavery if they default.

† Luke 8:15.

‡ I.e., he had no fixed opinion on when or how the soul enters into the conceived child, a matter of contemporary (and continuing) debate.

Book 10

1. Let me know you, you whose business is to know me, to vouch for me and plead for me*—let me know you the way I am known.† You, my soul's excellent mate, go into her and make her suitable to yourself, so that you can keep her and possess her without her having a spot or wrinkle.‡ This is my hope: it is why I speak,§ and in this hope I feel whatever wholesome joy I feel.

As for all the rest that belongs to this life, the more mourning for it there is, the less mourning it deserves; and those things that are commonly the occasion for less mourning should be

---

* God is the "knower," a pun on the word for a guarantor of identity or an attorney.
† 1 Corinthians 13:12, Galatians 4:9.
‡ Ephesians 5:27.
§ 2 Corinthians 4:13, quoting Psalms 116:10.

mourned for proportionately more. Look here: you have prized the truth,* and whoever performs the truth comes to the light.† I want to perform the truth in my own heart, in your presence, in my testimony; and with my pen I want to perform it before many witnesses.

2. But to you, Master, to whose eyes the deep chasm of the human conscience is laid bare,‡ what would be hidden in me, even if I didn't wish to confess it to you? I could hide you away from myself, but not myself from you.

As it is, because my groans are witness to my displeasure with myself, *you* are radiant, you please me and rouse my love and desire. I turn scarlet at the very thought of myself, and I throw myself away and choose you instead; I can please neither myself nor you unless it comes from you.

I am caught in the act then, Master, of being whoever I am. I have already said how I profit from confessing to you. I don't confess with physical words, with the sounds of speech, but with the words of my soul and the shouts of my thoughts—which are familiar to your ear.

When I am evil, testifying to you is no different from being at odds with myself; but when I am good, testifying to you is no different from not taking any credit for this goodness, because you, Master, bless a righteous person—but first you set his wickedness right.§

* Psalms 51:6.
† John 3:21.
‡ Sirach 42:18–20, Hebrews 4:13.
§ Romans 4:5.

Therefore my testimony, my God, given an audience before you, is inaudible and yet audible: there is no racket, only silence, but my feelings yell out loud. And I say nothing right to other human beings that you haven't heard from me first; and you hear nothing right from me unless you've first said it to me.

3. So what business do I have with other people, letting them hear my testimony, as if *they* were going to cure all my ills? Humankind is quite inquisitive about someone else's life, but quite lazy about correcting their own. Why do they ask to hear from me who I am, when they don't want to hear from you who they are? And how do they know, when they're hearing both about me and from me, whether I'm telling the truth? In fact, no one on earth knows what's going on in anyone—unless the spirit within the very self knows.*

If, in contrast, people hear from *you* about themselves, they can't say, "The Master is lying." What's self-knowledge, after all, but hearing from you about themselves? Who, then, has this knowledge yet says, "It's wrong," unless he's lying?

But since selfless love believes all things,† at least among those it binds to itself and thus unifies,‡ I, too, Master, will join in, testifying to you in such a way that other people can hear me at the same time. I can't prove to them that what I confess is the truth, but those whose ears love opens to me believe me.

---

* 1 Corinthians 2:11.
† 1 Corinthians 13:7.
‡ Colossians 3:14.

4. Nevertheless, you, the doctor at the core of my being, must make clear to me what the advantage is of my testimony. Well, when the confessions of my past wrongdoings—which you forgave and hid* so that you could make me happy in yourself, changing my soul with faith and your rite of baptism—are read and heard, they arouse the heart out of its sleep of despair, in which it says "I can't." It then lies awake in its passion for your mercy, and in the sweetness of your grace, through which every weak person gains power, when this grace makes him aware of his weakness.† It delights good people to hear about the past evil acts of those who are now free of them; it isn't a source of delight that these acts are evil, but rather that they are no longer going on.

But what's the advantage, then, my Master—to whom my conscience, more confident in your mercy than in its own innocence, makes its daily confession—please tell me, what's the advantage that I testify—in your presence, but relayed to humankind as well as through my writing—as to who I *am* as yet, instead of who I *was*? I've in fact seen and put on record the advantage of testifying to the latter.

As to who I am right now, at this very period when I'm writing my confessions, many people are eager to know this, both those who're acquainted with me and those who aren't, as they've heard something from me or about me; but their ears aren't laid against my heart, where I *am* whoever I am. That's why they want to listen as I testify about what I myself, inside myself, am, where they can't direct their eyes or their ears or their minds.

* Psalms 32:1.
† 2 Corinthians 12:9–10.

They want to hear, and they're ready to believe, but they're in no way able to *know*, are they? But the selfless love in them, which makes them good people, tells them that I'm not lying in my testimony about myself. It is this love itself, in them, that believes me.

5. But what is the benefit they want from this? Do they long to rejoice with me, when they hear how close I've approached to you, because you granted this? And to pray for me, when they hear how much I'm held back by the weight of what's in me? I'll point the finger at myself for such people.

It's no small benefit, God my Master, that many give thanks to you on our behalf,* and that on our behalf many plead with you. Let a brother's mind love in me whatever, according to your instruction, should instill love, and let it grieve for whatever in me, according to your instruction, should instill grief.

Yes, let the mind that does this be a brother's mind, not an outsider's, not the mind of other parents' sons, "whose mouth has spoken empty words, and whose right hands commit crimes"†— but a brother's mind, which when it approves of me, is joyful for me, and when it disapproves of me, is gloomy for me, because whether it approves or disapproves, it holds me dear. I'll point the finger at myself for people like that.

Let them sigh with relief for what is good in me; let them sigh with sadness for what is bad in me. What is good in me was ordained and given by you; what is bad is made up of my offenses and the sentences you have passed against me. Let my own peo-

* 2 Corinthians 1:11.
† Psalms 144:11.

ple sigh with relief for the former, and sigh with sadness for the latter, and let a song of praise, and let weeping, rise into your presence from brotherly hearts, which are your vessels for burning incense.*

And you, Master, in your delight at the fragrance of your holy temple, deal tenderly with me, according to your great tenderheartedness†—I ask it in your holy name. And by no means abandon what you've begun, but bring to culmination all that is incomplete in me.‡

6. *Here's* what is gained by my testimony about what I am, not what I was: that I testify not only before you, in secret elation, mixed with trembling, and in secret grief, mixed with hope; but also that I testify for the ears of the faithful sons of humanity, partners in my joy and sharers in my mortality, my fellow citizens and sojourners abroad with me, those who have come before me, and those who come after me, and those who accompany me in my life. These are your slaves, my brothers, but it was your will that they be your sons, and my masters, whom you commanded me to serve if it is my will to live with you and in reliance on you.

And this, your Word to me, would not have been enough as a mere precept spoken by you; it had to precede with action by you. And I myself carry out that Word with both actions and words; I carry it out under your wings; the danger would be too great unless my soul were under your wings§—and thus placed

---

* Revelation 8:3–4.
† Psalms 51:1.
‡ Philippians 1:6.
§ Psalms 17:8, 36:7.

in submission under you—and unless my weakness were known to you.

I am a little child, but my Father lives forever, and my protector is the right one for me. It is the very same self who begot me and guards me; you yourself are everything good that belongs to me; you are all-powerful, you are with me before I am with you. Therefore I will point the finger at myself for the sake of such people as you order me to serve, showing myself not as I was but as I am now, as I am up to this point—but I will not judge myself one way or another.* Showing myself this way, then, let me be heard.

7. You, Master, judge me thus. No one among humankind knows what it is to be a human being, unless that human's spirit within himself knows;† but there is nevertheless something in a human being that not even the spirit within himself knows. You, however, know everything about him, because you made him.

But as for me, though when I stand in your sight I have utter contempt for myself, and place my value at the level of dirt and ashes,‡ I nonetheless know something about you that I don't know about myself. To be sure, now we see in a riddling mirror, and not yet face-to-face,§ and so while I'm traveling in a country foreign to yours,¶ I am closer to myself than to you; and yet I know that it is impossible to disturb your sanctity. I, on the other hand, don't know which temptations I have the strength to resist, and which not. But there is hope, because you are faithful

* 1 Corinthians 4:3.
† 1 Corinthians 2:11.
‡ Genesis 18:37, Job 42:6, Sirach 10:9.
§ 1 Corinthians 13:12.
¶ 2 Corinthians 5:6.

and don't allow us to be tempted beyond what we can endure, but rather create, along with the temptation, a way out so that we can bear up.[*]

Therefore I will testify to what I know and don't know about myself, because you give me the light by which to know what I know; and what I don't know, I don't know only until my darkness becomes as bright as noon in the light of your face before me.[†]

8. It isn't with a wavering but with a sure awareness that I love you, Master. You struck my heart to the core with your Word, and I fell in love with you. But the sky, too, and the earth, and everything that's in them—look, from all directions everything is telling me to love you, and never stops telling all people, so that they have no excuse.[‡]

But deeper is the mercy you will grant to whomever you grant your mercy, and the tenderheartedness you will show anyone to whom you're tenderhearted.[§] Otherwise, the sky and the earth could speak your praises, but we would be deaf.

But what do I love, in loving you? It's not the beauty of material things, or any attractiveness of this time-bound world, not the pale gleam of the light, this light here which is so friendly to these physical eyes of mine; and not the sweet melodies of every sort, and not the agreeable aromas of flowers and perfumes and spices, and not manna or honey on the tongue, and not a body welcome in a physical embrace. I don't love these things in lov-

---

[*] 1 Corinthians 10:13.
[†] Psalms 90:8, Isaiah 58:10.
[‡] Romans 1:20.
[§] Romans 9:15, quoting Exodus 33:19.

ing my God, but I do love a certain light, and a certain voice, and a certain fragrance, and a certain food, and a certain embrace in loving my God: this is the light, the voice, the fragrance, the food, the embrace of the person I am within, where something that space does not contain radiates, and something sounds that time doesn't snatch away, and something sheds a fragrance that the wind doesn't scatter, and something has a flavor that gluttony doesn't diminish, and something clings that the full indulgence of desire doesn't sunder. This is what I love in loving my God.

9. But what is it that I love? I asked the earth, and it said, "It's not me," and everything in it admitted the same thing. I asked the sea and the great chasms of the deep,* and the creeping things that have the breath of life in them,† and they answered, "We aren't your God: search above us." I asked the gusty winds, and all the atmosphere there is, along with its inhabitants, said, "Anaximenes is deluded: I'm not God."‡ I asked the sky, the sun, the moon, the stars, and they said, "We're not the God you're looking for, either."

I told all those beings who stand around outside my body's gates, its senses, "Tell me about my God. You aren't him, but tell me something about him." And they declared with a shout, "He made us!"§ My question was the act of focusing on them, and their response was their beauty.

* Job 28:13–14.
† Genesis 1:20.
‡ A pre-Socratic philosopher who had argued for the divinity of air.
§ Psalms 100:3.

But then I turned myself toward myself and asked myself, "Who are you?" and I answered, "A human being." Here at my service were my body and my soul, the one of which is outward, the other inward. Which was the one I should use to seek my God—whom I'd already sought through material objects from the earth clear up to the sky, as far as I could send the message-bearing rays of my eyesight?

The soul within is certainly better for informing me, as all the messengers that are material objects relay to it their news, and it presides and judges the depositions of the sky and the earth and everything in them that says "We are not God," and "God made us." The inside person has found this out through the help of the outside person; my inside self found this out—I did, it was me, my mind working through my physical perception. I asked the whole huge universe about my God, and it answered me, "I am not God, but God made me."

10. But doesn't this beauty appear to everyone whose perception is unimpaired? Then why doesn't it speak the same words to everyone? Animals tiny and large see it, but they're not able to question it, because in them there is no judicious reasoning placed in charge of the physical senses that bring them news. Human beings, on the other hand, can question this beauty, so as to gaze at unseen things belonging to God and understand these through the creation.*

But people are in submission to their love for the creation, and those who are in submission, who are subordinate, are not

* Romans 1:20.

judges. And created things don't answer the people questioning them, unless these people *judge*. It's not as if the objects alter what they say—their beauty, that is—between the person who merely observes them and the other who observes and questions, so that their beauty is physically different in either case: it's just the same to the one person as to the other, but to one of these it *says* nothing, while to the other it speaks.

No, actually, it speaks to everyone, but it's only understood by those who compare with the truth inside themselves the voice taken in from outside themselves. It's the truth that tells me, "Your God isn't the earth and sky, or any material thing." The very nature of material things says this. Do you see what I mean? The universe is a physical mass, smaller in any part than in the whole. But *you*, my soul, are automatically better than that, I'm telling you, because you give energy to the mass of my body, giving it life, which no material object can do for another one. But your God is actually the life of your life.

11. So what do I love, in loving my God? Who is he who's so far over my soul's head? But I'll climb up to him by way of my soul just the same. I'll pass beyond my own vitality, with which I adhere to my body and fill its framework with vital essence. It isn't through this strength that I find my God, as in that case a horse or a mule could find him, too; they have no understanding,* but it's the same stamina that animates their bodies.

But there's a further power at play, one by which I endow not only with life but also with sensibility the physical being my Master crafted for me, commanding the eye not to hear, and the

---

* Psalms 32:9.

ear not to see, but rather the eye to see for me, and the ear to hear for me, and all of the other organs of the senses to perform their appropriate functions, doing their assigned jobs in their assigned places—all the various business that my own self alone, which is my awareness, carries out through my senses. But I'll pass beyond that contemptible capacity of mine, too, because even a horse or a mule shares it: they as well perceive through the body.

12. I will pass beyond even that power of mine, belonging to my nature, and climb step by step toward him who made me, and I am coming into the fields, the spacious palaces of memory. There lie the repositories of countless images hauled in by things of every conceivable kind that were perceived. There we lay up as well whatever we think up, whether that's by enlarging or diminishing or altering in any other way what perception has touched; and anything else that's entrusted to safekeeping and not yet swallowed down and interred in forgetfulness.

When I'm there, whatever it is I want, I ask for it to be produced. Certain things issue forth immediately; certain other things need a lengthy search, and it's as if they were being dug out from this or that obscure, neglected container; and certain other things charge at you in hordes: when you're asking and looking for something else, they rush into the open as if they're saying, "Is it maybe us you want?" But with the hand that's my inmost will, I swat these away from the face of my memory and wait until what I want emerges from the fog of recondite items and steps forth into my sight. But still other things are effortlessly supplied in flawless, uninterrupted order, just as they're requested, with those that come first falling back to make room for those that follow, and are stored away as they give way, though poised to issue forth again whenever I wish. All of this happens whenever I tell about anything from memory.

13. There in the storehouse is the whole lot laid up individually but according to type, lavishly bestowed, with each item coming through its proper entrance; the light and all the colors and the shapes of objects through the eyes, and all kinds of sounds through the ears, and all smells through the aperture of the nostrils, and all tastes through the mouth's ingress, while for its part the sense of touch in the whole body takes in what's hard, soft, hot, cold, smooth or rough, light or heavy, whether inside or outside the body.

The huge receptacle of the memory receives, in whatever hidden and indescribable hollows it has, all these impressions, to be recalled and reconsidered when necessary. All these impressions come in through their own gateways and are stashed in memory. The items themselves don't come in, but rather images of things perceived, which are at the service of thought and recollection.

Who can say how the images are crafted?—though it's clear which physical senses snatch them away and store them up inwardly. Even while I'm living in darkness and silence, I can (for example) bring out colors in my memory, if I want to, and can distinguish between white and black and any others I choose.

Sounds don't rush in and upset what I've drunk in through my eyes and am now contemplating—though sounds are there, too, and, in a way, hide elsewhere, where they're stored away. I call on the sounds, too, if I decide to, and there they are on the spot, and though my tongue is at rest and my throat is silent, I sing as much as I like. Those images of colors, which are still there just the same, don't push in or break in when some other collection of precious objects, which poured in through my ears, is being handled again.

In this way I remember, exactly as I please, all the impressions heaped on me and heaped up in me through all my physical senses. I tell a whiff of lilies from that of violets though I'm not catching a scent of anything. I prefer honey to the dregs of wine, and a smooth surface to a rough one, even when I'm not tasting or touching anything, but only remembering.

14. I do all these things inwardly, in the immense royal court of my memory. There the sky and the earth and the sea are ready to attend me, with everything in them that I've been able to perceive, except for what I've forgotten. There I run into myself and recollect myself: when and where I was doing which things, and how I felt while I was doing them. There is found everything I remember, whether I experienced it directly or accepted it, at second hand, as true.

Also, from the same abundance I take likenesses both of what I've experienced directly and what I've accepted, at one time or another, as true based on what I've experienced: I interweave these likenesses with past impressions, and on the strength of the result I actually contemplate future activities and occurrences and hopes, going over all of this as if it existed right now.

"I'll do this," or "I'll do that," I say to myself within myself in the enormous cavity of my mind, full as it is with so many images of such extensive things, and whatever it is that I've said I'll do follows. "If only this would happen!" or "If only that would happen!" or "May God prevent this!" or "May God prevent that!"—I say all of this stuff to myself, and while I'm still saying it, images of everything I'm speaking about are on hand out of this same storehouse of memory. But I wouldn't be able to say any of it in the first place, if not for those images.

15. The power of memory that I'm writing about is tremendous, my God—intimidatingly great: an extensive, a boundless innermost recess. Who has ever gotten to the bottom of it? This power belongs to my mind and is part of my nature—but I myself don't hold the whole of what I am. Is the mind too narrow to encompass itself, so that the question arises of where a place is for that part of itself it doesn't contain? That couldn't be outside itself instead of inside itself, could it?

In that case, how could it fail to contain itself? In the face of this question, a marveling bafflement overwhelms me, and bewilderment seizes me. People go where they can marvel at mountain heights and massive waves of the sea, and immensely wide waterfalls, and the ocean that encircles the continents, and the orbits of the heavenly bodies—but these same people leave themselves behind.

They don't bother to wonder that in saying all of what I've just said, I don't see the places with my eyes; and that, notwithstanding this fact, I couldn't say what I say unless the mountains and the streaming tides and the streams and the heavenly bodies that I've seen, and the ocean that I take on trust, were inwardly visible in my memory, in spaces as enormous as if I saw them outwardly. But I didn't swallow these things up by seeing them, when I saw them with my eyes, and it's not the things themselves that are with me, but the images of them; and I know which one has been imprinted in my mind by which physical sense.

16. But this immeasurable capacity of my memory doesn't carry only these things. In it is also everything I've learned from liberal studies—everything that hasn't fallen out of it, of course, and been moved off someplace further in what isn't really a place. Yet I don't carry around in me the images of these things, but the things themselves. As to the character of the literary arts, and the character of expertise in argumentation, as well as the many lines of scientific and philosophical investigation, whatever I know of these things doesn't exist in my memory as if I'd kept the picture but left the thing itself outside. It isn't like a voice, either, making a sound and then passing by, but imprinting through our ears a track by which the hearer can go over it again, just as if it's making the sound that in fact it's not making any longer. It isn't like a smell, either, transiting and evanescing into the winds but impacting on the sense of smell, through which it transfers onto the memory an image of itself that we can retrieve by remembering. It's not like the food that, for sure, has no taste once it's in the stomach but has a kind of taste in the memory. And it's not like something that's felt when it touches the body, and that even when it's apart from us, memory pictures to itself. These objects aren't of course injected into the memory, but the images of them alone are seized with

wonderful speed and laid up in wonderful storerooms, if you will, and wonderfully brought out by remembering.

17. No, here's what I mean instead. When I hear, for example, that there are three possible lines of inquiry about a thing (whether it exists, what its identity is, and what its qualities are), I do retain images of the sounds these words consist of, and I know that they've passed through the air making a sequence of noises and are there no longer. But in contrast, these matters themselves, which are signaled by those sounds, I don't take in through any physical perception, and I've never seen them anywhere except in my mind. In my memory, I've stored away not images of them, but what they actually are.

I leave it to them to say, if they can, from where exactly it was that they themselves entered my consciousness. I review all the sensory gateways into my body, and I can't discover by which of them these things could have gone in. The eyes say, "If the things were imbued with color, we relayed them." The ears say, "If they had a sound, we gave notice of them." The nose says, "If they had a smell, they went through us." The sense of taste has something to say as well: "If there's no flavor, don't ask me." The tactile sense says, "If it's not a solid body of a thing, I didn't touch it; if I didn't touch it, I didn't notify you of it."

So what's the source, and what's the route, for these things entering into my memory? I just don't know how it happened. When I learned them, I didn't rely on anyone else's heart, but in my own I recognized them and affirmed that they were true and entrusted them to that same heart, more or less putting them into storage in a place from which I could bring them out when

I wished. So they were *there* before I learned them, and yet they weren't in my memory.

So where and why, when they were stated, did I acknowledge them, saying, "That's the way it is, that's true"? They must have been in my memory already, but withdrawn so far, pushed so far out of sight, in—shall we say?—the better-concealed caverns, that unless they were unearthed under somebody else's direction, perhaps we couldn't think them at all.

18. On these grounds, we can ascertain just what it means to learn the things that we don't swallow down in the form of images, through our physical senses, but instead in their pure state, in themselves. What we do is take the things that memory holds in random and arbitrary arrangements and bind them together, as it were, by thinking about them, and care for them by paying attention to them.

The result is as if they're placed within easy reach in memory itself—where they were scattered and neglected before—and readily come to meet an application of mind that's closely associated with them. How many things of this kind my memory carries, which have been discovered so far in my life, and (as I said) are within easy reach—for which "having learned" and "knowing" are common terms!

If for middling spaces of time I'm remiss in gathering them in again, they naturally sink down and slide into the more out-of-the-way inner chambers, so that they have to be cogitated anew, as if they *were* new, from the same quarter (as there's no other space for them) and congregated again, so that they can be known.

This means, given that they're in a certain state of dispersion, they have to be (as we say) collected (*colligenda*); which is why we use the word for "[to keep driving together] / to think" (*cogitare*). In fact, the word for "I drive together" (*cogo*) and for "[I keep driving together] / I think" (*cogito*) are parallel to the pairs for "I drive / I act" (*ago*) and for "I keep putting into motion / I shake" (*agito*); and for "I do / I make" (*facio*) and "I keep doing / I keep making" (*factito*).

However, the *mind* claims the word *cogito* as its exclusive property, as nothing that's collected together in any other place, but only something that's collected together (*conligitur*)—or in other words driven together (*cogitur*)—in the mind is at this stage of the language properly said to be "thought of" (*cogitari*).

19. Likewise, the memory holds innumerable logical relationships and rules concerning numbers and measurements, none of which is imprinted by physical sensation, because these things in themselves are not colored, nor do they make sounds, nor do they have a scent, nor are they tasted or touched. I've heard the sounds of words that stand for these things in discussions of them, but we're dealing here with two completely different categories. The sounds vary between Latin and Greek, but the other things are neither Greek nor Latin, nor any other way of speaking.

I've seen lines on builders' diagrams, some as thin as you can imagine, but the lines of geometry are different: they're not the images of lines conveyed to me by my physical sight. Anyone who has recognized them inwardly, without any mediating conception of any kind of material object, knows them. I've also sensed, with all my physical senses, the numbers *which* we count ("one, two, three," etc., of a given number of any material things), but they're quite different from the ones *by which* we count (one, two, three, etc.); these aren't images of those other numbers, and for this very reason they do, prevailingly, exist. Let anyone who doesn't *see* them laugh at me when I say this, and I'll feel sorry for him even while he's laughing at me.

20. All of this I keep in my memory, and I keep in my memory the ways I learned it. Besides, I've heard many outrageously wrong arguments against these principles, and I remember those arguments, too. Though they're wrong, my memory of them is not wrong. I distinguished between the true statements and the false ones that were adduced against them, and I remember this as well. Also, I see that it's a different thing to distinguish now, and to remember that I often distinguished in the past, however often I thought about it.

So I both remember that I often exercised my understanding this way, and I also stash in my memory what I distinguish and understand now, so that later on I'll remember that I understand at this moment. Therefore, I remember remembering, just as, later on, if I recall the fact that I've been able to remember these things now, I'll undoubtedly recall it through the power of memory.

21. This same memory also contains attitudes of my mind— which is not as if the mind itself "has" them when it experiences them—no, it's very different from that: it's as if the power of memory "has itself" (as we say in Latin), or just is that way.

I remember having been happy, for example, even when I'm not happy, and I recall my past sadness though I'm not sad, and I recollect without fear that at one time I was afraid, or I'm mindful, in the absence of desire, of a long-ago desire. Conversely, in happiness I remember past sadness, and in sadness I remember past happiness.

This isn't a surprising kind of phenomenon when it concerns the body. The mind and body are two separate entities, so that if, while rejoicing, I remember past physical pain, it's not a big surprise. But suppose, at this juncture, that the mind is memory itself, a single thing. We do say, when we ask someone to commit something to memory, "Make sure you keep that in mind." And when we forget, we say, "I didn't have that in mind," and "It slipped my mind." With these expressions, we call the memory the mind.

But if that were actually the case, then how can it be that when I remember in happiness my past sadness, my mind has the happiness and my memory the sadness, and the mind is happy because of the happiness in it, whereas the memory isn't sad because of the sadness in it?

Is memory perhaps not an inherent part of the mind? Who would say that? Evidently, then, memory is a sort of stomach of the mind, and happiness and sadness are like food that's sweet and bitter: when they're entrusted to the memory, it's as if they're transferred into the stomach, and they can be laid up there but not tasted there. Yes, it's silly to think of these things as similar, but still they're not different in *every* respect.

22. But look here: it's from my *memory* that I bring it out, when I say that there are four strong emotions the *mind* can experience: desire, joy, fear, and sadness. Whatever I can argue about these phenomena, by dividing and defining individual cases by category and subcategory, the memory is where I find what I have to say, and it's from the memory that I bring it out.

I'm not, however, feeling strong emotion due to any of these strong emotions when, through remembering them, I recount them. Yet before they were recalled and reexamined by me, they were there, in my memory; that's the reason that, through reminiscence, they were ready to be produced.

Perhaps, then, it's like food brought up from the stomach for chewing the cud, when these phenomena are brought out of the memory by recollection. But why, then, is the sweetness of joy or the bitterness of mourning not felt in the mouth of thought by a person making some argument about these phenomena— that is, by a person remembering them?

Is this the great difference that can be found among the similarities between these two realms of experience, of remembering and of ruminating? I mean, who would willingly talk about such passions, if whenever we named "sadness" or "panic," we were forced to mourn or be frightened?

We wouldn't, however, be speaking of these things at all, unless in our memory we found not only the sounds of the terms, imprinted through our physical senses, but also concepts of the things themselves, which we haven't taken in through any physical gateway; instead, the mind itself, perceiving through the experience of its own passions, has committed these very things to memory, or memory on its own retained them, even without these things having been committed to it.

23. But who could easily say whether this happens through images or not? I call a thing "a stone," and I call another thing "the sun," when the objects themselves aren't available to my senses. But in my memory, certainly, images of them are on hand. I call a feeling "physical pain," but that thing isn't with me when I don't hurt at all. However, unless the image of pain was in my memory, I wouldn't know what to say, and in reasoning out the matter I wouldn't be able to tell pain from pleasure.

I call something "physical well-being" when I'm physically well, and in fact the condition itself is in me. Nevertheless, unless the image of it was in my memory, there would be no way for me to remember what the sound of this term meant; nor would sick people recognize what's been said when something's called "well-being," unless that same kind of image was retained by the power of memory even though the condition itself is absent from their bodies.

I name the numbers with which we count; right there they are, in my memory, not images of them, but themselves. I call something "the image of the sun," on the other hand, and this image is there in my memory; and it's not an image of an image that I recollect, but the original image itself: this is at my service as I remember. I call something "memory," and I recognize the thing to which I apply that term. But where's the place where I perform that act of recognition, unless it's in my memory itself? It isn't the case, is it, that that memory itself is present to itself through an image of itself, right? It's present to itself through its very self, isn't it?

24. Furthermore, when I call something "forgetting" and likewise recognize what I'm naming, how would I recognize it unless from memory? I'm not talking about recognizing, as the same, the sound of the word, but rather recognizing the thing that word signifies. If I had forgotten the thing, I certainly wouldn't have the power to recognize the power of that sound.

It follows that when I remember memory, memory itself is at its own service, through itself. When, on the other hand, I remember forgetting, both memory and forgetting are on hand: memory as the means of remembering, and forgetting as the thing I remember doing.

But what is forgetting if not an absence of memory? How, therefore, is forgetting present for me to remember, when, in the presence of forgetting, I'm not able to remember? But given that we retain through memory what we remember, and given that if we didn't remember forgetting, then by no means, in hearing the word "forgetting," could we recognize the thing that word signifies, then forgetting is retained by memory. Therefore, forgetting is present to the degree that we don't forget it, but in its actual presence, we forget.

Can it be understood from this that forgetting doesn't, as itself, exist in the memory when we remember it, but that instead an image of forgetting exists in the memory? This would be because, if forgetting were on hand as itself, it would result in our forgetting, not remembering. But who's going to track this down in the end? Who's going to grasp the way it is?

25. For sure, Master, I'm toiling here, and I'm toiling in myself. I've become my own land of hardship and pouring sweat.* And we're not now rummaging among the sky's zones, or measuring the distance from the earth to the stars, or asking how much the earth would weigh if you put it on a scale.† It's just me who remembers, I, my mind. It's no big surprise that whatever I'm *not* is far out of my reach, but what's closer to me than I myself?

And yet here we have it: the power of my own memory isn't something I can comprehend, though I can't speak of myself without speaking of that power. What am I going to say, when it's certain to me that I remember forgetting? Am I going to say that what I remember isn't in my memory? Or that forgetting is in my memory for the purpose of keeping me from forgetting? Both these options are totally ridiculous.

Then what about that third option, the image? But how am I to say that an image of forgetting is held in my memory, instead of the actual forgetting, when I remember forgetting? How am I to say even this, since in fact whenever an image of anything is impressed into the memory, it's first essential that the thing itself be present? The thing must impress that image on me.

This is the way I remember Carthage, and all the other places where I've been, and this is how I remember the faces of people I've seen, and other messages from my body's senses, and this is how I remember the physical health and suffering of my body itself. When these things were on hand, my memory captured images from them, so that I can gaze at these images and go over them right here, when I remember the things that are *not* here.

---

* Genesis 3:17–19.
† These were in fact all matters of astronomical and geometrical calculation from the time of the pre-Socratic philosophers.

If, therefore, forgetting were held in the memory through the image of forgetting, and not through forgetting itself, then forgetting itself was certainly there for its image to be seized. When forgetting would have been there, however, how did it compose its own image in the memory, when through its presence it erases even what it finds already marked down?

But nevertheless, somehow or other, if only by some means that can't be grasped or explained, I'm certain that I remember even forgetting itself, that thing by which what we remember is swallowed up.

26. The power of memory is great, a fearsome thing, a deep, endless complexity. Yet this is the mind, and this is me, myself. What am I, then, my God? What am I by nature? A life of many shades, existing by many means, and mightily immeasurable. Here I am, in the fields and grottoes and caverns of my memory, which are countless, and full of countless things of countless kinds—whether acquired through images, which is always the case for objects; or through their actual presence, which is the case for the learned disciplines; or through concepts or conceptualizations of some kind, which is the case for attitudes of the mind (and even when the mind doesn't experience them, it holds them in memory, as whatever's in the mind is in the memory): I'm scurrying around there in all directions, fluttering back and forth, and I do make my way in as far as I can, but there's no end anywhere.

That's how great the power of memory is—and that's only the power in the life of a person, who lives in the realm of death. What should I do then, tell me, my true life, my God? I'll pass through even that power of mine that's called memory, I'll pass through it because it must, with effort, lead to you at last, you, my sweet light.

What do you say to me? Here I am, climbing up to you through my mind, to you who remain above me; I'll pass through even that power of mine that's called memory, in my will to touch you, in whatever way you can be touched, and to cling to you through anything that allows clinging to you.

Even farm animals and birds have memory; otherwise they wouldn't be able to find their beds and nests again, or the many other things they become used to; they wouldn't in fact have the power to get used to *any* things, except through their memory. Therefore, I'm going to pass through memory, and into contact with the one who set me apart from the four-footed animals, and made me wiser than the winged creatures of the sky.* I'll pass through even memory, so that I find you—but where will I find you, you who are truly good, you who are sweetness that cannot be taken away? Where will I find you? If I find you somewhere beyond my memory, then I don't hold you in remembrance. But how will I find you in the first place, if I don't hold you in remembrance?

27. A woman had lost a drachma and searched for it by lamplight.† If she hadn't held it in remembrance, she wouldn't have found it. And once it had been found, how was she to know it was the actual one she'd been looking for, unless she'd held it in remembrance?

* Job 35:11.
† Luke 15:8.

I remember losing many things and finding them again, so I know how this works: when I was looking for one of these things, someone would say to me, "It's not this, by any chance, is it?" or "Not that, by any chance?" But I kept on saying, "That's not it," until I was shown what I was looking for. Unless I'd been holding in my memory whatever it was, even if I'd been shown it I wouldn't have *found* it, because I wouldn't have recognized it. That's the way it always is, when we look for and find something lost.

In actual fact, if something happens to vanish from our eyesight, but not from the memory—which is the case with any kind of visible material object—an image is held within and is sought, until the thing is presented to physical sight again. When it's found, it's recognized on the basis of the image within. We don't say that we've found the thing that's gone missing if we don't recognize it, and we can't recognize it if we don't remember it. It has in fact gone missing from the eyes, but it is retained in the memory.

28. What about the times when the memory itself has lost something, as happens when we forget and seek to recall? Where, after all, do we look but in the memory itself? And if we're shown the wrong thing, we reject it until we encounter what we're looking for, and when we do encounter it, we say, "That's it!" We wouldn't say that unless we recognized the thing, and we wouldn't recognize it unless we remembered it. Definitely, then, we would have forgotten.

Or is a "forgotten" thing not wholly fallen away, and is the part that's kept used to seek the other part? Thus, the memory perceives that it isn't reeling off all at once what it used to reel off all at once: limping on its maimed habit of remembering something, it demands that the missing part be returned to it.

It's like catching sight of or just thinking of a person we know, and we forget his name and want to know what it is. Whatever wrong name occurs to us doesn't connect, because we're not accustomed to thinking of it while thinking of the person; and so each name is rejected until one comes to us that allows our accustomed knowledge immediate acquiescence to an adequate fit.

Where does this solution come from, if not from the memory? It comes from there even when someone else prompts us into recognition. We don't simply *believe* what we hear, as if it's something new, but through our recall we certify that what's been said is correct. If, however, it's obliterated from deep down in the mind, we don't remember it even when reminded. Thus, we haven't in every sense forgotten a thing if we can remember that we've forgotten it. We couldn't even look for, as lost, this thing we've forgotten altogether.

29. So how do I seek you, Master? When I seek you, my God, I seek a happy life. Let me seek you so that my soul can live:* my body lives from my soul, and my soul lives from you. So how do I seek a happy life?—because I don't have it until I can say, "Fine: it's there."

But that "there" is where I need to say how I seek it: whether through recollection, as if I'd forgotten it, but still bore in mind that I'd forgotten; or whether through the desire to learn about

* Psalms 69:32, Isaiah 55:3.

this unfamiliar thing; and in that case, whether I never knew it, or whether I've forgotten it to the degree that I don't even remember having forgotten it.

Isn't this very thing the happy life that everybody wants, and that absolutely no one *doesn't* want? Where do people know it, given that they all want it? Where did they see her, *Vita Beata*, to fall in love with her? Presumably, we in *some* sense apprehend her.

There is some means by which each person can be happy at the time when he actually gets his hands on a happy life; but other people are happy in hope. They grasp happiness in a lower way than do those who are already happy in the thing itself, but the former are better off than those who are happy neither in the hope nor in the thing itself. Unless they had some kind of idea what happiness was, even hopeful people wouldn't want to be happy.

That they do want to be is beyond the slightest doubt. By some sort of means they know it, and thus they hold it in some sort of knowledge—which I'm flummoxed in trying to figure out. Is it in the memory, in which case we were already happy at some point in the past? I'm not asking now whether all of us were happy as individuals, or whether we were happy in Adam, that person who first sinned, in whom we all died,* and in whom we were all born into wretchedness. I'm simply asking whether a happy life is in the memory.

We wouldn't, of course, be in love with that life unless we knew it (or her). We hear the word "happiness," and all of us admit that we strive for the thing itself. It's not that we're delighted with the word's sound. If a Greek hears the word in Latin, he's

---

* 1 Corinthians 15:22.

not delighted, because he doesn't know what's been said. We, on the other hand, *are* delighted, as he would be if he heard it in Greek, since the thing itself is neither Greek nor Latin, yet speakers of Greek and Latin and all the other languages are drooling to get hold of it. Therefore, it's known to everyone, and if they could be asked by a single utterance whether they wanted to be happy, they'd answer without the slightest hesitation that they *did* want to. That wouldn't happen unless the thing itself, named "a happy life," were held in their memory.

30. Is it anything like remembering Carthage after seeing the place? No, a happy life isn't seen with the eyes, because it's not a physical thing. Is it anything like remembering numbers? No, a person who has knowledge of them doesn't go on trying to acquire them. We have a happy life, in contrast, within our knowledge, and on this basis we love it, and yet we still want to acquire it, so as to be happy.

Do we remember it the way we remember oratorical skill? No: granted, even those who aren't yet skilled speakers—and many long to be (from which it's clear that the skill is within their awareness)—recall the thing itself when they hear its name; yet it's through their physical senses that they've focused on skilled speakers, and were delighted, and desire to be the same. Granted, they wouldn't be delighted except through *inner* knowledge; nor would they want to be the same unless they were first delighted. Nevertheless, we don't use *any* physical perception to learn about the happy life in others.*

---

* I have repunctuated this passage slightly, as otherwise the sequence of thought does not seem workable.

Do we by any chance remember the happy life the way we remember joy? Maybe this is it. I remember my joy even when I'm sad, as a miserable man remembers a happy life, but I never saw or heard or smelled or tasted or touched my joy through physical perception; instead, I felt it in my mind at the time I was made glad, and the knowledge of it clung to my memory, so that I would have the power to recall it, sometimes with revulsion, and sometimes with longing, according to the various things I remember finding joy in. I have been flooded with a certain joy even from shameful things, and now when I call that joy to mind I curse and revile it. Sometimes my joy has been from good and decent things, and this feeling I recollect with yearning, although the things themselves may not be here. In this way, in sadness I call to mind joy long past.

31. So where and when have I experienced my happy life, so that I remember it and love it and desire it? And I'm not alone, or one of a few; no, we all, without exception, want to be happy. Unless we knew that with a firm knowledge, we wouldn't will it with a firm will.

But what *is* this "happy life"? If two men were asked whether they wanted to be in the army, it might be that one would answer that he wanted to, and the other that he didn't. But if they were asked whether they wanted to be happy, then both, without any hesitation, would say that this was their desire; and the one man would have no other reason for wanting to be a soldier, or the other character for not wanting to be one, than the wish to be happy. Wouldn't it be because the two have joy from these two different sources?

Everyone's agreement in their wish to be happy is in line with their agreement, should they be asked this question, in the answer: they want to have joy, and that joy is the very thing they call "a happy life." Though they have different pursuits, it's nevertheless only one goal they're all striving to reach, and that's to have joy. Since this is something no one can claim never to have experienced, it's consequently found in the memory and recognized when the term "happy life" is heard.

32. Far be it, Master, far be it from the heart of your slave, who testifies to you, far be it that, whatever kind of joy I enjoy, I consider myself *happy*. There's a joy that isn't given to the irreverent,* but to those who worship you with no expectation of a reward— those whose joy you yourself are. This is happy life itself: to rejoice in your presence, and through you, and because of you. This life is the actual happy life; there is no other kind. Those who think the happy life is different pursue another joy, and not the true one itself. Yet their inclination isn't turned away from *some* reflection of this joy.

33. Therefore it *isn't* certain that all people want to be happy, as those who don't want to be happy through you—which is the only happy life—don't really want a happy life at all. Or is it that everybody does want this, but since the desires of the body are against the Spirit, and the desires of the Spirit against the body, with the result that people don't do what they want,† they fall into what they merely have the willpower for and are con-

---

* Isaiah 48:22; modern English translations are much different.
† Galatians 5:17.

tent with it; and as for what they don't have the willpower for, they don't have enough will for it to have the willpower for it?

I ask everyone whether they'd rather have joy in the truth or in falsehood.* They hesitate as little to say they'd rather have joy in the truth as they hesitate to say they want to be happy. The happy life is, after all, joy in the truth. This is joy through you, God, who are the truth,† my illumination, the salvation of my face,‡ my God. Everybody wants this happy life; this life, which alone is happy, everyone wants; everyone wants joy in the truth.

I've known many people who wanted to deceive, but no one who wanted to be deceived. So where do they know this happy life, unless that's where they know the truth as well? They do love the truth, too, because they don't want to be deceived, and when they love a happy life—which is nothing other than joy in the truth—they by all means love the truth also. And they wouldn't love it if there weren't some knowledge of it in their memory.

So why don't they have joy in the truth? Why aren't they happy? It's because they're too powerfully engrossed in other things, which do more to make them miserable than the thing they re-member slightly can do to make them happy. There is still a small amount of light in human beings. Let them walk, let them walk on, so that the darkness doesn't close in on them.§

34. But why, then, does the truth give birth to hatred, and why did your man Paul, when proclaiming what is true, become the

---

* 1 Corinthians 13:5.
† John 14:6.
‡ Psalms 27:1, 42:11, and 43:5. The expression "salvation of my face" is from the Latin scrip-ture.
§ John 12:35.

people's enemy,* if the happy life is an object of love, and if this happy life isn't anything other than joy in the truth?

It must be that truth is loved in such a way that whatever else people love, they want this thing to be the truth; and because they wouldn't want to be deceived, they don't want it proved that they *have* been deceived.

That means they hate the truth for the sake of that thing they love in place of the truth. They love the truth when it lights up a thing, but hate the truth when it refutes a thing. Because they don't want to be deceived but want to deceive, they love the truth when it discloses itself but hate it when it discloses them.† For this reason, the truth will give them their due, forcibly revealing all those unwilling to be revealed, but not itself being revealed to them.

It's absolutely so, in fact: the human soul, in fact so blind and sick, ugly and unseemly, wants to lie low and unseen—but doesn't want anything else to lie low and not be seen by itself. The soul is paid back in that it can't hide from the truth, but the truth is hidden from it.

Yet even so, as long as it's miserable, the soul prefers to have joy in true things rather than in false things. This means it will be happy if, with no nuisance getting in the way, it has joy in the truth itself alone, through which all things are true.

35. This is how far I've ranged in my memory in search of you, Master, and I haven't found you except within it. I haven't found

* John 8:40, Galatians 4:16.
† John 3:20.

anything about you except what I've remembered from the time I learned of you—given that from the time I learned of you, I haven't forgotten you.

Wherever I've found truth, I've found my God, you who are truth itself—and since the time I learned the truth, I haven't forgotten it. Therefore, from the time I learned of you, you've remained in my memory, and there I find you when I recall you, and I delight in you. This is my most darling holy delight, which you granted me in your mercy, and in your concern for my poverty.

36. But where do you stay in my memory, Master? Where do you stay there? What kind of couch have you crafted for yourself? What sort of shrine have you built for yourself? You've granted to my memory the indulgence of remaining in it, but here's what I contemplate now: In what part of it do you remain?

When I remembered you, I went up beyond those parts of memory that animals have too, because I couldn't find you among the images of material things. Then I came to the parts of memory where I've stored up my mind's dispositions, and I didn't find you there, either. Then I entered into my mind's own headquarters, which it possesses in my memory, since the mind also remembers itself—but you weren't there, either.

You aren't an image of a material thing, or an inward experience of a living thing either, such as when we're cheerful or sad, or when we desire or fear or remember or forget, or other conditions of this kind; and you're equally not the mind itself, because you're the Master, the God of the mind. Also, all of these conditions change, whereas you remain unchangeable* above all things, yet you've condescended to live in my memory from the time I learned about you. But why do I ask in which *place* you live, as if there were actually places there? But you certainly live in the memory, since I remember you from the time I learned about you, and I find you in the memory when I recall you.

37. So where did I find you, so that I could learn about you? You weren't already in my memory before I learned about you. So where did I find you, to learn about you, if not in yourself, above me? But nowhere is there a place; try as we might to progress toward it or regress from it, there's no place anywhere.

You, the truth, give an audience everywhere to everyone consulting you, and you respond at the same time to everybody, even though they ask you about very different things. Your answers are as clear as water, but not everyone hears them so clearly. Everyone consults you as to what they want, but they don't always hear what they want. Your best functionary is the one who by preference doesn't pay regard as much to hearing what he wants from you, as to wanting what he hears from you.

38. I took too long to fall in love with you, beauty so ancient and so new. I took too long to fall in love with you! But there you were, inside, and I was outside—and there I searched for you, and into those shapely things you made, my misshapen self went sliding. You were with me, but I wasn't with you. Those things, which wouldn't exist unless they existed in you, held me

* Psalms 102:26–27.

back, far from you. You called and shouted and shattered my deafness. You flashed, you shone, and you put my blindness to flight. You smelled sweet, and I drew breath, and now I pant for you. I tasted you, and now I'm starving and parched; you touched me, and I burst into flame with desire for your peace.

39. Once I cling to you with all I am, I'll no longer have pain or hardship. My life will be alive when the whole of it is full of you. You lift whomever you fill, so that now, because I'm not full of you, I'm a dead weight to myself.

My gratifications that I ought to weep over struggle against the sorrows that ought to gratify me, and I don't know which side will have the victory. My wicked woes fight with my good joys, and I don't know which side will win out. What a wretch I am, Master! Have mercy on me! What a wretch I am! Here are my injuries: I don't hide them. You are the doctor, and I'm ailing. You heart is full of pity, and I'm pitiful.

Is human life on this earth anything but a trial?[*] Who would want troubles and hardships? You order us to put up with them, but not to be in love with them. Nobody loves what he puts up with, although he loves the ability to put up with it. Though he finds joy in his endurance, he does prefer for there to be nothing to endure.

If things go against me, I long for them to go my way, and when circumstances are in my favor, I fear they'll go against me. Where, between these two extremes, is the middle ground where human life isn't a trial? Woe to the world's advantages, on

[*] Job 7:1.

not one but two counts: the fear of a reversal, and ruinous gladness. Woe to the world's misfortunes, on not one or two but
three counts: the yearning for good fortune, the fact that misfortune itself is hard to bear, and the chance that endurance will
break down under misfortune. Is human life on this earth not a
wholly uninterrupted trial?

40. The whole of my hope is only in your powerfully great
mercy. Grant what you command, and command what you
wish. You order us to have self-restraint. "And when I knew,"
says a certain man, "that no one can be self-restrained unless by
the gift of God, this knowledge itself—that is, knowing whose
gift this was—partook of wisdom."*

By self-restraint we are tied tightly together, restricted and
reduced to the oneness from which we flowed out into multiplicity. A person loves you less if he loves, along with you,
something he doesn't love because of you. Oh, passion of love,
you who are always burning and never quenched; you, tender
love, my God, set me on fire! You command me to be self-
restrained: give what you command, and command what you
wish.

41. You certainly command that I constrain myself from lust of
the body, and lust of the eyes, and worldly ambition.† You commanded constraint from cohabitation, and as far as the conjugal
relationship itself goes, you counseled something better than

---

* Wisdom of Solomon 8:21. See the note on book 6, chapter 20.
† 1 John 2:16.

what you allowed. * And since it was your gift, it was done, even before I became a dispenser of your sacrament.†

But there still live in my memory (about which I've said so much) images of the kinds of things that my habits of the past nailed in there. When I'm awake, these images keep making attacks on me—though they don't have any strength then. In my sleep, though, they push me not only into enjoyment, but all the way to an accord with them, and into what's very much like the act. This illusory image in my soul has so much power over my body that the deceptive sights can convince me, while I sleep, to do what the real ones can't while I'm awake.

Could I really not be myself at such times, Master, my God? Yet there's so much difference between the two selves from the moment I pass from here into sleep or pass back from there to here. Where, in sleep, is the waking reason that resists such intimations and, even if the things themselves are thrust onto its notice, remains unshaken? Does this reason really close along with the eyes? Is it truly lulled to sleep along with the physical senses?

But then how does it happen that even in sleep we often resist, keeping our resolve in mind and standing fast very chastely in

---

* 1 Corinthians 7:1–6.

† Augustine's decision to be celibate long predated his becoming a *presbyter* (literally, an "elder"—a term from which the modern "priest" in English is derived) with the right to administer the Lord's Supper. In North Africa at this time he would not have absolutely needed to be celibate in order to be a *presbyter*. The New Testament's so-called pastoral Epistles make it clear that at least until the early second century, officials of the "assembly" (later, "church") were ordinarily family men. But from even earlier, celibacy developed enormous prestige (see Augustine's own remarks above at book 8, chapter 2, and book 9, chapter 5, for example), and as early as the fourth century the church hierarchy was issuing demands for it. Celibacy was, however, not an ineluctable requirement for the priesthood in the West until after the Second Lateran Council of 1139.

that resolve, so that we give no approval to such temptations? And yet the difference is so great that when things don't turn out this way, we return to a restful conscience once we're awake. The gap itself between the two kinds of occurrences reveals to us that it wasn't we ourselves who did what, in any event, we're sorry happened within us—however it happened.

42. Isn't your hand, all-powerful God, powerful enough* to heal all the diseases† of my soul, and through your grace as it flows more plentifully, can't your hand even quell the lewd movements of my sleep? Master, you will increase more and more your gifts in me, so that my soul follows me to you, its feet free of the glue trap of lust. Then my soul won't rebel against itself. Even in sleep it will not only stop committing those shameful acts, sources of corruption, because of brute images that succeed in making the body flow dissolutely out of itself; my soul will not even share in those sensations.

To prevent any pleasure at this juncture, or to allow only the tiny amount that can be suppressed at will during sleep by a chaste disposition, not merely during this whole lifetime of mine, but even during my youth, is no great task for an all-powerful being, with the strength to do more than we ask for or conceive.‡

But as things are, I've told my good Master the state I'm still in as to this kind of wickedness; I've trembled with the triumphant sense of what you've given me, lamented over what leaves me still unfinished, and hoped that you will complete your mercies

---

* Numbers 11:23.
† Psalms 103:3.
‡ Ephesians 3:20.

in me to the point of perfect peace, which both my inward and my outward selves will enjoy with you when death is swallowed up in victory.*

43. There is another evil of the present day, which I wish would be (merely) enough for it.† We restore the everyday damage to the body by eating and drinking, but only until you destroy food and the stomach,‡ killing our need with miraculous fullness, at the time when this perishable body will clothe itself in everlasting imperishability.§

But as things are now, the necessity of eating is sweet, and I fight against that sweetness so that I'm not taken prisoner by it. I fight a daily battle through fasts, quite frequently reducing my body to slavery,¶ and yet my sufferings are beaten back by pleasure.

Hunger and thirst *are* sufferings of a sort; they burn, and like a fever they kill, unless the medicine of sustenance comes to the rescue. Since this sustenance is at hand from the consolation of your gifts, through which the earth and water and the sky are slaves to our weakness, distress can be called delight.

44. This you taught me: when I'm going to take alimentation, I should resort to it the way I resort to medication. However, when I cross over to the calm of fullness from the irritation of needfulness, in that very crossover the snare of sensual desire is lying in wait for me. That crossover is a pleasure, and there is no

* 1 Corinthians 15:54, which quotes Isaiah 25:8.
† Matthew 6:34.
‡ 1 Corinthians 6:13.
§ 1 Corinthians 15:53.
¶ 1 Corinthians 9:27.

other route for getting across to where necessity drives me to go. Though health is the reason to eat and drink, much of the time an agreeable experience, a menacing minion following, tries to maneuver ahead, so that what I say I'm doing or want to do actually happens because of her.

And the same limits don't belong to both kinds of eating. What's enough for health is too little for dissipation, and often it's unclear whether the essential care of the body is asking for help, or hedonistic self-deceit is slyly demanding that I cater to her. At this uncertainty, the soul in its sorry state cheers right up and uses the excuse to write up a plea in its own defense, thrilled that it isn't self-evident what amount of food is enough for the management of well-being, and that the pretext of health can obscure transactions of self-indulgence. Every day, I try to resist these temptations. I call on your right hand, and take my churning perplexities to you, because I don't yet have a fixed resolve on this matter.

45. I hear the voice of my God commanding me, "Don't let your hearts be weighed down by too much drinking, or by drunkenness."* Actual drunkenness is a far cry from my life; you will be merciful and keep it from coming anywhere near me. But sometimes too much drinking creeps up on your slave; you'll be merciful in putting that, too, at a great distance from me.

---

* Luke 21:34. The Latin term *crapula* has given translators apparent difficulties; I don't find that either it or its Greek parallel ordinarily means anything but excessive drinking, and I think the rendering "gluttony" or "overindulgence" is overdelicate and obfuscating.

No one, of course, can be self-restrained unless you grant it.* You allot many things to us when we pray for them, and whatever good we receive even before praying for it we receive from you; and the recognition of this afterward is a gift we receive from you. I was never a drunkard, but I've known drunkards who were made sober by you. It's thus your doing that those who were never drunkards were never drunkards, and it's your doing that those who were once drunkards didn't have to be drunkards forever, and it's even your doing that either group comes to know who's done for them what's been done.

I've heard your words: "Don't go after the things you crave, and deny yourself pleasure."† By your gift, I heard the following words too, for which I have a great passion: "And if we eat, that doesn't make us prosperous, and if we don't eat, that doesn't make us needy."‡ That means, "And eating won't give me ample resources, and not eating won't render me distressed."

And I've heard still more words: "I have learned to be content in my circumstances, and I know how to be plentifully supplied and how to endure poverty. I can do everything through him who strengthens me."§ That's Paul there, a soldier in heaven's camp, and not the dust that we are.

But remember, Master, that we *are* dust,¶ and that you made humanity out of dust,** and that it had been lost but was found.†† Not

<hr>

* Wisdom of Solomon 8:21. See the note on book 6, chapter 20.
† Sirach 18:30.
‡ 1 Corinthians 8:8.
§ Philippians 4:11–13.
¶ Psalms 103:14.
** Genesis 3:19.
†† Like the prodigal son: Luke 15:24, 32.

even Paul was able to do anything in himself, because he was the same dust—though when you breathed your breath of power into him, he said such things that made me infatuated with him: "I can do everything through him who strengthens me."*

Strengthen me, so that I'm able, too. Grant what you command, and command what you wish. That man testifies to your gifts, and what he boasts of, he boasts of in the Master.† And I've heard someone else asking for a gift: "Take away from me," he says, "the ardent desires of my stomach."‡ From this it's clear, my holy God, that when what you order comes to pass, you're giving it.

46. You have taught me, good Father, that all things are pure for those who are pure,§ but that it is an evil thing for a person to create a stumbling block by what he eats;¶ and that all of your creation is good and nothing should be rejected that is taken with thanks;** and that a food doesn't secure God's favor;†† and that no one should disdain us as to food or drink;‡‡ and that the one who eats shouldn't judge the one who doesn't, and that the one who doesn't eat should not judge the one who does.§§

I have learned these things: thanks to you, praise to you, my God, my teacher, the batterer of my ears,¶¶ the enlightener of my

---

* Philippians 4:13.
† Romans 5:11, 1 Corinthians 1:31, 2 Corinthians 10:17.
‡ Sirach 23:6.
§ Titus 1:15.
¶ Romans 14:20–21. Paul is writing about Jewish dietary law and the potential for conflict and exclusion in the very early assemblies.
** 1 Timothy 4:4.
†† 1 Corinthians 8:8.
‡‡ Colossians 2:16.
§§ Romans 14:3.
¶¶ Revelation 3:20.

heart. Snatch me away from all temptation. I don't fear the uncleanliness of any dish, but the uncleanliness of greed. I know
that Noah was permitted to eat every kind of meat that was in
use as food;* that Elijah recovered his strength by eating meat;†
that John, a man endowed with marvelous self-denial, was not
defiled when animals—that is, locusts—were given to him as
food.‡

And I know that Esau was cheated through his avidity for
lentils;§ that David reproached himself because of his longing
for water;¶ that our king was tempted not by meat but by
bread.** Also, the reason the Hebrew people in the desert deserved to be blamed wasn't that they yearned for meat, but that
in their yearning for meat they complained against the Master.††

47. Positioned in the middle of these temptations as I am, then,
I engage in everyday struggles against inordinate desire for eating and drinking. These aren't practices I can simply decide to
cut myself off from and never touch again, as I could with sex.
Therefore, the reins around my gullet must be held with carefully managed loosening and tightening.

But who is there, Master, who doesn't get drawn some distance
off the track of necessity by the galloping racehorses? Whoever
he is, he's a glorious person, and let him glorify your name. But
that's not me, because I'm just a sinful human being;‡‡ yet I, too,

* Genesis 9:3.
† 1 Kings 17:6.
‡ Matthew 3:4.
§ Genesis 25:27–34.
¶ 2 Samuel 23:15–17.
** Matthew 4:3.
†† Numbers 11:1–3.
‡‡ Luke 5:8.

glorify your name; and the one who overcame the world* intercedes with you for my sins,† counting me among the weak parts
of his body. Your eyes have seen what was the unfinished state of
that body,‡ and all of us will be written in your book.§

48. I'm not overly stressed about the allure of smells. When
they're not there, I don't miss them. When they're there, I don't
dismiss them with contempt. I would in fact be ready to do
without them from now on.

This *seems* to me to be the state of my character in this regard.
Maybe I'm wrong about it. There remains of course that lamentable darkness in which my own aptitudes within me lie hidden
from me, so that the mind, asking itself about its own powers,
should judge itself hard to believe: even its contents are generally hidden, unless they're made clear by testing. Nobody in this
life—the whole of which is called a trial¶—should be confident
as to whether a person who's become better couldn't become
worse again as well. There is one hope, one faith, and one solid
promise: your mercy.

49. The pleasures of the ears had too clingingly entangled and
subjugated me, but you released and freed me. Nowadays, I
confess I find a fair amount of satisfaction in the sounds your
words fill with the breath of life, when these words are sung
with a smooth and skilled voice—but not to the extent that I'm
clinging to the performance: I can get up and go when I want to.

* John 16:33.
† Romans 8:34.
‡ Romans 12:5, 1 Corinthians 12:22.
§ Psalms 139:16.
¶ Job 7:1.

Nevertheless, in company with the messages from which they take their life and are given a hearing by me, these sounds seek in my heart a place of no little prominence, but I'm hard put to offer them an appropriate one. Sometimes I think I grant them more honor than is suitable.

I do find that our minds are more reverently and more fervidly moved by the holy pronouncements themselves, to kindle the flame of devotion, when they're sung this way than when they aren't; of all our spirit's feelings, in all of their variety, each has its own proper mode of expression in voice and in song, and each mode is evoked by some mysteriously deep connection.

But my physical delight often dupes me. It's wrong to hand over my mind to be weakened by that delight—and that happens when sense perception is the kind of attendant who doesn't submissively follow behind but actually tries to run ahead and lead reason, for whose sole sake it deserved to be allowed there at all. This is how I sin in these circumstances, and I perceive it only later.

50. Sometimes, though, I lose a sense of proportion in avoiding this deceit, and I err on the side of too much strictness; really, I can be quite extreme, so that I want all the melodious, sweet songs that are the common means for the recitation of David's book of Psalms removed from my hearing and even that of the church. At these times, the safer measure seems to me what I remember often hearing that Athanasius the bishop of Alexandria instituted: he had the psalm reader employ such a narrow range of pitch that the result was closer to merely reading aloud than to singing.

Yet when I remember the tears I poured out in the early days after recovering my faith, and when even now I'm moved not by the song itself but by its content, which is sung with a clear voice and a highly appropriate modulation, I again recognize the great usefulness of this tradition.

Thus I waver between the danger of pleasure and the experience of music's healthfulness; and my tendency—though I'm not offering an opinion impossible for me to take back—is more toward sanctioning the custom of singing in the church. Through the entertainment of the ears, a weaker mind can rise up to devotional feeling. Yet when in my own case it happens that the song moves me more than the subject, I confess I've committed a punishable sin, and then I'd rather not hear someone singing.

So here's where I am! Weep with me, and weep for me, all of you who are inwardly working out something good, from which action can issue. Those of you who aren't don't find these things important. But you, my Master and God, hear my prayers: have regard for me, see me,* have pity, and heal me. In my own eyes, I've become a puzzle, and that puzzle itself is my sickness.

51. Finally, there's the pleasure of these eyes of mine, belonging to my body. I'll voice a confession of this pleasure for the ears in your temple to hear—brotherly, devoted ears—and with this we can wrap up discussing the temptations the body's inordinate desires offer†—though these temptations go right on pum-

---

* Psalms 80:14.
† 1 John 2:16.

meling me, while I groan and long to put on my small heavenly home and live in it.*

The eyes are in love with beautiful and varied shapes, and with bright and pleasant colors. But these must not possess my soul; God must instead possess it, as he made all these things, which are in fact very good†—but he himself is *my* good, and they aren't.

Yet all day long, through all my waking hours, they touch me, and no rest from them is granted to me, as in the case of singing's sounds, and sometimes of all sounds, when there is silence. The queen of colors herself, this ordinary light, saturates everything we see, wherever I am throughout the day, and sweet-talks me with the myriad ways she falls on things, though I'm busy with something else and not paying any attention to her. But she works her way into me so powerfully that if she suddenly withdraws, I miss her and yearn for her; and if she's gone for long, this clouds over my mind.

52. You, the light Tobit saw, when his earthly eyes were closed but he taught his son the path of life and went ahead of him with the footsteps of affection, and never went astray!‡

And you, the light that Isaac saw, when the lighted eyes of his body were weighted down and shut by old age, and when he didn't earn the right to bless his sons through recognizing them, but through blessing them earned the right to recognize them!§

---

* 2 Corinthians 5:2.
† Genesis 1:31.
‡ Tobit 4–5. The righteous blind man Tobit instructs his son Tobias on how to behave conscientiously, and sends him on a journey to recover his inheritance.
§ Genesis 27. Through his mother's connivance, Jacob, the younger son, receives the blessing that signifies a great inheritance, but Isaac suspects the deception even as he complies.

And you, the light Jacob saw when he had lost his eyesight to his own great age but shed light out of his heart into the Hebrew people's future tribes, portended by his sons! And it was with deep meaning that he transported his hands apart in a special way and laid them on his grandsons by Joseph; their father, thinking only of what was outward, did not understand and corrected him, but he himself distinguished from within.*

This is the light, and it is a oneness, and all who see it and love it are as one. But that physical light of which I've been speaking flavors the life of this world with a sweetness that's enticing and threatening for her blind lovers. When, however, they know how to praise you for that light, you, "God, the Creator of All Things," they take her up to use in that hymn to you, and they aren't used up by her in their sleep.†

This is how I desire it to be with me. I take a stand against my eyes' seductions, so that the feet with which I walk your path aren't entangled; and I raise to you the eyes that can't be seen, in the hope that you'll snatch my feet out of the snare. You repeatedly have to snatch them out, as often as they're ensnared. You never stop pulling them out (while *I* continuously get trapped

---

* Genesis 48–49. The sons of Jacob (also called Israel) are the progenitors of the Twelve Tribes of Israel, and their dying father foretells and certifies their descendants' destinies. His two grandsons born to Joseph in Egypt receive special blessings, but the choicest blessing is for the younger brother: Jacob grants this by laying his right hand on him, crossing his arms so that the older brother, brought to face him at his right because of prior birth, is blessed only by the inferior left hand. Joseph objects, but Jacob affirms the prophetic correctness of what he has done. For the gesture, Augustine uses a word never attested elsewhere, *divexus,* to which I gave this particularizing translation.
† For Ambrose's evening hymn, with its praise to God for the beauty of light, see above, book 9, chapter 32. Augustine plays on the feminine gender of the different noun for "light" that he uses here. "She" is, like a woman, to be strictly controlled for legitimate use, but is a dangerous, debilitating seductress if she acts independently.

in the treacheries scattered everywhere), since you who guard Israel will not sleep or even grow sleepy.*

53. Utterly uncountable are the things made by the various arts and handicrafts—in the way of clothing, footwear, tableware, and other household gadgets, but also paintings and a variety of other images. In going beyond essential, restrained usefulness and religious meaning, these things are merely added by humankind to the already existing enticements of the eyes. People follow outdoors (into things external to themselves) what they make, but they leave indoors (neglected and unregarded) the one by whom they themselves were made, and they send clear into exile what they were made to be.

But as for me, even on this basis I recite a hymn to you, my God, my seemliness and comeliness, and I make an offering of praise† to the one who made an offering for me; because the beautiful things sent through souls and into skilled hands come from that beauty that is above all our souls—the beauty for which my soul sighs day and night.

The makers and admirers of outside beauties draw from this higher beauty the proper parameters for evaluating things, but not the proper parameters for using things. These latter parameters are right there, but aren't perceived: people shouldn't go too far out, and they should save their strength for you‡ and not scatter it to serve la-di-da forms of effete enervation.

* Psalms 121:4.
† Psalms 116:17.
‡ See Psalms 59:9.

I, however, who say this and make this distinction, get my own feet tangled up in these same lower beautiful things—but you pull me free, Master, you pull me free, because your mercy is before my eyes.* I am pitifully trapped, but in your pity you pull me free. Sometimes I don't even perceive the rescue, because I've fallen lightly, but sometimes the rescue hurts, because I was already quite stuck.

54. Besides these, there is another form of temptation, and it is dangerous in a variety of ways. Beyond inordinate physical desire—which has to do with delight in all the senses and pleasures, a delight whose slaves are utterly lost when they distance themselves from you†—the soul contains a certain shallow, curious cupidity, cloaked in the name of comprehension and knowledge, and catered to by these same physical senses but aimed not at physical enjoyment but at exploring phenomena through the physical. Since this is part of the urge to gain information, and since the eyes are chief among the senses for this, the name in holy scripture is "the desire of the eyes."‡

Seeing is an inherent property of the eyes, but we use the word "seeing" in the case of other senses, too, when their purpose is coming to know something. We don't say, "Hear how that gleams red," or "Smell how that shines," or "Taste how radiant that is," or "Feel how that flashes." All of these phenomena are said to be seen. But we say not only "See how that glows," which only the eyes can perceive, but also "See how that sounds," "See

---

* Psalms 26:3.
† Psalms 73:27.
‡ 1 John 2:16.

how that smells," "See how that tastes," and "See how hard it is."
For this reason, as a class of impulses, exploration of the senses
is named in scripture "desire of the eyes": the other senses also,
when inquiring into comprehending something, cause us to
speak habitually of the seeing function, of which the eyes are in
charge, as resembling what those other senses do.

55. On this basis, the distinction is more obvious between how
pleasure and how curiosity is expressed through the senses:
pleasure seeks things that are beautiful, melodious, sweet-
smelling, tasty, and smooth, whereas curiosity may actually
seek the opposite of these for the purpose of testing; not in
order to submit to some irritation, but from the itch to try
something and find out about it.

What pleasure is there in seeing the wounds on a mutilated
corpse, which make you shudder in horror? Yet if there's one
lying anywhere, people flock to it, in order to get depressed, to
turn white—and they're even afraid of seeing it later in a dream.
It's as if somebody's forced them to see it now while they're awake,
or as if a rumor of its beauty persuaded them to come running.

It's just the same for the other senses, but a full account would
take too long. Because of this sick craving, "amazing things" are
exhibited at shows. It also leads to examining in detail the secrets of nature, which is beyond us. There isn't the smallest benefit in knowing these secrets, and people don't yearn for anything
anyway but simply to know them.

This craving also explains instances of trying to achieve something through the magical arts, with the same goal of twisted

knowledge. And this is also why, in religion itself, God is tested, when signs and miracles are demanded[*] not in order to save anyone, but merely because they're called for in an experiment.

56. In this enormous forest, full of snares and other dangers, see how many things I've snipped away from my heart and tossed to all sides—as you granted me the power to do, God of my rescue. But when do I dare say, when everywhere around our everyday life so many things of this sort surround us with their racket—when do I dare say I don't become riveted on anything like them, so that I stare and get caught up in frivolous concerns? Certainly, the theaters no longer ravish me, and I'm not concerned to know the courses of the stars, and my soul never asked for advice from ghosts; I execrate all "sacraments" that are in fact desecrations.

But how many manipulating contrivances does the enemy use against me, to get me to look for some sign from you, my Master and God, to whom I owe lowly and single-minded service! But I beg you in the name of our king and our fatherland, Jerusalem, the single, the pure fatherland: let me stay, forever, as far away as I am now—or even farther away—from acquiescence in all *that* stuff. But when I pray to you to save someone else, I'm riveted on a much different goal, and you grant—and in the future will grant—that I willingly follow you as you do what you choose.

57. Nevertheless, who can count how many minuscule things, which we ought to disregard, entail an everyday trial for our

---

[*] Luke 11:16, John 4:48.

inquisitiveness—and how often we fall? How many times is it that, when we begin by putting up with people telling silly stories—and we give ourselves the excuse that we don't want to give offense to the weak-minded—we then gradually, and gladly, come to concentrate on what's being said?

I don't watch a dog chasing a hare when it's happening in the circus, but when it happens in the countryside I happen to be crossing, it may turn me away from something important I'm thinking about, and that hunt can turn me wholly to itself. It doesn't force me physically to take my mount off track, but it tilts my heart toward itself. If you didn't point out my weakness and quickly warn me either to raise my mind to you through some meditation on this sight, or to disregard it entirely and pass on, I'd grow paralyzed and empty-headed.

And what about the frequent times when I'm sitting at home, and a lizard catching flies, or a spider entwining in her net the flies falling into it, engrosses me? Just because these are *tiny* animals doesn't mean that the same predation isn't going on within me, does it? I proceed from there to praising you, the wonder-working creator and ruler of all things, but it's not on that basis that I *begin* to be mindful. Getting up quickly is one thing, not falling is another.

But my life is full of such incidents, and my one hope is your very great mercy. When our heart becomes a container for stuff like this, and carries around masses of it, an endless supply, then even our prayers are often broken in on and disturbed; and before your eyes, when we direct the voice of our hearts at your ears, an onrush of frivolous thoughts from somewhere or other cuts short this great undertaking.

58. How could we possibly class this problem, too, among the things to be disregarded? But will anything except your known mercy bring us back into hope? You *have* begun to change us. *You* know to what a great degree you've changed me, at first curing my itch to justify myself, so that you could become forgiving toward all of my other sins as well, healing all my diseases and buying back my life from rotting in the grave, and crowning me with your tender mercy and tenderheartedness, and satisfying my desire with good things,* after you suppressed my arrogance with the fear of you, and tamed me to take your yoke on my neck. I carry it now, and it sits on me lightly, since this is the promise you carried out;† the yoke truly was light, though I didn't know it when I was afraid to put myself under it.

59. But Master, you who alone hold mastery without a diseased pride, because you alone are the true Master,‡ having no master yourself—yet a third kind of temptation hasn't let me be, has it?§ And can it possibly let me be any time in my life? I mean the wish to be loved by other people, and for no reason except that it's a source of joy that's really not joy.

Instead, it's a miserable life and an ugly ostentation; these are perhaps the chief causes for not loving you and not fearing you with pure hearts.¶ For this reason, you stand against the arrogant and give your favor to the lowly,** and you thunder above worldly ambitions, and the foundations of the mountains shake.††

---

* Psalms 103:3–5.
† Matthew 11:29–30.
‡ Isaiah 37:20.
§ See 1 John 2:16; the Latin scripture refers to this fault as "the arrogance of life.".
¶ Psalms 19:9.
** James 4:6, 1 Peter 5:5, quoting Proverbs 3:34.
†† Psalms 18:7 and 13.

Since for certain positions in human society it's essential to be loved and feared by others, the enemy of our true happiness is after us, baiting his snares with "Bravo, bravo!" so that when we go to greedily, recklessly gather that up, we're caught. Then we remove our joy from your truth and move it into human deceits, and it pleases us to be loved not because of you but in place of you. That way, the adversary, having made us like himself, can hang on to us, not for caring concord but for communion in punishment.

He has elected to enthrone himself in the north,* so that over-cast, frozen people serve him, who imitate you by a twisted, distorted route. But as for us, Master, look, we are your own tiny flock†—you must take possession of it.‡ Hold out your wings, and we'll retreat under them. You must be our boast, our glory. We must be loved because of you, and your Word must be feared among us.

Anyone who wants to be praised by humankind while he finds fault with you won't be defended by humankind when he's judged by you, and he won't be rescued by them when he's con-demned by you. Even when it's not a sinner being praised for pursuing his soul's cravings, or a wrongdoer being blessed,§ but merely a person being praised because of some gift you've given him, and he has more joy in being praised than in having the gift that's the occasion for praise, then even that guy is blamed by you while he's being commended by human words. And who-ever has given the compliments is better than the one who got them. The first approved of God's gift that was evident in a

---

* Isaiah 14:12–14.
† Luke 12:32.
‡ Isaiah 26:13.
§ Psalms 10:3. The Latin is different from the standard English version.

human being, whereas the second has preferred a human gift—
the approval—to the actual divine one.

60. Every day we're tried by these trials, Master; we're tried
without a pause. The human tongue that praises us is the daily
furnace that tests the purity of our gold.* You command for us
self-restraint even in this area: give what you order, and you can
order what you wish. You know the groans of my heart directed
at you on this subject, and the rivers running from my eyes. It's
even hard for me to deduce how much I'm purified from this
infection, and I have great anxiety over my hidden faults,† which
your eyes are aware of but mine aren't.

With other kinds of temptations, there's some degree of capacity for putting myself to the test, but in this case there's practically none. I see how far I've come in my ability to rein myself
in from physical pleasures and from superfluous investigative
inquisitiveness, whenever I go without the stimuli, either by an
act of will, or simply because they aren't there: then I ask myself
how much more or less annoying it is for me not to have them.

There's wealth, moreover, which is sought after so that it can
serve one of the three inordinate desires I've described (or two
of them, or all of them, as the case may be): if someone isn't
fully clear in his mind whether he disregards the wealth he has,
it can be given up, so that he can test himself.

But to do without praise so as to test our ability to do without it,
are we supposed to live discreditably, and in such a depraved
and monstrous way that everyone who knows us reviles us?

* Proverbs 27:21.
† Psalms 19:12.

What greater lunacy could be spoken or thought of? If words of praise are the normal and fitting companions of a good life and good works, then it's as unsuitable for this accompaniment as for a good life itself to be abandoned. But I can't tell whether it would be with equanimity or with pain that I could do without something, unless that something is actually absent.

61. So what am I testifying to you about this kind of temptation, Master? What else but that I'm delighted with praise?

But I'm more delighted with the truth itself than with praise. If I had the choice whether to be raving mad and in error about everything while getting praise from the whole world, or to be firm and unshakable in the truth though everyone castigated me, I'm clear on which I'd choose.

On the other hand, I wouldn't want an endorsement coming from somebody else's mouth to increase my joy at something good in me. But such an endorsement does increase my joy, I admit—and not only that, but censure diminishes it.

But when I'm distressed by my wretched plight in this regard, the idea of an extenuation steals into me. You know what it's worth, God—though it leaves *me* unsure. Anyway, here it is: you commanded not only self-restraint for us (that is, you tell us from which things to withhold our love), but also justice (which means you tell us where to direct our love), and it has been your will that we love not only you but our neighbor as well.

Accordingly, it's often my impression that I'm delighted by the progress my neighbor is making, or by his potential for progress, when I'm delighted at his discerning praise. Conversely, when I hear him finding fault with either something he doesn't know anything about, or something good, I'm downcast about his fault. I'm also sometimes gloomy at praise of myself, when I myself don't approve of what's being praised in me, and also when my petty, trivial merits are more highly valued than they should be.

But then again, how would I know whether the reason my emotions are stirred up this way is that I don't want the person praising me to judge me any differently than I judge myself? It wouldn't, in this case, be that I'm stirred by the thought of what's in his interest, but that the same commendable things I like in myself are more agreeable to me when somebody else likes them, too. In a certain sense, I'm not being praised as long as my own opinion about myself isn't praised, which is the case when either things I don't like are praised, or things are praised more that I like less. Isn't the upshot that I'm unsure what my attitude is here?

62. So here it is: I see in you, who are the truth, that where praise of me is concerned, I ought to be touched not for my own sake, but because of what's in my neighbor's interest. But whether that's how it is with me, I don't know. In this connection, I'm less well known to myself than you are to me. I beg you, my God, inform on me to myself, so that I can confess the affliction I've found in myself to my brothers, who will pray for me.

Again, and more carefully this time, let me question myself. If, when I'm praised, I'm stirred by what's in my neighbor's interest, then why am I less upset when someone else is unjustly taken to task than if it's me? Why do I find such an affront more galling when it's against myself than if, right in front of me, it's launched against someone else with equal unfairness?

Don't I know the answers here, either? Even now, does this remain to be dealt with: that I, in myself, lead myself astray, and that before your eyes I don't behave truthfully, in my heart and with my tongue? Place a great distance, Master, between this insanity and me, so that the words of my mouth aren't a sinner's oil for smearing on my head to make it fat and stupid.*

63. I am needy and poor,† but better off if I moan in private out of unhappiness with myself and seek your mercy, until my shortcomings are overcome and come to perfection in that peace that an arrogant eye never sees.

But speech issuing from the mouth and actions that become popularly known carry with them extremely perilous temptations, due to the passion for praise. This passion cadges and amasses marks of esteem to enhance some sort of individual prominence. The passion for praise remains even when I take myself to task for it, by the very fact that I do so: often the boasting over contempt for fatuous boasting is *more* fatuous. Thus there's no boasting about actual contempt of boasting: while the boasting is going on, it can't be condemnation of boasting.

64. Also within humankind, within ourselves is another bad temptation in the category of pride: people have an emptifying, narrow self-approbation, while invoking either no reaction or

* Psalms 141:5.
† Psalms 109:22.

disapproval in others, and not even stirring themselves to seek anyone else's approval.

But in their self-satisfaction they're greatly unsatisfactory to you. They're gratified not only by things that aren't good, as if these *were* good, but also by good things that are yours, as if these were their own; or they go so far as to suppose that the good things coming from you are due to their own merits; or, astonishingly, while believing that good things come from you as your free gift, from your grace, they don't rejoice in the commonality of this, but are jealous of your grace toward other people!

In all of these perils and hardships, you see the trembling of my own heart, and I perceive that my injuries are repeatedly healed by you rather than not inflicted at all.

65. Where haven't you walked with me, Truth, teaching me what to avoid and what to seek out, whenever I passed on to you my lower observations—or as many as I could—and asked for your advice? As far as I was able, I scoured the outward world with my perceptions; I paid attention to my body's life originating from within myself, and to my own physical senses in themselves.

From there, I entered the inner rooms of my memory, the myriad extensive spaces marvelously full of innumerable provisions, and I contemplated them and was terrified;* and I could discern none of them without you, yet I didn't discover that any of them *was* you. And I myself wasn't you, either—I the discoverer, who scoured the entire lot and tried to sort it all out and rank it according to its various values, using my senses as messengers to pick out some things to investigate, judging that other

* Habakkuk 3:2.

things were blended with myself, and setting apart and numbering off those messengers themselves, and then, among the extensive wealth of my memory, going over some things, stashing away others, and digging out still others.

Even while I was doing this, I myself wasn't you—and I mean my power, by which I did it, wasn't you. You're the enduring light I asked to advise me about all these things, as to whether they existed, what they were, and what they were worth, and I continually heard you teaching and commanding me.

And I often do just that: it delights me, and to the extent that I can take respite from my essential activities, I take refuge in this pleasure. But in all of these things I run through, asking your advice about them, I don't find any safe space for my soul except in you. There everything of mine that's scattered can be gathered together, and nothing of me can withdraw from you.

And sometimes you allow me to enter into an emotion deep inside that's most unusual, to the point of a mysterious sweetness, and if this is made whole in me, it will be something this life can't ever be. But I fall back, under my anguished burdens, into these ordinary things, and am swallowed back into what I'm used to, and am stuck there; I weep powerfully, but then I'm powerfully stuck. That's what the baggage of habit is good for! I'm strong enough to be here, though I hardly long to be; I long to be there, though I'm not strong enough, so in either place I'm miserable.

66. Thus I examined the diseases of my sins in three categories of inordinate desire,* and I called on your right hand for my

* 1 John 2:16.

healing. I saw your shining light with my wounded heart, and was driven back when that light struck me. I said, "Who has the capacity for that?"

I was ejected from before your face, from before your eyes.* You are the truth† keeping watch over the universe, it was clear, and I didn't want to lose you through my greed, but I wanted to keep falsehood along with you—just as no one wants to tell a lie in such way that he himself doesn't know what's true. Thus I lost you, because you don't stoop to being kept along with falsehood.

67. Whom could I find to reconcile me with you? Should I canvass the angels? With what kind of prayer? With what rites? Many people trying to return to you but lacking the ability in themselves have tried this, I hear, and have fallen into a craving for odd revelations, and have been held fit only for illusions.

In their lofty flights, they sought you through snobbish scholarship, sticking out their chests with self-regard rather than beating them in repentance. They recruited those they resembled at heart, the powers of the air,‡ as fellow plotters and partners in pride, by whose magic powers they were hoodwinked. They were looking for a mediator to purify them, and this wasn't one.

The devil, of course, was the one taking the form of an angel of light§ and was very successful at luring in pretentious entities of the flesh, given that he himself didn't have any bodily being. They were mortal, and sinners, whereas you, Master, with

* Psalms 31:22.
† John 14:6.
‡ Ephesians 2:2. The devil is thought to be ruling demons in a sort of invisible principality.
§ 2 Corinthians 11:14.

whom they were trying to be reconciled in this egotistical manner, are immortal and without sin.

But a mediator between God and humankind* ought to be like God in one way, and like humankind in another way. If he were like humankind in both ways, he would be too far removed from God, and if he were like God in both ways, he would be too far removed from humankind, and could not be a mediator.

The devil, therefore, that fraudulent mediator by whom presumption deserves, according to your secret judgments, to be duped, has one thing in common with humankind, which is sin. He wants to look as if he has something in common with God: because he doesn't have a body, the clothing of mortality, he wants to pretend he's immortal. But since sin pays death as its wage,† he shares with human beings the thing for which he's condemned to death along with them.

68. The truthful mediator, whom in your mysterious mercy you sent and revealed to mankind, so that by his example they might learn that very same humility; that mediator of God and humankind, the human Jesus Christ, appeared between mortal sinners and the just immortal being‡—he was mortal with humankind, just with God. Since justice pays the wage of life§ and peace, through justice joined to God he was to cancel the death¶ of the ungodly** when they were justified, the death he was willing to share with them.

---

* 1 Timothy 2:5.
† Romans 6:23.
‡ 1 Timothy 2:5.
§ Romans 6:23.
¶ Romans 4:5.
** 2 Timothy 1:10.

He was revealed to his holy people of that time long ago, so that they would be saved through faith in his suffering that was to come, as we are saved through faith in his suffering that is past. Inasmuch as he was a man, he was a mediator, but inasmuch as he is the Word, he is not in the middle, because he is equal to God,* and is God in the presence of God, and one God together with him.

69. How you loved us, good Father, who did not spare your only son, but handed him over for the sake of us, the wicked!† How you loved us, for whose sake your son, though not considering it an act of robbery to be your equal, was subjugated and reduced clear to death on the cross!‡

But he was the only one among the dead with free will, having both the power to lay down his life and the power to take it up again.§ For our sake, he was both your victor and your sacrificial victim, and the victor because he was the victim. For our sake he was both your sacrificing priest and your sacrifice, and he was the priest because he was the sacrifice.¶ He was born from you yet acted as our slave, thereby turning us from your slaves into your sons.**

Deservedly on him rests my strong hope that you will cure all my diseases,†† through him who sits at your right hand and intercedes for us;‡‡ without him, I would have no hope. These are

* Philippians 2:6.
† Romans 8:32.
‡ Philippians 2:6–8.
§ John 10:18.
¶ Hebrews 7:27.
** Galatians 4:5.
†† Psalms 103:3.
‡‡ Romans 8:34.

many major diseases that I have, many major ones, but your healing art is more powerful than they are. We could have considered your Word debarred from any connection with humankind, and thus have lost hope for ourselves, if your son didn't become embodied and live among us.*

70. Appalled by my sins and the massive mound of my misery, I had deliberated in my heart and considered retreating into isolation, but you held me back and gave me your assurance, saying, "For this reason, Christ died for all of humankind, so that those who are alive no longer live for themselves, but for the one who died for them."†

Here, then, Master, I throw my troubles onto you, so that I can live,‡ and I will contemplate the wonders of your law.§ You know my callowness and my weakness.¶ Teach me and heal me.

Jesus, your only son, in whom all hoards of wisdom and knowledge are hidden away,** bought me back at the price of his blood.†† The arrogant must not slander me, since I contemplate‡‡ the price paid for me, and I eat and drink it and share it out.§§ As a poor man, I long to be filled full by it, among those who eat and are filled full.¶¶ And those who seek the Master praise him.***

* John 1:14.
† 2 Corinthians 5:15.
‡ Psalms 55:22.
§ Psalms 119:18.
¶ Psalms 69:5.
** Colossians 2:3, Revelation 5:9.
†† 1 Corinthians 6:20.
‡‡ Psalms 119:21–23.
§§ As an official of the church, Augustine presided over the rite of the Lord's Supper: see John 6:55, 57, 1 Corinthians 10:31, 11:29.
¶¶ Psalms 22:26, Luke 16:20–22.
*** Psalms 70:4.

Book 11

1. Master, since eternity belongs to you, you couldn't fail to know, could you, what I'm telling you? And you don't *see* according to time what *happens* in time, do you? So why, then, am I directing so many narratives at you? Certainly you don't know these things through *me;* but I do arouse my feelings toward you, and the feelings of those who read this, so that we can all say, "The Master is great, and is to be praised loudly."* I've already said, and I'm going to say again, that I do this out of passion for my passion for you.

We do of course entreat you through prayer, though the truth states, "Your Father knows what you need before you ask him

* Psalms 48:1, 96:4, 145:3.

for it."* We therefore open our feelings toward you in testifying to our miseries, and to your commiseration for us, so that you can set us free altogether—and you've already begun—and so that we stop being wretched in ourselves and become happy, become blessed in you—since you have called us to become poor in spirit, and gentle, and mournful, and hungry and thirsty for justice, and tenderhearted and pure of heart, and makers of peace.†

Look at how much I've narrated at you, according to my ability and my will—because *you* took the lead in willing me to testify to you, God my Master; because you are good, because your mercy is forever.‡

2. But when will I be up to articulating, with the pen that is my tongue here,§ all of your arm-twisting and threats, all your comforts and guidance, through all of which you led me to preach your Word and to share out your rite of Communion to your people? Even if I'm up to setting out these matters in the correct order, they still take a great deal of time: the water clock's dripping has a high price in my eyes.

But for a long time now, I've been incandescing to contemplate your law¶ and to testify to you, as to both what I know and what I don't know, as to the origins of my illumination and the remains of my darkness, until my weakness is devoured by your stalwart strength. I don't want to fritter away on anything else the hours I find free from the necessary physical relaxation,

---

* Matthew 6:8.
† Matthew 5:3–9.
‡ Psalms 118:1.
§ Psalms 45:1.
¶ Psalms 1:2.

mental concentration, and servitude—both what we owe to mankind and also what we don't owe but render anyway.

3. Master, my God, attend to my prayer and let your mercy hear my yearning, since it is not only for myself that this yearning seethes; it wants to be of use in love for my brothers and sisters— and you see in my heart that this is true. Let me give as a sacrifice to you the servitude of my thought and speech, and you give me what I can offer up back to you. I have nothing, you see; I am poor,* but you are rich for all who call on you† because, though you have no anxieties yourself, you carry ours.

Circumcise in spirit‡ my speaking, the speaking that happens both inside me and outside me, and keep it from any kind of recklessness and any kind of falsehood.§ Let my delight in your holy writing be pure. Don't let me be deceived in reading it; don't let me deceive others on the basis of it.

Master, listen and have pity, Master, my God, you who are the light of the blind, and the manly might of the weak, and for the sighted their light from the very start, and the manly fortitude of the strong. Listen to my soul and hear it shouting from the depths.¶ Unless your hearing is there in the depths, where will we go, to whom will we shout?

Yours is the day, and yours is the night.** By your will the moments fly by. Bestow out of that supply a space for our contem-

---

* Psalms 86:1.
† Romans 10:12.
‡ Romans 2:29, echoing a reported Old Testament metaphor of "circumcision of the heart."
§ Exodus 6:12.
¶ Psalms 130:1.
** Psalms 74:16.

plation concerning the mysteries of your law, and don't keep the door shut to those of us who are knocking.*

It couldn't have been for nothing that you wanted so many pages of dimly lit, recondite things written: those forests of words have stags native to them, who retire inward and revive themselves, walking around and grazing, reclining and ruminating.†

Oh, Master, make me whole, and unveil your pages. Your voice here is my delight, your voice is superior to a flood of delights. Give me what I'm in love with; I do love it, and you gave me my love for it. Don't desert your own gifts. Don't disdain the thirsty, sprouting field that belongs to you. Let me testify to you with whatever I find in your books. Let me hear the voice of praise. Let me drink you in and consider the marvels of your law,‡ here from the beginning when you made the sky and the earth, and clear to your everlasting kingdom, when we will be together with you in your holy city.§

4. Master, have pity on me and hear what I long for,¶ as I do think my longing isn't for the things of this earth—it's not for things made of gold or silver, or precious stones, or for handsome clothing, or distinctions and positions of power, or pleasures of the body. It's not even for the body's necessities, for what we need to sojourn in this life: when we seek your king-

---

* Matthew 7:7–8, Luke 11:9–10.
† Psalms 41:1.
‡ Psalms 119:18.
§ I.e., from Genesis 1:1 to the book of Revelation.
¶ Psalms 27:7.

dom and your justice, all these other things are given to us as well anyway.*

Look, my God, and see where my yearning comes from. Criminals told me stories about pleasures, but that's not what your law has told me, Master.† *There* is where my yearning comes from. Look, Father, look carefully and see and judge, and may it please you that within the sight of your mercy I find grace in standing before you, so that when I knock, the indoors of your discourse is opened to me.‡

I beg you by our Master, Jesus Christ your son, the man at your right hand, the son of humanity, whom you strengthened as your intermediary, your intermediary and ours, too,§ to seek us out when we weren't seeking you¶—no, you sought us *so that* we would seek you, meaning your Word, through which you made everything** (including me). This was your only son, through whom you called the believing people (including me) to be your adoptive children.†† I beg you in his name, because he sits at your right hand and intervenes with you for us,‡‡ and because all treasures of wisdom and knowledge are buried away in him.§§ I seek these treasures in your books. Moses wrote about him; he himself says so, the Truth says so.¶¶

---

* Matthew 6:33.
† See Psalms 119:85.
‡ Matthew 7:7–8, Luke 11:9–10.
§ 1 Timothy 2:5.
¶ Romans 10:20, quoting Isaiah 65:1–2.
** John 1:1–3.
†† Galatians 4:5.
‡‡ Romans 8:34.
§§ Colossians 2:3.
¶¶ John 5:46, 14:6. See footnote on next page.

5. Let me hear and understand how in the beginning you made the sky and the earth. Moses wrote this.* He wrote this, he wrote this and went away, he went from here to there, from you to you, and he is not in my presence. If he were, I would take hold of him and question him, and beg him in your name to open up these matters to me, and I would apply my body's ears to the sounds breaking out of his mouth.

If he spoke the Hebrew language, he would be knocking on my perception to no purpose, and nothing of what he said would reach my mind. But if he spoke Latin, I would know what he said. But then how would I know if he spoke the truth? Because if I were to know this, wouldn't I have to know it from him?

Inside me, for sure, inside where my thought is at home, the truth would speak not in Hebrew or Greek or Latin or a barbarian language, or with the voice of musical instruments; the truth would speak without any noisy syllables and say, "He's speaking the truth." And right away, in certainty and confidence, I would say to Moses, who belongs to you, "You're speaking the truth."

So, since I can't question him, it's you I ask, you, the Truth, which filled him when he spoke true things. My God, I beg you, show clemency to my sinfulness. You granted to Moses, your slave, the ability to say these things. Grant, even to me, the ability to understand them.

6. Here they are, the sky and the earth. They shout that they have been made. They change and they diversify. Whatever, on

---

* Genesis 1:1. The first five books of the Bible, the Pentateuch, are attributed by tradition to Moses's authorship.

the other hand, has not been made, yet exists, has nothing in it that was there before it; to contain anything that was not there before means to change and diversify.

They also shout that they didn't make themselves: "We exist because we were made. Therefore we didn't exist before we *could* exist; that would have meant we could come into being from ourselves." And the voice with which they speak is evidence in itself.

So you, Master, made them, you who are beautiful (for they are beautiful), you who are good (for they are good), you who exist (for they exist)—but they are not beautiful, and they are not good, and they do not exist in such a way as belongs to you, their Maker. Compared with you, they are not beautiful or good, and they don't exist. We know this—thanks be to you! But compared with your knowledge, our knowledge is ignorance.

7. But how did you make the sky and the earth? What was the machine with which you completed this massive work? You weren't like a human craftsman shaping a material object from another material object. Such a person does so through the inclination of his soul, which has the power to place on the material whatever form it likes, a form the soul sees within itself with an inward eye. (Where, by the way, would the soul, unless made by you, get this power?) The form is placed on something that already exists, that has some capacity for being. It could be earth or stone or wood or gold, or anything else of this kind.

But where would all that stuff come from unless you had ordained it? You made the workman; you made his body, and you made his mind, which governs all the outward parts of his body.

You made the material from which he makes something, and you made his talent, through which he takes possession of his craft and sees within himself what he's going to make outwardly. You made his physical perception, which is the go-between and transfers his creation from his mind to the material and then takes back to his mind the news of what has been made, so that within itself the mind can consult the truth presiding over it as to whether the object has been made well. All these things praise you, the creator of all things.

But how do you make them? How, God, did you make the sky and the earth? You certainly didn't make the sky and the earth *in* the sky, or *in* the earth, either; or in the atmosphere, or in bodies of water, since these belong to the sky and the earth. And you didn't make the entire universe *in* the entire universe, because before it was made, it didn't exist as a place where it *could* be made, so that it could exist. And you didn't hold in your hand anything that you used to make the sky and the earth, since where would you get this thing, which you yourself hadn't made but which you could use for making something?

What is in existence, after all, except because of your existence? And so you spoke and things were made, and in your Word you made them.*

8. But how did you speak? It couldn't have been the way a voice was created out of a cloud, saying, "This is my beloved son."† That voice was carried out and carried through, started and finished. The syllables made their sounds and passed by, the sec-

* Psalms 33:9.
† Matthew 3:17, 17:5, Luke 9:35.

ond one after the first, the third after the second, and so on, in their proper order, until the last one, after all the others; and then, after that last one, silence.

It's glaringly and strikingly obvious that the activity of some created being delivered that voice, and that this being—though itself existing in time—was a slave to your eternal will. And the outward ear brought the news of your words, which were created only for a time, to the sagacious mind, whose interior ear is set where it can hear your eternal Word, and that ear compared these words that made sounds for a time with your eternal Word that exists in silence, and the mind said, "Both the one and the other are far away from me. These material things are far below me, and they don't really exist, because they run off and pass away, whereas the Word of God remains above me for eternity."*

If in words passing by as they made sounds you spoke to cause the sky and the earth to come into existence, and that's the way you created the sky and the earth, then there would already have been a material creation *before* the sky and the earth, and that creation's voice would have run its course in time through movements that exist in time.

But there was no material object before the sky and the earth; or if there was, you had certainly not used a passing voice to create it—whatever it was, as the source of the passing voice with which you spoke to create the sky and the earth? But whatever that thing was from which you created a passing voice, unless that thing was created by you, it could not have existed in the first place.

* Isaiah 40:8.

So, through what sort of word did you speak, so that a material object could come into being, and the words "Let the sky and the earth be made" could come into being from that material object?

9. Thus you call us to understand the Word, God in your presence, God.* It is spoken forever, and in it all things are spoken forever. What is spoken does not end, so that another thing can be spoken and the whole can eventually be spoken; rather, everything is spoken forever at the same time. Otherwise, this would be time and change, and not true eternity or true immortality. I know this, my God, and I give thanks. I know it, I testify to you, Master, and along with me whoever is not ungrateful for certain truth knows it and blesses you.

We know this, Master, we know this inasmuch as whatever does not exist that used to exist, and whatever exists that didn't use to exist, dies and arises. In contrast, nothing, no part of your Word, gives place to or takes the place of anything, because your Word is truly immortal and eternal. For that reason, by means of your Word, which is one with you in eternity, you say everything that you say at the same time and forever; and whatever you say must come into being comes into being; and you don't create in any way except by speaking—however, not everything you create by speaking comes into being at the same time, or is eternal.

10. But please tell me, my Master and God—why? Somehow I see it, but I don't know how to state it except in the following

* John 1:1.

way. Everything that begins or ceases to exist does so at that moment when it is recognized that now it needs to do so; and this is recognized by an eternal reasoning, in which nothing begins and nothing ends.

This act of reasoning is your Word, which is also the *principium*, "the beginning," or "the first, guiding principle or authority," because it also speaks to us. In this way, in the Gospel the Word speaks through the flesh,* and this Word was heard outwardly by human ears so that we would believe, and so that inwardly the Word would be sought and found in eternal truth, where the good teacher, who is the only teacher,† teaches all his students.

There, inwardly, I hear your voice, Master, as you speak to me, because the one who speaks to us teaches us. On the other hand, if anyone doesn't teach us, even if he's speaking he's not speaking to us. What, then, teaches us if not the truth that stands fast?

Even when we're prompted by changeable creation, we're led to the truth that stands steady. There we truly learn, when we stand and hear him and rejoice beyond rejoicing at the voice of the betrothed,‡ and return, and restore ourselves to the source of our being.

In this way, it is the beginning, the starting point, the first authority or principle, because unless it stayed steady while we wandered around, there would be no place to return to. When we return from our wandering, we do that by an act of recognition. The Word teaches us, so that we can recognize it as the

---

* John 1:14.
† Matthew 23:8.
‡ John 3:29.

beginning and the first guiding principal or authority, which speaks to us.

11. In this *beginning,* or *principle,* God, you made the sky and the earth, in your Word, in your son, in your strength, in your wisdom,* in your truth, marvelously speaking and marvelously creating. Who will grasp it? Who will tell about it? What is it that shines straight into me and strikes through my heart without wounding it? I shake with terror, and I'm aflame with desire. I shake inasmuch as I'm not like this thing at all; I'm aflame inasmuch as I *am* like it.

Wisdom, wisdom is exactly what it is that shines through, tearing apart the fog that covers me again, when I falter in that murk, and under the heap of my punishments, because my vigor is broken down by my need,† and I can't bear up under the weight of my own goods, of my own good, until you, Master, who have shown yourself forgiving toward all of my wrongdoing, also heal all of my diseases; since you'll buy my life back too and keep it from rotting away, and you'll crown me with tenderness and tenderheartedness, and you'll satisfy my longing with good things, as my youth will be renewed, like an eagle's.‡

We're saved by hope, and in patience we wait for the fulfillment of your promises.§ Whoever can, let him hear you discoursing within himself. As for me, I'll confidently shout, on the basis of your oracle—which is my heart—how exalted are your works, Master: you've made them all with wisdom;¶ and wisdom is the

* 1 Corinthians 1:24.
† Psalms 31:10.
‡ Psalms 103:3–5.
§ Romans 8:24.
¶ Psalms 104:24.

beginning, the leading principle, the guiding principle, the authority, and in that beginning you made the sky and the earth.

12. Isn't it a sign of being completely out of date* that people say to us, "What was God doing before he made the sky and the earth? If he wasn't doing anything," they go on, "if he wasn't busy, then why didn't he stay off work from then on and forever, just as he always did before? If any new impulse, any new will arose in God, so that he undertook the creation, which he'd never undertaken before, how can there be 'true eternity,' given that a will arises that didn't exist before?

"God's will isn't a created thing; instead, it precedes creation, because nothing could be created unless the will of the Creator came before it. Logically, then, God's will belongs to God's actual substance. But if something arose within God's substance that didn't exist before, it can't be truly called that eternal substance you were talking about. If, on the other hand, God's will was eternal, and out of that eternal will he willed creation, why isn't creation also eternal?"

13. The people who say these things don't understand you yet—you, the wisdom of God, the light of our minds. They don't understand how things can come into being both through you and in you. They've tried to play the eternal wise guys, but even now their hearts are fluttering around past and future movements of things, and even now proving themselves pieces of pure frivolity.

---

* Colossians 3:9.

Who's going to take hold of their hearts and nail them down, so that they stand still for a little while, and for a little while are able to take hold of your splendor that stands still, always and eternally? Then they could compare it with periods of time that never stand still, and they'd be able to see that there's no comparison.

Their hearts would see that a long time can't become long unless it's composed of many past movements, which can't be drawn out all at once. In eternity, in contrast, nothing can pass by; the present is the entirety. But there's no *time* that's wholly present.

Their hearts would see that all of past time is driven out of the future, and that all future time follows out of the past, and that all past and future time is created by that time which is always present, and that it runs from there.

Who will hold the human heart, so that it stands still and sees how eternity, which is neither future nor past, stands still and decrees future and past times?

Surely my writing hand doesn't have the strength to bring this about? Nor, surely, can my speaking mouth, acting in place of my hand, manage such a considerable thing through its baby-talk?

14. So here's how I answer someone saying, "What was God doing before he made the sky and the earth?" I don't answer the way a certain person is reported to have done, by dodging this aggressive question with a joke: "He was preparing hell for deep probers like you."

A potshot is what insight is not. That's why I don't give that answer, but would prefer this one: "I don't know what I don't know." That's better than saying what results in laughter at somebody asking a deep question, and praise of somebody giving an answer that isn't true.

I say instead that you, our God, are the creator of all creation. And if we understand all creation under the heading "the sky and the earth," I boldly say, "Before God made the sky and the earth, he didn't make anything." If he was making something, what was it if not creation? And whatever's useful that I long to know, I wish I knew it as certainly as I know that no created thing came into being before creation could come into being.

15. And if anybody's mind wanders on inward wings through images of past time and is amazed that you, the all-powerful God, creator of all things, sustainer of all things, the craftsman who fashioned the sky and the earth, held off through uncountable ages from this work of creation before you performed it, let him wake up and take cognizance of being amazed at things that never happened.

How could those countless ages have passed by if you, the originator and creator of all ages, didn't make them?* What ages could there have been that weren't created by you? And how did they pass by, if they'd never existed?

Since you're the framer of all time, if there was some time before you made the sky and the earth, how can it be said that you weren't at work then? Time itself, in which you weren't working, is something *you* would have made, and no ages could have

---

* Hebrews 1:2. The standard English version is different from the Latin.

passed by before you created them. If, conversely, there was no time before the sky and the earth, why this question of what you were doing then? There was no "then" when there was no time.

16. You, God, don't precede time by means of time; otherwise, you wouldn't precede all time. Rather, you precede everything that is past, through a transcendent state of the eternity that is always present; and you are superior to everything that is to come in that those things are to come, and once they come they're going to be past. You, however, are always the same, you are yourself, and your years don't run out.* Your years don't arrive and depart, but ours do, so that they can all eventually arrive.

Your years all stand fast together because they do stand fast, and the ones departing aren't shut out by the ones arriving, as none pass by. Our years, on the other hand, will be complete when they're all gone. Your years are a single day,† and your day isn't every day but today, because your today doesn't give way to tomorrow, and your today doesn't replace your yesterday. Your today is eternity. Therefore, you begot someone who shared your eternity when you said, "Today I have begotten you."‡ You made all time, and you are before all time; and there wasn't any time in which there was no time.

17. So there hasn't been any time in which you hadn't made something, because you made time itself; and no periods of time share eternity with you, because you remain through all of

* Psalms 102:27.
† See Psalms 90:4, quoted in 2 Peter 3:8.
‡ Psalms 2:7, quoted in Acts 13:33 and Hebrews 1:5, 5:5.

them. If they remained continuously, they wouldn't be periods of time.

But what, after all, *is* time? Who could explain it easily and briefly? Who could grasp it so as to express it in words, or just comprehend it through cogitation? And yet what do we mention more offhandedly and self-assuredly in conversation than time? We do in fact understand "time" when we talk of it, and we also understand when we hear somebody else talking of it. So: What is time?

If nobody's asking me, I know. If I'm trying to explain it to somebody who asks me, I don't know. However, I can confidently say I know that if nothing passes by, there wouldn't be past time; and that if nothing arrives, there wouldn't be future time; and that if nothing existed, there wouldn't be present time.

So how is it that there can be these two kinds of time, the past and the future, when the past no longer exists and the future doesn't exist yet? As for the present, if it were always present and didn't go by into the past, it wouldn't be time but eternity. But then, if the present, in becoming time, comes into being in such a way that it passes into the past, how can we say that the present exists, either? The reason for its being is actually that it *won't* be. I guess, then, that we couldn't truly say that time exists, unless through its existence it aims at nonexistence?

18. And yet we do say "a long time" and "a short time"—but we don't say these things except about the past and the future. A "long time" in the past is what we call, for example, a hundred years ago, and likewise a "long time" in the future is what we

might call a hundred years from now. When it's "a short time ago," on the other hand, it's a term for, let's say, ten days ago, and "a short time in the future" might be ten days from now.

But in what way is something long or short, if it doesn't exist? The past doesn't exist anymore, and the future doesn't yet exist. Accordingly, let's not say, "It *is* a long time since ..." about the past, but rather, "It *has been* been a long time since ..."; and about the future, let's say, "It *will be* a long time until ..."

My Master, my light, at this point, too, doesn't your truth enjoy a good laugh at human expense? The time that was long—was it long when it was already past, or when it was still present? It could have been long at that time when it existed, as something that *could* be long; but as past time, it didn't exist anymore, with the potential to be "long," because it didn't exist as anything.

So let's not say "The past time was long"; we're not going to discover what was long then, because from the point that it's past, it doesn't exist. Let's say instead, "That time, when *present, was* long," because when it was present it was long. It hadn't yet passed by into nonexistence, and therefore it had the potential to be long; but after it passed by, it stopped being long because it stopped existing—both happened at the same moment.

19. Okay, then: let's see, my human soul, whether the present time can be long. It has in fact been granted to you to perceive stretches of time and measure them. How are you going to answer me? Are a hundred years of the present a "long time"?

But first, see whether a hundred years *can* be present. If the first of these years is passing, it's present, and ninety-nine are in the future and therefore don't yet exist. If, however, the second year is passing, one year is already past, the second is present, and the rest are in the future: and so on and so forth with any year within the sum of a hundred that we postulate as present. The past years will be before it, and after it will be the future years. In consequence, there can't be a hundred years in the present.

Okay, see whether at least one year that's passing can be the present. If the first month of this year is passing, the others are in the future; if it's the second month passing, the first month is already past and the remaining ones don't exist yet. Therefore, a year that's passing can't be wholly present either, and if it's not wholly present, it isn't present.

Twelve months make up a year. Of those twelve months, whichever single month is passing is present, while the others are either past or future; although the month that's passing isn't present, either, but instead it's a single day. If it's the first day, the rest are in the future. If it's the last day, the rest are in the past; if it's any day in the middle, it's between past and future days.

20. Look at how present time, the only time we found we should call "long," has shrunk to barely one day in length. But let's sift through even this day, because not even a single day is wholly the present. It's made of twenty-four nighttime and daytime hours. From the point of view of the first hour, the others are in the future, and from the point of view of the last, the others are in the past, and from the point of view of any hour in between, those behind it are the past, and those ahead of it are the future.

A single hour itself happens in fugitive small pieces. Whatever part of it has flown by is the past, and whatever part of it remains is the future. If any time can be conceived that can be divided into no further parts of intervals, or into only the most infinitesimal parts, that time alone can be called "the present." That time, however, flies past so quickly from the future into the past that it isn't stretched out to even the tiniest interval. If it *is* stretched out, it's divided into the past and the future; the present, in contrast, has no extent.

Where, in that case, is the time we could call "long"? Is it in the future? We don't in fact say of a future time "It is long," because it doesn't yet exist, so that it *could* be long. Instead, we say "It will be long." So when will *that* be? If even then, in the future, the time will still be in the future, it won't be long, because there won't yet be anything that *can* be long. If, on the other hand, it will be long when, out of the future that doesn't yet exist, the time starts to exist and becomes the present, and hence is something that *could* be long—well, at this point, the present shouts, using the arguments I've made previously, its denial of its own ability to be long.

21. And yet, Master, we perceive periods of time and compare them with one another, saying some are longer and others shorter. And we actually measure how much longer or shorter this one is than that one, and if we're asked, we answer that this one's double or triple or precisely or as good as the same amount, in comparison to another.

But when we measure time with our perceptions, we measure it as it passes by. As for past time, which doesn't exist any longer, or future time, which does not yet exist, who can measure either—unless somebody has the gall to say he can measure what doesn't exist? While it's passing, time can be perceived and measured, but once it's passed, it can't: because it doesn't exist.

22. I'm inquiring, Father, my God, not claiming anything as a fact. Take charge of me and direct me.

Who in the world would tell me there aren't three kinds of time, as we learned when we were boys, and as we've taught boys— the past, the present, and the future—but rather that there's only one, the present, given that the other two don't exist?

Or do they also exist, and it's just that when the present is made from the future, it proceeds from some hidden place, and when the past is made from the present, it recedes into some hidden place? If things in the future don't exist yet, where did those who intoned divination concerning the future see the future? That which doesn't exist can't be seen. And historians certainly couldn't tell accurately of the past unless they could divine it in their minds. If it doesn't exist at all, there's no way whatsoever they could make it out. Therefore, the future and the past do exist.

23. My Master, my hope, permit me to inquire more fully; don't let my concentration be disrupted. If future and past things exist, I want to know *where* they exist. But if I don't yet have the capacity to know that, I nevertheless know that wherever they exist, they don't exist there as the past or the future there, but as the present.

If they're there as the future, or the "to be" in Latin, they *are* not yet there. And if they're there as the past, "the passed by," they *are* no longer there. Wherever they are, then, and whatever they are, they *aren't* unless they're *present*.

The stories of past events brought out of our memory, true though they are, aren't the things that have gone into the past themselves, but words thought up on the basis of images of those things; the images have imprinted those things like footsteps in the mind, using the physical senses as the things go by.

My boyhood, which doesn't exist any longer, is in past time, which doesn't exist any longer. But when I recall it and tell about it, I look at an image of it in the present time, because that image is still in my memory.

Whether the prediction of future events has a similar cause, producing premonitions of things that don't yet exist through images that already do—this I confess I don't know, my God. But I certainly know this: we commonly contemplate in advance our future actions, but this contemplation in advance is actually present, whereas the action that's being so contemplated doesn't exist yet, because it's in the future. But when we've embarked on that action and have started to do what we were contemplating, then that action will exist at that time, as at that time it will be not in the future, but in the present.

24. However the mystic premonitions of future things are constituted, nothing can be seen that doesn't exist. But what exists now isn't in the future but the present. When things in the future are said to be "seen," that's not the things themselves, which don't exist yet, meaning that they're in the future, but rather their causes or perhaps their signs, which already do exist. Hence, not future but present things are there for people to see now, and from these present things future things can be predicted, once they're imagined in the mind. Again, these imaginings already exist, and those who predict the future gaze at them in the present within their minds.

Let the world's immense multiplicity communicate to me some example. I look at the dawn, and I predict the rising of the sun. What I look at is present, but what I predict is in the future. The sun isn't in the future—it exists already; rather, its rising, which doesn't exist yet, is in the future. If I couldn't picture that rising in my mind, as I'm doing right now while speaking of it, I wouldn't be able to predict it. The dawn I see in the sky isn't the sun's rising, although it precedes the sun's rising; and that act of imagination in my mind isn't the sun's rising, either. But these two, the dawn and the image, are perceived in the present, so that the sun's rising can be spoken of.

Thus things in the future don't yet exist, and if they don't yet exist, they don't exist, and if they don't exist, they absolutely can't be seen; but they can be predicted based on present things, which already exist and are seen.

25. You, therefore, ruler of your creation, what is the means by which you inform souls of the things that will be? You did inform your prophets of them. What in the world is your method for showing the future, given that to you, nothing is in the future? Or do you instead show things that are here now as a way to show the future? After all, what doesn't exist surely can't be shown.

Whatever your method, it's too remote for me to see: it's proved overpowering. On my own, I can't reach it*—but through you I

* Psalms 139:6.

can, when you grant me this, you, the sweet light of my inward, my underlying eyes.

26. By now, anyway, it's as clear as water that there exist neither future nor past things, and that it can't properly be said that there are three times, the past, the present, and the future. But perhaps it could properly be said, "There are three times: the present with respect to things that are past, the present with respect to things that are present, and the present with respect to things that are in the future."

There are, in fact, in the mind a certain three kinds of time I don't see elsewhere: the present with respect to past things, which is the memory; the present with respect to present things, which is contemplation; and the present with respect to future things, which is expectation. If we're permitted to say this, then I see these three different kinds of time, and I admit it: there are three.

But let people also say, "There are three kinds of time: the past, the present, and the future," which is the common misusage. Let them say that—because, look, I don't mind, and I won't argue about it, and I'm not saying anything against it, as long as what's said is understood, and nobody's saying that what's in the future exists already or that what's past still exists. There are a few things we properly say, and quite a few we improperly say, but it's recognized what we mean.

27. So, I said a little while ago that we measure periods of time as they're passing, in such a way that we can say, for example, that this period is twice as long as another, or that the two are equally as long, and so on and so forth for all other periods we can describe through measuring them. Hence, as I was saying, we measure time as it passes, and if somebody should say to me "How do you know this?" I can respond that I know because we *can* measure it, whereas we *can't* measure things that don't exist; and things in the past and the future don't exist.

But how do we measure present time, given that it doesn't have any extent? Well, when it passes it's measured, but when it's past it isn't measured, because there's nothing to measure. But from which point, and through which point, and to which point does it pass, when it's being measured? From which point could that be, if not from the future? And through which point, if not through the present? And to which point, if not into the past?

Therefore, it passes from what doesn't exist yet, through what lacks any extent, and into what doesn't exist any longer. But what do we measure unless it's time in some kind of extent? When we say "The original amount," and "Twice as much," and "Three times as much," and "Just as much," and whatever else we say about time, isn't it always about *extents* of time? So in what extent of time do we measure time as it's passing by? Do we measure it in the future, from which it passes? But we can't measure what doesn't exist yet. Do we measure it in the present, through which it's passing? But we can't measure a nonexistent extent. Or do we measure it in the past, into which it passes? But we can't measure what no longer exists.

28. My mind is on fire to solve this incredibly complicated co-nundrum. My Master, my God, good Father, by Christ I entreat you, don't close off these longed-for things that are both ordinary and obscure. No, Master, let my desire enter into them, so that they dawn for me as mercy's light is shed on them.

Whom am I going to question about these things, and to whom can I admit ignorance with more hope of advantage than to you? My fiercely flaming passion to understand your written Word isn't an annoyance to you. Give me what I love. I do love it, and my love for it is your gift. Give it to me, Father, because you truly know how to give good gifts to your sons.* Give it to me because I've undertaken to gain this knowledge, but the work must remain far in advance of me† until you open the way to it.‡

By Christ, I beg you, in the name of the holy of holies that he is, let no one shout me down. I, too, have believed, and it's for this reason that I also speak.§ This is my hope, for which I live: to contemplate the delight of my Master.¶ But see, you've done it, you've brought my days into old age, they pass by, and I don't know how.**

Yet we say about this or that time, or these or those periods of time: "What a long time it's been since that person said this!" and "What a long time since he did this!" and "What a long time it's been since I saw that!" and "This long syllable takes twice as long to say as this short one."†† We say these things, and we hear these things; we are understood, and we understand. They're absolutely clear and absolutely habitual, but at the same time

---

* Matthew 7:11.
† Psalms 73:16.
‡ Matthew 7:7–8, Luke 11:9–10.
§ 2 Corinthians 4:13, quoting Psalms 116:10.
¶ Psalms 27:4.
** Psalms 39:4–5.
†† Roman poetic meter was quantitative, based on the length of syllables, not qualitative, like English meter, which is based on accent, or the stressing of syllables.

these very same things are mysterious, and they must be figured out from scratch.

29. I once heard from a certain learned person that the movements of the sun and moon and the other heavenly bodies constitute time itself,* but I didn't agree. In that case, why shouldn't the movements of all objects constitute time?

Are we really to think that if the luminous objects in the sky stopped while a potter's wheel was still moving, there wouldn't be any time by which we could measure those rotations and say whether they were happening at equal intervals, or whether they were slower at some times and faster at others, or whether some rotations took longer than others?

And in these cosmic circumstances, wouldn't we also be speaking in time when we make these statements here? In the case of our own words, would there be any reason that some syllables are long and others short, except that the former made a sound in a longer space of time and the latter in a shorter space?

God, grant to humankind the ability to see in small things the shared signs of things both small and great. The stars and the great lights of the sky serve as earthly signs, for seasons, for days, for years.† These things truly exist; but I wouldn't say that the circuit of that little disc made of wood is a day—yet likewise neither should that learned man say that time, in itself, doesn't exist.

---

* This view was held by several ancient authorities (who would be, of course, only the ones we know about), so Augustine's source, or his source's source, is unclear.
† Genesis 1:14.

30. I long to know the power and the properties of time, by which we measure the motion of material objects and say, for example, that this motion takes twice as long as that one.

I have a question, since a day is defined not just as the interval in which the sun is above the earth—in which parlance day and night are different things—but also as the entire circuit of the sun from the east back to the east. This is what we mean when we say so many days have passed, and in that parlance it's that many days *and* the nights that go with them: the extent of the nights isn't reckoned up separately.

Since, then, in this sense a day is completed by the movement of the sun in a full circle from east back to the east again, I want to know which is a day: that motion itself, or the length of time it takes to happen, or both.

If it's the first, it would still be a day even if the sun completed its course in a stretch of time only an hour long. But if it's the second, it *wouldn't* be a day if the interval from one sunrise to another were as short as an hour: the sun would have to go around twenty-four times in completing a day. If both reckonings were in force, it couldn't be called a day if in the space of an hour the sun ran its entire circuit, but it also couldn't be called a day if the sun stopped altogether but as much time passed as was normally necessary for the sun to complete its whole circular course from one dawn to the next.

So at this point I'm not asking what that thing is we call a day, but rather what *time* is, the thing *by which* we could measure the orbit of the sun and be able to say, for example, that the sun had completed its course in half the usual interval, if it had in fact completed its course in the amount of time it takes twelve hours to pass. Comparing both stretches of time—that is, twenty-four hours and twelve—we would call one of them a single unit and another double that unit, even if the sun made its circuit from the east to the east in that single unit in one instance, and in double that unit of time in another instance.

So I don't want anybody telling me that the motion of the heavenly bodies constitutes periods of time. When in answer to a certain person's prayer the sun stood still* so that he could complete a battle and win it, the sun stood still but time kept going. That fight was fought and brought to an end through its own extent of time, which was adequate for it. To sum up, then, I see that time is a certain stretching out—but do I really see this? Or do I just see myself seeing it? *You* will show me this, you who are light, you who are truth.

31. Do you command me to assent if somebody says that time constitutes the motion of an object? You don't command this. I don't hear that any object moves unless it's within time: you say so; *but* I don't hear that this motion is time itself: you don't say so.

When an object moves, I measure in time how long it moves, from when it starts to when it stops. If I haven't seen from which point it begins to move, and if it goes on and on so that I don't see when it stops, I'm not able to measure—unless by chance I measure from when *I begin to see* it move to when *I stop seeing* it move.

* Joshua 10:13.

If I'm seeing it for a long time, I only report that it's a long time, not the length of time that it actually is. When we say how long something is, we say that by comparison, as in "This is just as long as that" or "This is twice as long as that" or whatever else along these lines.

If, however, we have the ability to mark physical space from where and to where a body goes that's moving—or parts of it are moving, as happens when a lathe is being turned—we can say how much time the object takes to move from this place to that, or the time part of it takes to move.

So since the motion of an object and the means by which we measure how long that motion takes are two different things, who wouldn't perceive which of these two we should call time?

What's more, if a material object has a variant motion, moving and stopping at different times, it's not only its motion but also its stasis that we're measuring in time. We say, for example, "It stood still for as much time as it moved," or "It stood still for double or triple the time it was in motion"—and whatever else our measurement either determined or made a rough estimate of: "more or less," as people like to say. In conclusion, time isn't the motion of an object.

32. But I admit to you, Master, that I still don't know what time is. On the other hand, I admit to you, Master, I know I'm saying all this stuff within time, and that I've already spent quite a while speaking about time, and that this thing itself that I call "quite a while" isn't quite a while except as an interval of time.

So how do I know this when I don't know what time is? Do I perhaps not know how to say what I know? Poor me, not even knowing what I don't know!* Here I am, God, before your face, not lying.† What I'm speaking is exactly what's in my heart. But you will light my lamp, Master, my God: you will light up my darkness.‡

33. Doesn't my soul testify to you, with a testimony that speaks the truth, that I'm measuring time? It's true, my God, I do measure time—but I don't know what I'm measuring.

I measure with time the motion of a material object. Don't I measure time itself likewise? Could I measure the motion of a material object—how long that lasts, how long a time that thing takes to get from one place to another—if I didn't measure the time in which it was moving?

So how do I measure time itself? Do I measure a longer space of time with a shorter space of time, the way you measure a rod with a cubit? This seems to be the way we measure the extent of a long syllable and say it's twice as long as a short syllable. In the same way, we measure the extent of poems, by means of their lines' extent; and we measure the extent of the lines by the feet's extent, and we measure the extent of the feet by the syllables' extent, and we measure the extent of the long syllables by the short syllables' extent.

We don't make these measurements on the pages—in that case, we measure spaces, and not time; rather, as the enunciated

---

* Socrates' foundational philosophical claim (backgrounded in Plato's *Apology*) was to know what he didn't know.
† Galatians 1:20.
‡ Psalms 18:28.

words go by, we say, "This is a long poem, because it's made up of so many lines; these are long lines because they consist of so many feet; these are long feet because they're stretched out in so many syllables; this is a long syllable because it's twice as long as a short one."

But a definite measure of time can't be provided for in this way, either. It can happen that a shorter line produces its sounds in a more extensive space, if the enunciation is drawn out, so that this line can take a longer time than a long line hurriedly enunciated; and the same thing for a whole poem, and for a foot, and for a syllable. Hence it seems to me that time is nothing else but a drawing out, but what that's a drawing out *of,* I have no idea. But I'd be surprised if the mind itself weren't the thing being drawn out.

Then I entreat you, my God, tell me, what is it I measure? Either I say approximately, "This space of time is longer than that," or actually with precision, "This space of time is double that." I *know* I measure time. But I don't measure the future because it doesn't yet exist. I don't measure the present because it isn't drawn out in any space. And I don't measure the past because it no longer exists. What do I measure, then? Do I measure time in its passing, but not past time? This is in fact what I said before.

34. Concentrate, mind of mine, and pay strenuous attention. God is our helper.* He made us—we didn't make ourselves.† Look to where truth is dawning.

* Psalms 62:8.
† Psalms 100:3.

So let's just posit that a physical voice begins to be audible, and it's audible, and it's still audible—oh, but here it's stopped. Now it's silent. That voice is past, and it's no longer a voice. Before it began to be audible, it was in the future, and it couldn't be measured because it didn't exist yet. Now it can't be measured because it no longer exists. It could, however, be measured then, at the time it was audible, because at that time it existed and so could be measured.

But even at that time, it wasn't stationary; it was passing, and passing by. Was it better able to be measured for that reason? In the act of passing by, it was—given that the actual present doesn't have any extent—stretched out into some space of time in which it could be measured.

Granted, therefore, that at that time it could be measured, let's say we posit another voice, which started to be audible and goes right on making sustained, unbroken, and undifferentiated sounds. Let's measure it while it's audible, because when it stops being that, it will have passed, and there won't be anything that can be measured. Let's just measure it and name its quantity.

But say it's still audible and can't be measured except from its beginning, where it starts to make sounds, clear up to its end, where it stops making them; it can't be measured because we measure an interval from some beginning to some ending. For this reason, a voice that hasn't ended can't be measured, and it can't be said how long or how short it is; nor can it be called equal to another sound, or half as long, or double it, or anything else.

When, however, it's over, it will have ceased to exist. By what means could it then be measured? And yet we do measure periods of time; not, apparently, those that don't yet exist, or those that no longer exist, or those that are drawn out completely unbroken, or those which don't have any boundaries. So we don't measure future or past or present or passing time, yet we do measure time.

35. "God, the maker of all things":* that line alternates between short and long syllables, eight in all. Now, four are short—the first, the third, the fifth, and the seventh—and they're each half as long as the four long syllables, which are the second, the fourth, the sixth, and the eighth. Each of the long syllables takes twice as much time to say as each of the short syllables.

Thus I pronounce and announce, insofar as self-evident sensory perception backs me up. Insofar as my physical sense is patently informative, I measure a long syllable by means of a short syllable, and I perceive that a long syllable has twice the content.

But since one syllable is heard after another, if the first one is short and the next one long, how will I hold on to the short one? And how will I, in measuring, hold it against the long one so that I can discover that this has twice the content, when in fact the long one doesn't start to be audible unless the short one has stopped being audible? I don't measure the long one itself while it's going on, do I, given that I don't measure it except when it's not over? But its ending is the act of passing by, out of existence.

So what is it that I'm measuring? Where is the short syllable that's my means of measurement? Where is the long one I'm measuring? They've both made their sounds, they've flown

---

* This is the first line of Ambrose's evening hymn, which Augustine renders more fully in book 9, chapter 32.

away, they've passed by and no longer exist. I, on the other hand, am here measuring, and I confidently answer—to the extent that in experienced physical perception there's any basis for confidence—that this one is half as long and that one is twice as long, plainly in a space of time. And I wouldn't be able to do this unless the syllables had gone by and were finished. Therefore, I don't measure these things themselves, which no longer exist, but I measure something in my memory, which is attached there and remains.

36. In you, my mind, I measure time. Don't shout me down with the protest that time is a thing in itself. Don't shout yourself down with the riot of your feelings. In you, I say, I measure time. This feeling that things create in you when they're passing by remains even once they've passed by, and I measure that feeling in itself, as current, and not those things that have gone by to create it. It's this thing itself that I measure when I measure time. So either this is time itself that I'm measuring, or I'm not measuring time.

What about when we measure silences and say this silence occupied the same amount of time that that voice occupied? Don't we stretch out our thought in proportion to a sound, as if one were audible, so that we're able to report something about periods of silence within a certain stretch of time? After all, if the spoken voice is idle, we do run through in our minds poems and lines of poetry and every other kind of discourse, and any manner of measure things in motion can evince, and we make a report about extents of time, how long this one or that one was in relation to another one, no differently than if we actually reproduced the sounds in question.

Suppose someone wanted to issue forth a speech that's a tad *long,* and resolved, deliberately in advance, just how long it was going to be. This character has at any rate gone through at least *that* time in silence; now, having entrusted the speech to his memory, he has begun to issue forth said speech, which makes noise until it can be brought to its planned ending.

But no: it *has* made noise and it's *going to go on* making noise, because the part of it that he's already passed through has no doubt *made* noise, and what remains of it *will* make noise, and thus the thing is executed until his purpose in the present has transferred the future into the past, with the shrinking away of the future and the growth of the past until, when the future is shriveled up, the whole is past.

37. But how does the future come to be shrunk or shriveled up, given that it doesn't yet exist? And how does the past grow, given that it no longer exists? Isn't it, in both cases, because in the mind there are three things at work? The mind expects, and pays attention, and remembers. What it expects becomes what it remembers through what it pays attention to.

Who would deny that things in the future don't yet exist? Yet there's already in the mind an expectation of future things. And who would deny that things in the past no longer exist? Yet there remains in the mind the memory of things past. And who would deny that present time lacks any breadth, because it passes by in an instant? Yet the act of paying attention persists, so that through it whatever's going to become present can become absent and past.

Therefore, future time, which doesn't yet exist, can't be long, but rather a "long future" is really a long expectation of the future; nor can past time be long, as it doesn't exist, but rather a "long stretch of past time" is really a long memory of the past.

38. Say I'm about to recite a psalm that I know. Before I start, my expectation stretches into the whole of the psalm. But once I've begun, my memory stretches through whatever amount of the canticle I've plucked off and placed in the past. The life of what I'm doing here is stretched out into my memory because of what I've recited, and into my expectation because of what I'm about to recite. Yet the attention I'm paying is present; it's through this act that what was in the future is taken across, so that it becomes the past. And while the recitation goes on and on, memory is prolonged to the same degree that expectation is shortened, until the whole of the expectation is used up; then, all of what I'm doing is finished and has passed into memory.

And in individual, small parts of that psalm, and even in its individual syllables, it's the same as in the whole. And it's the same in doing something over a longer period, out of which reciting that psalm is perhaps a small part. And it's the same in the whole of a person's life, the parts of which are everything that human being does. And it's the same in the whole history of the sons of humanity, the parts of which are all human lives.

39. But given that your mercy is superior to such lives,* look how my life is overextended and stretched out of shape; but your right hand has upheld me† in my Master, the son of humankind,

---

* Psalms 63:3. The New Revised Standard Version is different from the Latin.
† Psalms 18:35, 63:8.

the mediator between you the one and us the many,* who are spread thin through many things and over many things.

This way, I can grasp him in whom I am grasped, and following the one, I can be gathered together from my outdated days, forgetting things that are past†—and not stretched out of shape, but only stretched out, not into those things that are to be and to pass by, but simply into those things which are in advance of me: not with distention but with intention following toward the prize of the heavenly calling,‡ where I can hear the voice of praise§ and contemplate your delight¶ that neither comes nor goes. But now my years are spent in groaning;** yet you are my comfort, Master, you are my eternal father.

But as it is, I have exploded into pieces of time whose sequence I don't know; and in a riot of contradictory states of being, my thoughts, the inmost viscera of my soul, are mangled—and I'll continue this way until I'm cleansed in the fire of your passion and made fluid and run into you.

40. I'll stand and grow solid in you, my shapely mold, which is your truth; and I won't put up with questions from people who, in a sickness that's a punishment, are thirsty for more than they can hold and say "What was God doing before he made the sky and the earth?" or "Why did it enter his mind to make something when before this he'd never made anything?"

* 1 Timothy 2:5.
† Ephesians 4:22, Colossians 3:9.
‡ Philippians 3:13–14.
§ Psalms 26:7.
¶ Psalms 27:4.
** Psalms 31:10.

Grant them, Master, the ability to think straight about what they're saying and to realize that there's no saying "never" in a case where time doesn't exist. When somebody's said never to have done something, what does that mean but that he's done it *at no time?* Let them see that there couldn't have been any time without creation—so that they stop talking twaddle.* Let them also stretch out into the things that are before them;† and let them understand that *you* are *before* all of the ages, and that you're the eternal creator of all ages; and that no time is an equal sharer in eternity with you—nor is any created thing, even if there's some created thing above time.‡

41. Master, my God, what is that recess of your deep mystery, and how far from there have the results of my wrongdoings hurled me? Heal my eyes, and let me partake in the joy of your light.

For sure, if there's a mind with such a great deal of powerful knowledge, with such potent prescience that all things past and future are known to it as well as I know that one psalm I know best, that mind is really too wonderful, and so astounding that I'd shudder at it: nothing whatsoever happening in all the ages past or to come could hide from that mind, just as nothing in that psalm I'm singing hides from me, whatever part of it and however much of it is gone from the beginning, and whatever and however much remains until the end.

* Psalms 144:8.
† Philippians 3:13–14.
‡ I.e., the spiritual or angelic part of creation that is transcendent and unchanging. See below, book 13, chapters 8 and 9, for example.

But it's an outrageous thought that you, the creator of everything that is, the creator of souls and bodies—it's an outrageous thought that you know all things future and past in *this* way; in you, it's far, far more marvelous and mysterious. You don't have feelings that vary, or sense perception that's stretched out of shape, as in the experience of somebody singing things he knows, or of somebody listening to a psalm he knows. Such a person is subject to the expectation of future sounds and to the memory of past sounds. Nothing like that happens to you, who are unchangeably eternal—the truly eternal *creator* of minds.

Thus, just as in the beginning you knew the sky and the earth without any variation in your knowledge, in the same way, in the beginning you made the sky and the earth without any stretching out, any distortion of your activity.

Whoever understands, let him testify to you, and whoever doesn't understand, let him testify to you, too. Oh how exalted you are—yet the lowly in heart are your home!* You set upright those who are battered down to the ground;† and those whose loftiness is you yourself do not fall.

---

* Isaiah 57:15.
† Psalms 145:14, 146:8.

Book 12

1. In my destitute life, Master, my heart runs back and forth no end, battered by the words of your holy scripture. Hence, in general, our poor human intelligence has (if nothing else) a fulsome supply of discourse:* naturally so, because the act of searching is more voluble than the act of finding, the act of asking is longer than the act of obtaining, and the knocking hand is harder at work than the hand laying hold.

Yet we have the promise in our grasp. Who's going to falsify it? If God is for us, who's against us?† All of you, ask and you will receive, seek and you will find, knock and it will be opened to you. Everyone who asks receives, and everyone seeking will

---

* Echoes the Latin description of Martha's domestic distractions in Luke 10:40–42.
† Romans 8:31.

find, and to everyone knocking the door will be opened.* These are *your* promises, God, and who would be afraid of deception when it's the truth that promises?

2. The lowliness of my tongue testifies, in your lofty presence, that it's you who made the sky and the earth.† As to this sky I see and this earth I walk on, which is the source of the earth I'm made of and carry around with me, you made them.

But where is the heaven of heaven, Master, about which we've heard in the words of the psalm: "The heaven of the heaven belongs to the Master, but he gave the earth to the children of humankind"?‡ Where's the heaven we don't perceive, in the face of which all this that we perceive here is, in effect, the earth?

This material whole, everywhere composed of things that are not themselves whole, has even so been given a beautiful form in it lowest parts, the base being our land; but in comparison to that heaven of heaven even the sky of our earth is the earth. Both these material things, earth and sky, are cogently "the earth" in comparison to that mysterious sky that belongs to the Master, not to the children of humankind.

3. As is plain in the text, this earth had no visible form and no order; it was some sort of very deep abyss above which there was no light—because the abyss looked like nothing. Hence you commanded it to be written that "darkness was over the abyss."§

---

* Matthew 7:7–8, Luke 11:9–10, John 16:24.
† Genesis 1:1.
‡ Psalms 115:16. Augustine quotes the psalm through its Latin version, which makes a considerable difference in the content of this chapter. See pages xxix–xxx of the introduction.
§ Genesis 1:2.

But what was darkness other than the absence of light? Where would the light have been if not above, looming and illuminating? So where there wasn't yet any light, what was the presence of darkness if not the absence of light? Thus darkness was there above, because light *wasn't* there above, just as sound isn't in the place where silence is. What is the existence of silence in a place except the nonexistence of sound there?

Wasn't it you, Master, who taught this soul of mine, which now testifies to you? Wasn't it you, Master, who taught me that before you formed that unformed matter we're talking about, and sorted it out, there was no anything: no color, no shape, no object—or body; no wind—or breath—or Spirit of life? But no, wait: there wasn't *nothing* at all. There was a certain formless something that was hardly good-looking, that looked as if it couldn't even be classified.*

4. So, what was an apt term for that formless something, so that its character could be conveyed somehow even to those who're quite slow on the uptake?

Only some common word would do. And anywhere in the universe, what can be found that's closer to formlessness of every sort than earth and an abyss are?

They're less impressive-looking, as they're at the lowest level, lower than all the rest of the universe over them, which is resplendent and splendid in its light. So why shouldn't I accept that matter in its unformed state, which looked like nothing but from which you made the impressive-looking universe, has

* The Latin *species* means "appearance," "classification," "beauty," and other things. See page xxxvi of the introduction.

been suitably called unseen and unordered earth as a way to suggest to humankind what it was?

5. When human thinking seeks in that unseen and unordered earth something that the understanding can attain to, and says to itself, "This form isn't comprehensible the way life is, or the way justice is, because it's matter belonging to material objects yet isn't perceptible, since there's nothing to be seen or otherwise perceived in the unseen and unordered"—when human thinking says this to itself, is it trying to know this form through not knowing it, or to not know it through knowing it?

6. As for me, Master, if I testify to you with my voice and with my pen about the whole story—whatever you've taught me, that is, about this material whose name I'd previously heard but didn't understand when Manichaeans who didn't understand it themselves were telling me about it—then I testify this: I thought about it merely through countless different appearances, and for that reason I wasn't in fact thinking about it at all. My mind was turning over hideous and frightful forms, their order jumbled, but they *were* forms; which means I was applying the term "unformed" to things that didn't *lack* form, but instead had the kind of form that, if it appeared, would be odd and discordant, so that my perception would turn away from it in revulsion and my weak human sensibility would be upset.

But in actuality the thing I was persistently thinking about was unformed not in being the absence of all form, but only by comparison with beautiful forms. True reason urged that I should take away absolutely any kind of remainder of any form if I wished to think straightforwardly about the lack of form—but I couldn't. I could more readily decide that what was lacking any form didn't exist than I could think about something that was between a form and nothing, neither formed nor nothing, an unformed thing that was almost nothing.

And now on this matter my mind stopped questioning my spirit, which was full of images of formed things and was changing them and varying them at will. I now directed my attention to these objects themselves and took a deeper look at their change-ability, through which they cease to be what they were before and start being what they haven't been. I had an inkling that this actual transition from one form to another happened through some kind of formlessness but not through complete nothing-ness; yet I yearned for knowledge, not just an inkling.

But if my voice and my pen were to testify to you fully, explaining whatever knots you untied for me concerning this question, who among my readers could last until he took it all in?

But still, that's no reason for my heart to cease offering you honor and a song of praise for these very things about which it has such an inadequate capacity to compose an account. The changeability of things that change is quite able to hold all the forms into which changeable things change. But what *is* this changeability? It can't possibly be a mind, can it? Or a material object? Or the outward appearance of a mind or a material object? If it could be said, "It's a nothing/something," or "It is/isn't," I would call it either, and in any case it already somehow existed so that it could contain those visible and ordered appearances I've been writing about.

7. But whatever its nature, where did mutability come from un-less it came from you, from whom all things exist,* to the extent they do exist? Yet the farther things are from you, the less they're like you—but it's not of course a matter of geography.

Therefore you, Master, who aren't a different being in a differ-ent situation, or of a different nature in a different situation, but the very same, and the very same, and the very same, holy, holy, holy, Master, God, all-powerful:† in the beginning, which is from you, in your wisdom, which was born from your substance, you made something, and made it from nothing. You made the sky and the earth, but not from yourself. In that case, they would be equal to your only begotten son, and through this they would be equal also to you, and in no way would it have been right for what was out of you not to be equal to you.

But there also wasn't anything else, beyond you, from which you would have made those things, God, you who are a single Trin-ity and a threefold unity, and thus you must have made the sky and the earth—a big something and a small something—from nothing. You're all-powerful and good, so that they all would be made good: the huge sky and the little earth, two somethings, the one near to you and the other nearly nothing, the one to which you would be higher and the other in relation to which nothing could be lower.

8. But that heaven of heaven is yours,‡ Master. The earth, for its part, which you gave to the children of humanity to see and to

* Romans 11:36, 1 Corinthians 8:6.
† Isaiah 6:3, quoted in Revelation 4:8.
‡ Psalms 115:16. See pages xxix–xxx of the introduction.

touch, was not like the one we now see and touch. It was unseen
and unordered, and it was an abyss above which there was no
light—or the darkness was above the abyss, meaning that there
was more darkness there than in the abyss. In fact, that abyss of
waters visible to us now has a light of its own kind, even in its
depths, somehow perceptible to the fish and the crawling things*
alive on its floor.

However, the whole of that, before creation, was nearly nothing,
since it was altogether unformed, yet it already was something
that *could* be formed, as you, Master, made the universe out of
matter without form. And this matter without form you made,
out of nothing, as an almost-nothing. But from that you would
make great things, which we children of humanity wonder at.

This material sky is certainly very wonderful. It is the buttress
or prop or "firmament" between one realm of water and another, and on the second day after the creation of light, you said,
"Let it be made," and so this buttress was made.† You called it
"the sky,"‡ meaning the sky of this earth and sea, both of which
you made on the third day by giving a visible shape to unformed
matter, which you had made before there was any day.

You had already made heaven, too, before there was any day,
but it was the sky of this sky, the heaven of this heaven, because
(as it is written) in the beginning you had made the sky, or
heaven, and the earth. The earth itself, which you had made,
was unformed matter because it was unseen and unordered, and
darkness was above the abyss. And from this unseen and unordered earth, this unordered state of things, this almost-nothing,

* Genesis 1:20–22.
† Genesis 1:6.
‡ Genesis 1:8–13.

you made all these things of which the changeable universe consists and is inconsistent, the universe in which changeability is so clearly in evidence. In that changeability, periods of time can be perceived and counted off, because periods of time arise from changes in things, given that their types, or their visible appearances, diverge and diversify. But their common material component is that unseen earth described above.

9. Therefore, when the Spirit, your servant's teacher, tells about your having made the sky and the earth in the beginning, it says nothing about periods of time and is silent concerning days. Apparently, this heaven of heaven that you made in the beginning is some kind of creation with insight, although it's by no means equal in eternity with you, the Trinity or Three in One; yet as a sharer in your eternity, it powerfully suppresses its own changeability for the sake of the sweetness of ecstatically contemplating you; and by virtue of clinging to you without a single slip since the time it was made, it is superior to all of the rotations and alternations of time.

But even that unformed state of things, the unseen and unordered earth, isn't counted among the days of creation: where there is no shape or appearance or category, there is no order, and nothing comes or goes; and where this doesn't happen, there are certainly no days, nor in fact any alternation of time periods.

10. Truth, light of my heart! You, and not the darkness, must speak to me. I melted away, I dribbled down into those mere objects, and their gloom covered me. But from here, even from

here, I fell in love with you. I wandered off, yet I remembered you.* I heard your voice behind me, calling me to return—but those on whom no peace has been imposed nearly drowned out that sound for me.

Now look, I return, sweltering and gasping, to your fountain. No one's going to keep me away! I'll drink from it and live from what I drink. I must not be my own life. I had a sorry life on my own account, and I was my own death. In you, I come back to life. You, speak to me; you, converse with me. I've placed my reliance on your books, but their words are awfully recondite.

11. You've already told me, Master, with a loud voice in my inward ear, that you're eternal; you alone have immortality,† because you're changed in no appearance or figure and by no movement, and your will doesn't vary with time. An immortal will isn't one that's inconsistent with itself. Within your sight, this shows plainly to me, and may it become plainer and plainer, I beseech you, and may I be sober and constant in this revelation, sheltering beneath your wings.

Likewise you've told me, Master, with a loud voice in my inward ear, that natures and substances that aren't what you are and yet do exist were made by you. (Only one thing doesn't come from you, and that's what doesn't exist—and also any movement of the will away from you, who simply *exist*, toward what exists in a lower sense, because such a movement is crime and sin.) You've said that no one's sin either harms you or upsets the order of your reign, from the first to the last and lowest of

* Psalms 119:176.
† 1 Timothy 6:16.

that order. This shows plainly to me within your sight, and may it become plainer and plainer, I beseech if you, and may I be sober and constant in this revelation, sheltering beneath your wings.

12. Likewise you've said to me with a loud voice in my inward ear that not even that creation, the heaven of heaven, is an equal sharer in eternity with you. But you're its single enjoyment, and it drinks you in with an absolutely unshakable purity, nowhere and never obtruding its own capacity for change. You're always with it, and it clings to you with all its consciousness, having no future to anticipate, and never sending into the past what it remembers; it has no back-and-forth transformation, and it doesn't stretch out into any kind of time.

Blissful creation—if it does exist—that can fuse into your bliss! Blissful, with you living within it and lighting it everlastingly! I can't arrive at any designation I'd consider better for "the heaven of heaven, belonging to the Master"* than your home, which contemplates your bliss without any diminishing exit into anything else; your home is unsullied awareness, with the most harmonious oneness propped up by the peace of holy spirits, citizens of your city† in the sky's realms above these skies of ours.

13. From where shall the soul, which has gone far away to sojourn, gain understanding, if it's already thirsty for you, and tears have already become its daily bread, while people say to it day after day, "Where is your God?";‡ if it already asks urgently

* Psalms 115:16.
† Ephesians 2:19, 4:3.
‡ Psalms 42:2–3, 10.

for only one thing from you: to live in your house all the days of its life?*

And what is its life, if not you? And what are your days, if not your eternity? They are like your years, which don't fall short, because you are the same, yourself.†

From this, then, let the soul that's able understand how far above all time your eternal existence is: the heaven of heaven, your house, doesn't sojourn away from you, and though it's not an equal sharer in your eternity, still, by virtue of clinging enduringly and unfalteringly to you, it endures no alternations of time. This shows plainly to me in your sight, and may it become plainer and plainer, I beseech you, and may I be sober and constant in this revelation, sheltering beneath your wings.

14. But here we are with something formless or misshapen in these changes of the meanest and lowest things. Now, who's going to tell me, unless it's anyone straying and swaying among his own apparitions, from the sheer emptiness of his mentality— who but someone like that is going to tell me that, once every type of category or appearance or beauty is diminished and reduced to nothing, and nothing remains but the formlessness through which one type of figure was changed and turned into another, this formlessness could show alternations of time? It's entirely impossible, because without variety in movement, there are no periods of time, and where there's no variety, there's no figure.

* Psalms 23:6, 27:4.
† Psalms 102:27.

15. Once I've reflected on these things—which I can do only to the extent that you grant it, my God, rousing me to knock, and opening when I'm knocking*—I discover that you've made two things that are free of time, though neither is an equal sharer in eternity with you. One of them, the heaven of heaven, was formed in such a way that without any slip in its contemplation, and without undergoing any change over any period of time—because, though it's subject to change, it doesn't in fact change—it partakes of the ecstasy of your eternity and unchangeability.

The second, the abyss, was so formless that it didn't have the ability to be changed from any one form into any other—either a moving form or a stationary one—and so be subordinated to time. But you didn't abandon this thing and let it remain formless; instead, in the beginning, before there was any day, you made the sky and the earth, both of them, that I have been speaking of.

"But the earth was unseen and unordered, and darkness was over the abyss":† these words imply formlessness or misshapenness, as a special provision to lead along intellectually those who can't conceive the absence of any kind of well-composed figure or seemliness without this adding up to nothing in their minds. From this abyss was to come a *second* heaven, and the visible and ordered earth, and water with a composition lovely to look at, and next, in the establishment of this universe—including its days—everything that's mentioned as having been

---

* Matthew 7:7–8, Luke 11:9–10.
† Genesis 1:2.

made.* They are the way they are so that, through them, alternations of time are enacted, because of orderly changes of motions and forms.

16. If only for the time being, my God, here's how I interpret your scripture where I hear it saying, "In the beginning, God made the sky and the earth, but the earth was unseen and unordered, and darkness was over the abyss"†—but where there's no word as to the day on which you made these entities. If only for the time being, I think that reflects "the heaven of heaven" of which I've been speaking, the sky or heaven as a creation with insight, the sort of insight that consists of knowing all at once, not in part, not through a riddle, not in an indistinct mirror, but wholly, by direct revelation, face-to-face.‡ This isn't knowing different things at different moments, but (as I stated above) knowing everything at once, without any alternations of time.

And days' going unmentioned here is also due to the "unseen and unordered earth" not partaking of the temporal alternations that usually change an object's character from one moment to the next. Where there's no category or appearance, there aren't any such differences anywhere.

Because of both these entities, the one formed primordially, the other profoundly unformed; first the sky or heaven—that is, the heaven of heaven—and then the earth—meaning the unseen and unordered earth: I conclude at least for now that it's because of these two that your scripture says, without any mention of days, "In the beginning, God made the sky and the earth."

* Genesis 1.
† Genesis 1:1–2.
‡ 1 Corinthians 13:12.

The passage does immediately go on to describe what kind of earth it meant; and then in recording that on the second day the "firmament" or prop was made and called "sky" or "heaven,"* it implies that the heaven or sky spoken of first has nothing to do with days.

17. Your words have an astonishing depth—whereas the surface, baby talk for tiny children, is immediately before our eyes; but your words do have an astonishing depth, my God. It makes a person shake to look into that depth, and quake for the sake of its authority, and shudder with ardor for it.

I fiercely hate its enemies—if only you'd kill them with a double-edged sword!† Then they wouldn't *be* its enemies. Such is my passionate love for them that I want them killed in themselves so that they can live in you.‡

But here are some other people, who don't find fault with but rather praise the book of Genesis, and yet they say, "The Spirit of God, who through God's servant Moses composed this, meant *this* by these words—not what you say, but something else, which we say." With you as judge, God of us all, I give them the following answer:

18. Will all of you possibly call wrong the things that truth itself spoke with a loud voice in my inward ear concerning the true eternity of the creator? Truth told me that his substance by no means varies through time, and that his will isn't outside his

substance. Hence, he doesn't will different things at different times, but instead wills everything that he does will only once, but at the same time and for all time—not over and over, and not differently now and then; and he doesn't will later on what he didn't used to will, or not will what he used to will, because such a will is subject to change, and everything subject to change isn't eternal. But our God *is* eternal.

Likewise, I was told in my inward ear that the expectation of things to come becomes contemplation of them once they've come; and that once they've passed by, contemplation becomes memory. Thus, any kind of attention that varies is subject to change, and everything subject to change isn't eternal. But our God *is* eternal.*

I bring this all together and join it together, and I discover that my God, the eternal God, didn't establish creation by a new act of will, and that his knowledge doesn't undergo any transitory influence.

19. What are you going to say then, naysayers? Is what I've laid out here wrong? "No," they answer. So what do you mean by that "no"? Is it wrong that every being that's been given a form, and every material thing that *can* be given a form, doesn't exist except by virtue of the one who exists as the highest good, because he exists in the highest sense?

"We're not denying this, either," they answer. What are you denying, then? Are you denying that there's a certain transcendent creation that clings with such chaste love to the true and truly eternal God that, though not an equal sharer in his eternity, it

* Psalms 48:14.

doesn't fragment and sink away from him into the variations and alternations of time, but instead rests in the purely truthful contemplation of him alone—because you, God, reveal yourself to a creation that loves you as much as you command, and you're enough for it,* and therefore it doesn't veer down away from you and toward itself?

This creation is the house of God, which isn't material: it's not of the earth, and it isn't embodied through any mass that's part of the sky; it is of the Spirit, and shares in your eternity, because it goes forward into eternity without slipping. You founded it for the ages and the everlasting ages; you have ordained your edict, and it won't end. However, this creation isn't an equal sharer in eternity with you, because it does have a beginning, given that it was made.

20. We don't find time existing before this creation, the heaven of heaven—as wisdom was created before all other things.† But of course that wisdom is by no means the one evidently equal to you and a sharer in eternity with you, our God,‡ the father of *created* wisdom: that isn't the one through which, and in which beginning or authority, you created the sky and the earth. But no doubt this creation, the heaven of heaven, was that created wisdom, apparently an essence with the power of insight; and through the contemplation of light, it *is* light.

Although it was created, it is actually called wisdom; but between the light that illuminates and the light that's illuminated there's just as great a difference as between the wisdom that cre-

---

* John 14:8, 21.
† Sirach 1:4.
‡ Philippians 2:6.

ates and the wisdom that's created; as also between the justice that justifies and the justice that's brought into being by that justification. (We ourselves are actually called your justice; your slave Paul says, "so that we become the justice of God in Jesus Christ himself."*)

Therefore, a certain wisdom that was created was created before all other things, as a reasoning and insightful mind of your chaste city, our mother, which is above us, and free,† and eternal in the heavens‡ (and in what heavens would this be, unless "the heavens of heavens that praise you,"§ which are also "the heaven of heaven of the Master"?¶). We don't find time existing before it, because, being created before all other things, it naturally preceded time, too; nevertheless, the eternity of the creator himself is prior to it. Made by him, it took its commencement from him—not its commencement in time, because time didn't yet exist, but the commencement that was its own particular establishment.

21. Hence the heaven of heaven is from you, our God, but it's from you in such a way that it's clearly something other than you are, not the very same thing. Time doesn't just fail to precede it but doesn't even exist within it, we find, because the heaven of heaven is fit for always seeing your face,** and nowhere diverted down from there; and as a result, it doesn't vary through any kind of change. But it does in fact have the capacity for

* 2 Corinthians 5:21.
† Galatians 4:26.
‡ 2 Corinthians 5:1.
§ Psalms 148:4.
¶ Psalms 115:16. See pages xxix–xxx of the introduction.
** Matthew 18:10.

change, and could grow dark and cold if it didn't cling to you with a great passion, always shining and glowing hot like the midday sun because of you.

House full of light and brilliant beauty! I have cherished your loveliness and the place where my Master's glory lives˙—he is your builder and your owner. Let my distant sojourn sigh for you. I tell the one who made you that he must possess me also through you, because he also made me. I have wandered like a lost sheep† but I hope to be brought back to you on the shoulders of my shepherd,‡ your architect.

22. What have you got to say to me, you naysayers I was just speaking to? You do believe that Moses was the reverent servant of God, and that his books are oracles of the Holy Spirit? Is that house of God, though not an equal sharer of eternity with God, still in its own way eternal in the heavens§—where you waste your effort looking for alternations of time, because they aren't there to be found? That house of God, which finds it good always to cling to God,¶ transcends every stretching out and every interval of time's onward-rolling passage.

That's a fact, these people say. So then, out of all this that my heart has shouted to my God while hearing inwardly the sound of his praise—when it comes down to it, what do you argue is wrong? That in unformed matter there was no orderly arrangement, because there was no form? But it must follow that where there was no orderly arrangement, there could be no alterna-

---

* Psalms 26:8.
† Psalms 119:176, Isaiah 53:6.
‡ Luke 15:4–6.
§ 2 Corinthians 5:1.
¶ Psalms 73:28.

402 · Confessions

tion of time. And yet this almost-nothing, inasmuch as it wasn't absolutely nothing, certainly came from God, the source of whatever in any sense is anything. These people say, "We're not denying that, either."

23. In your presence, my God, I want to have a little talk with these people, who admit the truth of all of these things, about which your truth doesn't cease speaking inwardly, in my mind.

As for the people who refuse to accept these things, they can go on yapping as much as they want and drown themselves out. I'm just going to try to persuade them to give it a rest and give themselves a way forward through your Word. If they're unwilling and push me back, I appeal to you, my God, not to be silent to me.*

You, speak truthfully in my heart; you are, in fact, the only one to do so. Then I will send them on their way, outdoors, panting into the dust and stirring up dirt that gets in their own eyes, and I'll get into bed† and sing you love songs, groaning indescribably‡ in the midst of my sojourning away from you, and remembering Jerusalem, as my heart stretches upward toward her, Jerusalem, my fatherland, Jerusalem, my mother;§ and toward you, the ruler over her, the shedder of light, the father, the guardian, the husband, the pure and powerful captivation and unmovable joy, and all good things defying any description— everything good at once, because this is the one highest and true good.

* Psalms 28:1.
† Echoing Matthew 6:6, Jesus' command to go into a private room to pray.
‡ Romans 8:26.
§ Galatians 4:26.

And I won't turn away until you bind together the whole of what I am and gather it into the peace of that adored mother, the church, in which are found the first fruits of my spirit* and hence my assurance of those things I believe. Thus you, my God, my mercy, can rescue me from this dispersal and this dis- figurement, and give me a sure shape and sure strength for eter- nity.

But here's what I have to say to the people who aren't calling all these true things false but rather honoring your holy scripture— given that it was set forth by the saintly Moses—and along with us establishing it on the heights of authority to which we must accede; though they concede all this, they do have something to dispute with me, so I say this to them. You, our God, must be the judge between my testimony and their attempts to refute it.

24. They say, "Though all these things are true, Moses didn't have in mind the two things you've described when he said, through an unveiling by the Spirit, 'In the beginning God made the sky and the earth.'† He wasn't conveying, through the term sky, or heaven, that spiritual creation, or a creation with insight, which forever contemplates the face of God;‡ nor did he mean unformed matter in referring to the earth."

So what did he mean, then? They say, "What *we're* claiming is what that man thought, and here's what he's expressing by those words." And what's that? "He meant," they say, "at first to note, sweepingly but briefly, under the designation 'the sky and the earth,' the whole of this visible universe, so that afterward, by

* Romans 8:23.
† Genesis 1:1.
‡ Matthew 18:10.

counting off the days as headings, he could classify—point by point, as it were—all the things that the Holy Spirit chose to express in this way. At the time, you see, the people of the nation to whom he was speaking were uneducated and materialistic in their outlook, so that he considered he could bring to their favorable attention an idea of God's works only as things they could see."

But these people arguing with me do agree that "formless matter" is a suitable term through which to understand the unseen, unordered, dark abyss, from which it's subsequently indicated that all these visible things, familiar to us all, were made and set in order over the course of the days we read about in this account.

25. What if somebody else says that this same unformed and muddled state of matter was, in a *forward*-looking way, designated by the term "the sky and the earth" because out of this matter was created and brought to fulfillment *this visible universe,* with all its characteristics appearing in it with complete self-evidence—this universe that in fact is often called "the earth and the sky"?

What if still another person says that "the sky and the earth" is the apt term for the order of things both invisible and visible, and that *the whole of the creation,* which God made in wisdom—that is, in the beginning or in the first principle—is covered by these two words we read?

This person notes, however, that these things in their entirety were made from nothing and not out of God's actual substance, because they are not the very same as God; and that there is a degree of capacity for change in all of them, whether they endure as they are—as does the everlasting house of God—or whether they change, as do the human body and soul.

On this consideration, he adds that the common material of all things visible and invisible (material not yet formed but no doubt capable of being formed), from which arose the sky and the earth (meaning visible and invisible creation, from the point that both were formed), is expressed by the terms for the unseen and unordered earth and the darkness over the abyss.

But he makes the distinction that the "unseen and unordered earth" should be understood as physical matter before it got the property of form, whereas the "darkness over the abyss" must be spiritual matter before the control of its fluid overexuberance, so to speak, and before its illumination by wisdom.

26. A further thing that yet another person could say, if he wanted to, is that where we read "In the beginning, God created the sky and the earth," invisible and visible phenomena already brought to fulfillment and fully formed don't fall under the designation "sky and earth"; rather, still unformed and rudimentary material—from which entities *could* be formed and created—was called by these words. In this material, things were muddled and not sorted out according to their natures and forms, whereas now they're arranged in their proper ranks and called "the sky and the earth," the first being a spiritual and the second a physical creation.

27. Now that I've heard and considered all this, I don't want to squabble verbally: that's of no use for anything but undermining

and bringing down the people listening.* For building them up, in contrast, the law is good if used lawfully, because then its purpose is brotherly love from a pure heart, good conscience, and unfeigned faith:† I do know on which two commandments our teacher insisted the whole of the law and the prophets depend.‡

My God, the light for my vision in places where nothing is visible, when with burning zeal I offer you that testimony, what does it matter to me if divergent interpretations can be found in these words, interpretations that nevertheless are true?§ What, I ask you, does it matter to me if I discern differently than somebody else does about the author's discernment?

All of us readers are struggling to track down and seize the author's meaning, and as we believe him to be a teller of the truth, we wouldn't dare posit that he said anything we know or think to be false. In our common efforts to discern in the holy scriptures what the one who wrote them discerned in them, what harm is there if an individual discerns what you, light of all truth-telling minds, show him to be true—even if the author

---

* 2 Timothy 2:14.

† 1 Timothy 1:5–8.

‡ Matthew 22:34–40. The love of God and the love of one's neighbor subsume the whole will of God as expressed in scripture.

§ At this critical juncture, Augustine's phrasing is (as so often) ambiguous. Are the Bible's words or interpretations of the Bible's words "true"? One convention of Latin syntax suggest the former, as "words" is the closer of the two potential antecedents to the relative pronoun. But the resulting point might seem too obvious: scripture is always and inarguably true, in Augustine's eyes, as a matter of faith. Furthermore, the English "are" here is from the Latin subjunctive, which tends not to be used for straightforward fact like the truth of scripture according to Augustine's worldview. But are interpretations—if these are what is "true"—potentially or characteristically true? The subjunctive could suggest either, or something else. Moreover, the adverb *tamen* can mean "in any case" as well as "nevertheless." As a rule, I cannot drink enough to translate Augustine with the confidence other ancient authors afford.

he's reading didn't discern it, given that the author did see *something* true, though not this particular thing?

28. It's true, Master, that you made the sky. And it's true that the "beginning" or "first principle" is your wisdom, in which you made everything.* It's likewise true that this visible universe has as its major parts "the sky and the earth," words that are a brief summation of all entities made and established.

It's also true that everything capable of change suggests to our awareness a certain formlessness, by which a thing takes on form, or alters, or is transformed. It's true that a thing isn't subject to any change if it clings to an unchangeable form in such a way that, though it *could* change, it doesn't. It's true that formlessness, which is nearly nothing, can't reflect the back-and-forth course of time.

It's true that a thing can have, though this is just a manner of speaking, the name of the thing from which it comes: hence the sky and the earth can be called whatever kind of formlessness it was from which the sky and the earth were made. It's true that of all things with forms, none is more like what's unformed than earth and an abyss. It's true that not only what's created and formed, but also anything that *could be* created and formed was made by you, the source of everything.† It's true that everything formed out of what's formless is first formless, and then formed.

29. These are all a range of statements not doubted by those to whom you granted the ability to see such things with the inward

* Psalms 104:24.
† Romans 11:36, 1 Corinthians 8:6.

eye, and who unshakably believe that Moses, your servant, spoke in the spirit of truth.*

From all these statements, a person picks out one when he says, "In the beginning, God made heaven and earth," meaning that God, in his Word, an equal sharer in eternity with himself, made the creation that we can grasp with our minds *and* perceive with our senses—or *both* the spiritual and physical creation.

Picking out another statement, another person says, "In the beginning, God made heaven and earth," meaning that God in his Word, an equal sharer in eternity with himself, made this whole mass of the *physical* universe (only), *with* all the characteristics that are self-evidently known to us.

Picking out another statement, another person says, "In the beginning, God made heaven and earth," meaning that God in his Word, an equal sharer in eternity with himself, made the *formless material* of *both* spiritual and physical creation.

Picking out another statement, another person says, "In the beginning, God made heaven and earth," meaning that God in his Word, an equal sharer in eternity with himself, made the formless material of physical creation (only), and that in it the sky and the earth were still muddled together, though they're now things we see as separate, fully formed parts of this universe's mass.

Picking out another statement, another person says, "In the beginning, God made heaven and earth," meaning that *at the very start of his making and working,* God made *the formless material en-*

---

* Moses was the purported author of the Pentateuch, or first five books of the Bible.

closing the sky and the earth in a muddled state; and that, *formed from that source,* these now stand out clearly, along with everything that is in them.

30. Likewise for the words that follow in the text: out of all true ways of understanding them, a person picks one out in saying, "But the earth was unseen and unordered, and darkness was over the abyss," with the meaning that *the physical substance* that God made was still (only) *the unformed material of physical things,* but without order or light.

Another person picks out another way of understanding in saying, "But the earth was unseen and unordered, and darkness was over the abyss," with the meaning that *the whole, named "the sky and the earth,"* was still unformed and dark material, from which the *physical* sky and the *physical* earth would be made, with *everything* in them that is known to the physical senses.

Another person picks out another way of understanding in saying, "But the earth was unseen and unordered, and darkness was over the abyss," with the meaning that the whole, named "the sky and the earth," was still unformed and dark material, from which would be made the *comprehensible* sky—which elsewhere is called the "heaven of heaven"*—and the earth, which is apparently all of *physical* nature, under which name the physical sky as well can be understood; thus the whole "sky and earth" would be the source of all creation, seen and unseen.

Another person picks out another way of understanding in saying, "But the earth was unseen and unordered, and darkness was over the abyss": the scripture does *not* name that formlessness

* Psalms 115:16. See pages xxix–xxx of the introduction.

"the sky and the earth"; rather, such a person claims, actual formlessness *already* existed and was called "unseen and unordered earth" and "the dark abyss," from which God, in the words coming just before, was said to have created the sky and the earth—evidently, the spiritual and physical creation.

Another person picks out another way of understanding in saying, "But the earth was unseen and unordered, and darkness was over the abyss," with the meaning that a certain formlessness was *already* the material from which scripture had said, in the words coming just before, that God had created "the sky and the earth," evidently the whole mass of the *physical* universe divided into two giant parts, above and below, with all the ordinary created things in them that we know.

31. Someone might dispute these last two interpretations, in the following terms: "If you don't wish it to appear that this material in its unformed state was called 'the sky and the earth,' it follows that there was something that God *hadn't* made, yet *from which* he made the sky and the earth. Scripture, you see, hasn't told us that God made that material, unless we were to understand that it were signaled by the words 'sky and earth' or only the word 'earth,' where the text says, 'In the beginning, God made the sky and the earth.' As to the words that follow, 'But the earth was unseen and unordered,' though this was how it was seen fit to name formless material, we nonetheless have no choice but to understand that this is the material God made, according to the words coming before: 'he made the sky and the earth.'"

Defenders of one or the other of these two views—whether the first or the second—that we placed at the end of the last passage, when they hear this objection, will answer by saying the following: "We don't in fact deny that that unformed material was made by God, the source of all very good things.* While we say that a thing is *better* for being *created and given form,* we do admit that the less good thing that's made, and is only *susceptible* of being created and given form, is in any case good. We note, however, that this scriptural text hasn't mentioned that God created this formlessness, just as it hasn't mentioned many other things, like the cherubim and the seraphim,† and the things the apostle clearly speaks of, 'thrones, dominions, empires, dominions'‡—all of which, nevertheless, God self-evidently made.

"And," they continue, "if everything is included in the statement 'He made the sky and the earth,' what are we to say about the 'waters' on which 'the Spirit of God was carried'?§ If the 'earth' that's been named is understood in conjunction with these 'waters,' how then can formless, unsightly material be taken under the designation 'earth,' when we see how lovely to look at waters are?

"Or if we do take 'waters' under that designation, why is it written that the support or firmament was made from that same formlessness and called the sky, whereas it wasn't written that the waters were made? Formless deformity and invidious invisibility don't *still* characterize the waters we perceive to be flowing with such a becoming appearance.

"And," they continue further, "if they got that appearance when God said, 'Let the water that is under the firmament be gath-

* Genesis 1:31.
† Mentioned in Genesis 3:24, Isaiah 37:16, and elsewhere in the Bible.
‡ Paul, in Colossians 1:16. Paul refers to hierarchies of both earth and heaven.
§ Genesis 1:2.

ered together," so that this gathering together is an actual formation, what will be your explanation for the waters that are *above* the firmament?† In an unformed state, they wouldn't have deserved so honorable a position, but scripture doesn't say what words were spoken for forming them.

"Thus, even if Genesis is silent about God's having made something, neither sound faith nor solid comprehension allows any doubt that God made it; and it follows that no sober teaching will dare to assert that those waters are equal sharers in eternity with God just because we hear them mentioned in the book of Genesis without, however, finding there any indication that they were made. Why then can't we, under the instruction of truth, understand that that unformed material also, which this scripture calls 'unseen and unordered' and 'a dark abyss,' was made by God out of nothing, and therefore isn't an equal sharer in eternity with him, although the account leaves out any report of when the material was made?"

32. Having heard these things and taken a thorough look at them, according to my feeble ability—which I acknowledge to you, who already know it—I see two kinds of disagreement that can arise when truthful messengers communicate something through the signals of language. One kind of disagreement is about the truth of the matters at hand; the other is about the intention of the person communicating. We have one way of inquiring about the nature of the creation, and another of in-

---

* Genesis 1:9.
† Genesis 1:7.

quiring what Moses, an outstanding household servitor of your faith,* wanted the reader and hearer to understand.

As to the first kind of disagreement, I banish from my company all those who think they know something that's in fact not true. Likewise as to the second, I'm banishing from my company all those who think Moses said things that aren't true. Let me rather be joined in you with those, Master, who feed like flocks on your truth in all the wide range of love,† and rejoice along with them. Let us approach together the words of your book and seek in them your intention through the intention of your servant, through whose pen you shared out these words to us.

33. But who of us can find that intention among so many true things that, in these words, present themselves with various meanings to inquirers? If someone *could* find that intention, he would be able to say, with equal confidence, that Moses held a given opinion and wanted it to be understood in that account; and that it's the truth, whether it was an opinion Moses held or not.

Look at me, my God, your slave, who pledged to you a sacrifice of testimony in my writing—and I pray that, through your mercy, I will fulfill my pledge;‡ look how assuredly I state that in your unchangeable Word you made everything, seen and unseen. But could I possibly say with equal assurance that Moses wasn't focused on something else when he wrote, "In the beginning, God made the sky and the earth"? In your truth, I see the

---

* Hebrews 3:5.
† Ephesians 3:18–19.
‡ Psalms 116:18.

above interpretation as an indisputable fact, but I can't with the same certainty see in Moses's mind what he was thinking when he wrote those words.

He could have been thinking "at the very start of making things" when he said "in the beginning." He could also have wished it to be understood that "the sky and the earth" were not yet a fully formed, finished entity, whether spiritual or physical, but that either was in a rudimentary, unformed state.

I do see that any of the interpretations stated above could have been stated truly, but I *don't* with the same clarity see which one of them Moses had in mind when he wrote these words. Nevertheless, whether it's one of the above interpretations, or another I haven't mentioned, that was contemplated by such a great man when he produced these words, I wouldn't doubt that he discerned the truth and expressed it suitably.

34. From now on, I don't want anybody bothering me* by saying, "What Moses thought isn't what *you* say; he thought what *I* say." But if he said to me, "How do you know that Moses thought *this* way, as you assert about these words of his?"—in that case I would need to take it calmly, and perhaps I would answer as I have immediately above; or to some degree more fully, if he were more than ordinarily hardheaded.

But when he says, "What Moses thought isn't what *you* say; he thought what *I* say," yet without denying that the statement made by either of us is true—then, ah, I appeal to you, God, who are the life of the poor, and in whose bosom backtalk finds

* Galatians 6:17.

no home: rain your mollifying interventions into my heart, so that I can endure such people with forbearance.

They don't say this to me because they have miraculous powers and have seen what they say in your servant Moses's heart. Rather, they're arrogant: they don't know Moses's opinion but are in love with their own, not because it's true, but just because it's their own. If that weren't the case, they would love another true opinion equally, the way I love what they say when they say something true—not because it's theirs, but because it's true; and the very fact that it's true makes it not their own, personally. If, on the other hand, they love it because it's true, then it belongs to both them and me, because it's held in common by all the lovers of truth.

As to their contention, however, that Moses didn't view this the way I say, but rather the way they say, I reject it, and I don't love it, because even if it's the case, that boldness of theirs doesn't come from knowledge but from presumptuousness: not vision but brain-fevered pride gave birth to it.

Therefore, Master, your judgments should be shuddered at, because the truth belongs to you, and not to me, and not to anybody else. All of us possess it whom you publicly call to share it, fearsomely warning us not to try keeping it as our private property, so that we risk being deprived of it.* Whoever claims as his personal province what you've put before everyone for their profit, whoever wants as his own what belongs to everybody, is expelled from the commonality into what's only his own—that

* 1 Timothy 6:5.

is, from truth into a lie. Whoever speaks a lie is speaking of what's his alone.*

35. Listen, God, you who are the most excellent judge and the truth itself, listen to what I tell this back-talker—listen. In your presence I say it, and in the presence of my brothers, who make use of the law as the law commands, for the purpose of love.† Listen and see what I say to him, if you will. I offer him this brotherly, peacemaking speech:

"If we both see that what *you* say is true, and if we both see that what *I* say is true, then please tell me where we see that? Certainly I don't see it in you, and you don't see it in me; rather, we both see it in the unchangeable truth that's above our own minds. So as long as we're not at odds over the actual light of God our Master, why are we at odds over a fellow human being's thinking, which we *can't* see, in the way the unchangeable truth is seen?

"If Moses himself had appeared before us and said, 'This is what I was thinking,' we wouldn't *see* it as he did, but we would simply *believe* it. So let's not be swollen-headed with partisanship against each other, going above and beyond what's written.‡ Let's be devoted to the Master our God with all our heart and soul and mind, and our fellow human being as ourselves.§ Whatever Moses's opinions were in those books he wrote, they were based on those two commands to love selflessly; if we don't believe that

* John 8:44.
† 1 Timothy 1:5, 8.
‡ 1 Corinthians 4:6.
§ Matthew 22:37–39, Mark 12:29–31, Luke 10:27, and 1 John 4:7, all echoing Deuteronomy 6:5 and Leviticus 19:18.

this was so, we'll make a liar out of the Master* by claiming something different about the mind of our fellow slave than what the Master taught.

"Look, now, how stupid it is, amid such an abundance of true opinions that can be dug out of those words, to crash ahead in asserting which one of them Moses most likely held, and with destructive arguments to blunder against the love for whose sake the man whose words we're trying to explain said everything he said."

36. Even so, my God, you who are the exaltation of my lowliness and the rest from my toil, who hears my confessions and forgives my sins: since you command me to love my fellow human being as myself,† I can't believe, concerning Moses, your very faithful servant, that he received less of a gift from you than I would hope and long for in my own case, if I had been born in that era and you had placed me in that same position, so that through the servitude of my heart and tongue those writings would be given out, carrying such great benefit for all the races of mankind for such a long time afterward, and destined, by means of their preeminent authority everywhere in the world, to overcome the words of all false and outrageous teachings.

I would want, if at that time *I* were Moses (well, we all come from the same lump of clay‡—and what is a human being if you're not mindful of him?§)—if, back then, I were what he was, and you charged me with writing the book of Genesis, *I* would

* 1 John 1:10, 5:10.
† Matthew 22:37–39, Mark 12:29–31, Luke 10:27, and 1 John 4:7, all echoing Deuteronomy 6:5 and Leviticus 19:18.
‡ Romans 9:21.
§ Psalms 8:4.

want to be given such skill at speaking and such an effective manner of weaving discourse, that not even people as yet unable to understand how God creates would resist what I said, on the grounds that it was beyond their capacity; and those already able to understand wouldn't find passed over, in the few words of your servant, whatever true opinion they had arrived at through their reflections; and whatever other opinion anyone else had seen in the light of truth, I wouldn't want it—comprehensible in the same words—to be missing, either.

37. Just as a spring, itself occupying only a small space, is more abundant and furnishes its flowing waters for more streams and over a greater area than do any of the individual streams having this same spring as a source yet spreading over an immense landscape, so the account given out by your scriptural steward* sends gushing up, from just a small measure of language, floods of crystalline truth for the good of a quite considerable crowd of commentators. From this plenty, each person variously draws for himself whatever true conclusions he can about these matters, through twists and turns of his longer (though more trivial) discourses.

Some, when they read or hear these words of scripture, think of God as some sort of human being, or as some kind of mass endowed with immense power. They think of this being making, in a place outside itself (in a distant region, as it were), and as the result of a fresh, a sudden decision, the sky and the earth; and they picture the sky and the earth as two huge physical bodies, above and below, in which all things were to be contained.

* Titus 1:7.

When these people hear, "God said, 'Let such and such a thing be made,' and it was made," they think that the words were begun and finished, making their sounds in the course of time and passing by, and that after they passed by, what was ordered to exist immediately existed—and so on, however what they're physically accustomed to happens to guide their ideas.

In such creatures, who are still tiny and weak* and are carried in the scriptures' extremely humble phrasing as if held against a mother's bosom, faith is wholesomely built up; and through this faith they can know and retain in their minds, as definite, that God made all the entities that, in their miraculous variety, physical perception notes all around.

If any of them disdains as cheap what's been said in scripture, and in the arrogance of his weakness stretches his head out beyond the cradle where he's being nurtured—then, alas, the poor thing falls out. Have pity, our God and Master, and keep those who are walking down the road from trampling into nothing the chick who has no feathers yet, and send your angel to put him back in the nest, so that he lives until he can lift himself on his wings.

38. But other people, for whom your words are no longer a nest but a whole shady grove, see the fruit latent among the leaves, and they flutter there in glee, chattering as they poke around and pluck it. They see, as they read or hear these words, eternal God, that all past and future time is bested by your unshakable lastingness; yet they recognize that there is no creation in time that you didn't make, and that because your will is the same as

---

* 1 Corinthians 2:14–3:3.

you are, it was not by any kind of changed will, or by one arisen that didn't exist before, that you made everything. You made it not from yourself, as a likeness of yourself*—which is the form of all things—but rather from nothing, *un*like yourself and *un*-formed, but able to be formed through your likeness when it returned to you, the one; each thing in accordance with its or-dained capacity to do this, as granted to every being in the uni-verse, appropriately for its kind: and thus all these things could be made very good,† whether they remain around you, or whether, removed from you by degrees of distance, they effect and are subject to their beautiful changes through time and space. These people see these things and rejoice in the light of your truth, to the very limited extent they're capable of doing so in this present existence.

39. But one of these people focuses on the statement "In the beginning, God made ..." and considers the "beginning" or "first principle" to be wisdom, because wisdom also speaks to us.‡ Likewise, another focuses on the same words and under-stands "beginning" as the initial creation of things and takes "In the beginning, he made ..." as if it meant "First he made ..."

Furthermore, among those who understand "In the beginning" as meaning that in wisdom you made the sky and the earth, one believes that what this text terms "the sky and the earth" is actu-ally the material from which the sky and the earth were able to

---

* Genesis 1:26–27.

† Genesis 1:31.

‡ John 8:25. This is an outstanding instance of the difference made by Augustine's primary use of the (derivative) Latin scriptures. The New Revised Standard Version translates, "They said to him, 'Who are you?' Jesus said to them, 'Why do I speak to you at all?'" The last part in the Greek text *may* be read, "'What have I told you from the beginning?'" The Vulgate has "'I am the beginning / first principle, who also speak to you.'"

be created; while another believes that's already a pair of fully formed, distinct entities. Yet another places under the name "sky" a single, fully formed spiritual entity, and under the name "earth" a separate, unformed entity made of physical material.

Further, those who understand, by the terms "sky" and "earth," a still unformed material from which the sky and the earth would be formed, don't themselves all understand it in the same way. One of them thinks this material is the source from which was brought to completion the creation that can be grasped through the mind *and* the creation that can be grasped through the senses. Another thinks it's only the source of this perceptible physical mass containing thoroughly and readily visible entities in its ample interior.

And those who believe that in this passage created things already divided and arranged in different positions are called "the sky and the earth" don't believe it in the same way. No, one of them thinks the division is between the visible and the invisible, and another thinks that the whole of it is visible, in which we see the light-filled sky and the murky earth, and whatever things are contained in both.

40. But the person who takes "In the beginning, he made ..." as if it were stating "At first, he made ..." has no right way of understanding "the sky and the earth" as anything but the material the sky and the earth, and plainly these would be the entire creation, both what's grasped with the mind and what's grasped with the senses. If someone meant the whole *fully formed* creation, then he could be cogently asked what God made next, if he made that first. He won't find any answer as to what was made

after the universe, and he'll hear—though he doesn't want to—another question: "How could that act of creation come first, and nothing after it?"

But if he says that first God made formless and then formed creation, he's not devoid of sense, as long as he makes suitable distinctions concerning what is meant by preceding *in eternity, in time, by choice,* and *by origin.* If it's eternity, then it's about God preceding everything. If it's time, then an example is a flower preceding a fruit. If it's choice, then the fruit comes before the flower. If it's origin, then it's like sound coming before a song.

In these four possibilities for creation that I've laid out, the first and the last are the most difficult to understand, and the second and third the easiest. It's a rare act of seeing, Master, excessively hard to picture in the mind, how your eternity in an unchangeable way could be making changeable things, and therefore having to come before them.

As to the fourth circumstance, who is so shrewdly perceptive in his intellect that he has the power to distinguish, without immense effort, how sound comes before a song? The reason for this is that a song is fully formed sound. Now, something *not* formed can certainly exist, but on the other hand, what doesn't exist in the first place can't be formed.

Accordingly, a material precedes what is made out of it; but it doesn't precede in the sense that it brings about this making, as on the contrary it *is made.* And it doesn't precede by the mere means of an interval of time. We don't, at an earlier time, produce unformed sounds without a tune, and at a later time adjust them and fashion them, like pieces of wood used to fashion a chest, or silver used to make a container for liquids. Such materials naturally precede, in time as well, the forms of the things made out of them, but where a song is concerned, it's not like this.

Only when a song is performed is its sound heard; it doesn't first make sounds without form, and then take the form of a song. In fact, as soon as a sound is made in any way, it passes by, and you won't find any trace of it that you can recover and fit together again through skill. Therefore, a song operates through its own sound, the sound that is its material. This material, as one might expect, is formed so as to be a song; and thus, as I was saying, the material of making sound precedes the form of singing.

But it doesn't precede through the power to create: the sound is not the artisan of singing. Rather, it is available to the singer's soul from his body, from which he makes the song. Nor does the sound precede in time: it is issued simultaneously with the song. Nor does sound precede by choice: sound isn't superior to song, since in fact a song is not just a sound but also a beautiful sound. But it does precede in origin, because a song is not formed so that there can be sound, but rather sound is formed so that there can be song.

Through this analogy, if anyone has the ability, I invite him to understand that the material of the universe was "made first" and called "the sky and the earth" because the sky and the earth were made from it. But this material wasn't made first in time, because the forms of things in the universe produce periods of time; whereas this material was formless.

Now, within periods of time, this material comes to our attention together with them. But no account can be given of formless matter except one that suggests priority in time—whereas this material is lowest and *last* in its worth, because certainly fully formed things are better than unformed things. And certainly it is "preceded" by the Creator's eternity, so that it could come from nothing and become something.

41. Among all these different true interpretations, let Truth itself beget agreement between our hearts, and may our God in his mercy let us use the law lawfully, for the purpose for which it was made, which is unsullied love.*

Accordingly, if someone asks me which of these interpretations your renowned servant Moses espoused, I have to say simply, "I don't know"; otherwise, my language here wouldn't be characteristic of sincere testimony. And yet I know that these are all true interpretations. I'm not speaking here of people who have a physical picture of God, of whom I think I've said enough; but they're just promising young children, not scared by your book's words, which are lofty in their lowliness and rich in their brevity.†

But all of us who I admit can discern and articulate true things in these words, must love one another, and must with equal fervor love you, our God,‡ the flowing fountain of truth, if we're really hungry for the truth and not trivia. And we must to such a degree honor Moses—the steward of your writing, who was full of your Spirit—as to believe that when he wrote these things, he set his mind on whatever in them was superlative both in the light of truth and in productive usefulness—because you unveiled to him whatever that was.

* 1 Timothy 1:5–8.
† See chapter 37 above.
‡ Leviticus 19:18, Deuteronomy 6:5, Matthew 22:37–39, Mark 12:30–31, Luke 10:27, 1 John 4:7.

42. Thus, while one person says, "Moses interpreted the way I do," and another says, "No, the way I do!" I think it's more reverent for me to say, "Why not both instead, if both are true? And if there's a third or fourth true interpretation, or absolutely any further one seen in these words, why shouldn't all these views be credited to Moses, through whom the one God modulated these sacred writings in due proportion for the sensibilities of many people, allowing them to view varied verities in them?"

I, at any rate, declare the following fearlessly from my heart: if I were to write anything aiming at the peak of authority, I would prefer to write in such a way that my words echoed whatever truth each person could grasp concerning these matters; that would be better than to give one true interpretation quite blatantly, for the purpose of excluding all other interpretations—though I'm not speaking, of course, of those interpretations that are problematic for me simply because they're false.

I don't want, then, my God, to recklessly believe that you didn't allow Moses, that great man, deservedly to do the same. Absolutely, what he perceived and thought about these words, while he was writing them, was whatever truth we've been able to find in them, *and* whatever truth we couldn't—or couldn't yet—find in them that *can* nevertheless be found in them.

43. Finally, Master, you who are God and not flesh and blood:* even if in any respect a human being has seen less than what he might, surely it would still be impossible for your good Spirit— who will lead me into the land of justice†—not to find out what-

---

* Matthew 16:17.
† Psalms 143:10; the Latin scripture conflates the idea of straightness or levelness and rectitude.

ever you yourself, in person, were going to reveal to the readers of future ages. And the same would hold even if Moses, through whom these things were spoken, perhaps was thinking of only one interpretation, out of many true ones.

If that were the case, the interpretation he was thinking of would be the loftier one. To us, Master, point out either that interpretation or any other true one that you choose. Whether you reveal to us either what you revealed to Moses, or something else opportune conveyed by the same words, it must be you who are pasturing us, and not straying error that amuses itself with us.

I appeal to you, my Master and God! Look at how much I've written, and it concerns so few words! What strength of ours, what length of time will be enough for all of your books, if this is my approach?

Therefore, let me testify to you more briefly through scripture, choosing some single thing into which you have breathed to make it true, something certain and good, even though many things may have come to my attention in passages where they had the power to do so.

In the course of this, my faithful testimony aims at saying what your servant had in mind, which is correct, and the best, and of course it behooves me to attempt it. But if I don't achieve that, let me still say what your truth meant to say to me through his words, seeing that your truth also spoke to him what it willed.

BOOK 13

1. I call on you, my God, my mercy, who made me, and who didn't forget me even when I forgot you. Through my desire for you, which you breathed into me, I call you into my soul, which you prepare to take you in. But now, don't abandon me when I call on you—you who, before I called on you, got in ahead of me* with proliferating and multifarious utterances, so that I could hear from far away and turn around, and call on you who were calling me.

In fact, Master, you erased the whole record of unworthy things I did, so that you wouldn't have to pay me back for the work of my hands by which I failed you; but you anticipated all my wor-

* Psalms 59:10.

thy works, so that you could pay yourself back for your own hands' work, by which you made me.*

Before I was, you were; and at the time I wasn't even in a state to which you could provide existence. And yet here I am, for the reason that your goodness anticipated all of this: both your making me and the means by which you made me.

And it's not that you needed me, or that I was a sort of good thing that could help you, my Master and my God. The purpose of my creation wasn't for me to serve you, if that meant keeping you from tiring in your activity. Your power wouldn't be less great if deprived of my obedient service. I don't need to tend to you like the land, as if you would go untended if I didn't tend to you. I was created to serve you and tend to you and reverently attend to you so that I could do well because of you, from whom I have the capacity to be someone who *could* do well.

2. Your creation stood fast out of the fullness of your goodness. In this way, the good, though it in no way benefited you, nor was a part of you and thus equal to you,† nevertheless wouldn't fail to exist, and this is because it came into being because of you.

What did the sky and the earth, which you created in the beginning, do for you? Let the spiritual and physical entities, which you created in your wisdom, say what they did for you. Still-rudimentary and unformed things—in their different categories, either spiritual or material—depended on your wisdom, prone as they were to pass into uncontrolled activity and a re-

* Psalms 119:73.
† Philippians 2:6.

mote unlikeness to you. But a spiritual being even without a form was superior to what it would have been as a material object with a form; and for its part a material object even without a form was superior to complete nonexistence.

Thus these things, in their unformed state, had to depend on your Word, until they were called back by that same Word to your oneness, and so were given form and existed out of you, the highest good, and could be very good,* every one of them. But what had they done to deserve from you their existence as mere unformed things, as they couldn't even have existed to that degree unless from you?

3. What did physical matter do for you to deserve that it be merely unseen and unordered?† It couldn't even be this unless you made it. Because it didn't exist, it couldn't earn its existence from you.

And what did that rudimentary arising of spiritual creation do for you to earn its existence as merely a wavering darkness like the abyss, and not like you—until, through that same Word, it could be turned or converted to that same Word, by which it was made, and from that Word could be illuminated and become light; although not on an equal basis with you—and yet in conformity to a form equal to you?‡

Just as for a physical object, existence is not the same as formally beautiful existence—otherwise an object could not be "malformed"—in the same way, even for a spiritual creation to

---

* Genesis 1:31.
† Genesis 1:2.
‡ The incarnated son of God has material existence in common with the created universe. See Romans 8:29 and Philippians 2:6.

live is not the same as to live in wisdom; if this were not so, such a spirit would be unchangeably wise.

It is, then, good for that spirit always to cling to you,* so that it doesn't lose, by turning away from you, the light that it gained by turning toward you, and in losing it, slip back into a life like the dark abyss.

We ourselves, who by virtue of the soul are a spiritual creation, were at one time darkness in that life when we turned away from you, our light.† And we struggle in what is left of our darkness until we can be your justice through your only son,‡ like the mountains of God: for when we were your judgments (or the objects of them), we were like the huge abyss.§

4. You said, when you were first creating, "Let there be light," and there was light.¶ I understand those words to mean (because this explanation wouldn't lack cogency) that this light was your spiritual creation, because there already did exist some kind of life for you to illuminate. But it didn't earn from you existence as the kind of life that *could* be illuminated; and likewise, when it *did* already exist, it didn't earn from you its illumination.

Rather, the unformed state of that life couldn't be pleasing to you unless it became light. And it became light not simply through arising but through gazing at and clinging to the light illuminating it. In this way, both the fact that this being lived in

* Psalms 73:28.
† Ephesians 5:8.
‡ 2 Corinthians 5:21.
§ Psalms 36:6.
¶ Genesis 1:3.

the first place, and the fact that it lived in bliss, were due to nothing but your free gift.

Thus, this entity was turned or converted—by transforming into something better—to that which can change neither for the better nor for the worse. This is you alone: you alone are undifferentiated existence: for you, to live isn't something different than to live in blessedness or bliss, because you *are* this.

5. So what would have been missing in you, as far as the good goes—the good you are in yourself? For that matter, those created things could have been nothing at all, or could have remained unformed. You didn't make them because of any shortcoming of your own, but rather out of the fullness of your goodness you confined them and converted them to form.

It's not as if your joy is completed by them. It's because to you in your perfection their imperfection is displeasing, so that they need to be perfected out of you and to please you—it's not, in contrast, as if you were imperfect and needed to be perfected by means of their perfection.

Your good Spirit, or "wind," or "breath," carried itself above the waters;* it wasn't carried by them, as if it were resting on them. It's said that your Spirit rests on certain people,† but in fact it causes them to rest in itself.

So, then, your imperishable and unchangeable will carried itself above, being entirely self-sufficient: it carried itself above that life you had made. To that life, living was not the same as living

---

* Genesis 1:2.
† Luke 4:18, 1 Peter 4:14, echoing a repeated locution in the Old Testament.

in bliss, because that life *lives* even while sloshing around in its own darkness. It remains for that life to be turned to him from whom it was made, and to live more and more on the fountain of life, and to see light in his light* and to be perfected, and filled with light, and filled with bliss.

6. Here, now, there appears to me, like a riddle,† the Trinity, which is you, my God. You, the father, made the sky and the earth. You made it in the beginning of our wisdom, that is, your wisdom born from you, equal to you, and sharing in eternity with you: that is, you created the sky and the earth in your son.

We have said a great deal about the heaven of heaven,‡ and the earth that was unseen and unformed, and the dark abyss with its roving instability of spiritual formlessness.§ It needed to be turned to him, who had caused it to be life (such as that life was); it needed to become, through illumination, life that was beautiful—fit to be seen, so to speak. It needed to become his heaven of heaven, which was created afterward between one realm of water and another.¶

By this point I could grasp, under the name of God, the father who made these things; and, under the name of "the beginning" (or "the first principle"), the son, in whom God made these things. Then, believing that my God is three in one, as I did believe, I searched in your holy words and there it was: your Spirit carried itself above the waters." There it is: the Three in

One and my God, the creator of all creation: the Father and the Son and the Holy Spirit.

7. But what was the reason for phrasing it this way? Truth-telling light, I bring my heart close to you, to keep it from telling me nonsense. Scatter its darkness and tell me—I beg you by Love, our mother—I beg you, what was the reason that after naming the sky (or heaven) and the unseen and unordered earth, and the darkness over the abyss, only then, finally, does your scripture name your Spirit?

Was it proper to introduce the Spirit by saying it "carried itself above" or moved? That couldn't be said unless there were first a mention of the thing above which your Spirit could be understood as moving. It didn't move above the father or the son; and yet it couldn't be correctly described as moving above if it were moving above nothing. First, it needed to be said *what* the Spirit was moving above, and then the Spirit itself could be spoken of; and there was no proper way to describe it except by saying it carried itself above or moved above.

But *why*, then, was it not appropriate to introduce the Spirit except by saying that it moved *above*?

8. From this point, if anybody has the mental ability, let him follow with his understanding what your apostle Paul says about your love having been spread through our hearts by the Holy Spirit, which has been given to us.* The apostle explains and exemplifies, while speaking of spiritual things,† the *transcendent*

* Romans 5:5.
† 1 Corinthians 12:1.

path of love, the path rising above.* For our sake, he kneels to you, praying that we may acquire *transcendent* knowledge of Christ's love.† So from the start the Spirit *rose up above* and *carried itself above* or *moved above* the waters.

So to whom should I speak, and how should I speak, about the weight of desire dragging down into the sheer abyss; and about love's action of lifting up through your Spirit, which moved above the waters? To whom shall I speak, and how shall I speak? There aren't, of course, any actual places in which we're submerged and from which we emerge. But what's more similar, and what's less similar?

These are feelings, these are passions: the filth of our spirit running down lower through a passion for all that preoccupies us on the one hand; and on the other, your holiness raising us upward, so that, in our passion to be free of care, we can take our heart upward toward you,‡ where your Spirit is moving over the waters. Then we can come to transcendent rest, when our soul has come through the waters, which give us no place to stand down here underneath, no sub-stance.§

9. The angel plunged down,¶ the human soul plunged down, giving evidence that all creation endowed with the Spirit would have found its way to the bottom of the dark pit if you hadn't from the start said "Let there be light," and if the light hadn't

---

* 1 Corinthians 12:31–13:13.
† Ephesians 3:14–19.
‡ Colossians 3:1–2.
§ Psalms 124:1–5.
¶ From a quite early stage in Christianity, Satan was identified as the rebellious, "fallen" angel.

come into being,* and if every obedient understanding in your
heavenly commonwealth hadn't clung to you and rested in your
Spirit, which moved unchangeably over what was changeable.

Otherwise, even the "heaven of heaven" would have been, in
itself, a dark abyss; but as things are, it is light in the Master.†
Even in that wretched restlessness of spirits plunging down and
displaying their darkness, stripped of your light's clothing, you
demonstrate clearly enough the greatness of the thinking creation you've made, to whom nothing less than what you are suf-
fices in any way for a happy rest—and who, consequently, is not
a self-sufficient creation. *You*, Master, light our darkness;‡ our
clothes of illumination arise from you,§ and our darkness will be
like noon.¶

Give me yourself, my God, restore yourself to me. See, I'm in
love with you, and if it's too little, let me be more powerfully in
love with you. I can't measure and know how much is missing
from my love, how insufficient it is for allowing my life to run
into your arms and not turn away from you, but stay until it's
hidden away in your hidden presence.** I only know that except
for you, things go badly for me, not only on the outside but on
the inside, and that all the wealth that isn't my God is poverty.

10. It couldn't possibly be that either the Father or the Son
moved or "was carried" above the waters? Well, if it were like a
physical object in a place, then the Holy Spirit didn't do so, ei-

* Genesis 1:3.
† Ephesians 5:8.
‡ Psalms 18:28.
§ Isaiah 61:10.
¶ Isaiah 58:10.
** Psalms 31:20.

ther. Yet if it were about the transcendence of unchangeable divinity over everything that can change, then the Father *and* the Son *and* the Holy Spirit moved above the waters.

So why is only the Holy Spirit said to have done this? Why has a place (which in fact isn't a place) been suggested for this being that alone has been spoken of as your gift?*

In your gift, we rest; *there* we delight in you. Our rest is our place. Love lifts us up there, and your good Spirit† raises on high our lowliness from the gates of death.‡ In a good will is our peace.§

A material object works its way toward its own place by means of its own weight. A weight doesn't simply direct its course to the lowest level, but to its own proper place. Fire moves up, stone down. These things are in motion through their own weights, and they seek their own places. Oil poured underneath water rises to the top, and water poured on top of oil sinks underneath. They are set in motion by their own various weights, to seek their own places. Things that are not set in the order they should be are restless; once set there, they rest.

My love is my weight. I'm carried by it wherever I'm carried. Through your gift we catch fire and are carried upward; we go up in flames, and up we go. In our heart we ascend the ascending staircase, and we sing the song of the rising steps.¶ By your

---

* Acts 2:38.
† Psalms 143:10.
‡ Psalms 9:13.
§ Luke 2:14.
¶ Perhaps the original Hebrew Bible label is for a psalm like 122 (quoted immediately after this), sung while climbing the steps of the Temple.

fire, by your good fire, we go up in flames, and there we go, since we go up to the peace of Jerusalem; since I rejoice in those who said to me, "We will go to the Master's house."* Good will is going to set us in the right place there, in such a way that our will is for nothing but to remain there for eternity.†

11. What a happy creation that knows nothing else—though it would have been something else itself had it not been raised up as soon as it was made, with no time intervening, through your gift, which is carried above all that is changeable; this happened through your calling and saying "Let there be light," and making the creation into light.‡

But in us, time makes a difference, because we were darkness, and we are made complete as light.§

But for that other creation, it's otherwise; it's merely stated what it would have been had it not been illuminated, and that's stated as if it was unstable and dark beforehand.¶ This is to make plain why it was made different from that: namely, when turned to the unfailing light, it would be light.

Let whoever is able to understand this understand it, asking you to explain. Why is such a person bothering me,** as if *I* could illuminate any person coming into this world?††

---

* Psalms 122:1, 6.
† Psalms 23:6, 27:4.
‡ Genesis 1:3.
§ Ephesians 5:8.
¶ Genesis 1:2.
** Galatians 6:17.
†† John 1:9.

12. Who's going to understand the all-powerful Trinity? But who doesn't speak of it?—if it's *it* they're actually speaking of. It's a rare soul who, when talking about it, knows what he's talking about; yet people quarrel and battle about it—though no one who is without peace can see that sight.

I would like people to think about three things that they possess within themselves. These three are very different from the actual Trinity, but I'm giving people examples by which to exert and test themselves and experience just how very far away the examples are from the reality.

I'm naming, in any case, three things: to be, to know, and to will. I am, and I know, and I have a will. I am a being that knows and wills, and I know that I am and that I have a will, and I have a will to be and to know. Let anyone who's able see how insepa- rable a life there is among these three: one life and one mind; and one essence or being, and at the end of the day how unpars- able any distinction is between them—and yet there *are* distinc- tions. Certainly a person has himself; he is face-to-face with himself, as it were. Let him turn his attention toward himself and have a look, and tell me what he sees.

But when he finds something among these three and tells about it, he mustn't then think he's found what is unchangeable above this stuff, what exists without change and knows without change and wills without change.

Anyway, whether it's through and in these three acts that there is a Trinity, or whether all of these three are in each part of the Trinity so that each possesses all three, or whether both these propositions are valid, given the Trinity's marvelous singularity and multiplicity, its endless end within and for itself, so that it is and is known to itself and sufficient unto itself, unchangeably the very self in the plentiful vastness of its oneness—who can easily work this out in his mind? Who could in any way articulate this problem? Who would, in any way whatsoever, make a stab at announcing his own view?

13. Go forward in your testimony, my faith; say to God your Master, "Holy, holy, holy, my Master and God,* in your name we were baptized, you the Father and the Son and the Holy Spirit";† because among us as well, in his Christ, God made heaven and earth, the people of the Spirit and the people of the flesh in his church.‡

And the earth we are made of, before it took form from teaching, was unseen and unordered,§ and we were covered over in the darkness of ignorance; you disciplined mankind as a payment for sin,¶ and your judgments are like a deep abyss.** But because your Spirit moved above the water, your pity didn't abandon our pitiful state, and you said "Let there be light."††

"Make your repentance, because the kingdom of heaven has come near to you."‡‡ "Make your repentance." "Let there be light." And since our soul was roused against ourselves, we remembered you, Master, from the land of the Jordan River and from the mountain§§ that was as high as you but lowered itself for

* Isaiah 6:3, Revelation 4:8.
† Matthew 28:19.
‡ 1 Corinthians 3:1.
§ Genesis 1:2.
¶ Psalms 39:11.
** Psalms 36:6.
†† Genesis 1:3.
‡‡ Matthew 3:2, 4:17, Mark 1:15.
§§ Psalms 42:6.

our sake.* And our darkness was offensive to us, and we turned to you, and light came into being. So there it is: we were once darkness, but now we are light in the Master.†

14. But that is still only through faith, and not yet through sight, as we have been saved through hope.‡ Hope in something we can see is not hope.§ One abyss still only calls to another—but now in the voice of your floodgates.¶

Even Paul himself, who says, "I wasn't able to speak to you as spiritual beings, but only as physical ones,"** doesn't yet think he has a grasp; he merely forgets the things that are behind and stretches toward those that are ahead,†† and groans with his burdens‡‡ and thirsts in his soul for the living God, as deer thirst for flowing springs, and he says, "When will I arrive there?"§§—at his shelter, his covering, his clothing, which is from heaven, and which he yearns to put on;¶¶ and he calls to the abyss below, saying, "Don't conform to this world, but instead transform yourselves by giving yourselves new minds,"*** and "Don't let your thinking turn you into children; rather, be mere youngsters when it comes to malice, but adults in your thinking,"††† and "Oh, you idiot Galatians! Who's cast a spell on you?"‡‡‡

* Philippians 2:6.
† Ephesians 5:8.
‡ 2 Corinthians 5:7.
§ Romans 8:24, 2 Corinthians 5:7.
¶ Psalms 42:7.
** 1 Corinthians 3:1.
†† Philippians 3:13.
‡‡ 2 Corinthians 5:4.
§§ Psalms 42:1–3.
¶¶ 2 Corinthians 5:2.
*** Romans 12:2.
††† 1 Corinthians 14:20.
‡‡‡ Galatians 3:1.

But now he doesn't speak in his own voice, but in yours, God, as you sent your Spirit from the heights,* through the one who ascended on high and opened the floodgates of his gifts,† so that the rushing streams would gladden your city.‡ Paul, the friend of the bridegroom, sighs for that city.§ He already has the first-fruits offering of the Spirit, because the bridegroom possesses them, but he sighs within himself, waiting to be adopted, and to have freedom bought for his body.¶

The bridegroom's friend sighs for him (as he's part of the bride's body) and is jealous on behalf of the bridegroom (whose friend he is)—not on his own behalf: in the voice of your floodgates, not his own voice, he calls on the other abyss.** He is protectively jealous on behalf of it, in his fear that, in the way the snake deceived Eve with his cunning, the people's understanding will be corrupted and alienated from the chastity that is in our betrothed, your only son.††

What is that light of beauty that will appear? It's when we'll see him as he is,‡‡ and the tears will pass away that have become my daily and nightly bread, while people say to me every day, "Where is your God?"§§

---

* Wisdom of Solomon 9:17.
† I.e., Christ; Psalms 68:18.
‡ Psalms 46:4.
§ John 3:29.
¶ Romans 8:23. Adoption gave full rights as a legal heir, while "redemption" meant buying a person out of slavery or captivity.
** Psalms 42:7.
†† 2 Corinthians 11:2–3, the core of this passage's metaphor: "I feel a divine jealousy for you, for I promised you in marriage to one husband, to present you as a chaste virgin to Christ. But I am afraid that as the serpent deceived Eve by his cunning, your thoughts will be led astray from a sincere and pure devotion to Christ."
‡‡ 1 John 3:2.
§§ Psalms 42:3.

15. But I also say, "Where is my God?" Right here is where you are. I find in you a little breath of rest when I pour out my soul* over myself in words of rejoicing and confession, the sounds of someone celebrating a feast day.†

But still my soul is sad, because it falls back and becomes an abyss—or rather it feels it's still an abyss.‡ My faith, which you lighted as a guide on my nighttime pathway,§ says to it, "Why are you sad, my soul, and why do you trouble me? Hope in the Master.¶ The light for the path before your feet is his word.** Hope and hold on, until the night, the mother of the wicked, passes by, until the Master's anger passes by.†† We too were once sons of that anger;‡‡ we were darkness,§§ and we carry traces of that darkness in our body, which is dead because of sin,¶¶ until the dawn approaches and the shadows draw back.*** Hope in the Master."

In the morning, I will stand in his presence and contemplate him;††† always I will testify to you. In the morning, I will stand and see the salvation of my countenance, my God,‡‡‡ who will bring to life even our deathly bodies through the Spirit, which makes

---

* Job 32:20.
† Psalms 42:4.
‡ Psalms 42:5, 11, 43:5.
§ Psalms 119:105.
¶ Psalms 42:5, 11.
** Psalms 119:105.
†† Isaiah 26:20.
‡‡ Ephesians 2:3.
§§ Ephesians 5:8.
¶¶ Romans 8:10.
*** Song of Solomon 2:17.
††† Psalms 5:3–5. The Latin in the Vulgate is quite far from both the original Hebrew and modern translations.
‡‡‡ Psalms 42:5, 11, 43.5.

its home in us,* because in mercy it was carried over what was dark and unstable within us.

From this source, we have, in our sojourning in this life, been given a pledge that we are already light.† Up to now we have been saved by hope‡ and made sons of light and sons of God, not sons of night and darkness, which we were before.§

Between those and us, given the continuing uncertainty of human knowledge, you alone distinguish, testing our hearts, and you call the light day and the darkness night.¶ Who can tell us apart, if not you? But what do we have that we haven't received from you?** You made us containers for functions held in high esteem, but used the same lump of clay, as it were, for other containers with degraded functions.††

16. Or did anyone but you, our God, make a supporting vault‡‡ of authority over us through your holy scripture? The sky will be folded together like a book,§§ but now it is stretched like a tanned hide over us.¶¶ Your holy scripture in fact has more authority

---

* Romans 8:11.
† Ephesians 5:8.
‡ Romans 8:24.
§ 1 Thessalonians 5:5.
¶ Genesis 1:5.
** 1 Corinthians 4:7.
†† Romans 9:21.
‡‡ Genesis 1:7–8.
§§ Isaiah 34:4. In the original Hebrew, it is "rolled up like a scroll"; there were no books of the modern type in ancient Israel.
¶¶ Psalms 104:2. Behind the following perhaps odd-seeming conceit of stretched skin are two facts of material culture that might immediately have evoked cogent images in the minds of Augustine's contemporaries. Tents were made of animal skins, a circumstance resonant with many Hebrew Bible stories; and the material of a codex Bible in Augustine's time was vellum, or animal skin, which was prepared on stretchers at one stage.

now that the mortals through whom you provided it to us have met their death (for what that was worth).

But you know, Master, you know how you clothed humankind in animal skins when through sin they became mortal.* Accordingly, you stretched like a tanned hide the vault of your book— your by all means harmonious discourse—that you placed over us by means of mortals' service. By their very death, the solidification of authority in your words given out through them is transcendently extended over everything below, whereas while they lived here on earth it was not extended in this way. You had not yet stretched out the sky like a hide; you had not yet spread the fame of their death everywhere.

17. Let's look, Master, at the heavens, the works of your fingers.† Brush aside from our eyes the clouds with which you've covered the heavens underneath. *There* is your evidence, furnishing wisdom for little children.‡ Make mature, my God, your praise from the mouths of babies still at the breast.§

We don't know of any other books that tear down lofty arrogance so thoroughly,¶ so thoroughly destroying the enemy and the defender, who repels reconciliation with you by shielding his sins. I don't know, Master, I don't know any other words so pure,** which could urge confession on me and tame my stiff

* Genesis 3:21.
† Psalms 8:3.
‡ Psalms 19:7.
§ Psalms 8:2, quoted in Matthew 21:6.
¶ Ezekiel 30:6.
** Psalms 12:6.

neck under your yoke* and draw me to worship you with no expectation of a reward. Let me understand these words, good Father. Give this to me in my place here underneath them, because you made them firm and sound for those under them.

18. There are other waters above this supporting firmament,† I believe, and they're deathless and set apart from earthly deterioration. Let them praise your name, let the nations of your angels above the sky praise you. They have no need to look up at this firmament and learn your Word by reading it. They always see our face,‡ and there they read, without the syllables of time, what your eternal will wills. They peruse it, they choose it, and they lose themselves in love for it. They read always, but what they read never passes by. By choosing and loving without reservation they peruse the actual changelessness of your plan. Their volume doesn't close; their book isn't folded shut,§ because for them this is you yourself, and you are forever. You marshaled them above that firmament, which you made firm over the infirmity of the peoples below it, where they look up and learn your mercy, which proclaims in time you who made time.

Your mercy and truth, Master, are in the sky, clear up to the clouds.¶ But the clouds pass by, and the sky remains. The preachers of your Word pass by out of this life into another life, but your scripture stretches itself over the nations until the end of

* Matthew 11:29–30.
† Genesis 1:7–8.
‡ Matthew 18:10.
§ Isaiah 34:4; see note on chapter 16 above.
¶ Psalms 36:5.

the world. Yet the sky and the earth will pass away, whereas what you speak will not pass away.* The hide will be folded up and the meadow grass over which it is stretched will pass away in its bright beauty, but your Word remains for eternity.†

This now appears to us in riddling form in the clouds, and in the sky's dim mirror, and not as it is:‡ this is because, although we have been beloved by your son, what we will be hasn't yet appeared. He has looked through the lattice of the body and spoken endearments to us, and kindled our love for him, and we run after the fragrance he gives off.§ But when he will appear, we will be like him, since we will see him as he is.¶ It will be in our power, Master, to see him as he is; but this power doesn't yet belong to us.

19. Just as you alone exist absolutely, you alone absolutely know, as you unchangeably are and unchangeably know and unchangeably will. Your being knows and wills unchangeably, and your knowledge is and wills unchangeably, and your will is and knows unchangeably. With you, it is not seen as right that the unchangeable light should be known by the changeable, illuminated being in the same way that the light knows itself. For this reason, my soul is like waterless land before you;** just as it can't be enlightened from itself, it can't satiate itself. The fountain of life is in your presence, just as in your light we will see the light.††

* Matthew 24:35.
† Isaiah 40:6–8.
‡ 1 Corinthians 13:12.
§ Song of Solomon 1:3–4, 2:9.
¶ 1 John 3:2.
** Psalms 143:6.
†† Psalms 36:9.

20. Who herded all the bitter, briny people into a single fellowship?* They in fact have the same goal of happiness in time and on earth, and everything they do is because of this, although they're washed back and forth by their countless variety of anxieties.

Who was that, Master, but you, who commanded that the waters be herded together into a single flock and that the dry land appear, thirsty for you,† since the sea as well is yours, and you made it, and your hands formed the dry land?‡ Thus it wasn't bitterness in human impulses but water herded together that is called the sea.

But you also discipline the evil desires of souls and set fixed limits, saying how far the waters can advance,§ so that the waves in them are lessened, and in this way, in your orderly rule over all things, you make the sea.

21. But as for the souls that thirst after you and appear before you,¶ and are kept apart by another boundary from the fellowship of the sea, you water them with your secret, pure spring, so that the earth as well can yield its harvest.**

As the earth yields its harvest, so our soul at your command, its God and Master's command, produces the works of mercy "according to its kind"††—humankind, that is; the soul cares lov-

---

* Genesis 1:9.
† Psalms 63:1.
‡ Psalms 95:5.
§ Job 38:10–11.
¶ Psalms 63:1–2.
** Psalms 85:12.
†† Genesis 1:11–12.

ingly for its neighbor* by giving help for the body's needs. According to similar experiences, it bears within itself the seed of sympathy, since from a sense of our own weakness we suffer along with others, which leads us to assist those in need, succoring them the same way we would like help brought to us, should we find ourselves in the same need. This is not only in easy matters, like grass going to seed, but in protective support as firm as oak wood, such as a fruit-bearing tree gives: the service of rescuing a victim from powerful hands, and the provision of shading protection under the strong oak of just judicial proceedings.

22. So, Master, so, I appeal to you, let there arise—as you grant already, giving us good cheer and the ability to do good works— let truth rise from the ground, and let justice look down from the sky,† and let there be lights made in the vault, the firmament.‡ Let us break our bread to share it with the starving, and bring the destitute and homeless man under our roof. Let us clothe the naked, and not look down on our household slaves, who were born from the same seed as ourselves.§

See how good it is when this harvest is born in the earth.¶ But let our light sprout forth in a timely fashion. After this lower harvest of practical activity, let us enter into the delights of contemplation; possessing ourselves on high of the supporting word of life, let us appear like stars in the universe,** by clinging

* Matthew 22:37, 39, Mark 12:30, 33, Luke 10:27, 1 John 4:7, echoing Leviticus 19:18.
† Psalms 85:11.
‡ Genesis 1:14–15.
§ Isaiah 58:7–8.
¶ Genesis 1:12.
** Philippians 2:15, 1 John 1:1.

to the firmament of your scripture. There you discourse with us, so that we can tell, as we tell day from night, things of the mind from those of the physical senses, and so that we can tell souls dedicated to things of the mind from those dedicated to things of the senses.

This means that it is no longer you alone, in your recondite discernment, dividing the light from the darkness, as when the firmament didn't yet exist; it is also your people of the Spirit, set on that same firmament and showing distinct through your grace that's self-evident throughout the world, who shine above the earth and divide night from day. They mark periods of time,* because the old has passed away, and look: the new has been created;† and because our salvation is more imminent than we believed, as the night is far advanced, and the day is approaching;‡ and because you bless your year with the chaplet of celebration,§ sending your workers to reap the harvest,¶ though others labored at the sowing;** and sending them also into another sowing, whose harvest comes at the end.†† Thus you grant the prayers of the hopeful, and you bless the passing years of the just—but you are the same, yourself, and in your years, which don't fall short,‡‡ you prepare a granary for our years that pass by. Through your eternal plan, you give heavenly goods throughout the earth at the proper times.

* Genesis 1:14.
† 2 Corinthians 5:17.
‡ Romans 13:11–12.
§ Psalms 65:11.
¶ Matthew 9:38.
** John 4:38.
†† Matthew 13:39.
‡‡ Psalms 102:27.

23. So one person is given, through the Spirit, the discourse of wisdom like a more brightly shining heavenly body,* for the sake of those who are gratified by the light of clearly seen truth, like the light at the day's beginning, or like the light that rules the day. But another person, by the will of that same Spirit, is given the discourse of knowledge, like the lesser light, the moon. Another is given faith, another the gift of healing, another the working of miracles, another the discernment of whether supernatural creatures are good or bad, another prophecy, another the ability to speak many languages through divine inspiration. These gifts are all stars. One and the same Spirit is at work in all of them, giving each person what is right for himself, just as it wishes,† and making heavenly bodies appear self-evidently for useful ends.

The discourse of knowledge, however, in which are contained all sacred signs‡ that vary in time like the moon, and the other gifts enumerated above, which are set out in a list and compared to stars, govern in the night, differing as they do from the incandescent brightness of wisdom, in which the day I cited delights.

They are necessary to those whom your shrewdest servant, Paul, couldn't address as people of the Spirit, but only as people of the flesh; he spoke actual wisdom only to fully developed intellects. A human as a mere living being, like a tiny child in Christ, still nursing,§ must become strong enough for solid food and fortify his eyesight to look at the sun; but before then, he shouldn't consider his night abandoned, but instead be content with the light of the moon and stars.

* Genesis 1:16.
† 1 Corinthians 12:4–11.
‡ 1 Corinthians 13:2.
§ 1 Corinthians 2:14–3:3, Hebrews 5:12–14.

These things you discuss most wisely, our God, in your book, in your firmament, so that we're able to distinguish everything in a miraculous contemplation, although as yet this is only by means of signs and times and days and years.*

24. "But first bathe, be clean, remove the evil from your souls and from the sight of my eyes"—so that the dry land can appear. Learn to do good, give your judgment on the orphan's side, and give justice to the widow, so that the earth produces the green stalks yielding fodder, and trees bearing fruit. "And come, let's weigh the matter up," says the Master,† "so that lights come out in the sky's support, to shine over the earth."

The rich man was asking the good teacher what to do in order to acquire eternal life. The good teacher—who he thought was nothing more than a human being (but the reason he's good is that he's God)—says to him that if he does aim to arrive at eternal life, he must keep the commandments, separating himself from the briny bitterness of evil-mindedness and ill will, should not murder, should not commit adultery, should not steal, should not perjure himself, so that the dry land can appear and grow honor for his mother and father and love of his neighbor.

"I have done all of this," the rich man says. So where do all these brambles come from, if your land is so fertile? Come on, root out the overgrown thorn-thickets of greed, sell what you possess, and fill yourself with a harvest by giving to the poor, and you will have treasure in the heavens. Follow the Master‡ if you wish to grow to maturity, and to be in fellowship with those

* Genesis 1:14.
† Isaiah 1:16–18.
‡ Matthew 19:16–22, Mark 10:17–22, Luke 18:18–23.

among whom he speaks wisdom. He knows what to allocate to the day and the night, and you will know it as well, so that lights in the sky's support can be yours. That won't happen unless your heart is there; by the same token, it won't happen unless your treasure is there, as you have heard from the good teacher.* But the barren earth is darkened over with gloom,† and thorn bushes have choked the Word as it tried to sprout.‡

25. But you, the race of the chosen,§ weak things of the universe,¶ who have given up everything to follow the Master:** go after him and put the strong things to shame.†† Go after him, with your feet beautiful to see,‡‡ and shine in the firmament, so that the heavens tell of his glory, as they make a division between the light of those who have come to maturity and fulfillment (but who are not yet angels) and the darkness of the little children (who are not beyond hope).

Shine over the whole earth, and day radiant with the sun will give forth to day the speech of wisdom, and night luminous with the moon will make known to night the speech of knowledge.§§ The moon and the stars shine for the night, and the night doesn't darken them, as they illuminate the night as much as is proper for them.

---

* Matthew 6:21.
† Luke 18:23.
‡ Matthew 13:7, 22.
§ 1 Peter 2:9.
¶ 1 Corinthians 1:27.
** Matthew 19:27.
†† 1 Corinthians 1:27.
‡‡ Isaiah 52:7, quoted in Romans 10:15.
§§ Psalms 19:1–2, 1 Corinthians 12:8.

Look! It's as if God were saying "Let there be light," so that lights emerged in the sky's vault,* and suddenly there came a sound from the sky, as if a powerful wind were moving, and split tongues were seen, as in a fire, and a tongue sat upon each of the people;† and there emerged lights in the sky's vault, and these possessed the Word of life.‡

Scatter, running everywhere, holy flames, lovely flames. You are the light of the world, and you're not under a basket.§ The one to whom you've clung is raised on high, and he's raised you, too. Scatter and make yourself known, make yourselves clear as day to all peoples.¶

26. Let the sea as well conceive and give birth to your works, and let the waters bring forth creeping things with the breath of life or living souls in them.** In dividing the precious from the worthless, you all will be the mouth of God,†† through which he said, "Let the waters give birth to"—not the kind of breathing life or living soul the land produces, but creeping things with this in them, and winged creatures winging their way above the earth. Your holy rites, God, through the works of your holy ones, have crept through the center of the wavy deep, this world's temptations, to dye all peoples with your name in your baptism.‡‡

* Genesis 1:15.
† Acts 2:2–3.
‡ Philippians 2:15–16, 1 John 1:1.
§ Matthew 5:14–15.
¶ Matthew 28:19.
** Genesis 1:20.
†† Jeremiah 15:19.
‡‡ Matthew 28:19.

Among these creations are mighty and marvelous works,* such as huge whales, and the voices of your messages flying over the earth close to the firmament of your book, which was placed in authority over them, so that they would fly under it wherever they went. There are no kinds of speech, no kinds of discourse that are not heard in their voices, when sounds issue from them to every land and their words reach the ends of the earth†— since you, God, by blessing these creations have caused them to multiply.‡

27. Could I possibly be lying, befuddling my readers with a lot of balderdash? Or am I correctly distinguishing clear conceptions of these things in the sky's firmament from material works in the wavy sea and under the sky's firmament?

Conceptions of these things are firm and within boundaries that don't grow from generation to generation; they are like the lights of wisdom and knowledge. But the same things have many different physical functions, and by one thing growing out of another, they multiply under your blessing,§ as you, God, have soothed the tedium of our mortal perceptions: in the mind's contemplation a single thing is pictured and verbally expressed in many ways with the help of mere physical movements.

The waters produced these things, but this was in your Word. The needs of peoples alienated from the eternity of your truth produced them, but this was in your Gospel; the actual waters

---

* Genesis 1:21, Acts 2:11.
† Psalms 19:3.
‡ Genesis 1:28, Psalms 107:38.
§ Ibid.

cast forth these things, and a bitter, briny sickness of the waters was the reason for them to come forth from your Word.*

28. But with you making them, all things are beautiful, and—look!—you who made all things are indescribably more beautiful. If Adam hadn't fallen away from you, the sea's salty water would not have poured out of his belly and spread in all directions, in the form of the human race, troubled to its depths, stormily swollen, and uncontrollably sloshing back and forth.

And had it not been like this, there would have been no need for your stewards† to be physically and intellectually at work in many waters with words and acts of holy mystery.

It strikes me now that creeping and flying things are like the physical rites in which people are to be imbued and initiated. But such people could make no further progress unless their souls come to life in the Spirit, at another, higher step; and so after the Word of the initial, initiatory stage, the soul can look toward the fulfillment.‡

29. Thus, in your Word, not the depths of the sea but the earth, which was set apart from the sea's bitterness, cast up out of itself—not creeping things with the breath of life in them, and not flying things, but the living soul.§

---

* The passage is moving from signs or wonders toward sacraments. The pronouns (though one expresses mild contempt) are even more obscure than in most places. Unable to slap the author until he explains, I can merely construe that he is still talking about the material elaboration of eternal abstractions.

† 1 Corinthians 4:1.

‡ Hebrews 6:1–2. Here both miracles and rites are cited.

§ Genesis 1:24.

And it no longer has any need for baptism—which the pagan nations do need—as it had when it was covered with waters; there being no other way to enter into the kingdom of heaven, from the time you established that it must be entered this way.*

And the soul does not require mighty prodigies of portents to foster its faith; nor does it fail to believe unless it sees signs and miracles,† since the faithful and committed earth is now separate from the earth's waters, which are bitter with faithlessness; and speaking in tongues is a sign for the benefit of the faithless, not the faithful.‡ Nor does the land, which you set on a firm foundation above the waters,§ stand in need of the kind of flying thing that the waters brought forth at your Word.¶

Send your Word to the earth by your messengers instead. We're telling about their labors, but it's you who labor in them, so that they can labor over the living soul. The earth puts the soul forth, because the earth is the cause of these things being active there, as the sea was the cause of activity for things with the breath of life in them, and the flying things under the sky's firmament—which the earth no longer needs, although it eats the fish raised from the deep,** on the table you laid in the sight of believers:†† it was raised from the deep for the purpose of nourishing the dry land.

Birds are the offspring of the sea, yet they multiply over the earth.‡‡ The faithlessness of humankind arose as the reason for

* John 3:5.
† John 4:48.
‡ 1 Corinthians 14:2.
§ Psalms 24:2, 136:6.
¶ Genesis 1:20.
** Christ resurrected and consumed in the Eucharist.
†† Psalms 23:5.
‡‡ Genesis 1:22.

the first voices bringing the Gospel's good news; but the faithful also are urged on and blessed by these voices many times from day to day.

The living soul, in contrast to the flying things, takes its *start* from the earth; only to those who are faithful and committed already is it of benefit to keep themselves chaste,* free of passion for this world, so that their soul lives for you;† it was dead when it spent its life in pleasure‡—the pleasure that brings death, Master. You are the life-sustaining pleasure of the pure-hearted.

30. Therefore, let your servants now go about their work on the earth, but not in the way they worked in the waters of faithlessness. That was by proclaiming and discoursing through miracles and sacred rites and mysterious words, in a place where ignorance, the mother of amazement, could be riveted by the fear of esoteric signals. The entrance into faith is like this for the sons of Adam who have forgotten you, hiding themselves from your face§ and becoming the abyss.

Let the servants rather go about their work as if on dry land, apart from the whirlpools of the abyss, and let them be fully formed beings in the eyes of the faithful, by living before them in plain sight and encouraging imitation.¶ Thus, it's not only for the sake of hearing but for the sake of doing that the faithful hear the words "Seek God, and your soul will live,"** so that the

* James 1:27.
† 2 Corinthians 5:15.
‡ 1 Timothy 5:6.
§ Genesis 3:8.
¶ 1 Thessalonians 1:6–7.
** Psalms 69:32.

earth brings forth a living soul. Don't take on the form of this world;* hold yourselves back from it."

The soul lives by leaving alone the things it dies pursuing. Hold yourselves back from the monstrous wildness of arrogance, from the loafing pleasures of dissipation, and from the fraudulent heading "knowledge,"† so that the animals are domesticated animals, the herds tame and obedient, and the snakes harmless. These are impulses of the soul as depicted in allegory.

But the conceit of those who get above themselves, the self-indulgence of lasciviousness, and the poison of officious curiosity are the impulses of a dead soul.‡ The soul doesn't die in such a way that it's altogether inert; it dies by leaving the flowing spring of life§ and is taken up by the world as this passes by; thus the soul takes the form of the world.

31. But your Word, God, is a flowing spring of eternal life,¶ and does not pass by. Therefore, in your Word, that act of leaving is checked when we are told, "Don't take the form of this world."** This is how the earth, with its spring of life, can bring forth a living soul. And in your Word, through your bringers of good news, this soul achieves restraint by imitating Christ's imitators.††

---

* Romans 12:2.
† 1 Timothy 6:20.
‡ 1 John 2:16.
§ Jeremiah 2:13.
¶ John 4:14.
** Romans 12:2.
†† 1 Corinthians 4:6, 11:1.

This is "[every creature] according to its kind,"* since that means a person emulates his friend.† Paul says, "Be like me, all of you, since even I am like you."‡ In this way, in a living soul there will be good animals, gentle in their paths of action; gentle to lead, if you will. You gave the command, saying, "In gentleness bring your works to their conclusion, and everyone will love you."§

And the good animals of the herd, if they eat, don't eat to excess, and if they don't eat, aren't in need;¶ and the good snakes aren't harmful and destructive, but shrewd and cautious,** reconnoitering the character of time-bound things, but only to the extent needful for looking carefully at eternity and understanding it through the things that are made.†† These living creatures labor in the service of reason when, kept back from that forward motion that brings death, they live and are good.

32. Our Master and God, our creator, here it is, then: once our feelings—in which we were dying by living badly—are held back from passion for the world, and our soul begins truly to live by living in goodness, and your word, which your apostle expressed as "Don't take on the form of this world," is accomplished, there will follow as well what you immediately added, saying, "But rather be re-formed by the renewing of your mind."‡‡

* Genesis 1:24–25.
† Ecclesiastes 4:4. Standard English translations are different.
‡ Galatians 4:12.
§ Sirach 3:17.
¶ 1 Corinthians 8:8.
** Genesis 3:1, alluded to in Matthew 10:16.
†† Romans 1:20.
‡‡ Romans 12:2.

That will no longer be "according to [your] kind" as if you all were imitating your neighbor, whoever is going ahead of you, or as if you were living under the authority of a better person. You, God, did *not* say, "Let a human being be made according to its kind," but rather, "Let us make a human being in the image and likeness of ourselves"*—so that we human beings ourselves can show the reality of *your* will.†

That was the purpose of your steward, Paul, who begot sons through the good news.‡ He didn't want them to be tiny forever, needing to feed on milk§ and be carried in a nursemaid's arms,¶ as it were; so he said, "Be re-formed by the renewing of your mind, in order to verify for ourselves what the will of God is: meaning that which is a good thing, and an acceptable one, and has come to maturity or fulfillment."

Therefore, you don't say "Let there be a human being," but rather "Let us make ..." You don't say "according to its kind,"** but "in the image and likeness of ourselves." A person renewed in his mind and contemplating your truth that is understood†† doesn't need another person as a guide; he is not to imitate his *own* kind.

Rather, with you as a guide he validates on his own what your will is, which is a good thing, and an acceptable one, and has come to maturity or fulfillment,‡‡ and you teach him, now that

---

* Genesis 1:26.
† Romans 12:2.
‡ 1 Corinthians 4:15.
§ 1 Corinthians 3:1–2.
¶ 1 Thessalonians 2:7.
** Genesis 1:24.
†† Romans 1:20.
‡‡ Romans 12:2.

he's able, to see the Trinity in its unity and the unity of the Trinity. Thus, once it's been stated, with a plural subject, "Let *us* make a human being," the text continues with a singular subject: "And *God* made a human being." And when it's been stated, with a plural possessive adjective, "in *our* image," the text continues "in the image *of God*."*

In this way, a human being is renewed by the recognition of God, according to the image of his creator,† and being completed as a spiritual being he judges all things—all that should be judged, at any rate; but he himself is judged by no one.‡

33. That a believer judges all things means that he has power over the fish of the sea and the flying creatures of the sky, and all livestock and wild animals, and the whole earth and the crawling things that crawl over the earth.§ He exercises this power through his mind's understanding, by which he apprehends which things belong to the Spirit of God.¶

Otherwise, a man in a prestigious position *hasn't* been able to understand. He has been compared to irrational beasts of burden, and in fact has become like them.** Therefore, our God, in your church, according to your free gift or grace—which you gave to the church,†† since we who belong to it are what you have shaped, creating us for good works‡‡—not only do those who are

---

* Genesis 1:26–27.
† Colossians 3:10.
‡ 1 Corinthians 2:15.
§ Genesis 1:26.
¶ 1 Corinthians 2:15.
** Psalms 49:12, 20.
†† 1 Corinthians 3:10.
‡‡ Ephesians 2:10.

spiritually in charge judge spiritually, but those who are spiritually placed beneath them do so as well.* (You made the male and
the female person in your spiritual grace in such a way that
there is no difference between the masculine and the feminine
according to physical gender, as there's no difference between
Jew and Greek or slave and free person, either.†)

People of the Spirit, then, whether they are in charge or in compliance with these, judge in the Spirit. This does not, however,
apply to spiritual conceptions that shine in the firmament, since
it's not proper to judge concerning such sublime authority. And
it doesn't apply to your book itself, even if something's unclear
there, since we subordinate our understanding to the book,
being sure that even whatever in it is shut off from our view has
been rightly and truly stated. Thus, a person, though he's already of the Spirit and renewed by the recognition of God according to the image of the one who created him,‡ ought to be a
doer of the law, and not a judge of it.§

Nor does a person of this kind judge about that division I've
been discussing—I mean between people of the Spirit and people of the flesh: they are all known in your sight, Master, but as
yet they have not become plain to us by their works so that we
can learn about them through the harvests they produce.¶ But
you, Master, know people already and have separated them in
their two groups** and called them in secret, before the vault of
heaven came into being.

---

* 1 Corinthians 2:15, and several other New Testament verses.
† Galatians 3:28.
‡ Colossians 3:10.
§ James 4:11.
¶ Matthew 7:20.
** Matthew 25:32–34.

Nor does a person, though spiritual, judge concerning the savage peoples of this world. What business does he have passing judgment on these outsiders,* when he doesn't know who's going to come from among them into the sweetness of your grace, and who's going to remain in the unending bitterness of ungodliness?

34. For this same reason, humanity, whom you created in your image, did not receive power over the lights of the sky or the hidden part of the sky itself, or the day and night, which you named before the establishment of the sky, or the waters herded together, which is the sea.† But humanity did receive power over the sea's fish and the sky's flying things, and all herd animals, and the whole earth, and everything that crawls on the earth.‡

Hence, a human being judges and approves what is right, and disapproves of what he finds wrong, whether that's in the solemn rites for the initiation of those whom your mercy has searched out in many waters;§ or in the rite where the fish, raised from the deep to be eaten by the reverent earth, is set out;¶ or in verbal signals, language placed under the authority of your book—like flying things under the firmament—and used in interpreting, expounding, discussing, and discoursing, and in blessing and invoking you; symbolic utterances break out of the mouth, so that the congregation says "Amen."

The reasons for all this language being expressed physically are the abyss of the world and the blindness of our physical being:

---

* 1 Corinthians 5:12.
† Genesis 1:6–9.
‡ Genesis 1:26.
§ Baptism; see Song of Solomon 8:7 and Jeremiah 51:13.
¶ The Eucharist or Lord's Supper.

things thought out cannot be seen, and so have to be blared into the ears. Thus, though the communicative flying things multiply over the earth, they nonetheless draw their origin from the chaotic waters.

A person of the Spirit also judges by approving what is right and disapproving what he finds wrong in the works and ethics of the faithful, in their acts of charity like the fertile earth. And he judges concerning the living soul, with its disposition made gentle by chastity, by fasts,* by reverent meditations on these things that are perceived by the physical senses. He's said, in sum, to exercise judgment in matters in which he also has the authority to correct people.

35. But what is this here, and what sort of mystery is it? Here you are, Master, blessing humankind so that they swell in number, and multiply, and fill the earth.† But are you giving us no hint here, to allow us to understand anything further?

Why did you not bless in this way the light, which you called the day, or the sky's firmament, or the luminous sun and moon, or the stars, or the earth, or the sea? I would say, our God, you who created us in your image, I would say that you wanted to bestow this gift of a blessing on humankind in particular, had you not blessed the fish and the whales in this way, so that they would swell in number and multiply and fill the waters of the sea; and blessed the flying things so that they would multiply over the earth.‡

---

* 2 Corinthians 6:5–6.
† Genesis 1:28.
‡ Genesis 1:22.

By the same token, I would say this blessing applies to the sorts of things that procreate by reproducing themselves from their own bodies, if I found the words applied to trees and bushes and herd animals of the earth. But no, it's not plants, not timber, not animals or snakes that are told, "Grow in numbers and multiply," even though all these things as well, like fish and birds and human beings, increase and secure their species' continuation through reproduction.

36. My God, you who are the truth, what do I say, then? That this language is a void, that these statements have no content? By no means, father of fearful reverence. It would be outrageous for the slave of your Word to say this.

If I myself don't understand what you mean by this phrasing, let better people than I am—I mean people with more understanding than I have—put the phrasing to better use, according to the amount of discernment you gave each one of them.*

But let my testimony, too, find favor before your eyes. I do confess to my conviction, Master, that there is some cause for your speaking this way, and I won't pass over in silence what occurs to me when I come across this passage. The thing *is* true, after all, and thus I don't see what should stop me from construing the metaphoric statements in your book as I'm doing.

I know that something understood a single way by the mind can have a number of physical meanings, and that a thing with a single physical meaning can be understood in a number of ways by the mind. Look, for example, at the love of God and of one's neighbor as a singularity, which is expressed, physically, in mul-

* Romans 12:3.

tiple rites and multiple languages and multiple kinds of phrasing in any given language. That's how the waters' offspring grow in number and multiply.

But look again, whoever's reading this: you see scripture setting out and the voice sounding out something in one manner: "In the beginning, God made the sky and the earth." Can't it be understood in multiple ways—not through mistakes' deceiving us, but through different kinds of true understandings? That's how *humankind's* offspring grow and multiply.*

37. Therefore, if we conceive of the actual natures of things not allegorically but factually, the command "Grow in numbers and multiply" suits everything that reproduces by fertility or "seed." If, on the other hand, we treat these words as if they were meant figuratively (and I rather think that the scripture aimed to do that, as there couldn't be any reason whatsoever for assigning this blessing to the offspring of aquatic creatures and humankind alone), then we find multiples in other things as well.

These multiples are in spiritual and physical creations, corresponding to the sky and the earth;† and in righteous and wicked souls, corresponding to the light and the darkness;‡ and in the holy authors through whom the law was provided to us, corresponding to the prop or firmament which was solidified between one realm of water and other;§ and in the gathering together, the fellowship of embittered, agitated peoples corresponding to

* Genesis 1:28.
† Genesis 1:1.
‡ Genesis 1:4.
§ Genesis 1:6–7.

the sea, and in the zeal of reverent souls corresponding to the dry land;* and in works of mercy in this life† corresponding to the plants that bear seeds and the trees that bear fruit;‡ and in the spiritual gifts made self-evident for useful purposes,§ corresponding to the lights of the sky;¶ and in feelings given the shape of self-restraint, corresponding to the living soul.** In all of these we meet with multiples and plentiful supplies and increases.

But whatever grows in number and multiplies—so that one thing is expressed in many ways and one expression is understood in many ways—we don't find it except as it's given out in physical signs and in matters thought out in a comprehensible manner.

We have understood signs issued physically as the begetting activities in the waters, because of the inescapable conditions of the physical abyss humankind finds itself in, for now; the things thought out so as to be comprehensible, on the other hand, we have understood as human begetting activities, because of the fertility of the intellect. And thus we have come to believe that to both these kinds of beings it was said by you, Master, "Grow in number and multiply."

By this blessing, I take it, you granted to us the ability and the power to express in many ways what we have understood and borne in mind in only one way; and to understand in many ways

---

* Genesis 1:9–10.
† 1 Timothy 4:8.
‡ Genesis 1:11.
§ 1 Corinthians 12:7.
¶ Genesis 1:14–15.
** Genesis 1:20, 24, 30.

what we've read if it's expressed in a single, obscure manner. Thus the waters of the sea are filled, and they don't move except through the different meanings of the sea's changes. Thus also the earth is filled with human offspring; the earth's dryness is clear in desirous, zealous effort or thirst, and reason is clearly master over the earth.

38. I also want to say, my Master and God, what the following passage in your scripture prompts me to. I'll say it, and I won't be afraid. With you breathing inspiration into me, I will say things that are true, just as you've wanted me to say about these words. I don't believe, either, that I speak the truth if anyone besides you inspires me, since you *are* the truth, whereas every human being is a liar,* and therefore whoever speaks falsely speaks from what is his own.† So in order to speak the truth, I speak from what is yours.

Here we are: For food, you gave us every sort of sown grass that engenders seed anywhere on earth, and every tree that has on it the produce of planted seed. And you gave this food not to us alone, but to all the birds of the sky as well, and to the animals of the earth, and to the reptiles—but not to the fish and the great whales.‡

We were saying that the meaning of the produce of the earth, and the allegorical picture it paints, is works of mercy, which are delivered from the productive earth for the needs of this life. The reverent Onesiphorus, or Help-Bringer, was this kind of earth. You showed mercy to his house because he often gave

* Psalms 116:11, quoted in Romans 3:4.
† John 8:44.
‡ Genesis 1:29–30.

your Paul cool and shady refreshment—and didn't blush at the chain the apostle wore in prison.*

Paul's brothers in the faith did likewise and were fertile in such fruits of the earth, making up his shortfall with supplies from Macedonia.† But how he grieves that certain trees haven't bestowed on him the harvest they owed, his comment being, "When I first had to defend myself in court, no one stood by me; they all deserted me; may it not be held against them!"‡

Food is owed to those who furnish reasoned teaching through their discernments concerning holy mysteries, and in this sense it is owed to them as human beings. But it is owed to them as living souls,§ when they make themselves available as examples to imitate in all kinds of their own self-denial. Likewise it is owed to them as if they were flying things, because of their words of blessings, which multiply over all the earth,¶ since the sounds they make have gone out into every land.**

39. The people nourished on this food are those who delight in it; those whose god is their belly†† don't delight in it. And for those who provide these foodstuffs, not what they give but rather the intention in which they give it makes up the harvest.

So as to Paul, a slave to God and not his belly,‡‡ I can see plainly where his joy comes from; I see it and I heartily concur in it. He

---

* 2 Timothy 1:16.
† 2 Corinthians 11:9.
‡ 2 Timothy 4:16.
§ Genesis 1:20, and several verses following.
¶ Genesis 1:22.
** Psalms 19:4.
†† Philippians 3:19.
‡‡ Romans 16:18.

received from the Philippians what they'd sent him through Epaphroditus*—but I see the actual source of his joy as something else.

The source of his joy is the source of his nourishment, because, in the truth, he says, "I had tremendous joy in the Master, because at long last the taste for me that you used to have sprouted again; you had in fact been sick of me."† Thus, through that lengthy sickness or irksomeness they'd withered and dried up, so to speak, and were no longer producing that harvest of good work; but Paul has joy in them, because they've sprouted again.

The joy isn't for himself, in that they've come to his aid while he's in need; hence he follows up by saying, "I'm not saying I lack anything; I've learned to make do with what I have. I know how to go without, and what to do with more than enough. In all circumstances and in every way I've been schooled in being both full and hungry, in having more than I need and in enduring poverty: I can do everything in the one who strengthens me."‡

40. So what is the source of your joy, eminent Paul? Where does joy, where does nourishment come from for you, a person renewed through the recognition of God, according to the image of the one who created you;§ for you, a living soul with such self-denial, and a voice on the wing, speaking of mysteries?¶ Such breathing, living creatures are in fact owed that food. So what is it that nourishes you?

---

* Philippians 4:18.
† Philippians 4:10.
‡ Philippians 4:11–13.
§ Colossians 3:10.
¶ 1 Corinthians 14:2.

It's delight. Let me hear what follows: "Nevertheless, you did good in making common cause with me in my straits."* This is where his joy, his nourishment comes from: that they did good, not that the tight place he's been in has eased. He says to you, God, "In my straits, you made room for me to escape,"† because he knows what to do with more than enough, and how to endure poverty, in you who strengthen him.

"You know," he says, "you the Philippians, that at the start of my mission to deliver the good news, when I set out from Macedonia, no church shared with me in the business of giving and receiving, except you alone, in that you sent money for my needs to Thessalonica, not once, but twice."‡ Now he's delighted that they've returned to good works and sprouted again, as if a field's fertility is coming back to life.

41. But could it have been because of his own needs that he said, "You sent money for my needs"?—could that be the reason for his joy? That's *not* the reason. But why do we know this? Because he himself follows up by saying, "It's not that I'm looking for something to be given or paid over to me, but that I'm looking after the produce, the proceeds, the profit."§

I've learned from, you, God, to distinguish between what's given and the produce from it. The given is the actual thing given by someone who shares material necessities, such as money, food,

---

* Philippians 4:14.
† Psalms 4:1, 118:5.
‡ Philippians 4:15–16.
§ The verses (ibid.) add "that accumulates to your account." Paul is employing an investment conceit: what is "given / paid over" will actually accumulate spiritual interest for the giver.

drink, clothing, shelter, or other assistance. The produce or profit from it is the good and righteous intention of the giver.

The good teacher Jesus doesn't say only, "Whoever takes in a prophet"; he added, "in the name of a prophet." And he doesn't say only, "Whoever takes in a just man"; he added, "in the name of a just man." That means that the one benefactor will receive a prophet's payment, and the other will receive a just man's payment.

He didn't say only, "Whoever gives one of my lowliest followers a cup of cold water to drink"; he added, "only in the name of a student or disciple," and accordingly he added onto that, "Truly I tell you, he won't fail to receive the payment he deserves."*

What is given is to take in a prophet, to take in a just man, to hand a cup of cold water to a disciple; the harvest, the earnings are to do this in the name of a prophet, in the name of a just man, in the name of a disciple. Elijah was nourished with produce, with profit by the widow who knew she was nourishing a man of God, and nourished him for this reason. But he was nourished by the crow merely with what was given. Elijah wasn't nourished inwardly then, but only outwardly, although for lack of this food as well he could have broken down and perished.†

42. In this respect, I will say in your presence what is true, Master: when people without knowledge or faith—whose admission and acquisition for the profit of our cause requires initiatory rites and mighty, miraculous works, which we have reckoned to

* Matthew 10:41–42.
† 1 Kings 17:4–18.

be signaled by the words "fish" and "whales"*—take in your children to care for them or to help them in some other need of this present life, they aren't really grazing or feeding them, and these draw no true nurture from them. That's because the former don't do this work with a holy and righteous will, and the latter have no delight in what's given them by those people, as they see no yield from it, no return on it as yet.

Hence, the mind is nurtured from the source of its delight. And therefore, fish and whales don't forage on the food that springs forth nowhere but on land, which is set off and separated from the bitterly salty sea waves.

43. And you saw, God, everything you had made, and there it was, very good;† because even we see it, and there everything is, very good. As to individual kinds of your works, once you had commanded them to be made, and they had been made, you saw one after another as good.

Seven times, as I've counted, it's written that you saw what you'd made as good. The eighth time here, it says you saw *all* that you'd made, and there it was, not only "good," but "very good"—as if all of it together was very good: the individual things were merely "good," but all things together were both "good" and "very."

Every beautiful material object also testifies to this, because an object is far more beautiful, in consisting of all its beautiful parts, than are its individual parts, given that the whole is made

* Genesis 1:20–21.
† Genesis 1:31.

up of these parts in a highly orderly union—although, taken singly, they're also beautiful.

44. I set my mind on finding out whether, when your works pleased you, it was seven or eight *times* that you saw they were good. But in your act of seeing them, I couldn't conceive of any actual periods of time, and so it made no sense to me that you saw so many *times* what you had made.

And I said, "Master, your scripture here must be true, mustn't it? You, the truthful one, the truth itself,* set it forth. Why, then, do you tell me that in your seeing there is no time, whereas this scripture of yours tells me that over the course of separate days you saw that what you had made was good, and when I counted I found out how many times that happened?"

You answer me, since you are my God and you speak with a loud voice in your slave's inward ear, breaking through my deafness with a shout: "You, who belong to humankind! Certainly what my scripture says, I myself say—and yet it says these things in time. Time, however, does not impinge on my Word, which remains steadfast with me, in an eternity equal to mine. In this way, the things you all see through my Spirit, I myself see; likewise, the things you all say through my Spirit, I myself say. But in conjunction with this, whereas you all see these things in time, I myself don't; just as, although you say these things in time, I myself don't."

45. And I've heard, my God and Master, I've licked a drop of sweetness from your truth. I've grasped that there are certain

* John 3:33, 14:6.

people who don't like your works, and they say that you made many of them, such as the framework of the sky and the arrangements of the stars, under the force of necessity; and that the material was not your own, but was created elsewhere and from another source than you: you only gathered it into one place and fastened it together and fashioned it, after you had conquered your enemies and set to work on the world's bullwarks, so that those constrained by that edifice couldn't revolt again.

They say that there are other things you didn't make or even assemble, such as all animate creatures, including the tiniest living things and whatever clings to the earth with its roots. Rather, they say, a consciousness at war with you, an alien essence not created by you, but opposed to you, gives birth to and shapes these things in the lower regions of the world.

Lunatics say these things, because they don't see your works through your Spirit, and thus they don't recognize you in these works.*

46. Whoever sees these things through your Spirit, you see in these people. Thus, when they see that these things are good, you see that the same things are good. And whatever things are pleasing because of you, you are pleasing in these things. And whatever things are pleasing to us through your Spirit, they are pleasing to you in us.

Who among humankind knows what's in a human being, unless a human being's own spirit knows it? In the same way, no one but the Spirit of God knows the things that belong to God. "But

---

* This passage recaps Manichaean cosmology.

we," Paul continues, "have received not the spirit of this world but the Spirit that comes from God, so that we may know the gifts that have been given by God to us."*

I feel myself prompted to say, "Certainly no one, except the Spirit of God, knows the things that belong to God. But how, then, do we actually know the things that are given to us by God?" The answer presented to me is that, in actual fact, no one but the Spirit of God knows the things we know through God's Spirit.

Just as it was correctly said to those who were speaking in the Spirit of God, "It's not you yourself who are speaking,"† it is correctly said to those who know in the Spirit of God, "It's not you who know." It's then equally correct to say, to those who see in the Spirit of God, "It's not you yourselves who see." Thus, whatever people see, in the Spirit of God, as good, they themselves don't see it as good; rather, God does.

So whoever considers something to be evil that is actually good—which is the view of the Manichaeans, cited just now—is committing one kind of error. Another error is that someone sees as good something that is in fact good—and your creation is pleasing to many people simply because it *is* good—without your being pleasing to them *through* it, as they want to enjoy *it* rather than you.

But it's something else again when a person sees something as good because God in him sees that it's good; plainly this happens so that God can be loved in what he has made: we can't

* 1 Corinthians 2:11–12.
† Matthew 10:20.

lose our hearts to God unless it's through the Spirit that he has given, since the love of God is poured out and spreads through our hearts through the Holy Spirit, which has been given to us;* through the Holy Spirit, we see that whatever in any manner exists is good, coming as it does from the one who doesn't exist in any particular manner, but *is* being.†

47. We give thanks to you, Master! We see the sky and the earth—whether that means the physical regions above and below, or the spiritual and physical creation. And as an adornment of these parts—which make up either the whole material mass of the universe, or the whole creation in sum—we see the light that has been made and separated from the darkness.

We see the firmament or support of the sky, whether this is between the spiritual waters above and the physical ones below, which were the initial physical objects of the universe; or whether the firmament is simply this space of the air, as this is called the sky as well. Through it wander the winged creatures of the sky, between the waters: those waters that are carried above them like mist and also drip dew during calm nights, and the waters below, which, because of their weight, only undulate on earth.

We see the beauty of the waters herded together over the plains of the sea, and we see the dry earth, either stripped bare, or fashioned so that it could be sightly and ordered as the maternal material for herbage and trees.

* Romans 5:5.
† Exodus 3:14.

We see the lights gleaming above, the sun satisfying the day's needs, the moon and the stars comforting the night, and all of them marking and giving meaning to periods of time.

We see the watery element stretching endlessly in all directions, burgeoning with fish and monsters and birds—as the density of air, which bears up birds in their flight, is congealed from the waters' evaporation.

We see the face of the land made lovely by land animals, and we see humankind, in your image and likeness, placed above all unreasoning living things because of this very image and likeness, meaning excellence in reasoning and understanding.

And in the pattern of two different kinds of activities in his soul, deliberating and ruling on the one hand, and submitting and complying on the other, woman also, in physical terms, has been made for man. In her mind, of course, she has an equal natural endowment for reasoning intelligence, but in her physical sex she is in subjection to the male sex, in the same way that the impulse for action is subjugated for the purpose of conceiving, from the mind's rationality, shrewdness in acting rightly.

We see all these things, and we see that individually they are good, and that all of them are very good.

48. Your works praise you* to make us love you, and we love you, making your works praise you. They have a beginning and an end in time, a rising and a setting, they make headway and they decay, they have a shape, shapeliness, beauty, and they lose it.

* Psalms 145:10, Daniel 3:57.

Thus they have a morning and an evening following on each other, partly hidden and partly apparent.

They were made out of nothing by you, not from you; and not from something that was not yours and came before you, but from what was "created together," meaning material created simultaneously by you, because you turned its formlessness into form without any gap in time.

The material of the sky and the earth is different from the beauty, or the formal order, of the sky and the earth; you made the material from absolutely nothing, whereas you made the beauty from formless matter; but you made both simultaneously, so that with no interruption, no pause, form could follow matter.

49. We have also looked closely at the allegorical purpose for which you willed these things to arise in a series like this, or to be written about as arising in a series like this, and we have seen that they are individually good and together all very good, in your Word, in your only son. They are the sky and the earth, and the head and the body of the church, and they were determined beforehand, before all time,* without a morning or evening.

But then you began to carry out in time the things determined beforehand, so as to make plain what was hidden† and place in order what was disordered in us. This is because our sins were a burden on us from above,‡ and we had moved into the dark

---

* Colossians 1:17–18.
† Psalms 51:6.
‡ Ezekiel 33:10.

abyss, away from you; but your good Spirit was carried above to our rescue at the fitting time.

You made the godless righteous* and separated them from the evildoers, and you solidified the authority of your book among those in a higher position, so that they would be teachable by you; and among those in a lower position, so that they would be placed under it; and you herded the community of the faithless into a single cabal.

This meant the zealous impulses of the faithful could be brought into the open, and thus the faithful could bring to birth for you works of mercy and even share out among the poor their earthly means,† so as to acquire heavenly wealth.

And then you lit certain lights in the firmament, your holy ones, possessing the Word of life‡ and shining with the exalted authority displayed through spiritual gifts.

And then, from physical bases, for the edification of the faithless races you brought forth visible rites and wonders, and expressions in language in accordance with your book's firm support, with all of which the faithful also could be blessed.

And next, through feelings brought into order by the energy of self-restraint, you formed in the faithful a living soul; and then you renewed according to your image and likeness the minds§ that was brought under your command and needed no human authority to pattern itself on, and you placed reasoning action under the power of superior understanding, as you placed

---

* Romans 4:5.
† 1 Corinthians 13:3.
‡ Philippians 2:16.
§ Romans 12:2, Colossians 3:10.

woman under man. And you willed that for the benefit of all your officers, who are essential for the full maturing of the faithful in this life, these same faithful people should render services of practical usefulness in this world of time, bringing bounty in the world to come.

We see all of these things, and they are very good, since you see them in us. It was you who gave us the Spirit in which we could see them and love you in them.

50. God, our Master, grant us peace—because you have provided everything for us: the peace of rest, the peace of the Sabbath, peace without an evening. All of this surpassingly beautiful arrangement of things that are very good will run through its own limits and will pass away—naturally, because both the morning and the evening were made among these things.

51. But the seventh day is without an evening and has no setting sun; you made it holy so that it could remain steadfast for all time. You made it after your other very good works. You made them all, of course, when you were at rest, so this expression in your book, that you rested in the seventh day,* is meant to foretell to us that after our works, which are very good in that you granted them to us, we, too, will rest in you on the Sabbath of eternal life.

52. At that time also you will rest in us as you now work in us, and your rest through us will be like your works through us now. But you, Master, are always at work and always at rest, and

* Genesis 2:2–3.

you don't see things in time or move in time or rest in time; and yet you make both things for us to see in time and time itself—and rest outside of time.

53. Thus *we* see the things you made because they exist; but they exist because you see them. And we see both outwardly that they exist and inwardly that they are good, but you saw them made at that point when you saw that they needed to be made.

Even we at one time were moved to do good, and that was after our heart conceived from your Spirit; but at an earlier time, when we abandoned you, we were moved to do evil. You, however, the single, the good God, have never stopped doing good. There are certain good works of ours, which are in fact your gift to us, but they are not for all time. We hope that after these works we will rest in your great power to make us holy. But *you* are goodness that needs no goodness, and so are always at rest, since your rest is your very self.

But who among humankind can offer another human being a way to understand this? What angel could offer it to another angel? What angel could offer it to a human being? We must ask you for it, and look for it from you; we must knock at your door: in this way, we will receive it, we will find it, and you will open the door to us.*

* Matthew 7:7–8.

Acknowledgments

To Sam Nicholson, the editor of this book, and to Will Lippincott, its agent, I owe profound thanks.

Without the aid of Brown University's world-class research facilities, this manuscript could not have gone forward. Christopher Beeley of Yale offered generous advice on matters of patristics and early Christianity. (He is not responsible for my choice of "Master" over "Lord"—that was me.) Rhodes College, Thomas Aquinas College, and Mount Saint Mary's University were extremely helpful in allowing me to present portions of my draft to their communities and discuss this project with them.

A Creative Nonfiction Grant from the Whiting Foundation allowed me to finish the translation I had undertaken with even less than my usual caution in the face of an ancient author's neglected genius in making style serve his ideas. I am grateful not only for the practical support but also for the warm encouragement this grant has entailed.

The Latin text I used for this translation, and the main commentary I consulted, are James O'Donnell's in his *Augustine: Confessions* (1992). I am particularly indebted also to Robin Lane Fox for *Augustine: Conversion to Confessions* (2015).

SARAH RUDEN was educated at the University of Michigan, Johns Hopkins, and Harvard, from which she graduated with a Ph.D. in classical philology. She has translated six books of classical literature, including *Lysistrata, The Golden Ass,* and *The Aeneid,* and has also translated Aeschylus's *Oresteia* for the Modern Library collection *The Greek Plays.* Her translation of Augustine's *Confessions* is her first book-length translation of sacred literature. Her articles have appeared in *The Wall Street Journal, Books & Culture,* and other magazines. She is a winner of a Guggenheim fellowship and a Whiting Creative Nonfiction Grant, and is the author of *Paul Among the People: The Apostle Reinterpreted and Reimagined in His Own Time* and *The Face of Water: A Translator on Beauty and Meaning in the Bible,* as well as a book of poetry, *Other Places.* Ruden is a visiting scholar at Brown University and lives in Hamden, Connecticut.

sarahruden.com